THE *Hiring & Firing* BOOK

A Complete Legal Guide for Employers

Steven Mitchell Sack

Legal Strategies Inc.

OTHER BOOKS OF INTEREST BY STEVEN MITCHELL SACK:

The Salesperson's Legal Guide, Prentice Hall (1981)

Employment Law: A Printer's Handbook on Hiring & Firing, National Association of Printers & Lithographers (1991)

Sales Rep Strategies For Dealing With Principals Successfully: Negotiations, Contracts, Working Relationships & Terminations, The Sales Rep's Advisor (1991)

The Employee Rights Handbook: Answers To Legal Questions From Interview To Pink Slip, Facts On File, Inc. (1991)

LIBRARY OF CONGRESS CATALOG NUMBER: 93-077045

ISBN: 0-96363-060-1

1 2 3 4 5 6 7 8 9 0

THE *Hiring & Firing* BOOK

Acknowledgments

Due to the size and complexity of this book, there are many people I wish to thank.

I am grateful to I. Gregg Van Wert, President of the National Association of Printers and Lithographers, for permitting me to use extensive material from articles I furnish NAPL as general labor counsel in *Printing Manager* magazine and from publications I have drafted for NAPL, including the *NAPL Employee Handbook* and *Employment Law: A Printer's Handbook On Hiring and Firing*. A special word of thanks also goes to Patrick Henry, Director of Communications; Don Lupo, Publications Editor; and Rhona Bronson, Director of Marketing, who have encouraged me in many NAPL projects throughout my career.

Kudos are extended to my editor, Mary O'Hara Smith, Vice President at BRP Publications, Inc. In addition to acting as my editor, Mary assisted me in most phases of the planning and publishing of this book and I am appreciative of her knowledge, skills and support. I also wish to thank Diane Cramer, Production Editor; Krishnendu Mandal, Production Assistant; and Elmer Ellentuck, Esq. for their assistance and editorial comments. Of course, Harry Greenwald, Chief Financial Officer at BRP, is also acknowledged for giving me the green light for this project, for permitting me to incorporate extensive material, case studies and other written information contained in BRP newsletters, and for allowing me to use BRP's resources to produce this book.

I offer thanks to friend and fellow attorney Stanley M. Spiegler, who taught me more about the practice of labor law than he could ever realize. I also acknowledge the friendship and expertise of Shirley and Larry Alexander, who helped me acquire an understanding of the publishing industry and who introduced me to BRP Publications, Inc.

Thanks are extended to Chicago attorney James J. Oh for permitting me to excerpt portions of his comments in the section on sexual harassment and include his valuable checklist for sexual harassment investigations. I also wish to thank Mary Ann Mandell, President of Publications Management, Inc., for her valuable suggestions.

Richard Frishman, President of Planned Television Arts and the entire staff at PTA, including Curtis Hougland and Paul Schwartz, are acknowledged for their competent public relations skills and support of all my labor work and publishing activities.

Of course, personal thanks are extended to Dr. Subhi Gulati, my brother and law partner Jonathan Scott Sack, Esq., Joan and Sidney Pollack, my mother Judith and my extended family for their constant love and encouragement.

I wish to express my love to my wife Gwen, who put up with my long hours in creating and writing this book, and to my son Andrew for future dreams. Finally, as always, I wish to express my appreciation and gratitude to my father, Bernard, whose insights and dreams helped make this book a reality.

Author's Note

The information in this book is an attempt to reduce complex and confusing law to practical general strategies for employers to follow. These strategies are meant to serve as helpful guidelines—concepts to think about—when you experience problems with your employees. They are not intended as legal advice per se, because laws vary considerably throughout the fifty states and the law can be interpreted differently depending upon the particular facts of each case. Thus it is important to consult experienced counsel regarding the applicability of any strategy or point of information contained herein.

Additionally, this publication is sold with the understanding that the publisher is not engaged in rendering legal, accounting or other professional services. If legal advice or other expert assistance is required, the services of a competent professional must always be sought.

Finally, fictitious names have been used throughout the work where appropriate and any similarity to actual persons, places or events is purely coincidental.

Contents

How To Use This Book

This book was written to save your company money and aggravation.

Beginning in the 1960s, some state legislatures began scrutinizing the fairness of the employment-at-will doctrine. Under this traditional rule of law, employers hired workers at will and were free to fire them at any time, with or without cause and with or without notice. From the nineteenth to mid-twentieth century, employers could discharge individuals with impunity. But beginning in the 1960s, courts began handing down rulings to safeguard the rights of non-unionized employees, and Congress passed specific laws pertaining to occupational health and safety, civil rights and freedom to complain about unsafe working conditions.

Thirty years later, there has been a gradual erosion of the employment-at-will doctrine in many areas. For example, some states have enacted public policy exceptions which make it illegal to fire workers who wish to perform jury duty or military service. Some courts have ruled that statements in company manuals, handbooks and employment publications constitute implied contracts which employers are bound to follow. Other states now recognize the obligation of companies to deal in fairness and good faith with longtime workers. This means, for example, that they are prohibited from terminating workers in retaliation when an employee tattles on abuses of authority (i.e., whistle-blowing), or denying individuals an economic benefit (e.g., a pension that is vested or about to vest, commission, bonus, etc.) that has been earned or is about to become due.

Most employers are unaware that in the past thirty years, the amount of employment-related litigation has increased more than 2000 percent. The average jury verdict in wrongful discharge cases now exceeds $500,000, and the amount of litigation stemming from discrimination charges has skyrocketed, due in part to the more liberal amendment to Title VII in the form of the Civil Rights Act of 1991 and the recently enacted Americans With Disabilities Act. From pre-hiring considerations to on-the-job rights of privacy, freedom from lie detector tests, and enhanced rights upon discharge, new rulings are emerging every day that give employees greater rights.

Federal and state laws are continually being passed that grant employees access to their personnel records, prohibit companies from firing female employees on maternity leave, make it more difficult to fire workers who are performing inadequately, permit union employees to be represented by union delegates when accused of disciplinary violations, and protect employees in many other ways.

In the past, employers could fire workers with or without cause or notice, with little fear of legal reprisal. This has changed. More and more terminated workers are successfully arguing and proving that company promises made at the time of the hiring interview are binding on the employer. Years ago, terminated employees would merely bow their heads and shuffle out the door after hearing they had been fired. Now, terminated workers are questioning these decisions and negotiating better severance packages and other post-termination benefits. In fact, the guiding maxim I offer to personnel executives, recruiters and owners of businesses is, "No good deed out of kindness goes unpunished." If you think about this apparent contradiction for a moment, you will begin to understand the problems employers currently face.

No company, regardless of its size or industry, is immune from this growing trend. The evolution of new laws, and the philosophy that a job is an integral part of a person's life and not just a vehicle for earning a living, is creating problems for employers and giving workers ammunition with which to fight back. Thousands of independent salespeople are also receiving protection from principals who fail to pay commissions due them in a timely fashion. In the past few years, 31 states have enacted sales rep protection laws which guarantee prompt payment of commissions upon termination or resignation and award double and triple damages, plus reasonable attorney fees and costs of litigation, in the event companies fail to comply with the appropriate provisions of each applicable state law.

Statistics indicate that 3.8 of every 100 employees are fired or resign from their jobs each month. Experts suggest that more than 350,000 workers are terminated unjustly and illegally each year, exposing their employers to hundreds of millions of dollars in potential damages, not including lost manpower costs and bad publicity, and tens of millions of dollars in unnecessary legal fees and expenses. A recent story in *The New York Times* reported that "in almost every industry, unfair discharge litigation has proliferated and the amount of money involved in settlements runs into hundreds of millions of dollars annually." The Wall Street Journal confirmed in a 1987 article that more than one-third of the New England companies interviewed indicated they were involved in legal actions with terminated employees, which in most cases were settled for cash payments ranging from $1,000 to $50,000, not including other benefits.

The Hiring & Firing Book: A Complete Legal Guide For Employers evolved from the variety of services I perform as labor counsel. In the mid-1980s, I was invited to address printing industry employers at a dinner in New York City. My topic was how to hire and fire employees properly in view of recent, drastic changes in the law. After the dinner meeting, I. Gregg Van Wert, then Executive Vice President of the National Association of Printers and Lithographers (and now President), inquired if I would create a special full-day seminar for NAPL employers to cover the wide spectrum of legal issues and problems currently faced by printing companies. Following the seminar, NAPL commissioned me to write a simple manual, complete with checklists and forms, for its 3,700 printing company members, entitled *Employment Law: A Printer's Handbook On Hiring And Firing*. This manual was written to give company executives charged with interviewing, hiring, disciplining and firing employees, an overview of and assistance in understanding the multitude of court rulings, regulations and laws which protect workers.

Based on the manual's positive impact in the printing industry, I decided to write a major, comprehensive book for employers in *all* industries throughout the country which would combine up-to-the minute changes in the law with the expertise gained in my professional experience as a practicing labor lawyer representing thousands of employees.

My career was stimulated, in part, from an interview about my work which appeared in *The Wall Street Journal* in the fall of 1984. Many actual cases cited in this book are derived from the numerous terminated executives and workers who hired me after reading the article and my subsequent book, *The Employee Rights Handbook: Answers To Legal Questions From Interview To Pink Slip*. Thus, you will note I have used real cases in a conscious attempt to make this book as comprehensive and practical as possible.

A few examples illustrate the potential cost to employers who fail to understand the issues. In one case, I obtained a quick cash settlement of $37,500 for a man who was fired after being falsely accused of drinking too much at lunch. Another executive with nine-plus years of accumulated work time was fired suddenly, late one November day. During negotiations, I argued that the firing was unjustified and deprived him of a large year-end bonus he was anticipating and a pension due to vest at the beginning of his tenth year of service. The company eventually paid my client a bonus of $50,000 plus severance pay totaling $75,000 (representing one month's salary for each year of service) and agreed to keep him on unpaid leave for the duration of the year so he would qualify for his vested pension.

Based on actual true case experiences, the text was written to reveal the hidden traps for well-intentioned employers who do not understand the scope and force of employees' rights. In addition, the book provides ammunition on how to fight back.

In this litigious age, it is *crucial* that employers take a preventive approach. By implementing the suggestions contained in this book, you can significantly reduce the chances that your company will be successfully sued by a former or current employee. Many of the self-protective steps outlined herein can enable your business to avoid ongoing disruption due to claims of sexual harassment, discrimination, invasions of privacy, breach of contract and unfair firings.

Regardless of the number of workers your company employs, its location or industry, *The Hiring & Firing Book* offers hundreds of preventive strategies your company can take to avoid such problems. The book covers pre-hiring and post-hiring considerations as well as the traditional problems associated with the hiring and firing stages essential to minimizing litigation. In fact, most lawsuits that arise after a firing could have been avoided by proper planning long before the hiring stage. With this book as your guide, you will be able to implement new policies within your company if none already exist, and alter current policies where warranted. Obviously, while this book suggests what company policy should be, it is not a per se statement of a particular policy. Rather, it provides various strategies which can be modified and implemented as required.

This book can reduce the odds of your company being sued unfairly and advises you and your lawyer how to minimize claims if you are sued. For example, some states allow terminated workers to sue in tort (as opposed to asserting claims based in contract) and recover punitive damages and money for pain and suffering arising from the firing. Employees who assert tort claims for wrongful discharge sometimes recover large six-figure and more jury verdicts as a result. Also, innovative lawyers are asserting federal racketeering (RICO) claims seeking criminal sanctions and treble (triple) damages against companies. This is in addition to fraud and misrepresentation claims against individuals responsible for making wrongful termination decisions. By reading this book, you may be in a better position to tell if an individual is able to assert such theories and reduce your company's exposure to such claims.

Since non-union employees have greater options than union members in many instances, and since these options are what make the new legal developments so dangerous to non-union companies, this book deals primarily with topical problems of non-union employees. The information contained herein can help you hold back the tide in this potentially dangerous area. Using the text as a guide and reviewing and incorporating the numerous contracts and other agreements where warranted, you can help your company anticipate and avoid legal hassles before they occur.

The Hiring & Firing Book contains all the practical information my clients receive, but at a fraction of the cost. Thus, keep this book in an accessible place and read the applicable sections *before* making a decision. Although each case depends on its unique facts, I have tried to reduce complicated court rulings, regulations and labor laws throughout the United States into simple strategies that companies in all states can understand and follow.

The Hiring & Firing Book is organized into four sections. Chapter 1, Pre-Employment Considerations, discusses a multitude of points and procedures to implement within your company before a candidate is hired. This includes how to avoid asking illegal questions at the hiring interview, how to design advertisements, brochures and employment applications properly, and how to negotiate the candidate's job.

Chapter 2, Benefits and Financial Considerations, discusses many financial and benefit concerns of newly hired workers which most employers fail to understand and incorporate into standard hiring and operating procedures.

Chapter 3, On-The-Job Employment Considerations, advises companies of the numerous on-the-job rights available to workers today. For example, this information will discuss rights to smoke in the workplace, whether it is illegal to fire pregnant workers, how to minimize claims of sex harassment and other rights of privacy currently available. Employers will learn how to deal fairly and legally with their workers on-the-job and how to implement internal policies by using employee handbooks, manuals, progress appraisals and performance evaluations effectively to minimize exposure in this area.

Finally, in Chapter 4, Firing and Termination Decisions, you will learn the right principles to follow when firing workers to avoid charges of unfair discharge, breach of contract and other common legal wrongs frequently asserted today. The chapter will cover, for example, when and how to negotiate a firing, when it is adviseable to offer severance and other benefits, and how to use references properly. Since all of these suggestions are tried and true, your company will now be able to review and implement many of these same strategies to your benefit.

You are about to learn that knowledge is power and that employers have significant rights at their disposal. Many of the items discussed in the following pages encompass simple rules of common sense and reason. The body of employment law has been created to further fairness and justice; it is there to protect your company, but it will not help you unless you participate in your own defense and know how to detect improprieties and avoid common labor problems. Thus, know the law and above all, good luck.

—Steven Mitchell Sack, Esq.
New York City, New York

About The Author

Steven Mitchell Sack is a nationally known attorney who devotes substantial time to labor problems and employment litigation avoidance. Since 1980, he has maintained a private law practice in New York City devoted primarily to representation in contract negotiations, disputes and litigation, and general labor law.

A prolific writer, Mr. Sack is the author of seven other books on legal subjects. Since 1986, his advice on labor issues regularly appears in The Legal Brief column carried in NAPL's *Printing Manager Magazine.* He has also authored numerous articles in business publications which discuss many subjects including hiring and firing salespeople, anti-trust issues, and avoiding age and sex discrimination problems.

In addition to conducting a private law practice, Mr. Sack serves as General Counsel for many trade associations, presides in commercial arbitrations as an arbitrator for the American Arbitration Association, and has conducted corporate seminars for companies throughout the United States both in-house and with the American Management Association.

A Phi Beta Kappa graduate of Stony Brook University and a graduate of Boston College Law School, he is a member of the American Bar Association (Labor and Employment Division), NewYork County Lawyer's Association, New York State Bar Association, and is admitted to practice before the United States Tax Court.

Mr. Sack's advice about company exposure to employment-related litigation has appeared nationally in such publications as *The New York Times, The Wall Street Journal, Alert* (published by the Research Institute of America), and many other business journals. He has appeared on hundreds of radio programs and national television including *The Oprah Winfrey Show* and the *Salley Jesse Raphael Show.* His recent books in the consumer market include *The Salesperson's Legal Guide* (Prentice Hall, 1981), *Don't Get Taken* (McGraw-Hill, 1985), *The Complete Legal Guide to Marriage, Divorce, Custody and Living Together* (McGraw-Hill, 1987), and *The Employee Rights Handbook: Answers To Legal Questions From Interview to Pink Slip* (Facts on File, Inc. 1991).

CHAPTER

1 Pre-Employment Considerations

Successful strategies to reduce litigation exposure begin with a variety of considerations and procedures before a candidate is ever actually hired. This involves correctly designing advertisements and brochures during job recruitment, proper techniques for screening applicants, conducting the hiring interview legally (with particular care to avoid asking questions that could lead to charges of discrimination), and properly investigating a candidate's references and statements on the employment application while avoiding charges of defamation and invasion of privacy actions. Employers must also be careful to avoid misrepresenting the job and to spell out carefully and clearly the remuneration, duties, and responsibilities of the job offered. These are just a few of the many pre-hiring considerations that careful employers must follow and which will now be explored in greater detail.

ADVERTISEMENTS AND BROCHURES

The employment relationship begins with the prospective employee's first contact with the company, which is often in the form of an advertisement or brochure. There are many major problem areas employers should be concerned with when drafting advertisements and brochures.

Companies should avoid using descriptions implying that the job is secure. For example, avoid using words such as "long-term growth," "permanent," "secure," or "career path." Such words may create an inference that the employee was hired in a manner other than at-will. If this were the case your company might have difficulty firing the employee suddenly, without notice or cause, because the employee would argue that he/she could not be fired without a warning or unless there was a good reason (e.g., fighting or sleeping on the job). Rather, the use of words such as "full-time" or "regular" is preferable in ads because they minimize the inference that long-term tenure was to be given to an employee after he/she was hired. The same care with words must be taken during job interviews and is discussed in the section "Promises of Job Security."

Additionally, companies must take proper steps to insure that advertisements and brochures are properly worded to comply with various federal and state discrimination laws. For example, companies are prohibited from publishing advertisements indicating any preference, limitation, specification or discrimination based on age. The Department of Labor has published an Interpretive Bulletin stipulating that Help Wanted notices or advertisements containing phrases such as "must be 18," "age 25 to 35 preferred," "recent college graduate," "sales trainee, any recent degree," and "sales executive, 2 yrs. out of college" and others of a similar nature discriminated against the employment of older persons when used in relation to a specific job and were considered to violate the law.

Counsel Comments: *Requesting an experienced, mature worker in an advertisement is not illegal since this does not discriminate against older workers.*

Under the federal Civil Rights Act, Equal Employment Opportunity Commission (EEOC) regulations make it a violation of the Act to indicate limitations or exclusions from job opportunities on the basis of race, color, religion, sex or national origin in help-wanted ads, unless the specific job is a "bona fide occupational" exception under its regulations. This caveat applies to advertisements which favor men over woman, whites over blacks, and so forth. Thus, words such as "youthful," "male," "Gal Friday," "Amish," "Chinese," or "married" must never be used. The reason that it is so important to draft advertisements and brochures properly to comply with the law is that discriminatory advertising is a "smoking gun" and is certain to be used as evidence against an employer when a related complaint is filed.

Effect Of The Americans With Disabilities Act

Additionally, due to the enactment of the Americans with Disabilities Act of 1990 (the ADA), employers must be certain that recruitment and job application procedures do not discriminate against qualified job applicants based on their disabilities. The first step in demonstrating lawful conduct can be accomplished through use of positive statements in your company's advertisements and brochures. In fact, it is recommended that all advertisements and brochures be rewritten to contain the following text or similar words: "Our company is an Equal Opportunity Employer and does not discriminate on the basis of a physical or mental handicap." Insertion of such language is important because all companies employing more than 25 workers (and more than 15 workers as of July, 1994) must take reasonable steps to accommodate the needs of handicapped workers under the ADA. Persons with disabilities cannot be disqualified from applying because of the inability to perform non-essential or marginal functions of the job. Inserting similar language in your ads and brochures will demonstrate your company's desire to comply with the law and not initially exclude qualified but disabled applicants from the potential job pool.

Misrepresentation

Due to various state laws enacted to crack down on unscrupulous companies whose help-wanted ads prey on the unwary, employers must be careful to avoid drafting help-wanted ads that misrepresent the job. These laws primarily penalize employers for painting overly rosy job descriptions which mislead applicants about the true nature of the job and ultimately disappoint them. In New York State, for example, the law prohibits false advertising about "the kind, character, terms or conditions of any employment opportunity if such advertising is misleading in any material respect." Disgruntled employees misled by such an ad (e.g., told in the ad that the job offered was an important position with supervisory duties when in fact it is not) can sue the new employer for money damages; the employer might have to pay for the employee's job-related losses resulting from resigning from the previous job or relocating.

Advertising Agencies

Employers should recognize they are probably liable for false or discriminatory ads conceived and designed by an outside advertising agency. Although an employer's exposure might depend on a number of factors (i.e., whether the ads were supposed to be reviewed and approved before distribution), generally, employers may be liable unless it can be shown that the language in the ad was a mistake and renounced immediately upon discovery.

Counsel Comments: *If this happens to your company, you should immediately send a certified letter, return receipt requested, to the advertising agency alerting them to the mistake and seeking a retraction and/or indemnification from the mistake. Such a letter could demonstrate that no intent to practice discrimination was involved.*

Also, under the ADA, if your company uses an employment agency to recruit, screen and hire, you cannot escape liability when the employment agency fails to hire qualified but disabled workers. Thus, be sure the employment agency is familiar with the ramifications of this new law.

In light of the serious penalties imposed by the ADA, including damages which range up to $300,000 and attorney *fees, some companies are now inquiring whether the employment agency is aware of its obligation to "send over" disabled workers for screening and are demanding that this be done. For additional protection, include an indemnification clause in your contract with all employment agencies providing that your company be paid for legal defense and damages caused by illegal acts committed by the agency against disabled job applicants and workers.*

Finally, to avoid mistakes in this entire area, it is suggested that your company designate one person to handle the drafting and review of all advertisments and brochures. Such a person would coordinate the placement of all recruiting ads to minimize the possibility of legal problems. Instruct that person to save copies of all ads and record the number of responses and number of hires. On any discrimination investigation or audit, copies of all previous ads will be one of the first items you are requested to produce, so be sure they are collected and stored in an accessible place for easy retrieval.

JOB REQUIREMENTS

When preparing job criteria, do not set a higher requirement than is needed for the job simply to attract a better caliber of applicant. The reason is that you may be inadvertently discriminating against a particular class of applicant. For example, in the case of *United States vs. Georgia Power Company,* decided by the Supreme Court in the early 1970s, the requirements of a high school diploma and aptitude test scores raised the central concern of whether the requirements really were related to successful job performance. Since many local black and other minority applicants did not have high school diplomas in rural Georgia when the case was initially brought, the company's requirements effectively excluded minorities from jobs. However, the diploma requirement was found to be unlawful because any requirement must measure the person for the job and not the person "in abstract." In this case the Supreme Court ruled that the qualification of a high school diploma did not measure the individual's ability to do the job (i.e., to work on power lines) and was therefore illegal.

As a result of cultural obstacles and discriminatory educational practices, older applicants, women and persons belonging to minority groups may be affected unfairly by job standards based on a level of educational achievement. Courts and anti-discrimination agencies insist that educational requirements be related to the successful performance of the job at hand.

Counsel Comments: *Be sure that all requirements are directly job-related. Avoid denying employment to persons who lack formal education credits or requirements when education is not relevant to the job skills sought. Choose the person with the best demonstrated skills for the job to avoid problems in this area. Recognize that it is not sufficient to show a lack of discriminatory intent if your company's selection process discriminates against one group or class of applicant over another.*

Age Discrimination

Courts are aware that age discrimination is often difficult to prove by direct evidence. That is why, at the start of a case, the plaintiff is allowed to benefit from an inference of discrimination simply upon proof that the employee was in a protected age category (e.g., over 40) and that he/she was refused a job that was then given to a younger person with no better credentials. The burden then shifts to the employer to produce a non-discriminatory reason for the person's non-hire, following which the applicant has the burden to demonstrate that the proffered reason was a mere pretext not to hire the aging employee.

In one recent case the court stated: "It seems that often an old employee never has the right combination of credentials to fit into existing openings. The principal reason advanced by the employer during litigation for refusing to hire the worker is because he is overqualified. For those individuals in the protected age group, such a reason may often simply be a code word for too old." The court noted that employers should not have preconceived notions and stereotypes of what a candidate for an entry level position should look like and should not refuse to hire an older applicant based on such a reason.

Counsel Comments: *Instruct all personnel in charge of hiring never to tell or admit to an older applicant that they* *"lack formal education credits," "are overqualified," "are overspecialized," or that the company is "looking to hire someone with a more recent college degree." Recent cases demonstrate it may be illegal to refuse to hire an older applicant by successfully arguing that being* overqualified *for a position means the person is* unqualified *for the position. Such words are a "smoking gun" likely to stimulate the older rejected applicant's desire to file a discrimination lawsuit or to contact the Equal Employment Opportunity Commission (EEOC) for more information. Be sure that such words are never directly mentioned to the applicant or placed in memos written after the applicant has left the interview.*

On the other hand, a company *may* be able to reject job applicants because they are college graduates without violating age discrimination laws. In one recent case, a 58-year-old retiree on a pension from a federal job sought employment in the private sector. A help-wanted ad placed in a local newspaper drew his attention. The ad invited applications for openings for "customer service representatives." The individual was soon granted an interview but the colloquy hit a snag when the interviewer asked about his education. When told he was a graduate from Westbrook College cum laude, the interviewer stated that the company had a policy of not hiring college graduates for this entry level position.

The man brought a lawsuit in which he charged that the employer's no-college-graduates policy was a stratagem to practice age discrimination. When the case came to court, the employer responded that:

1. Its refusal to hire college graduates as customer service representatives did not constitute age bias since it applied the same no-hire policy to young college graduates as well as to older applicants;

2. The reason for the refusal to hire was justified—college graduates, whether young or old, do not typically remain long at customer services jobs since they find such jobs to be lacking in challenge and to be low paying;

3. To avoid heavy turnover, the company limited the jobs to employees who lack college educations since they were more likely to be content to stay with these jobs.

Even though the company was unable to produce statistical evidence proving that college graduates had a high turnover in customer service employment, the U.S. Court of Appeals rejected the claimant's argument that such a policy was a smokescreen to conceal a discriminatory policy aimed at not hiring older applicants. The court concluded that the company's policy was truly designed to reduce turnover and not to discriminate.

What about the employee who conceals his college education when he's accepted for a menial job? Can he be fired when his employer discovers the truth? Typically, the answer is yes, except when the individual is a union member entitled to grieve the termination in arbitration. This happened recently with a man who was fired after working six months for a company. When the company discovered that the new employee held a B.A. and master's degree, the man was fired because he had stated on his job form that he had only a high school education. He was fired for "falsifying his job application." The union which represents employees at the company fought for the employee's reinstatement and forced the issue into arbitration. The arbitrator ordered reinstatement after finding that the company had not suffered any "injury sufficiently grave to justify termination" and scoffed at the company's argument that only employees with a limited education would be content with a utility position.

Counsel Comments: *Simply showing that a younger individual was hired over a qualified older applicant does not prove age discrimination if the employer can show its decision was based on an honest evaluation of the candidate's qualifications (e.g., the prospective employee would be bored or likely to leave upon finding a better job, or both.) Furthermore, an employer is under no obligation to provide a laid-off employee with a job for which that person is overqualified. And, when eliminating a position, an employer does not assume an obligation to retain or create a position for the displaced employee simply because the employee is within a "protected class."*

Disabled Applicants

Scrutinize all job requirements to insure that your company is not inadvertently screening out qualified disabled applicants. Under the ADA, an employer may deny a job to an individual with a disability if the individual fails to meet a selected criterion under the Act. However, it is unlawful to exclude applicants with disabilities and fail to hire them if the criterion can be satisfied by the applicant with a reasonable accommodation by the employer. According to the Senate Labor and Human Resources Committee, which was responsible for drafting the bill:

Suppose an employer has an opening for a typist and two persons apply for the job, one being an individual with a disability who types 50 words per minute and the other being an individual without a disability who types 75 words per minute. The employer is permitted to choose the applicant with the higher typing speed.

On the other hand, if the two applicants are, one, an individual with a hearing impairment who requires a telephone headset with an amplifier and the other, an individual without a disability, both of whom have the same typing speed, the employer is *not* permitted to choose the individual without a disability because of the requirement to provide the needed reasonable accommodation.

Counsel Comments: *A disabled applicant can only be rejected if the person cannot perform essential job functions, even with reasonable accommodation. However, your company must avoid setting too high a standard of job requirement which purposely or inadvertently excludes qualified but disabled or handicapped applicants.*

The following rules summarize some important points in this area:

a. Any qualifications which are not job-related and which tend to screen out applicants, must be eliminated;

b. Educational requirements cannot be overstated (for example, a higher educational degree than is necessary). This can be illegal;

c. No age limit or preferred sex should ever be mentioned except where absolutely necessary for the job in question; and

d. Review your hiring policies regarding disabled applicants.

AFFIRMATIVE ACTION

Today the trend in the corporate community is to attract and cultivate a diverse workforce. Affirmative action involves making a specific effort to recruit individuals on the basis of classifications such as race, sex, religion, veteran status, etc., and taking positive action to insure that such individuals, when employed, have an equal opportunity for benefits and promotions. According to a 1987 Supreme Court decision, an employer's voluntary affirmative action plan is legal if there is a "manifest imbalance" in the makeup of the employer's workforce for a particular job category, the plan has a limited duration and the legitimate expectations of other workers are not trampled upon.

Initially, affirmative action programs were begun to comply with federal regulations imposed upon employers having government contracts or subcontracts worth in excess of $10,000. As a result of recent Supreme Court decisions, voluntary, reasonable affirmative action programs established by employers will be upheld and not found to constitute reverse discrimination provided company plans have flexible goals rather than rigid quotas which exclude a whole class of applicant (e.g., white males). Additionally, a company must be able to justify, statistically or otherwise, the need for an affirmative action plan and the plan must be capable of being eliminated or altered when certain goals are met.

Counsel Comments: *Since there is no private duty to institute affirmative action policies, do not establish them without conducting a thorough statistical analysis of your workforce. Unless a valid reason exists for implementing affirmative action, think twice before establishing such a plan. If an affirmative action plan is in place, review the program annually. Monitor all areas of employment and establish obtainable goals and timetables. Designate one person to discover potential problems, correct deficiencies and monitor the results. Avoid setting rigid quotas and creating low-quality standards and reverse discrimination.*

APPLICANT SCREENING

Screening takes place before job applicants are formally interviewed. Proper screening procedure begins with the development of an accurate, detailed job description so that applicants know the type of job that is being offered. In addition, candidates should be requested to complete a formal application form which contains general information, the candidate's educational background, work experience, references, and other pertinent information.

Job Descriptions

A preliminary job description for an established position should be reviewed by several persons, including a supervisor. The description must be written in a precise manner, using care to select words which convey specifically the meaning intended. The format of the description should include the job title and name of agency or unit, a job summary and precise description of the job's physical and mental qualifications. The purpose is to explain directly what the job involves and what is expected to be done.

Disabled Workers

The need for a precise job description has become even more important as a result of the enactment of the Americans With Disabilities Act of 1990. The ADA prohibits discrimination against a qualified individual based on his/her disability with regard to recruitment and job application procedures as well as hiring policies. The law demands several rules be followed to assure a fit between job criteria and an applicant's actual ability to do the job:

1. Persons with disabilities are not to be disqualified because of their inability to perform nonessential or marginal functions of the job;

2. Any selection criterion that eliminates or tends to screen out must be job-related and consistent with business necessity; and

3. Reasonable accommodation to assist persons with disabilities to meet legitimate criteria must be provided.

Written job descriptions defining job duties and responsibilities must be carefully reviewed before insertion in advertising or use when interviewing applicants. This is to insure that qualified individuals capable of performing the job are able to participate in the interviewing process. Employers cannot deny access to, segregate, or classify applicants in a way that adversely impacts the opportunities or status of the applicant because of disability.

Counsel Comments: *Job descriptions must now be carefully reviewed because this is the first place the EEOC will look to determine whether handicap discrimination in violation of the ADA has taken place. When in doubt, include* all *essential job functions in the description to demonstrate that certain jobs are incapable of being performed adequately by disabled workers and that these criteria were established* before *the interviewing process took place.*

The act also makes a distinction between an essential job function and a minimal job function which employers must identify in a job description. If you describe essential job functions which the plaintiff could not perform, your case will be stronger, whereas including only minimal job functions in the description weakens your case. For example, if you fail to note the essential functions of a particular job, such as heavy lifting as well as typing and telephone answering, you may have to hire a wheelchair-bound applicant who desires the job.

Under ADA, the importance of complete and accurate job descriptions cannot be overstated; properly written job descriptions prepared before job applicants are interviewed can be used as evidence of essential job functions and what the job entails. Employers who draft job descriptions that are current and accurate and which include all essential job functions can defeat a charge in discrimination lawsuits that such descriptions were tools of your own stereotypical thinking and consequent discrimination.

Summary Of ADA Rules To Remember During Hiring

Always consider the reason the individual is being hired, including the degree of expertise and skill the job requires. Are there some job duties that cannot be given to others? What duties are current employees actually performing? For example, don't claim that typing 105 words per minute is an essential function if your current secretaries actually type 75 words per minute. What will happen if an employee is not capable of performing the desired task? It is probably not a good idea to reject a disabled worker if the inability to perform a desired task creates only minimal problems.

During the hiring process:

1. **Avoid disability-related questions in interviews.** (Note: There is an exception for companies which are federal government contractors. Under the Rehabilitation Act of 1973, those companies are required to give applicants an opportunity to provide information about their disability but such facts cannot be used against the applicant in a hiring decision.);

2. **Never inquire what kind of accommodation the person needs in order to perform the job properly if hired;**

3. **Only request a medical exam *after* hiring and be sure it is made a condition of employment for *all* entering employees in that position;**

4. **Asking questions about the person's ability to perform specific job-related tasks or the job's requirements is legal;**

5. **Never keep written notes on observations about an applicant's disabilities since they can serve as a "smoking gun" against your company in the event of a lawsuit.** If information on accommodations has been obtained by an applicant tracking system or notes in a personnel file, be sure that such information is not used to discriminate against the individual regarding hiring or future job opportunities. Discuss access to and future use of such information. Develop written policies to minimize claims that your company unlawfully acquired and used such information to that person's detriment.

The Philadelphia law firm of Blank, Rome, Comisky & McCauley in the June 1, 1992 issue of *Management Policies and Personnel Law* newsletter, suggests the following excellent steps in order to comply with the ADA:

- Develop job descriptions in order to determine if an individual is "qualified."
- Examine employment applications to make sure that language is non-discriminatory.
- Examine employment tests and other selection criteria to make sure that those with disabilities are not screened out.
- Examine pre-employment drug testing procedures to make sure that they do not eliminate applicants because of prescription drugs taken for a medical reason.
- Reevaluate medical exam procedures so that exams are performed only after an offer of employment is made and confidentiality of examination results is maintained.
- Evaluate your workforce in order to accommodate those who have identified themselves as disabled.
- Train the workforce to deal with disabled co-workers.
- Reconsider your safety programs to include the disabled.
- Reconsider and revise personnel policies to make them more neutral, as well as fair to the company. For example, the ADA doesn't entitle those with disabilities to more paid leave than other employees.
- Prepare and post ADA notices throughout your company.
- Develop contacts among organizations for the disabled.
- Prepare reasonable accommodation options.
- Prepare both work and other areas such as rest rooms and lunchrooms to accommodate the disabled.
- Review performance appraisals to be sure they are neutral, and that they allow for documenting all negative as well as positive incidents.
- Consider a peer review panel to give feedback on employment practices and decisions.
- Document all efforts to accommodate applicants and employees who are disabled.
- Review contracts with employment agencies, unions, etc., and review all insurance plans to be sure they are non-discriminatory.

Enforceability Of Job Descriptions

Can a disgruntled ex-employee or employee compel companies to live up to job descriptions via lawsuits? Ordinarily, a company is free to change a person's duties and responsibilities after a hiring. Problems arise, however, when job descriptions and corresponding benefits are deliberately misstated to induce a worker to accept a position; they then become similar to misleading job opportunity ads and can become the subject of damage claims.

For example, this recently occurred to a lawyer who left a law firm for another after being promised that the new employer had secured a large environmental law client and had formed a department in environmental law which the person would head. However, after joining the new firm, it became apparent that neither environment clients nor the department existed. Disagreements arose, and the person was fired two years later.

A lawsuit was brought in federal court for breach of contract, negligent misrepresentation and fraudulent inducement. The Second Circuit authorized a trial to proceed on the fraud charges since factual assurances had been made to the employee (that a large environmental client had been secured), which had been relied upon and were the basis for the employee taking the job in the first place.

> **Counsel Comments:** *To avoid liability in this area, your company should indicate in a handbook or personnel manual, employment application, contract or in the job description itself, that the duties and responsibilities of the job are subject to change without notice.*

EMPLOYMENT APPLICATIONS

Employment applications are helpful in defeating lawsuits that may arise down the road. Despite the advantages of having an application form, many companies fail to use them effectively. For example, employment applications can be used to dispel contractual presumptions, reduce an employer's exposure when investigating past employment and other information, and can give the employer added grounds for immediate termination if false statements contained in the application are discovered.

In one case a job applicant filled out an employment application containing the following language:

"The purpose of this application is to get truthful answers. The fact that you tell the truth will receive more consideration for this position than any good impression you may try to make by untruthful answers. Providing false information shall be sufficient cause for rejection or dismissal."

Ten months after being hired, the man was fired for "falsifying company records" and failing to reveal two previous employers, of whom one had fired him for insubordination and the other had forced him to resign for unsatisfactory work.

The man sought reinstatement via a union arbitration hearing. He argued that he did not list one of the positions for fear that the employer would think he was a union organizer. The other job was not listed since he only worked there a short time. He also stated that his employer waited too long after his probationary period to fire him for the omissions and that such a delay constituted a waiver of the company's right to fire him on this basis.

The company argued that it acted as soon as it received the information (from a co-worker) and that the employment application clearly stated that omitting the names of past employers would lead to dismissal. The arbitrator ruled for the company and ordered that the man stay fired. The decision stated that the prime purpose of an employment application is to enable a company to assess the qualifications of a prospective employee. In order to effectuate this purpose the employee must give a full and accurate account as to the information requested on the form. Without such information the company is unable to render an informed judgment as to whether to employ the applicant. In this case, particularly since the application form itself stated the importance of truthfulness and that an untruthful answer would be sufficient cause for dismissal, the company's position was upheld.

> **Counsel Comments:** *Some companies purchase employment applications from books and other sources that do not adequately cover their particular interests. Many of the employment application forms acquired from these sources contain discriminatory questions, do not reflect recent changes in federal and state law and do not clearly cover a company's specific needs and concerns. Thus, it is best to have an experienced labor lawyer draft the application form or review it thoroughly before implementation.*

Well-drafted employment applications can give your company much legal protection. For example, the following language was taken from an employment application recently drafted by the author and illustrates the points cited above:

"I acknowledge that I have given (name of company) the right to make a thorough investigation of my past employment, education and activities without liability, and understand that any false answer, statement or implication made by me in my employment application or at any job interview, shall be considered grounds for my immediate discharge.

"If hired, I agree to conform to the rules and regulations of (name of company) in all respects. I understand that my employment with and compensation from (name of company) can be terminated at any time without notice or cause at the option of either of us. I also acknowledge that no representations or promises regarding continued employment for any specified period of time have been made to me during job discussions.

"Just as I am free to resign at any time without notice, so may (name of company) terminate me at any time with or without cause and with or without notice. Upon my resignation or termination, I agree to return all company property in my possession or under my control at the company's request."

[Applicant's Signature] [Date]

Counsel Comments: *All prospective employees should be required to complete an application form, even if they submit a resume. All employment applications should contain a space for the applicant's signature and date, particularly when disclaimers similar to the above have been included. You may wish to print such disclaimers in boldface type or place them on a separate page to stress their importance. Better still, you can insist that candidates initial each disclaimer on the right-hand margin of the application form for greater protection.*

Generally, it is not necessary to use more than one application form (i.e., one for managers and another for salespeople or clerical workers) provided the form is thoroughly drafted and contains many of the disclaimers mentioned above. If you are concerned about a particular skill, for example, how many words a clerical worker can type per minute, but do not believe this is relevant for a managerial candidate, you may still place this question on the form and ask all applicants to answer it. You can simply disregard the manager-candidate's answer. Requiring everyone to complete the same form may eliminate potential claims of bias.

Application forms are the subject of considerable litigation under federal and state discrimination laws. The Equal Employment Opportunity Commission has indicated that it regards as discriminatory all questions that are not specifically related to the elements of the job or based on business need. Thus, be sure to review current employment applications to determine if they comply with all applicable federal and state laws (especially equal employment opportunity laws), and whether they help your company collect important information which will enable you to select candidates worthy of an interview. Employers may screen applicants for evidence of motivation, ambition and job interest, but cannot ask discriminatory questions on the employment application or in person at the hiring interview. (Note: A detailed review of legal and illegal questions is provided in a later section of this chapter.)

JOB RESUMES

How long must job resumes and employment applications be kept on file to avoid charges of discrimination and unfair hiring practices? The law differs in this respect. The Civil Rights Act requires all resumes and applications to be retained for six months after the document is submitted or after action is taken on the application, whichever is later. The Age Discrimination in Employment Act requires that job applications of individuals between the ages of 40 and 70 be retained for one year.

Counsel Comments: *Courts do not burden employers to retain job resumes and applications indefinitely in order to defeat charges of discrimination. In fact, a U.S. Circuit Court of Appeals held that a systematically applied policy of not saving applications beyond one year was not discriminatory. Thus, keep all applications for at least one year to be safe. Never segregate applications or treat some differently from others. For example, if you retain certain applications in an active status for a specified period, you must retain* all *applications for the same period.*

If your company receives unsolicited resumes, it is advisable to return them since many resumes contain discriminatory information that your company is not supposed to read. This can minimize charges that such information was used in the hiring process. Smart companies return all resumes immediately with a note requesting that the applicant complete the company's standard application, which is enclosed.

IMMIGRATION CHECKS

Companies must be mindful of many potential problems relating to hiring aliens, immigrants and minorities. For example, The Immigration Reform and Control Act of 1986 states that employers should hire only U.S. citizens and aliens who are authorized to work in the United States. The law requires every employer to verify the employment eligibility of every worker hired to avoid civil fines and criminal penalties for failure to comply with the law's recordkeeping requirements. The law requires each company to follow fixed guidelines regardless of company size or the number of employees being hired. The Immigration and Naturalization Service has developed a Form I-9 that employers must complete and retain in order to verify employment eligibility for all employees.

Essentially, employers have five verification obligations:

1. Employees must be instructed to fill out their portion of the Form I-9 when they begin work;

2. Employers must check documents establishing employees' identity and eligibility to work;

3. Employers must properly complete the remaining portion of Form I-9;

4. Employers must retain the Form for at least three years or until one year after a person leaves employment, whichever is later; and

5. Employers must present the Form for inspection to INS or Department of Labor officials upon request after three days' advance notice.

All companies must verify the identity and work authorization of every person hired. Evidence must be examined, collected and saved by the employer to refute charges that it knew it was hiring an unauthorized alien.

The list on the following page of acceptable documents will help establish identity and employment authorization.

Form 1-9 must be completed and attested to by the new employee at the time of hiring; the company must review all documentation and submit the Form within three business days of the hiring. The applicant has 21 additional business days to furnish documents which are lost or are not yet processed. Copies of the INS Form may be obtained from any district INS office and photocopied for future use by other applicants.

All completed I-9 Forms must be saved for at least three years after the hiring, or for one year after the person is terminated, whichever occurs later; these rules apply to temporary workers and independent contractors as well. However, companies are not obligated to verify employment eligibility for people working as employees for such independent contractors.

Employers failing to follow the law are currently liable for fines ranging from $250 to $2,000 for each unauthorized alien hiring for a first offense; $2,000 to $5,000 for each unauthorized alien for a second offense; and $3,000 to $10,000 for each unauthorized alien for subsequent offenses. The law also imposes criminal penalties against companies and their principal officers up to $3,000 for each unauthorized alien with respect to whom a violation occurs, or imprisonment for not more than six months, or both.

Counsel Comments: *If an employer can show that he or she has complied with the Form I-9 requirements, then the employer has established a "good faith" defense with respect to a charge of knowingly hiring an unauthorized alien, unless the government can show that the employer had actual knowledge of the unauthorized status of the employee. However, violations of the law exist when employers fail to comply with the Form I-9 requirements, engage in a pattern or practice of knowingly hiring or continuing to employ unauthorized aliens, engage in fraud or false statements, misuse visas, immigration permits and identity documents, or engage in unfair immigration-related employment practices.*

The above information is not meant to be all-inclusive; rather, it gives you a good idea of the kind of scrutiny that must be made to comply with The Immigration Reform and Control Act of 1986. If you have questions or require specific details as to what types of documents qualify for verification purposes, speak to an immigration attorney or representative at a local INS office.

LIST OF ACCEPTABLE DOCUMENTS

LIST A

Documents that Establish Both Identity and Employment Eligibility.

1. U.S. Passport (unexpired or expired)

2. Certificate of U.S. Citizenship *(INS Form N-560 or N-561)*

3. Certificate of Naturalization *(INS Form N-550 or N-570)*

4. Unexpired foreign passport with I-551 stamp or attached INS Form I-94 indicating unexpired employment authorization

5. Alien Registration Receipt Card with photograph *(INS form I-151 or I-551)*

6. Unexpired Temporary Resident Card *(INS form I-688)*

7. Employment Authorization Card *(INS Form I-688A)*

8. Unexpired Reentry Permit (INS Form I-327)

9. Unexpired Refugee Travel Document *(INS Form I-571)*

10. Unexpired Employment Authorization Document Issued by the INS which contains a photograph *(INS Form I-688B)*

OR

LIST B

Documents that Establish Identity

1. Driver's license or ID card issued by a state or outlying possession of the United States provided it contains a photograph or information such as name, date of birth, sex, height, eye color, and address

2. ID card issued by federal, state or local government agencies or entities provided it contains a photograph or information such as name, date of birth, sex, height, eye color, and address

3. School ID card with a photograph

4. Voter's registration card

5. U.S. Military card or draft record

6. Military dependent's ID card

7. U.S. Coast Guard Merchant Mariner card

8. Native American tribal document

9. Driver's license issued by a Canadian government authority

For persons under age 18 who are unable to present a document listed above:

10. School record or report card

11. Clinic, doctor, or hospital record

12. Day-care or nursery school record

AND

LIST C

Documents that Establish Employment Eligibility

1. U.S. social security card issued by the Social Security Administration *(other than a card stating that it is not valid for employment)*

2. Certification of Birth Abroad issued by the Department of State *(Form FS-545 or Form DS-1350)*

3. Original or certified copy of a birth certificate issued by a state, county, municipal authority or outlying possession of the United States bearing an official seal

4. Native American tribal document

5. U.S. Citizen ID Card *(INS Form I-197)*

6. ID Card for use of Resident Citizen in the United States *(INS Form I-179)*

7. Unexpired employment authorization document issued by the INS (*other than those listed under LIST A*)

Related Discrimination Concerns. Companies should also be aware that the Act contains anti-discrimination elements. For example, companies with more than four employees are forbidden from hiring, recruiting or discharging any person (other than an unauthorized alien) on the basis of race, sex, national origin or citizenship status. Sanctions can be imposed ranging up to $2,000 for each employee discriminated against in addition to the more common damages asserted and collected by litigants in Equal Employment Opportunity Commission (EEOC) discrimination cases.

> **Counsel Comments:** *To avoid problems in this area, it is suggested that companies do not ask an applicant to produce identity and authorization documents until* after *the decision to hire has been made and accepted; you may be accused of violating the law if you decide not to hire a person after viewing documentation that he/she is a legal worker. If you discover that the person is an illegal alien, you then have the right to deny employment on that basis without risking exposure under The Immigration Reform and Control Act. You would also avoid exposure to a case litigated by the individual with private counsel or in conjunction with the EEOC or the state's Division of Human Rights. Recognize that the points mentioned above provide only a thumbnail sketch of your responsibilities. If you are uncertain regarding any aspects of this law, consult with experienced legal counsel immediately.*

Finally, the following points may answer some of the more common questions employers have regarding this law:

- Citizens and nationals of the United States need to prove they are eligible for work.
- Companies need not complete I-9 Forms for everyone who applies for a job; only for those actually hired.
- The Form need not be filled out when the person is hired—only when the person actually begins working.
- Anyone receiving remuneration (i.e, anything of value, even if only food and lodging) must complete the Form.
- I-9 Forms need not be filled out for independent contractors, but you cannot knowingly use this loophole to circumvent the law.
- If the person hired is unable to produce the required documents within three days after hire, the employee must produce a receipt showing that he or she has applied for the document and must present the actual document to you within 90 days of the hire.
- Your company can fire any employee who fails to produce the required documents within three business days, provided this practice is applied uniformly to all employees.
- If the employer properly completes a Form I-9 and the INS discovers that the employee is not actually authorized to work, a good faith defense exists and your company should not be charged with a verification violation.
- The employee may choose which documents he or she wishes to present from the list of acceptable documents.
- Employers are required to examine carefully the documents presented to verify their authenticity.
- Employers may accept an expired United States Passport.
- Laminated Social Security cards may not be acceptable; Social Security Administration printouts are also not acceptable - only a person's official Social Security card will suffice.
- Employers may not accept photocopies of documents. The only exception is a certified copy of a birth certificate.
- It is not essential to make copies of all documents presented; but if your company does make copies, be sure to do so for all employees.
- When re-hiring a person who previously filled out an I-9 Form, you need not complete a new Form if the rehiring is within 3 years of completion of the original Form.
- You do not need to complete a new I-9 Form for promoted or transferred employees.

Immigration Policies

In a related area, the Immigration Act of 1990, which took effect on October 1, 1991, significantly restructured immigration and nationality policies by allocating 140,000 immigrants per year to enter the United States for employment purposes. Priority workers and professionals, defined as aliens with extraordinary ability (such as professors with three years relevant experience), will now find it easier to immigrate; unskilled workers will find it more difficult to immigrate. Section 122 of the act creates a pilot program whereby the Secretary of Labor will determine or "precertify" labor shortages for up to 10 occupations. For those categories, there will be no requirement to obtain labor certifications. Otherwise, labor certification from the U.S. Department of Labor, certifying that American workers are unavailable and that prevailing wages are to be offered, is required, as in the past, for all aliens, whether professionals, skilled or unskilled workers. The act is a complex law that affects all aspects of accepting foreign nationals into this country; every classification of employee has complicated procedures regarding visas and related areas that must be complied with by employers to avoid problems.

Hiring Preferences

Can U.S. applicants be given hiring preference over qualified aliens? If your company is considering hiring an alien, it must seek labor certification from the Department of Labor. The certification process is designed to preserve available jobs for qualified U.S. workers. If any *qualified* U.S. workers have applied for a position, they must be given preference, even if they are *less qualified* than the alien.

Language Rules

With more foreign-born employees entering the workforce, a wave of English-only regulations has been spreading among companies throughout the United States. Some of these regulations are very restrictive (only English may be spoken on company premises); others are fairly loose (only English may be spoken when customers are present); and many more are merely the verbal equivalents of informal company policy. But except in the rarest of circumstances, they're all *illegal.*

The Equal Employment Opportunity Commission (EEOC) has published strict guidelines relating to "English-only" rules. These guidelines recognize that "The primary language of an individual is often an essential national origin characteristic. Prohibiting employees...from speaking their primary language or the language they speak most comfortably, disadvantages an individual's employment opportunities on the basis of national origin." The guidelines continue, "It may also create an atmosphere of inferiority based on national origin, which could result in a discriminatory working environment. Therefore, the commission will presume that such a rule violates Title VII and will closely scrutinize it."

Advocates of "English-only" rules proclaim that job opportunities for minorities will not improve until they master the English language. For example, a 1990 study by a national Hispanic policy organization found that approximately 56% of Hispanic adults are functionally illiterate in English. Thus, the English-only advocates say, it is essential that minorities be forced to master the English language, and the easiest place to do this is in the workplace. However, even in states where English has been designated as the official language (e.g., California), the courts have ruled that employers have no legal right to dictate what language an employee speaks, absent *compelling business necessity.*

Depending on the circumstances, it may be permissible to regulate use of a foreign language in cases where groups of employees are performing hazardous tasks and fast and precise communication among all of them is essential. The burden of proving such a compelling business necessity falls on the employer, who faces an uphill battle in light of current law and reported case decisions in this area.

Counsel Comments: *Where applicable, the person in charge of hiring should go to great lengths to explain that the job being offered is dangerous, that other workers in the prospective employee's area speak only English, and that an"English-only" rule is essential for employee safety. This may demonstrate your company was reasonable in applying such a policy.*

However, the law is extremely protective of minorities on the job in many areas. Begin with the assumption that any rule restricting an employee's ability to speak a language other than English will violate federal and state discrimination laws. Although there are limited exceptions to these rules for compelling business necessity, speak to a knowledgeable labor lawyer before implementing any exceptions to avoid problems in this area.

THE HIRING INTERVIEW AND DISCRIMINATORY QUESTIONS

Twenty years ago, employers could ask almost any question they wanted of an applicant or employee. Questions could be asked about marital status, past arrests, alcohol and drug use, credit history, childbearing plans and age. Now, however, such questions are illegal, because employers are supposed to consider applicants as they presently are, not as they were in the past or may be in the future. Employers cannot use any application process which screens out a disproportionate number of women or minorities. All inquiries concerning an applicant's race, color, religion or national origin, either direct or indirect, may be regarded as evidence of discrimination.

Female applicants are frequent targets of discriminatory questions. Some employers ask questions about child care of female applicants but not males (e.g., "Who will look after your child?" "What birth control do you use?" "If you become pregnant, would you have an abortion?" "Are you married?" "Do you plan on having children?"). *These are all now illegal.* Just asking such a question exposes your company to a lawsuit, whether or not you hire the applicant.

The previous section discussed problems associated with "English-only" rules for minorities. Other violations pertaining to color, national origin, citizenship, language and relatives frequently occur before hiring. Recognize that under federal EEOC guidelines and state regulations it is illegal to ask applicants the following at the hiring interview:

Color: What is your skin color?

National origin: What is your ancestry? What is your mother's native language? What is your spouse's native language? What is your maiden name?

Citizenship: Of what country are you a citizen? Are your parents naturalized or native-born citizens? When did they acquire citizenship? Are you a native-born citizen?

Language: What is your native tongue? How did you acquire the ability to read, write and speak a foreign language?

Relatives: Names, addresses, age and other pertinent information concerning your spouse, children or relatives not employed by the company. What type of work does your mother or father do?

Availability for work: Are you available to work weekends?

> **Counsel Comments:** *Since employers are required to accommodate the religious practices of job applicants, it is unwise to ask any questions probing a person's religious beliefs until after a job offer has been made.*

Birthplace: Where is your birthplace?

Age: What is your date of birth?

> **Counsel Comments:** *Your company may be permitted to ask questions regarding a person's age or date of birth before hiring* provided *such inquiries are accompanied by a statement that federal and state laws prohibit age discrimination and the company does not tolerate or engage in age discrimination.*

Child care: Do you have children? Who will care for them while you are working?

Economic status: Have you ever declared bankruptcy, experienced a loan default or wage garnishment?

Military service: Did you ever serve in the military of another country?

Union membership: Are you a member of any union?

Name: Was your name ever changed? If so, how and what was it previously?

Employers may legally pose questions that test a candidate's motivation, maturity, willingness to accept instruction, interest in the job, ability to communicate and personality. The following are examples of the kinds of questions that may be asked:

- What are some of the responsibilities you had in previous jobs?
- What skills and traits do you have that suit the needs of our company?
- What attracted you about the position?
- What are some of your outside interests?
- How would you describe your relationship to those with whom you work?
- What are some of your short and long-term goals?

- Why do you want to change jobs?
- What form of supervisory style do you prefer?

However, inquiries into an applicant's race, color, age, sex, religion and national origin which further discriminatory purposes are illegal under Title VII of The Civil Rights Act of 1964, as amended. This law applies to private employers, employment agencies, labor organizations and training programs. In addition, each state has its own discrimination laws, which often go further in protecting the rights of applicants during job interviews. Particularly stringent states include New York, California, Michigan and Illinois, among others.

Innocent questions often result in companies having to defend against costly and time-consuming charges of discrimination filed with the federal EEOC and various state agencies, including the Human Rights Commission and the Attorney General's Office. If discrimination is found, an applicant may be awarded damages including a job offer, attorney costs and other benefits. Following enactment of the Civil Rights Act of 1991, successful claimants may also demand jury trials and recover compensatory damages (i.e, money paid for emotional pain and suffering) and punitive damages up to $300,000, plus money for expert witnesses who testify at the trial. Thus, in addition to lost worker-time, poor publicity and expensive legal fees, costs and verdicts, sloppy pre-employment interviewing techniques may also force you to hire someone you had no intention of bringing on board!

The chart on the following page illustrates many interview questions that are legal, as well as those found illegal under EEOC guidelines and state regulations. Note that the same question can be either legal or illegal depending on your intent in asking. For instance, asking a woman her maiden name is legal if you need the information to verify past employment records, but not if your intent is to check family background. Additionally, although it is legal to ask an applicant if he/she has any relatives working for the company, it is not legal to ask the names of any relatives in general. Thus, if the applicant responds that no relatives are employed by the company, never follow up the question by asking for names of other relatives.

Counsel Comments: *To avoid the problems of asking discriminatory questions during the hiring interview and committing other illegal acts, all intake and screening personnel must be trained as to what questions are and are not legal. It is a good idea to prepare a standard questionnaire which lists legal questions for interviewers. You can develop a list by consulting the following examples of legal and illegal questions. By referring to such a list, you could demonstrate at an EEOC or Human Rights Commission hearing that an applicant's testimony was incorrect (i.e., that discriminatory questions are never asked of candidates because the interviewer only asks questions prepared from the list and is instructed not to deviate from those questions.) Since discrimination hearings in this area frequently boil down to the word of the applicant versus the word of the interviewer, this document may help to convince the hearing examiner that discriminatory questions were not asked at the interview, and therefore, to dismiss the charges.*

Interviewing job candidates is a delicate business. Companies should also refrain from the following for additional protection:

- Asking for photos before hiring;
- Asking for clergy references before hiring;
- Asking questions of females that you would not ask of males;
- Asking questions about the applicant's military service in countries other than the U.S.;
- Asking questions about the applicant's military record or type of discharge.

Pay special attention to the following areas, where charges of employment discrimination often loom.

Arrests

Employers are not permitted to ask applicants about past arrests because these are often overcome by acquittal, dismissal, withdrawal of charges, or by overturning the conviction, and their use in employment decisions tends to discriminate against minorities. Even when administered evenly, a policy against hiring workers with arrest records may have an adverse impact on minorities when compared with other groups and is therefore illegal.

In limited situations in a few industries, such as day care, employers have an obligation to inquire thoroughly about an applicant's past, including ar-

CHECKLIST OF LEGAL AND ILLEGAL HIRING QUESTIONS

Subject	You May Ask	You May Not Ask
IDENTITY	What is your full name? Have you ever used an alias? If so, what was the name you used? What is the name of your parent or guardian? (Ask only if the applicant is a minor.) What is your maiden name? (Permissible only for checking prior employment or education.)	Have you ever changed your name by court order or other means? What are the names of friends and relatives working for the company? What kind of work does your mother, father, wife, or husband do? (Do not ask for information about spouses, children, or relatives not employed by the Company.)
RESIDENCE	What is your address? How long have you lived in this state/city? What is your phone number?	Do you rent or own your home? How long have you lived in this country? If you live with someone, what is the nature of the relationship? Do you live in a foreign country?
RACE, NATIONAL ORIGIN	Do you speak a foreign language? If so, which one?	What is your skin color? Your ancestry? Your maiden name? Where were you born? What is your mother's native language? What is your native tongue? How did you learn to speak a foreign language? What is your spouse's nationality?
CITIZENSHIP	Are you a citizen of the United States? If not, do you intend to become one? Can you provide documents required to prove that you have a legal right to work in this country?	Of what country are you a citizen? Are you a native-born or naturalized citizen? Your parents? Your spouse? When did you/they acquire citizenship?
CHILD CARE	Do you know of any reason why you might not be able to come to work on time, every day? (Caution: permissible only if the question is put to every applicant, regardless of sex.)	Are there children at home? How many? Their ages? Who looks after them? If you plan to have children later on, who will take care of them while you work?
DISABILITY	Would you be willing to take a company physical if offered the job?	Are you disabled or impaired? Have you ever received compensation for injury or illness? Have you ever been treated for...(do not present a checklist). In your last job, how much sick time did you have?
PERSONAL HISTORY	Have you ever been convicted of a crime? Do you hold a valid driver's license? Do you belong to any groups or clubs related to this job or field?	Have you ever been arrested? Have you ever pleaded guilty to a crime? Have you ever been in trouble with the law? To what societies, associations, lodges, etc, do you belong?
AGE	Are you of legal job age? If you are younger than 18 or older than 65, what is your age?	How old are you? When were you born? What makes you want to work at your age?
RELIGION		What is your religion? What church are you a member of? What religious holidays do you observe? Can you work on the Sabbath?
MARITAL STATUS	What is your marital status?	Are you married, single, divorced, separated, widowed, or engaged? Should we call you Miss, Ms., or Mrs.? Where does your spouse work? What does your spouse do? Is your spouse covered by a medical/health insurance plan? Are you the head of your household? Are you the principal wage earner?
GENDER ISSUES		Do you plan to marry? Will you have children? Do you believe in birth control or family planning? Do you consider yourself a feminist? What do you think about ERA?

rests, but this should only be done where permitted by law and if absolutely necessary. Under federal law, however, it is legal to inquire about convictions of a felony that took place within the not-too-distant past (i.e., within seven years).

Nevertheless, many states have laws that are considerably more restrictive. For example, in Massachusetts, an employer may not ask about first convictions for certain offenses such as speeding or simple assault and is prohibited from asking about convictions if the applicant was released from jail more than five years before. Under New York law, if an affirmative response is received that the applicant was convicted of a felony within the past seven years, the employer still has the burden of showing that the nature of the conviction impacts on the person's honesty or trustworthiness necessary for the *job in question* (i.e., a bank teller or pharmacist); if there is no correlation or if the job is not security sensitive, the employer may be required to hire that individual to avoid charges of discrimination!

The EEOC suggests that employers consider the following when evaluating an applicant's conviction record:

1. How long ago did the conviction take place? (If a long time has elapsed, the conviction may not now be relevant.)

2. Was the offense a minor crime or serious one?

3. Was it the first offense?

4. How long has the applicant been employed since the last conviction?

5. Has the applicant sought treatment? If so, what kind and for how long?

6. Does the applicant's history have a direct impact upon the particular job being offered?

Counsel Comments: *To avoid charges of discrimination, never consider the job and the applicant in the abstract. Be sure that any decision is documented and demonstrates a legitimate business purpose. For example, to avoid any appearance of wrongdoing, do not ask for a valid driver's license on an employment application. Rather, state that employment is subject to possession of a valid driver's license and offer the job to the applicant. Then, when the applicant cannot produce the valid license, refuse to extend the position.*

Know your state's law in this area and keep all acquired information confidential to avoid charges of defamation and invasion of privacy. When verifying information regarding convictions, it is best to conduct background checks rather than rely on information provided to you in an employment application, since the information you receive directly from an applicant may not always be reliable.

Disability

Enactment of the Americans With Disabilities Act of 1990 requires employers to change their hiring policies toward handicapped workers. This new law directly impacts pre-hiring questions. Now, any question asked at the hiring interview probing an applicant's medical history is probably illegal. This includes such questions as, "Have you ever been hospitalized?" and "Did you ever file a workers' compensation claim?"

In the past, you could legally ask an applicant, "Do you have any impairments that interfere with your ability to work in this job?" Now, however, *this question cannot be asked.*

Counsel Comments: *To overcome this problem, attach a detailed job description which states* essential *duties of the job (see the "Job Descriptions" section earlier in this chapter). For example, the description can state "The job being offered requires extensive work on weekends and overtime, often without much advance notice."*

Questions that could then be asked legally include: "Can you work overtime?" "Are there any problems meeting the job's demands of working overtime or on weekends without lengthy advance notice?" Such a policy may prove that you alerted all applicants regarding important elements of the job beforehand and were not necessarily singling out disabled workers.

Alcohol And Drug Addiction

Federal laws state that it is illegal to be denied employment or fired from a job as a result of current participation in a drug or alcohol treatment program if enrollment does not interfere with a person's ability to do the job.

Medical Exams

The ADA now prohibits pre-employment physicals even if all applicants are required to take physicals in the screening process. Now, only post-employment physicals are permitted provided the job is sufficiently strenuous (i.e., firefighter) to mandate the taking of physicals. In such cases, all individuals would be offered jobs on condition of successful results of physicals and are sufficiently advised about this requirement for the work to be performed.

> **Counsel Comments:** *The job description should state that offering the job in question is contingent upon successful completion of the physical. To avoid charges of handicap discrimination, only make the physical a final requirement for consideration* after *making the job offer; be sure that top physical condition is absolutely essential for the job and that all entering employees within the same job category are required to undergo the same examination. And be sure that your company pays for the cost of such exams.*
>
> *Some companies violate the law by unknowingly designing medical history forms that contain discriminatory questions; avoid this. Be aware that company doctors often ask discriminatory questions during the examination; employment cannot be denied on the basis of such illegal questions. Instruct company doctors that where a disability is evident, inquiries as to the nature or severity of the disability cannot be made.*

All candidates who receive physical examinations to detect disabilities that would substantially interfere with successful job performance of a particular job should be notified by an appropriate personnel officer when the results of the physical examination have been received and the company is content with their accuracy. Avoid disseminating the results to non-essential third parties to avoid charges of defamation and other violations of privacy rights.

Medical Conditions And Their Effect On Insurance Plans

Refusal to hire an applicant because you fear the applicant's condition will adversely impact your company's insurance plan is illegal. A company cannot deny employment to a qualified applicant because a spouse or child with a serious illness would create an insurance expense. Also, EEOC regulations and interpretive guidelines state that a qualified handicapped applicant cannot be denied a job because a company's health or liability insurance does not cover his or her disability or because of the increased cost of insuring that disability.

> **Counsel Comments:** *The ADA does not require that an employer offer health coverage; it merely requires that qualified handicapped individuals enjoy equal access to current health coverage. Some companies may eliminate or reduce health plan coverage to take advantage of this exception, provided it can be proved that such a decision was made independently of one person's effect on the company plan. For example, rather than merely excluding AIDS care, a company might eliminate expensive procedures and coverage for open heart surgery and cancer. Since the EEOC's interpretive guidelines do not affect the employer's ability to deny coverage for preexisting conditions in health insurance policies (even if they adversely affect individuals with disabilities), some companies are implementing cost-containment plans offering lower or no health benefits for preexisting problems, provided all workers are affected.*
>
> *Due to constantly evolving case decisions and statutory developments, including the ADA, employee benefits practices must be carefully scrutinized with labor counsel immediately to develop appropriate, legally permissible approaches for your company.*

Most importantly, to avoid any potential problems on hiring and application forms and at the pre-hiring interview, eliminate all improper questions. Then, obtain desired medical, insurance, and other information *after* the decision to hire has been made and include this data on a separate post-employment form.

Credit Reports

The Fair Debt Credit Reporting Act restricts employers from using credit reports for hiring or employment decisions. If such a report is made, companies are required to advise the applicant or employee that the report is being ordered, together with the name and address of the credit agency supplying it. Finally, the report can be ordered only if it serves a legitimate business purpose.

Discriminatory Questions After The Formal Interview

Discriminatory questions are sometimes asked after the formal interview with the applicant has been concluded (i.e., taking the applicant out to lunch after the interview) but before the decision to hire is made. Information solicited in this way may not be considered in the hiring process: the ramifications of asking such questions in informal settings are just as serious.

Testing And Other Attempts To Discover Discrimination

Recently approved federal policies allow your company to be "tested" for civil rights violations. Lawsuits resulting from the practices of testing are already in place and the use of testers is becoming more widespread as news of specific techniques travels. Will your company be tested for discrimination in hiring? Since testing could be a way of entrapping unsuspecting employers, supervisory-level employees who interview applicants should be trained to avoid certain kinds of conversations.

EEOC policy guidelines make it clear that the agency upholds the rights of any person applying for a job "whether or not a person intends to accept a position for which he/she applied." Organizations using testers may file complaints with the EEOC or go directly to court with the company allegedly committing the violation. One public policy organization recently conducted two employment discrimination studies using testers and found that the Immigration Reform and Control Act was used as a pretext to discriminate against Hispanic applicants. The other study found that white applicants were three times more likely to be favored over minority applicants.

A company may consider itself justified in refusing to hire a minority applicant and the employer will concoct reasons why a black, Hispanic, woman, Asian or other member of a protected group could not do the job properly. Such judgments, however, are frequently found to be illegal and testers are eager to uncover discrimination at the hiring stage.

Counsel Comments: *With the enactment of the Civil Rights Act of 1991, the stakes have risen and companies can no longer afford to discriminate during hiring or at any other stage of the employment process. Implementation of the Act exposes employers to a variety of additional, significant damages. This includes recovery by plaintiffs of compensatory and punitive damages up to $300,000 in certain cases, jury trials where damages are available, more difficult burdens of proof for employers arguing job relatedness and business necessity in disparate impact cases, express prohibition of compensatory adjustments to test scores in employment based upon race or other protected characteristics, express provision for extraterritorial application of Title VII and the employment provisions of the ADA to employment of citizens of the United States in foreign operations of U.S. employers, plus a provision for witness fees, attorney fees and interest against the employer. No longer will your company be exposed solely to awards of reinstatement of jobs, retroactive back pay and related benefits. (Note: The Civil Rights Act of 1991 will be discussed in great detail in Chapter 3.)*

It is *critical* that your company act properly and avoid discrimination during the hiring process. Since the use of testers will grow and the enactment of the Americans With Disabilities Act will likely utilize testers to uncover violations, more employers will be caught at this time because they are unfamiliar with the ADA and its ramifications.

Thus, never assume an individual really wants the job: be aware that he/she may be a discrimination expert-tester. Follow the law and treat everyone similarly. Hire employees on merit and avoid stereotypes. For example, do not refuse to hire a woman as a traveling salesperson because to do so may amount to unlawful discrimination. In one recent case the EEOC overruled arguments that such a position would expose the woman applicant to difficult-to-handle socialization. Similarly overruled was an argument that the woman's roles as a mother and wife would make traveling extra-difficult.

Avoid denying a minority applicant an interview or appointment. Finally, never ask discriminatory questions at the hiring interview, probing for responses on the basis of race, sex, national origin or citizenship status.

JOB MISREPRESENTATION

When hiring employees, particularly sales applicants, interviewers should be careful of "overselling" by making guaranteed earning claims. For example, when you tell an applicant, "If you come to work for us, I have no doubt you'll make $100,000 in commission this year based on what our other salespeople make," you may be making an illegal statement. The Federal Trade Commission considers such statements to be an unfair and deceptive trade practice if you promise an amount that exceeds the average net earnings of your other salespeople. In fact, the applicant has the right to ask you to show him/her the wage statements (i.e., W-2's or 1099's) of other salespeople within the company to prove your claims.

One of the oldest ways of luring an executive salesperson away from a current employer is to predict increased earnings if they come to work for you. Unless the recruiter talks specific numbers ("The last man in your job earned $50,000 last year. You'll do even better.") or presents records that falsify previous earnings, your company should avoid the likelihood of the misled executive winning damages in a lawsuit. Typically, many recruiters talk rosily about future earnings, but it is prudent to discuss potential earnings with applicants using words such as "it is possible," or "you may make," rather than making guaranteed earning claims, to avoid problems.

A company does not commit fraud merely by painting a job with glowing colors to a prospective employee and suggesting that a great future may await him or her. When a company representative predicts probable earnings, these predictions are mere opinions and not statements of fact actionable by law. However, a company should be careful about making special promises based on *conditions that do not presently exist.*

The facts of a true case illustrate this point. A supervisor lured a man who worked for a rival company and made him an offer. "Come to work for us. You'll make more money than you're making now because you'll receive bonuses based on your Division's net profit plus your salary."

Swayed by this statement, the man resigned his current position and went to work for the new employer. It didn't take him long to regret his decision; he learned that his Division had been losing money during his predecessor's stewardship and was continuing to lose money. He sued the company for fraud and misrepresentation and detrimental reliance, among other causes of action, and argued:

1. The company lured him away from a safe and comfortable job with lies about the financial state of the Division and his future earnings; and

2. The lies were told him knowingly and he relied on these misrepresentations to his detriment.

The company argued that the statements were common, optimistic remarks and with some hard work and ingenuity, they would have come true.

The court ruled in favor of the worker and stated that although the promises of potential earnings would not sustain a verdict in his favor, the statements regarding the company's financial history and current condition were misrepresentations, entitling him to damages.

PROMISES OF JOB SECURITY

Courts in some states are ruling that employees have the right to rely upon representations made before hiring and during the working relationship. In a growing number of recent cases throughout the country, discharged employees are suing and winning lawsuits against ex-employers for breach of oral agreements promising secure employment and even jobs for life. While courts have generally recognized that employers may be bound by written assurances and statements made in employee manuals, handbooks and work rules, they are now increasingly willing to consider oral contracts extended by management and company officers having the apparent authority to make such promises.

It is important to recognize that informal, off-the-cuff oral assurances can bind your company to devastating results. For example, a Michigan jury recently awarded $1.1 million to a worker, based on a claim of an oral promise of lifetime employment. In that case, the jury found the existence of a valid, oral contract and ruled that the company unjustifiably breached that contract when the worker was terminated.

To avoid similar problems, all of your company's hiring policies should be clearly spelled out so they cannot be misunderstood or misinterpreted by prospective job candidates and present employees. Interviewers, recruiters and other intake personnel must be careful not to say anything at the hiring interview that can be construed as a promise of job security. Avoid using words at the hiring interview which imply anything other than an at-will relationship. For example, use of the words "permanent employment," "job for life," or linking the phrase "just cause only" with termination, as well as broad statements concerning job longevity, assurances of continued employment (e.g., "Don't worry. No one around here ever gets fired except for a good cause."), or specific statements regarding career opportunities, should be avoided at all times, unless they are being stated as deliberate reflections of considered commitments.

As a first line of defense, your company should include language such as the following in the employment application:

"I understand that no promises regarding continued employment have been given to me about this job. If I am offered this position, I have the right to be terminated at will, with or without cause or notice, and may resign at any time. The foregoing is not to be construed as a guarantee of employment for a specific time."

> **Counsel Comments:** *It's not unusual for job interviewers to be over-exuberant in their job descriptions, leading to unrealistic expectations by the applicant and possible suits for damages. Take the precaution to word your applications so as to avoid problems arising from promises which hiring personnel might make without your company's approval. The use of language like that suggested above can be helpful.*

The following case demonstrates what can happen when employers fail to act properly:

An executive worked for 32 years without a written contract, then was suddenly fired. He sued his company and argued that he had done nothing wrong to justify the firing. At the trial, the executive proved that:

- The company's president told him several times that he would continue to be employed if he did a good job;
- The company had a policy of not firing executives except for cause;
- He was never criticized or warned that his job was in jeopardy;
- He had a commendable track record, his employment history was excellent and he had received periodic merit bonuses, raises and promotions.

The executive won the case because the facts created an implied promise that the company could not arbitrarily terminate him without "just cause."

> **Counsel Comments:** *In certain situations a company stumbling upon hard times may not reduce its overhead by firing longtime employees previously hired under "just cause understandings." Additionally, be aware that employees are now being advised by attorneys to reconstruct all promises that are made when they are hired (i.e., what was said, who said it, where the words were spoken, and the names of any witnesses). Remember, some courts have ruled that oral promises of job security are binding even though employment is not for a definite term.*

Promises Of Lifetime Employment

Even when employee handbooks and written personnel guidelines make it clear that no employee's job is guaranteed, there are circumstances when an oral assurance of secure lifetime employment can bind the employer assuming:

1. The discharged employee can prove such a statement was made;

2. The statement was a crucial factor in the decision to accept the job or decline a job with a competitor; and

3. The employee reasonably relied on such a promise and suffered damages as a result.

These were the facts with a worker who served for four years as a national sales manager with a New Jersey company and then was fired. He claimed that four months earlier the president had persuaded him to turn down a job offer from a competitor by a promise of lifetime employment. Although the company argued that the words were merely "friendly assurances" and weren't enforceable, the court ruled that the president's remarks had persuaded the employee to stay and could constitute a contract. In this case, it was proved that a better employment opportunity was turned down based on an employee's reliance on that oral promise of lifetime employment.

Companies are protected to a certain extent in this area because many employees have difficulty proving that such statements were made. However, when a supervisor who allegedly made such a statement has died, or no longer works for the company and can't be located or left under unpleasant terms, companies may be unable to rebut the employee's statements if a lawsuit is commenced.

Counsel Comments: *The best way to avoid problems is to notify your interviewers, recruiters and intake personnel not to say anything at the hiring interview that can be construed as a promise of job security. It may be a good idea for the person offering the position to have a colleague present when the offer is made, to serve as a witness that no additional promises were stated. In addition, it is beneficial to furnish a memo to the worker after he/she is hired which specifically denies that promises of job security have been made, or to include such a statement in a written employment contract which the worker is required to sign. In addition, pay special attention to welcoming letters sent out by company executives, particularly those in marketing and sales, which may talk in inflated terms and sometimes make statements or promises that the company never intended to keep.*

Just as it is critical to train recruiters, it is equally important to train hiring managers and other interviewers regarding what they may and may not say in this area. Be sure they understand that, since their oral statements may be treated as enforceable contracts, broad statements regarding job longevity or assurances of continued employment must be avoided. Some courts have ruled that conversations conducted in an atmosphere of critical one-on-one negotiation regarding terms of future employment may give rise to a contract of lifetime employment. One court held that an employee could be terminated only "for cause" where the employee had inquired about job security during the job interview and the employer had agreed that the employee would be employed "as long as he does the job."

Counsel Comments: *With respect to promises of lifetime employment (i.e., "jobs for life"), even though promises of lifetime employment from low or middle-level company officials may not bind your company, instruct all officers, no matter what rank, to avoid making any representations regarding a person's future employment status. It is also a good idea to state in your employment manual that no one other than the president has the authority to make promises regarding job security and that any other employees discovered making such unauthorized promises will be summarily discharged. In many cases even the president does not have the authority to give a lifetime contract without the written approval of the company's Board of Directors and in some states, notably California, employment contracts which exceed a specified number of years are unenforceable.*

Employment Agencies

If you use recruiting agencies, instruct them not to make any oral representations during the hiring process that may be binding on your company at a future date.

Counsel Comments: *Incorporate this provision in your contract with the employment agency and include a provision indemnifying your company for damages awarded in the event your company is sued and/or held liable. For maximum protection, the indemnification should also include legal fees and court costs.*

CHECKING REFERENCES

The majority of states limit an employer's ability to make pre-employment inquiries regarding criminal arrests and convictions beyond a certain number of years and restrict the use of such information. Nevertheless, all companies should conduct a complete background check of applicants before hiring. In fact, when companies fail to investigate an applicant's background and hire a person unfit for the position who causes harm or injury to another, they may be liable to others under a legal theory referred to as *negligent hiring and retention.*

Under this negligent-hiring doctrine, in most jurisdictions, employers have a duty of reasonable care in hiring individuals who, because of employment, may pose a threat of injury to fellow employees and members of the public. Negligent-hiring claims have been made against employers for murders, rapes, sexual assaults, physical assaults, personal injuries and property losses allegedly committed or caused by an unfit employee. In one recent case a McDonald's worker in Colorado, while on the job, sexually assaulted a 3-year-old boy. The fast-food restaurant had hired the man without a complete background check, which would have shown a history of sexually assaulting children. The family sued and a jury awarded the victim $210,000.

A realty company was found liable for the acts of its agent since it was aware that its agent had forged documents for a former employer, had been convicted of passing bad checks and had lied about obtaining a realty license. Despite this knowledge, the company vouched for her character. Knowledge of the risk the agent posed to customers made the company liable for her subsequent misconduct.

In another case, an apartment complex owner was found liable in the amount of $30,000 for the rape of a tenant by a building caretaker who used a passkey to enter the victim's apartment. The court found that the owner failed to make a reasonable investigation of the assailant's background and work history, including the reasons why he had not been employed during a previous five-year period. During this time, the caretaker had been incarcerated for armed robbery and burglary; a routine check of his employment references would have revealed that he had not told the truth on his employment application.

However, liability may not be found under the negligent hiring theory in cases where the employee's acts are not foreseeable and where the pre-employment investigation of an employee's qualifications did not give rise to actual or constructive knowledge of a potential problem. For example, a union was held not liable for recommending the hiring of a cruise ship employee who committed a homosexual assault upon another seaman while both men were vacationing on shore after working together on the cruise ship because evidence of his propensity for aggressive behavior did not show up in the union's standard pre-employment investigation.

Unfortunately, although companies are forced to undertake extensive pre-employment checks in this area, the fact that a person has an arrest record may not be a valid ground to refuse to hire. For example, in some states, including New York, no application for employment shall be denied by reason of the applicant's prior conviction of one or more criminal offenses or by reason of a finding of lack of "good moral character" based on such conviction, unless there is a direct relationship between one or more previous criminal offenses and the specific license or employment sought.

Thus, since the law is quite complicated in this area, companies must undertake thorough pre-employment checks but consult competent legal counsel whenever a potential problem arises. This is necessary because employers can be held liable to the applicant and to employees under legal claims including defamation, intentional infliction of emotional distress and violations of the implied covenant of good faith and fair dealing when references are not investigated properly or are leaked to nonessential third parties. In one case a man terminated from an insurance company several years ago discovered that his former boss, in reference checks, had called him "untrustworthy, disruptive, paranoid, hostile, irrational, a classic sociopath." He sued and a jury decided those characterizations were out of line, a mistake that cost the company $1.9 million.

Such cases typify the legal dilemma employers face with reference checks. When hiring, if they miss a potential problem, some courts find them negligent. But when giving references, if they say too much, they may be liable for defaming former workers. Thus, employers must be familiar with local, state and federal laws regarding information investigation. It is important to be aware that the majority of applicants are guilty of lies or omissions on their resumes. In fact, in a random sample of cases, investigators found 10 crimes for every one acknowledged on job applications!

The first step toward protecting your company is to obtain authorization from prospective employees either by permission to investigate information in the employment application or by a separate signed release that permits the company to contact former employers, schools, etc., to verify information supplied by the applicant. To avoid any impropriety on application forms or in pre-hiring interviews, as has been stated before, eliminate all illegal questions on the application. Obtain information necessary for insurance, physical checks, security purposes and so forth on a separate post-employment form and only begin the investigation *after* a favorable hiring decision has been made which is now subject to this investigation.

Counsel Comments: *Some companies allow the person to start work for a proba-*

tionary period while the investigation is taking place. Continued employment is then offered pending satisfactory results. This is a poor idea and should be avoided, if possible.

All employment applications should be verified. Former employers should be contacted by telephone or in writing to determine dates of employment, job titles and responsibilities, satisfactory work performance, attendance and eligibility for rehire and reasons why the person is no longer employed. When investigating such information, be on the alert for "red flags" (i.e., periods without employment, failure to provide addresses, etc.). If an applicant has no job experience, the applicant's educational background should be investigated. Schools should be asked about the applicant's attendance record and courses taken pertinent to the position applied for. In positions that require a certain educational level, transcripts need to be verified in addition to the work record. Additionally, if driving is an important function, require a valid driver's license *and* consider an independent investigation of the person's driving record with the State Department of Motor Vehicles.

In the event the applicant has made a false statement of material facts in the application or has a record of conviction for an offense directly related and important to the position in question, the person should be rejected for the position. Results of all investigations should be carefully guarded, particularly where damaging information is discovered. Avoid communicating such information to non-essential third parties to avoid charges of defamation or libel. Keep in mind that libel suits filed by discharged employees and job applicants now account for approximately one-third of all defamation actions and the average winning verdict in such cases exceeds $100,000, according to Jury Verdict Research Inc., a company that monitors this kind of litigation.

Investigation Of Medical Records

During the investigation process, can a company demand to see all of a worker's past medical records? In one case, a man was operated on for a peptic ulcer about 18 months after he joined the company. The company's personnel director decided to look at his file. On the hiring application, the man stated he had never suffered from stomach ulcers. The employee (union member) was then asked to sign a form authorizing "any physician, hospital or insurer" to release to the company any and all records they had pertaining to him and his dependents. After refusing to sign, the man was fired.

The union argued that the company's request was an unwarranted invasion of his privacy. The arbitrator agreed, ruling that the language on the form was so broadly written that any prudent person would think twice about signing it and ordered the employee reinstated. The form in this case gave the employer access to medical reports related even to the employee's family and covered every bit of data held by a wide range of sources: hospitals, doctors, and insurance carriers. Demanding that an employee authorize so grave an invasion of his privacy was an abuse of managerial discretion.

Counsel Comments: *The entire affair could have been handled better by the company. The arbitrator pointed out that it would have been relatively simple for the company to limit the terms of inquiry on the form to specific matters with which the company was concerned, requesting only the employee's specific data and no one else's.*

Under the ADA, investigation of a person's medical history has been seriously curtailed; proceed with caution in this area.

Investigation Of Bankruptcy Records

Can an applicant be denied a job because he or she has gone bankrupt? According to the Bankruptcy Code, no private employer may terminate the employment of, or discriminate with respect to employment against an individual who is or has been a debtor or bankrupt under the Bankruptcy Act, or an individual associated with such debtor or bankrupt, *solely* because such debtor or bankrupt is or has been a debtor or bankrupt under the Bankruptcy Act, has been insolvent before the grant or denial of a discharge or has not paid a debt that is dischargeable in a case under the Bankruptcy Act.

Counsel Comment: *If your company runs a credit check on an applicant which reveals that he/she has a poor credit history, always document* other *valid reasons for denying the applicant the job, if possible. However, since the law specifically forbids discrimination against those seeking or receiving the protection of bankruptcy law, you may fare better deciding* *not to hire an individual with credit problems than one who has declared formal bankruptcy!*

When considering minority candidates, case law and the Equal Employment Opportunity Commission advise against refusing to hire based on poor credit rating because minorities often have more difficulty paying their bills. In fact, the EEOC has ruled that it is illegal to refuse to hire minority applicants (particularly Afro-Americans) with a poor credit rating since minorities are more likely to be unable to pay their bills and such a policy effectively excludes a class of applicant from the job market.

In the majority of states and under the federal Consumer Credit Protection Act, it is illegal for a company to fire a person being sued for the nonpayment of a debt or when the company is instructed to cooperate in the collection of a portion of the person's wages through garnishment proceedings for any one indebtedness. Enforcement of this federal law is tough - violations are punishable by a fine of up to $1,000 and imprisonment for up to one year. Discharge for garnishment for more than one indebtedness is not prohibited, however, but such a policy may be restricted by Title VII of the Civil Rights Act of 1964 when it has a disproportionate effect on minority workers. And, since many states have even more strict laws on the books in this area (i.e., some states prohibit garnishment altogether or garnishment of pensions while others only allow garnishment on delinquent spouse or child support arrears) and problems often ensue when employers receive multiple garnishment orders (which one to pay first?), always check your state's law when faced with obeying a garnishment order.

Under the federal Fair Debt Credit Reporting Act, employers are generally forbidden to use credit reports for hiring or employment decisions unless the job is security-conscious or the financial integrity of the applicant is essential to successful job performance. When such reports are made, be sure to obtain the applicant's formal written consent before seeking such information. In addition, it is a good idea to give the applicant a copy of any credit reports received, together with the name and address of the credit agency supplying it. This way the applicant may be able to explain important errors that sometimes need to be corrected on credit reports.

Strategies To Protect The Employer

When sued for breach of contract and other matters, more and more companies are now asserting counterclaims seeking damages against employees for submitting fraudulent employment applications. In one case the court ordered a full-dress trial and acknowledged that misstatements in an employment application with respect to material misrepresentations of a person's background, training and skills may have caused the employer to give the employee additional job responsibilities, resulting in inadequate performance.

Counsel Comments: *To be successful, the employer must be able to prove that the alleged fraud proximately caused asserted losses.*

Always have job applicants sign release forms that approve reasonable background checks on credit, criminal and work histories to protect your company in this area. At the very least, companies should check work histories back five to seven years. That's beyond any government-mandated checks, such as driver's license histories for driving jobs.

What happens when you hire and then find out the person withheld material information concerning health or financial status? Can the person be fired for misrepresentation? The answer depends on the type and severity of the information withheld, and, most importantly, whether withholding the information is protected under numerous discrimination laws. The following two cases illustrate this point.

In one case an applicant was not offered a job because he lied about his financial status on his employment application. The employer was careful about the people it hired, requiring job applicants to submit to a pre-hiring investigation to determine if anything in their background made them unfit to join the company. The applicant appeared to qualify for an important job, but his background check revealed he was delinquent in making child-support payments to his former wife and owed money to various merchants. The personnel director gave him a rundown of the report, adding: "When you straighten out your financial problems, we'll be glad to take you on. But we'd hate to become involved with courts and creditors right from the start."

After representing that all his arrears had been "taken care of," the man was offered the job. However, less than one week later, the company learned that he had not told the truth and that his bills were still unpaid. When confronted, the employee replied that he needed the job to pay off his debts and that if he had told the truth he wouldn't have been offered the job. The company took the position that he was properly fired because he had lied.

The man hired a lawyer, who brought a suit against the company. According to the attorney his client was discharged not for lying, but because he was in debt and the law prohibits firing an employee because of the threat of garnishment. The court disagreed and ruled in favor of the company, commenting that because the employee lied to his employer at the time he was hired, the termination was legitimate. The court added that the garnishment statute does not immunize an employee who is guilty of lying merely because there is a possibility that he might be garnished in the future.

Another applicant told his prospective supervisor that if hired, he would need one day off a month to attend a manufacturer's meeting for a line of baby products he sold on the side. After he began working, the company became suspicious and discovered that the man was HIV positive and needed to go for medical treatment once a month. He was then given the option of resigning or being terminated. When he refused to resign, he was fired. His application for unemployment benefits met with strong opposition from his ex-employer.

At the hearing, the company argued that the man was fired because he was untruthful about his reason for being absent from work and defied the sales manager's demand that he end his once-a-month absences. The ex-employee argued that all of his once-a-month absences did not exceed what would have been his sick leave time, had he admitted to testing HIV positive. He also stated that revealing his disease to the employer would have been a breach of his right to privacy, and that he did not act willfully nor harm the company in any way, and therefore was not guilty of misconduct.

The unemployment court ruled that the man's actions did not evince a willful and wanton disregard of his employer's interests. The leave time taken was basically allotted to him by the company and he exhibited no disloyalty or untruthfulness except regarding his medical condition. Such deception was designed to protect his privacy and did not harm the employer in any fashion.

Counsel Comments: *The case was decided before the enactment of ADA. Now, it appears that an ex-employee having AIDS, AIDS-related complex or the HIV virus would have every protection available to qualified handicapped individuals in all aspects of employment.*

In conclusion, it is important to conduct your own thorough background checks for most positions so you can avoid charges that defamatory or inadequate job references were given your company by an ex-employer. Always obtain written releases and indemnification from the applicant authorizing you to inquire into personal facts. Be aware, however, that even if you receive damaging information, you may *not* be able to refuse to hire the applicant if the unique facts suggest a case protected under discrimination laws. And stick to the facts when discussing the person's background. Don't add personal impressions. If the person was fired, you can also state truthfully that your company would never re-hire the individual.

Not every exaggeration on an employment application should lead to automatic dismissal, even when the applicant attests to the truthfulness and completeness of the answers he or she has provided by signing the application form, which typically contains the following or similar language:

I affirm that my answers to the questions in this application are true and correct, and that I have not knowingly withheld any facts or circumstances which would, if disclosed, affect my application unfavorably. I understand that any misrepresentation will be cause for my immediate discharge.

Once the employer can prove that misconduct has occurred (i.e., a fabrication of an important fact was made), your company should then consider whether discharge is appropriate under the circumstances. Arbitrators are sometimes persuaded otherwise by a number of factors, including the employee's length of service, track record, length of time that elapsed before the misrepresentation was discovered, and other mitigating circumstances. One arbitrator proposed helpful guidelines when determining whether a falsification could be used as grounds for discharge:

1. Was the misrepresentation deliberate or willful?

2. Was it material (i.e., sufficiently prejudicial that a reasonable employer would not have hired

the individual knowing the truth) to the job at the time it was made?

3. Has a sufficient period of time elapsed, making the misrepresentation no longer that important or significant?

4. Did the employer act in good faith (i.e., without malice) as soon as the falsity surfaced?

5. Has the employer consistently punished similar offenders in the past or is an exception being made of this person?

6. Is the employee being unfairly treated because of a personal characteristic (i.e., being a female, over 40 or member of a minority)?

> **Counsel Comments:** *Although most arbitrators and judges recognize the employer's need to receive accurate information and to punish severely by immediate discharge employees who submitted false or inaccurate information or omissions on job applications, there may be times when it is prudent to consider carefully* all *the facts and circumstances before a termination.*

The following information summarizes a few points to keep in mind when instituting a background checking system:

- Tell the applicant what you're doing. Spell out the company's system on interviews, references and hiring procedures. Applicants and employees should be told how decisions are made and who is responsible for making hiring decisions.
- Ask the applicant to sign consent forms permitting your background investigation.
- Save all records and information you obtain about the applicant during each step of the selection process.
- Know the law. Conduct your screening system legally. For example, checking must be done on *all* candidates in the same manner so that all results are fair and accurate. An applicant's race, religion, gender, etc. must have no bearing on the investigatory process.
- Devise a formal written policy for background checks. Having a detailed internal policy in writing lets company people know what their role is in the hiring process.
- Keep all information received about an applicant confidential to protect his/her privacy rights.

Experts suggest that most applicants exaggerate about past jobs (salary or title), college degrees, job skills, and fail to include criminal arrests on application forms. To detect misrepresentations, it may be a good idea to have two people review the submitted application form; some items to watch out for include:

- Significant gaps in the applicant's employment history. Are the dates vague? If there are periods where no employment is shown, find out why.
- Any applicant's willingness to accept a drastic pay cut. There may be a logical reason for this, but employees with serious financial problems can pose problems. (Note: Be aware, though, of the legality of obtaining and using financial and credit information in making hiring decisions, as discussed previously.)
- Admissions of criminal behavior. If so, investigate further. Candidates who admit to what appears to be a small crime may be covering up involvement in more serious criminal activity. (Note: Be aware, though, of the legality of obtaining and using knowledge of criminal convictions in making hiring decisions, as discussed previously.)
- An emphasis on past jobs rather than the most recent employment.

Management should advise supervisors of the proper and systematic way to check references. This includes instruction on who to call at a previous employer to verify employment. For example, speaking with the personnel department is sufficient to verify the qualifications of an hourly worker but you may wish to speak to the immediate supervisor and relevant company officers when considering hiring a high-level executive.

> **Counsel Comments:** *A good initial question is, "Is the person eligible for rehire?" This may help you discover more information without offending the person with whom you are speaking. Also, always scrutinize relevant military service and education records.*

If you have decided not to offer the applicant the job on the basis of a credit investigation, but have another valid reason for the rejection (e.g., another applicant is more qualified), consider using the "better applicant" excuse as the reason for refusing to hire to avoid potential problems in this area.

TESTING

Experts estimate that more than 50 percent of the major corporations in the United States now engage in drug and alcohol screening before hiring new employees; such tests are on the rise, particularly in high technology and security-conscious industries. As a result of such frequent testing, the number of applicants who test positively for drugs is down sharply to under 5 percent.

Some state laws passed since the mid-1980s protect employers' right to test applicants. Many drug and alcohol tests have generally been upheld as legal, particularly with respect to job applicants (as opposed to employees asked to submit to random tests as a requisite for continued employment) because applicants have less legal right to protest such tests than employees. One basic reason is that such tests are generally not viewed as violating job-seekers' privacy rights since applicants are told in advance they must take and pass the test to get the job, and all applicants must submit to such tests after a job offer as a condition of employment. This freedom of choice for applicants (no one is forcing them to take the test or apply for the job) reduces their claim of legal harm.

To be absolutely certain your company is operating properly in this area, it is essential to research applicable state and local municipal laws regarding the legality of pre-employment drug and alcohol testing. Some states, including New York, *prohibit* pre-employment drug testing even though this is in conflict with the majority of states and federal law.

Drug And Alcohol Tests

Drug and alcohol tests of job applicants are neither encouraged nor *prohibited* by the ADA and the EEOC proposed rule and the results of such tests *may* be used as a basis for disciplinary action. The reason is that an employer does not have to hire an applicant who poses a direct health threat to the health or safety of himself/herself or others. In determining whether an individual poses such a threat, the nature and severity of the potential harm, duration of the risk, and the likelihood and immediacy that potential harm will occur are all factors to consider.

An employee or applicant who is currently engaging in illegal drug use is *not* protected under federal ADA law. Additionally, a current alcoholic who cannot perform his/her job duties or whose employment presents a threat to the safety of others is not protected under the ADA.

Counsel Comments: *Former drug users or alcoholics who have been rehabilitated or who are participating in a supervised rehabilitation program are protected under the ADA and must be considered for the job. Of course employers may prohibit the use of illegal drugs and alcohol at the workplace and require that employees not be under the influence of illegal drugs or alcohol while at work. Since the ADA is neutral on the issue of drug and alcohol testing, your company is free to test applicants provided state and local law authorizes same and many procedural safeguards are followed.*

The right to test does not give potential employers the right to handle test results carelessly. Unwarranted disclosure of this information can result in huge damages to companies. In addition, applicants may have rights in the event they are refused a job on the basis of an alleged failure to pass a test and it is later determined that there was a mistake with the test results (i.e., the applicant really passed the test).

Counsel Comments: *If you decide to screen applicants for drug or alcohol use, your company should adopt a plan and record it in work rules, policy manuals, employment contracts, and/or collective bargaining agreements. This will both reduce perceived privacy rights of applicants and document company policy in this area. When preparing employment applications, state that the applicant authorizes drug and alcohol tests and agrees that a positive result will mean forfeiture of a job offer. Make the applicant sign such a statement.*

Handle the results of drug/alcohol tests as you would any other confidential information. Unwarranted disclosure of this information, even within your company, could result in expensive, time-consuming litigation for breach of privacy rights, including defamation. Six-figure verdicts are being awarded routinely in this area so be careful that the test results are not disclosed to non-essential third parties.

Counsel Comments: *Since a failure to hire or termination based on a positive test which later proves inaccurate could lead to a multitude of legal causes of action, including wrongful discharge, slander and invasion of privacy, be sure you hire a reputable testing company. If the testing company doesn't carry an "errors and omissions" policy or other insurance protecting itself and your company from lawsuits arising from false test results, look for another firm to hire. Only hire testing companies who carry such liability coverage, for your protection.*

Polygraph Testing Of Applicants

The use of polygraph or lie detector exams by private employers has become the subject of increased scrutiny and criticism. In the past, employers resorted to such tests to verify statements on job applications and reduce employee theft and other forms of dishonesty. However, the tests generally came to be viewed as violating a person's fundamental rights regarding free speech, privacy, self-incrimination and the right to be free from illegal search and seizure. Consequently, the federal Polygraph Protection Act of 1988 was enacted to curb such abuses. Prior to that legislation, only 24 states and the District of Columbia either limited or prohibited the use of lie detectors in the employment context. The law now *forbids* the use of such tests in all states which previously allowed them and prohibits the use of such tests (defined as any mechanical or electrical process used to render a diagnostic opinion regarding honesty) in all pre-employment screening as well as in discharge and disciplinary proceedings. Thus, applicants generally *cannot* be requested to submit to such tests; do not even consider offering them to applicants before speaking with experienced labor counsel.

Psychology Tests

Many states have enacted strong laws protecting job applicants from stress tests, psychological evaluator tests and other honesty tests. In other states, the trend is to eliminate or strongly discourage the use of such tests. To be safe in this area, you are strongly advised to speak to a knowledgeable attorney who can advise you on the current status of such laws in your state. Additionally, all tests presently being used should be carefully reviewed and modified if necessary since pre-employment psychological testing has been seriously curtailed. Although legitimate psychological tests may exist, be certain that any tests you are using have been designed legally to comply with existing federal and state law.

Counsel Comments: *Even if such tests are legal they may be discriminatory by causing a different effect, positive or negative, on any race, sex or ethnic group when compared with another group. Any tests which cannot work as well with minorities as with other groups are illegal under EEOC guidelines. Thus, investigate whether inherent discrimination problems exist with such tests so that all tests given do not contain hidden bias or unfairly penalize one group over another.*

Skills Tests

Employers must be aware of several important concerns when testing the basic skills level of job applicants. Since failure to pass such tests could be viewed as the result of an attempt to exclude certain groups on the basis of race, age, sex, national origin or religion, companies must be very careful in testing. Title VII of the Civil Rights Act of 1964 as amended prohibits the use of discriminatory tests in making any employment decision.

To avoid liability, the employer must be able to show that any form of literacy or math skills test offered to job applicants has a high degree of validation (i.e., that a high test score is a strong indication of good future work performance). Under guidelines adopted and disseminated by the EEOC, the Civil Service Commission, and the Departments of Labor and Justice, all literacy tests for prospective employees must be job-related and must adequately evaluate the person's ability to perform the required duties and tasks. Such tests cannot be used to exclude significant numbers of protected minority groups.

Furthermore, the difficulty of such tests cannot be unreasonably related to the job being offered. For example, although a company can test a skill at a level higher than the position being offered if job promotion to that level will ensue in the reasonable future, a company cannot test applicants for skills that are not required in a basic entry position (if that is what is being offered). By setting unnecessarily high standards, companies often exclude qualified minority applicants who lack formal education credits and educational skills but who nonetheless can perform adequately in the basic entry-level position. Be sure to use tests that are at an appropriate level of difficulty and that test basic skills for the position offered.

Counsel Comments: *If your company requires applicants to enroll in basic skills programs to evaluate their skills as a condition of employment, you may be required to pay for such courses and pay overtime wages for participation under some circumstances.*

WRITTEN CONTRACTS AND DOCUMENTATION

Recruiters and interviewers are obligated to discuss all the terms, conditions and responsibilities of the job with the applicant up front, no matter what type of job is being offered. This is essential to maintaining positive relations with your employees and minimizing breach of contract and wrongful termination lawsuits. Always remember that the company is in a position to dictate the terms of the job before an offer is accepted. Thus, it is important to be thorough and to discuss carefully and completely all important points of the position. Since most interviewers fail to discuss one or more key points, the Employment Negotiating Checklist at the end of the chapter lists most of the key terms to cover. Please note the separate Negotiating Checklist to use when hiring sales employees or independent sales representatives.

Confirm The Deal In Writing

Once the company and applicant have agreed to key terms, it is important to confirm the deal in writing. I have observed that legal disputes often arise because many companies hire people on a handshake. A handshake, or oral agreement, only indicates that the parties came to some form of agreement; it does not specify the details of the agreement. The failure to spell out important terms often leads to misunderstandings and disputes. Even when key terms are discussed, the same spoken words that are agreed upon can have different meanings from the employee's and company's perspectives. Written words limit this sort of misunderstanding.

Companies can benefit from the use of written contracts for other reasons. One is the arbitration clause: you can compel the employee to resolve his/her dispute by arbitration rather than litigation, which may make the company's defense cheaper and less burdensome. In addition, since many attorneys believe that juries tend to favor individuals over companies, it may be better for your case to be decided by an arbitrator (usually a successful business person or attorney), rather than a jury.

Counsel Comments: *Arbitration provisions which specify the location of the hearing (i.e., "Any arbitration between the parties shall take place in the city of* X *where the company is located") are highly advantageous, particularly when you are hiring an employee or sales representative who lives and works in a distant state. Selecting the locale for the proceeding ahead of time can save your company unnecessary travel, related costs and hardship and may force the litigant to think twice before commencing arbitration that requires travel to a distant site.*

However, since the arbitration procedure is more streamlined than regular litigation and there is usually no right to appeal the decision, the agreement to arbitrate must be contained in a contract, typically an employment contract. Speak to counsel about the merits and pitfalls of arbitration, if applicable.

Restrictive Covenants

Another advantage of a written contract arises from the use of a restrictive covenant when an employee leaves the company. Such a clause can:

1. Restrict an ex-employee from working for a competitor of the former employer;

2. Restrict an ex-employee from starting a business or forming a venture with others that competes against the former employer;

3. Restrict an ex-employee from contacting or soliciting former or current customers or employees of the former employer;

4. Restrict an ex-employee from using confidential knowledge, trade secrets, customer lists and other privileged information learned while working for the former employer; and

5. Restrict an ex-employee from any of the above both in geographic or time limitations.

The above points are illustrated by the following clauses taken from actual employment agreements:

"For a period of one (1) year following the termination of your employment for any reason, it is agreed that you will not contact or solicit or be employed by any person, firm, association or corporation to which you sold products of the Company during the year preceding the termination of your employment."

"Upon termination of the Doctor's employment under this Agreement for any reason, the Doctor shall not engage in the practice of neurology or open his own office for the practice of neurology or associate himself with other physicians within a five (5) mile radius of any hospital for which the Doctor has worked on behalf of the Corporation for a period of one (1) year after the effective date of termination."

"In consideration of compensation paid to me as an employee, I hereby recognize as the exclusive property of the employer and agree to assign, transfer and convey to the employer, every invention, discovery, concept, idea, process, method and technique which I become acquainted with as a result or consequence of my employment and agree to execute all documents requested by the employer to evidence its ownership thereof."

"During the period of this Agreement and for a period of one (1) year thereafter, the employee agrees that he or any company he is affiliated with, shall not induce, hire, solicit or otherwise utilize the services of any employee or sales rep currently employed by the Company."

Without a written contract containing a restrictive covenant (also called a covenant not to compete) you cannot stop a former employee from working for a competitor except in the rare instance where you can prove that the employee has stolen and is using trade secrets. However, by inserting in the contract a restrictive covenant of reasonable geographic scope and duration (i.e., six months), you can pursue such a tactic if someone goes over to a competitor. This is of particular significance to companies that train their own employees in a skill, only to lose them soon to a competitor.

For many reasons, it is best to require all new executives and sales employees whose duties involve access to company secrets to sign a written confidentiality agreement or employment contract containing restrictive covenants. This will put your company in a better position to undermine the defense of ex-employees who typically claim that the subject matter was not a trade secret, and increase the odds that you will obtain an immediate legal remedy known as an injunction. Even the "chilling effect" such clauses have, through the implied threat that the company may institute legal action after a person's resignation or termination, can effectively discourage employees from contacting prospective employers and customers in your industry or trade and/or establishing a competing business.

> **Counsel Comments:** *Companies that sue ex-employees to enforce a restrictive covenant typically don't win. The enforcement of such measures varies on a state-by-state basis and depends on a number of factors. The primary focus of inquiry by a court is usually the reasonableness of the covenant in terms of geographic scope and time constraints. Therefore, it is wise to limit the covenant where practical. To enhance the chances of enforceability, it is best to keep the covenant short in terms of geographic location (i.e., never prohibit the employee from calling on customers located throughout the "entire United States" or your state) and not to draft covenants exceeding six months to one year.*
>
> *Most importantly, remember that courts respond favorably to situations where companies have paid the employee additional compensation, such as $1,000, an extra week's vacation or greater severance pay, in exchange for the employee's signing a contract containing a restrictive covenant. Better still, if the contract is drafted to state that the employee will receive $X per week (i.e., one-third of his/her regular salary) while the restriction is in effect after the termination of the contract, this may constitute adequate consideration to allow the covenant to continue undisturbed.*

Confer with counsel as soon as a problem develops. Cases demonstrate that if your company fails to take action (like sending a strong cease-and-desist letter to the ex-employee and the company he/she is now working for, or filing an injunction) *immediately* after learning the covenant has been violated, you may weaken the case. You should also recognize there is a greater chance of losing the right to enforce a restrictive covenant when you require employees who are already on-the-job to sign employment contracts containing such clauses. The reason is that in many states such a request by an employer will not be viewed as conferring any additional consideration (benefit) upon the employee to make such a clause valid.

> **Counsel Comments:** *If you desire to impose such contracts on current employees, an offer of substantial additional monetary benefits increases the odds that such arrangements may be enforceable. Speak to experienced labor counsel to inquire how this best may be done.*

Although a written contract cannot guarantee that you will be satisfied with the performance of your employee, it can provide the company with additional remedies in the event of a worker's nonperformance. That is why the mood is changing in most industries from hiring on a handshake to hiring by a written agreement. Most employers are learning that they can still fire an employee without notice (which was the main reason why companies previously hired on a handshake), but can better protect themselves by including favorable clauses in clearly drafted contracts. For example, by specifying in writing that an individual waives the right to a trial by jury, identifying the remedies associated with a breach of the agreement, or stating that the company is not obligated to honor prior commitments in the event of a merger or sale to a successor, your company can reduce the chances of eventually losing large damages in the event of a lawsuit.

Written contracts can also eliminate potential misunderstandings arising from representations given to the employee by outside job recruiters. Often, the job recruiter or employment agency makes promises which the company has no desire to live up to, for example, promised bonuses after a certain period of employment, and additional benefits.

To avoid liability, companies can protect themselves through the use of written contracts which specifically state that the employee does not rely on any representations not pointedly included in the contract, and that the contract supersedes and replaces all prior agreements and understandings. By using written contracts in this fashion, your company need not exercise direct control over statements made by outside job recruiters because the employment contract with an employee can specifically disaffirm any such representations or promises.

Contract Execution

When employment contracts are issued, be sure that all changes, strikeouts and erasures are initialed by a company officer and the employee. If your company uses a standard employment contract, be sure all blanks are filled in. If additions are necessary, include them in a space provided or attach them to the contract itself. Then, note on the contract that addenda have been accepted by both parties. This prevents questions from arising if addenda are lost or separated; it's often difficult to prove their existence without mention in the body of the contract.

A standard "formal" contract is not required to satisfy the strategy of putting key points of the deal in writing. I often recommend that companies issue simple letters which state the terms of employment and end with the following in the last paragraph:

"If any of the terms of this letter are ambiguous or incorrect please advise us immediately before signing this agreement. Otherwise, it is agreed that this letter will serve as an accurate reflection of our intentions but may be modified at any time by us with or without notice. If accepted, please sign in the space below where indicated and return it to us; you may keep a copy for your records."

Clearly drafted letters can serve as a contract in most situations; thus, don't forget to use them when appropriate.

> **Counsel Comments:** *Always review any comments or proposed amendments to the contract you may have received from the potential employee. Sales managers, supervisors and others sometimes shove letters of protest or modification in a drawer without responding. The failure to respond to such a writing may prejudice the company so always respond immediately* in writing *to any document received from a potential employee.*

Be sure that your agreement is signed by the employee. One company made the mistake of failing to check whether its contract had been signed and was forced to defend itself in a breach of contract claim as a result. In that case a mortgage company had courted a closing agent and offered him a job. The man indicated he would accept the position provided he was given a contract of one year's duration plus a monthly salary and commissions.

The man was invited to the annual company Christmas party where he was handed a one-year contract signed by the company president. He accepted the contract but, during the festivities, neglected to sign and return the contract. Thereafter he reported to work on January 4th of the following year. Six months later, when the company advised him that it was cutting his commission and base salary, he resigned and sued the company.

He argued that although the contract was never actually signed, he reported to work and acted as if it had been signed. At trial it was admitted that the president had signed the agreement. The company argued there was no breach of contract because the man never signed the agreement and therefore, the company was free to modify important contract terms at whim, without notice.

The Arkansas Court of Appeals ruled in favor of the employee. In its ruling the court stated: "There is no general requirement in the law of contracts that a contract or agreement be signed by both parties, although the statute of frauds requires certain contracts to be signed by the party to be charged...Unless otherwise indicated by the language or the circumstances, an offer invites acceptance in any manner reasonable under the circumstances. Here the evidence would support a finding that the employee accepted the employer's offer either verbally or by his subsequent performance."

Counsel Comments: *The law does not favor the destruction of contracts because of uncertainty. While it is true that a "meeting of the minds" is a requirement for the formation of a contract, a manifestation of assent may be made wholly by spoken words or by conduct. To avoid problems in this area, it is essential to prepare clearly drafted written contracts which specify that they must be signed by the employee in order to be valid. Had such a requirement been imposed in the cited case, the court might have decided the case in the company's favor.*

It is also important to understand the effect of the statute of frauds on written employment agreements. The statute of frauds is a legal principle requiring certain agreements (such as any sale of land exceeding $500.00, or promises to pay another's debt) to be in writing. In most states, employment agreements *exceeding one year* must be in writing and signed by both parties to be enforceable under this principle. Thus, if you desire to hire an employee for more than one year, be sure to prepare a written employment agreement evidencing this intent or your oral promise will probably not be legally valid.

Counsel Comments: *If you confirm arrangements with newly hired employees by letter and do not wish to prepare and send a formal employment agreement, be certain to specify all salary and bonus payments, benefit plan participation including health and insurance coverage, vacations, etc. together with a statement enunciating your right to discharge the employee at-will with or without cause. If you fail to state the at-will reservation in such a memo or letter, your ability to fire the employee suddenly could become the focus of a lawsuit. Always include a description of the job, incentives (i.e., raises), and other important concerns such as that the agreement will cease if the employee works for a competitor, discloses company secrets, etc. Always tailor such letters, memos or agreements to each particular hiring and get them reviewed by counsel before they are sent to avoid the many potential problems that often ensue.*

Understand the kinds of points to negotiate and include these in a written contract to protect the company. During negotiations with the applicant, experienced managers, supervisors and personnel executives in charge of hiring must discuss *all* important employment terms in advance and include these in a written contract for the company's protection.

Staff in charge of hiring have a duty to discuss carefully all the terms and responsibilities of the job with the applicant, no matter what type of position is being offered. This is essential to maintaining positive relations with your workforce and minimizing breach-of-contract and wrongful termination lawsuits.

Counsel Comments: *The employer holds most of the cards at the interview-*

ing-negotiation stage and can insist on almost any term it desires prior to the hiring. The worst that happens is that the applicant will attempt to modify or negotiate a particular point to his/her benefit. Thus, understand the company's position with respect to all employment terms, do not deviate from them—try to offer the same deal to different applicants—and confirm all the terms of employment in writing before the individual begins working.

The checklists at the end of the chapter outline many of the key negotiating points that should be discussed. One checklist offers a comprehensive list of key points to discuss no matter what type of job is being offered; the Sales Employment Checklist provides valuable negotiating strategies to discuss when hiring a sales employee or independent rep and may give you useful ideas of the kinds of fall-back positions to take for key terms during negotiations. At the end of the book, you will also find sample employment contracts which illustrate and include many of these points.

EMPLOYMENT AGENCIES

Problems pertaining to employment agencies typically arise when the parties fail to specify clearly the arrangement regarding payment for services rendered and how fees are deemed to be earned. To avoid problems in this area, *always* study carefully agency agreements submitted to your company. Insist that any exceptions or contingencies be spelled out in writing. Be sure there is a clear understanding among the agency, your company and the applicant at the time of hire as to who pays what and when. If your company agrees to assume all or part of the fee for an applicant, this should be documented in writing. Request reimbursement of the fee if the employee only works a short time and get this guarantee of a rebate in writing for your protection.

Commission arrangements with employment agencies are subject to the same legal rules affecting other contracts. Ambiguous clauses or careless omissions can cause problems. When disputes arise and no clear written agreement exists to resolve the problem of fees, most courts will award fees to the agency when: (1) The agency discussed the applicant with the employer; (2) The employer agreed to interview the applicant; (3) The applicant agreed to interview with the employer; and (4) The agency or the employer set the arrangements in motion for the interview.

But what happens in the event an unsolicited resume or applicant from an employment agency winds up as a job offer? Can the absence of a signed agreement destroy an agency's right to a fee? Although each case depends on its particular facts, numerous cases reveal the entitlement of an agency to a fee under equitable theories, including quantum meruit, when a placement is made and it is unjust to allow a company to retain the benefit of the employee's services without paying an agency reasonable value for its services. In some instances, courts impose "quasi-contracts" to insure that companies not enrich themselves unjustly at the agency's expense when a placement is made. However, the right to a fee does not extend indefinitely. In Illinois, for example, an employment agency which makes the first referral of a job candidate earns the recruitment fee if the applicant is offered the job within one year, notwithstanding an intervening referral by another agency.

What happens if the applicant leaves the job before the expiration of a 90-day probation period? In a recent New York case, the court ruled in favor of the agency, which demanded a $6,250 fee for placing a job applicant in a $25,000-per-year job. The company refused to pay the bill because the employee walked off the job after only 44 days. In ruling for the agency, the court drew the employer's attention to a state law that allows an agency the right to collect a fee after it has referred a job applicant to a company and the applicant has been selected for a job. Laws differ among the various states, however, as to when and how an employer incurs a hiring agency fee. In some states payment is due upon employment and there is no statutory requirement for an employment agency to provide any guarantee period at all.

Counsel Comments: *To protect your company from these and other problems, the following guidelines are recommended whenever hiring an employment agency:*

1. Always negotiate the placement fee and confirm this in writing.

2. Receive stipulations in writing from employment agencies that fees are payable after the completion by the employee of a minimum period of employ-

ment. Specify what that period is. Negotiate for use of a sliding scale (i.e., 25% of the fee upon acceptance, 25% upon completion of initial 30 days etc.) for greater protection.

3. If the law in your state does not prohibit applicants from paying the fee, require the employee to pay the agency fee, to be reimbursed by the company if he/she is still on the job at the end of a specified period of time.

Although an agreement by an applicant to reimburse the employer for a portion of an agency fee if he resigns during a trial period may be legal, it cannot *be enforced by deductions from the worker's pay.*

4. Always investigate the agency. Is it licensed and bonded? What services are you to receive? Does the agency check the history and reliability of the applicant? Will your company be indemnified and held harmless in the event the agency makes false representations to the applicant or fails to check applicant references carefully?

5. To avoid problems with competing agencies, hire only one or two at the same time. Institute a policy of time-stamping resumes so you will know how and when referrals were received. When several agencies submit the same resume, you are only obligated to pay the agency which submitted the resume first. *Thus, have all resumes enter your company through one source so you can document when and how they were received, to prove your position.*

6. Advise agencies you deal with that your company's policy is not to discriminate.

7. Discuss realistic job requirements, duties and terms for best results.

Outplacement Firms

Understand what role the outplacement firm plays and how such organizations differ from employment agencies and executive recruiters. Outplacement firms are typically retained by employers to help terminated employees move out. Fees for this service often range from a flat fee of several thousand dollars up to a small percentage of the employee's total annual compensation, depending on the extent of services provided. Outplacement firms typically ease the separation by providing professional career assessment, interview training techniques and helping develop a resume. Some firms even provide space for a desk and telephone to assist the terminated worker in calling on prospective employers.

Because not all outplacement firms are the same and some have better track records than others, always obtain references from candidates and companies who have used the service. Carefully scrutinize all contracts with outplacement firms before hiring and prepare written agreements. Discuss how additional fees may be incurred and resist these. If possible, try to structure a flat fee arrangement to limit costs and negotiate a discount in the event you terminate a number of employees who collectively wish to use the services of the firm.

Counsel Comments: *Consider the possibility of offering paid outplacement firm services as a negotiating tool in designing the severance package. Since there is no legal obligation to provide a terminated worker with outplacement services paid for by the company, this employee benefit may be used to your advantage by requiring the employee to sign a release before you grant such a paid benefit. This strategy will be discussed in greater detail in Chapter 4.*

PART-TIME POSITIONS

Companies are free to dictate the terms of employment with any employee, whether he/she is a full-time or part-time worker. The key is to specify in writing all employment terms and this rule applies to whatever job is being offered. Part-time workers must comply with the same company rules, policies and procedures as full-time employees; the only difference is that they may be excluded from company pension and profit-sharing plans, medical and other insurance benefits. In most cases, employees who regularly work fewer than 25 hours per week are considered to be part-time employees. Most policies contain clauses granting coverage to employees who work *more* than a stated number of hours per week, depending on the specific insurance policy. However, under

ERISA, employees who generally work 1,000 hours in a pension plan year must be included in pension plans.

> **Counsel Comments:** *Contact your nearest office of the Department of Labor to be sure that your company complies with all appropriate benefits laws affecting part-time workers. In some states, part-time workers must be paid overtime, vacations, lunch breaks and coffee breaks like regular workers. Whenever hiring new part-time employees, be sure to explain carefully what fringe benefits are* not *available to them. For example, failing to explain to a new part-time worker that he/she does not qualify for medical benefits could lead to devastating consequences for the worker and her family. Thus, always use written contracts with your part-time workers as well as with your full-time employees to confirm the benefits offered/not offered.*
>
> *Some companies offer pro-rated fringe benefits for part-time workers such as shorter holidays, vacations, paid sick leave, health/medical insurance and life insurance (i.e., employees working 25 hours per week would be entitled to half of the benefits given to full-time employees, etc.) Your company may be interested in implementing a similar policy.*

It is worth noting that under the federal Equal Pay Act, part-time workers and temporary employees may not be subject to the strict rules that men and women doing the same work must be paid equally.

If your company uses temporaries to supplement its full-time personnel, such a practice may be attacked by a union on the grounds that bargaining unit employees are deprived of job opportunities and overtime. In one recent case, a company's 1989 figures disclosed an extraordinary leap in the number of temporary workers hired. Early in 1990, the union instituted a grievance seeking an outright ban on the hiring of temporaries.

At the hearing, a unionist expounded that the company used the hiring of temporaries to reduce the number of employees in the unit. This affected job security, he argued, which is an essential part of any labor contract. The fact that temporaries had been hired in the past did not establish a binding past practice. He also asserted that the union's past acquiescence in the use of such employees did not take place under the same circumstances that now existed (i.e., with the union's existence now being threatened).

The company argued that the union contract did not forbid the use of temporary workers, that the company acted in good faith and at no time did the company deprive bargaining unit members of employment. The company also stated that past practice confirmed the legitimacy of its right to hire temporaries. However, the arbitrator ruled in favor of the *union* and placed a sharp limit on the practice. Although the employer was entitled to use temporary workers for legitimate business purposes, the arbitrator ruled this was not an unqualified right.

He stated: "The Arbitrator is convinced from all the evidence in this case that the company is engaging in a systematic plan to prevent the growth of the collective bargaining unit...It would be inappropriate to order the company to cease and desist altogether from the use of such temporary employees but there must be some limitation imposed. The company should not be permitted to use temporary employees in any week that a unit member is on lay-off status or that the number of unit employees falls below the level of the previous year, nor should any temporary employees be assigned overtime hours without such overtime first being offered to unit members."

> **Counsel Comments:** *In the absence of language in a contract limiting the hiring of employees to perform non-unit work, arbitrators are not inclined to apply a limitation on the employer when there is a reasonable exercise of discretion. However, when the overall impact is not simply incidental but strikes at the very existence of the bargaining unit, then arbitrators are likely to step in to protect the unit. Speak to experienced labor counsel for further details if applicable.*

EFFECTIVE POLICIES AND PROCEDURES

Even before the decision to hire a particular applicant has been made and the job is accepted in writing, companies can take many important steps to minimize discharge, breach of contract and other litigation stemming from alleged violations during the pre-employment relationship. This section will recommend practical strategies that should be implemented.

Employee Handbooks And Manuals

Effective personnel relations and a successful plan for litigation avoidance begin with an employee manual. In addition to giving employees a clear description of their benefits, a proper manual sets the rules for on-the-job behavior (i.e., reporting absences, authorized use of telephones, handling complaints, etc.), discusses criteria used for evaluating job performance, and reduces legal suits relating to "guaranteed" job security, unfair discharge and other claims. In addition, it may boost employee morale.

Despite these advantages, many companies do not use employee manuals; others fail to keep current with changing EEOC regulations and employment laws, and to incorporate such changes in their own publications. If staffing doesn't afford time to create a manual, this is one area where a company would be well advised to hire a consultant or lawyer to draft one. A few thousand dollars spent on a manual today can save you tens of thousands of dollars in a lawsuit tomorrow.

If the employer drafts a fair and reasonable policy which the employee violates, a jury is more likely to side with the company in the event of a lawsuit. Moreover, an employee who fails to exhaust the employer's internal complaint resolution procedures may find that his/her subsequent lawsuit is barred. In addition, a properly drafted manual - one which discusses how workers are hired, evaluated, disciplined and fired - will assist the company in discrimination lawsuits brought by disgruntled employees.

Remember, however, that your company must act according to the policies set forth in the manual, since the slightest deviation can create problems. Be aware that courts in many jurisdictions are ruling that manuals and handbooks can create contractual rights between employers and employees. Companies that fail to follow policies as presented in their manuals (e.g., if one were to terminate an employee without implementing progressive disciplinary measures called for in the manual), may be found liable for breach of contract. The following true case is a good example.

A man worked as a copywriter for a major publishing company. He did not sign an employment contract when he was hired. However, during negotiations, he was assured that the job was secure because the company never terminated employees without just cause, and his employment application stated that employment was subject to the provisions of the company manual on personnel policies and procedures. The manual stipulated that "employees will be fired for just and sufficient cause only" after internal steps toward rehabilitation had been taken and had failed.

For eight years the employee received periodic raises and job promotions, and turned down a number of offers from other companies. Despite that, the employee was fired suddenly, without warning. He sued the company, claiming he had been wrongfully discharged. The court ruled in the employee's favor, stating that the facts created a company obligation not to deviate from termination procedures as stated in its policy manual.

When your company uses a manual or revises one that is presently being used, be sure to follow *all* policies and procedures contained therein. Although not recommended, it is not uncommon for manuals to spell out the following:

- Who is authorized to fire;
- Whether a firing decision must first be approved by a committee;
- Whether an employee must be given written reasons for firing;
- Whether a terminated worker can appeal a firing decision before it is effective;
- Whether a terminated worker must first be asked if he/she would be willing to take a job demotion;
- Whether an employee can be fired only for cause;
- Whether there are set rules regarding huge severance benefits;
- Whether a final warning must be given before a firing is effective.

The reason such clauses are not recommended is that the company may be giving additional rights to workers which are unnecessary. If your manual contains any or all of these provisions, or similar ones, you would be well advised to make sure that each successive step has been implemented before an employee is fired to avoid legal exposure.

Counsel Comments: *Recent Supreme Court decisions and other legal developments indicate that companies may not be* *bound to promises in manuals regarding future medical, health and other benefits, provided clearly drafted and conspicuous language in the manual sufficiently states that such benefits may be eliminated or modified without notice, at the company's sole discretion. Be aware of this and be sure to review and amend your company's manual to take advantage of this recent development by drafting legally sufficient language where appropriate. For example, a company may state in the introduction that the booklet itself does not constitute an employment contract. Language should also be inserted stating that the handbook can give an indication of some of the company's present policies and personnel functions, including benefits, but that:*

"The Company may at any time change the policies, procedures, benefits, and benefit plans with or without prior notice since nothing in the handbook should be construed as a contract of employment or promise of continued benefits. Specific questions should be directed to the Supervisor or to the Personnel Department and the programs outlined in the booklet should be regarded only as guidelines, not guarantees, which the Company may change as needed in order to conduct its work to the Company's benefit."

Additional conspicuous language should also be displayed throughout the handbook that the company adheres to the employment-at-will doctrine, which enables either the employee or the employer to terminate the employment relationship at any time.

Oral Promises

It's not unusual for job interviewers to be over-exuberant in their job descriptions, particularly when impressed by an applicant's qualifications. This can lead to unrealistic expectations by the applicant over possible job security, advancement or expected benefits, with possible suits for damages. Since some courts may believe the applicant's version, avoid making such promises. Loose oral promises such as "the job is yours as long as you want it," or "you have a job with us forever," and similar words encourage disgruntled workers to commence lawsuits over what was intended, in turn, exposing your company to unnecessary and expensive litigation.

One job applicant was specifically told by the company president, "We have no mandatory retirement here. So long as you do your job, you can be here until you're a hundred." When fired three years later, the ex-employee recalled the president's euphoric forecast with bitterness, which was articulated in an expensive lawsuit, with the words repeated in legal papers. The court ruled that the president's statement did not amount to an expression of intent to create a binding lifetime contract but was rather, under the particular circumstances of the case, merely encouragement and optimism not to be taken seriously.

Counsel Comments: *Despite the result of the above case, courts in many states have held that conversations conducted in an atmosphere of critical one-on-one negotiation regarding the security of future employment or other terms may give rise to a valid, enforceable contract provided the use of such words can be proven.*

Finally, watch out for oral statements such as "the job is open as long as you want it" to avoid potential liability and legal exposure in this area. It is also strongly recommended that you avoid inducing someone to resign from another position to take a job with your company, particularly if major relocation expenses and hardship are involved, without adequately protecting the company. This could be done, for example, by issuing a written agreement confirming that no promises of continued, long-term employment were given, even to the person relocating with great hardship.

Job Offers

When making a job offer, it is also important to clarify just how long the offer will be held open. Courts and legal authorities on the subject of hiring contracts have consistently held that when an acceptance to a contract of employment does not correspond with the offer in every respect, no contract is formed. The following actual case illustrates this concept:

By a letter dated May 3, 1983, a university dean offered a teacher an 11-month appointment as chairperson and associate professor of the university's history department. The letter concluded: "If the terms of this letter are acceptable to you, please sign the enclosed copy and return to my office." When the professor failed to respond, the dean notified him by express mail dated May 25, 1983: "Unless an answer to our letter offer is received in my office by June 2, 1983, the offer for the position of Chairperson and Associate Professor...is withdrawn."

On June 2, 1983, the professor at last telephoned the dean and left a message with his secretary that he accepted the position, effective July 15, 1983. However, on June 7, 1983, the dean notified the professor that, since he had failed to accept in writing by June 2nd, the job offer was revoked. The professor thereupon filed a lawsuit for breach of a contract of employment, arguing that he did accept the job offer before the deadline expired by telephoning on June 2, 1983 and that he followed the call up with a confirming letter on June 11th. He also argued that the confirming letter should have been sufficient to create an employment contract since the university had not suffered any material damage by receiving his telephone message as opposed to a letter.

The university maintained that written correspondence set a deadline for the professor's acceptance of the job offer. His acceptance had to be received by the dean in writing no later than June 2nd. Moreover, the position offered to him was effective July 1, 1983. He telephoned that he would not be available until July 15, 1983 and this was unacceptable to the university.

The Ohio Court of Appeals ruled in favor of the university. Two aspects of the professor's case caused the revocation of the job offer, the court ruled. The court found: (1) He failed to respond in the precise manner and place of acceptance set forth in the May 3rd letter—that a copy of the letter be signed and the copy returned to the dean's office; and (2) The professor's admitted unavailability for employment on July 1st. "A reply to an offer which purports to accept but is conditional on the offeror's assent to terms...different from those offered is *not* an acceptance but a counteroffer," the court concluded.

Counsel Comments: *Companies can use this legal principle for their benefit. When offering jobs to applicants, you can be quite specific in the timing and manner of acceptance. For example, it may be a good idea to state what information, materials, data etc. the applicant must provide by the start date in order to begin the job. Making the job offer contingent upon receiving this information and requiring the applicant to sign a formal contract with non-compete and confidentiality provisions can provide your company with a number of options and legal strengths before the effective starting date. If the applicant refuses to sign such a document, that may be adequate grounds not to hire him/her.*

Refusal To Sign Confidentiality Agreements

In many situations, a refusal by an employee to sign a confidentiality agreement document after he/she begins working can constitute misconduct and cause for discharge.

In one case a technical writer was asked to sign a "Classified Information Agreement" by his supervisor after a few months of working. The supervisor told him that "The Company is asking all employees to sign one." The document stated, "I will not remove or divulge to anyone, either during my employment or for five (5) years after the termination of my employment, any information acquired by me concerning formulas, processes, methods of engineering or other classified and confidential information of the Company."

When the employee refused to sign the document, he was fired. The company opposed his claim for unemployment compensation and claimed that it was in the company's vital interest to protect the confidentiality of its methods and processes. Since all other employees signed the agreement, the employee's failure to sign was an act of insubordination. The employee stated that the wording of the agreement was too vague because it did not mention the specific material he was expected to keep confidential. Furthermore, he claimed that if he had signed the document his prospects for earning a living after leaving the company would have been impaired. Finally, he testified that he refused to sign the document because he was given no choice in the matter - it was either sign up or get out.

The Minnesota Court of Appeals ruled that his failure to sign the document constituted misconduct and he was therefore not entitled to receive jobless pay. The court noted that a state law requires that a manufacturer take reasonable steps to maintain its trade secrets. The document was judged to be reasonably calculated to protect its interests. Furthermore, the court noted it could not see how signing such a document would impair the individual's future job opportunities.

> **Counsel Comments:** *Confidentiality agreements should not be confused with non-compete agreements, whereby an individual commits him/herself not to compete with an employer for a designated period of time and in a designated geographical area after he/she is terminated. In many states, the refusal to sign an agreement containing a reasonable restrictive covenant will* not *constitute misconduct (although it may justify a termination) in the absence of additional consideration (i.e., two extra weeks pay, an additional week of paid vacation, etc.) offered by the company. Thus, understand this distinction and use it to your advantage.*

EMPLOYEE VERSUS INDEPENDENT CONTRACTOR STATUS

Companies often violate the law by not understanding the distinction between employee and independent contractor status. This distinction has become crucial due to increased IRS investigations. The IRS generally opposes independent status because companies who employ independents don't have to withhold income or employment taxes. Additionally, since the independent contractor can manipulate his/her earnings (they are entitled to claim all of their business-related expenses on Schedule C where expenses offset gross business income), many dollars of compensation go unreported.

Other problems can be involved as well. For instance, to obtain greater damages outside of Workers' Compensation benefits, a worker injured on-the-job may resist the Workers' Compensation Law prohibition of a direct cause of action against the employer for personal injury by claiming that he was not an employee but an independent contractor at the time of the incident.

No precise legal definition of an independent contractor exists. In fact, each state has its own laws that determine whether an individual is an employee or an independent contractor. When the courts attempt to determine the difference, they analyze the facts of each particular case. The most significant factors that courts look at when making this distinction are:

1. The company's right of control over the worker;

2. Whether the company carries indemnity or liability insurance for the worker;

3. Whether the individual works exclusively for the company or is permitted to work for others at the same time; and

4. Whether the parties have a written agreement which defines the status of the worker.

The distinction between an employee and an independent contractor is that the former undertakes to achieve an agreed result and to accept the employer's directions as to the manner in which the result shall be accomplished, while the independent contractor agrees to achieve a certain result but is not subject to the orders of the employer as to the means which were used. In each case, the court looks at the specific facts in making its determination. For instructive purposes, the company's right of control is best explained by the use of examples. Courts have found workers to be employees if the companies:

- Had the right to supervise the details of the operations;
- Required salespeople to collect accounts on behalf of the company;
- Provided the worker with a company car and/or reimbursement for some or all expenses;
- Restricted the worker's ability to work for other companies, or jobs (i.e. required full-time efforts);
- Required the worker to call on particular customers;
- Provided the worker with insurance and Workers' Compensation benefits;
- Deducted income and FICA taxes.

This list is not meant to be all-inclusive, but rather, to help you determine whether your personnel fall into either the employee or independent category. Since the law is so unsettled and frequently varies from case to case and state to state, and since the IRS has increased its scrutiny and activity in this area, federal legislation was presented in the Senate several years ago to introduce some standards. Although the bill was not passed, it is instructive and outlines a set of rules that can be used as guidelines. By following these rules, your company may minimize problems and/or better document your position in the event of an audit.

According to the parameters set forth in the proposed bill, an independent contractor:

1. Controls his or her own work schedule and the number of working hours;

2. Operates from his or her own place of business or pays rent if an office is provided and supplies his/her own stationery, business cards, etc., *not* at the company's expense;

3. Risks income fluctuation since his or her earnings are a result of output (i.e., sales, rather than the number of hours worked); and

4. Has a written contract with an employer before work begins that states he or she is not considered an employee for purposes of the Federal Contributions Act, the Federal Unemployment Tax Act, and income is not withheld at the source. The contract clearly states that the individual must pay self-employment and federal income tax.

Following these rules and the information contained in the 20 factor test cited on the next page can go a long way toward applying the correct status determination. When attempting to prove employee status in worker injury cases, the company's right of control may be the most important factor. According to Anthony F. Tagliagambe and Randall John Chiera, attorneys and authors of an article which appeared in the February 1992 issue of *The New York State Bar Journal*, all pertinent individuals, such as the worker's personnel manager, supervisor and co-workers, should be interviewed and prepared to testify on behalf of the company in this regard.

Some of the factors a court may look at when deciding a case in this area include:

- The method by which the individual was hired.
- The method of payment. For example, if the individual was paid hourly or weekly, rather than in a lump sum, this implies that an employer/employee relationship existed.
- Whether the company furnished equipment for the worker as opposed to requiring the worker to bring his own equipment.
- Whether the company required its workers to arrive at work and remain until a specific time.
- Whether the individual was required to wear any type of uniform or identifying logo which would indicate he/she worked for the company.
- Whether the worker had established, set times for lunch and breaks.
- Whether the worker was required to report to a particular supervisor at the beginning of the work day or during the course of the work day.
- Whether the worker received constant supervision and instructions regarding the means and methods of performing work.
- Whether the parties signed a written employment contract or agreement which stated that the worker was to be considered an employee rather than an independent contractor.

Although most companies desire the finding of the worker as an employee rather than an independent contractor at a Workers' Compensation hearing, thereby limiting exposure and damages, employers may have the opposite motive when involved in a tax case commenced by the IRS, state or local taxing authority. Here it is likely that your company may wish for a ruling finding independent contractor status (particularly when hiring sales reps) to minimize potential tax liability such as failing to withhold Federal Unemployment Tax (FUTA), Federal Insurance Contributions Tax (FICA), and the collection of income tax at the source of wages and other taxes on behalf of the individual-employee.

Generally, the IRS considers that an employer-employee relationship for tax purposes exists when the person for whom the services are performed has the right to control and direct the individual who performs the services, not only as to the result to be accomplished by the work, but also as to the details and means by which that result is accomplished. In this connection it is not necessary that the employer actually direct or control the manner in which services are performed; it is sufficient if the firm has the *right* to do so. The designation or description of the relationship of the parties as anything other than that of an employer and employee is immaterial and if such a relationship exists, the IRS considers it of no consequence that the employee is designated as a partner, agent, independent contractor or the like.

Rev. Rul. 87-41 contains a restatement of the so-called 20 factor test used by the IRS in similar determinations. The following is a list of the IRS' 20 factors which courts often consider. (Note: Courts do consider other relevant facts and circumstances not contained in the IRS list and may overrule initial IRS determinations where warranted.)

1. Instructions given to the individual
2. Training given to the individual
3. Integration
4. Services rendered personally by the individual
5. Hiring, supervising, and paying assistants working for the individual
6. Exclusive duties by the individual (not working for anyone else)
7. Set hours of work by the individual
8. Full-time duties by the individual
9. Doing work on the employer's premises
10. Following orders in sequence
11. Filing oral or written reports
12. Payment by the hour, week or month
13. Payment of business and/or traveling expenses
14. Furnishing of tools or materials
15. Significant training or investment in the individual
16. Realization of profit or loss from the individual
17. Right to discharge or terminate at any time without incurring a liability
18. Collection of money by the individual for the employer
19. Services provided on a continuing basis
20. Individual works under the firm name.

An excellent discussion of these rules is contained in Section 3121 of the IRS Regulations. Additionally, you may find the Basic Rules Summary on the next page a helpful reference .

Counsel Comments: *If an initial determination is made by the IRS finding employee status, costly damages, penalties and interest can ensue. Often the IRS has the right to impose additional taxes on your other employees similarly situated when a determination is found against your company with respect to the first employee, so act quickly. Speak to a competent attorney or accountant* immediately *upon receiving an initial IRS request for facts into such a matter. Competent advice and guidance may help "nip a problem" before it gets out of hand in this area.*

Summary Of Rules To Determine Employee Versus Independent Contractor Status

1. Instructions

Employees follow instructions about when, where, and how work is to be performed; contractors establish their own hours and have no instructions regarding how the job should be completed.

2. Training

Employees typically receive training via classes and meetings regarding how services are to be performed; contractors establish their own procedures and receive no training.

3. Coordination Of Services

Supervisors coordinate the work of employees with others; coordination of services between the contractor and others may not be apparent.

4. Services Rendered Personally

Services are typically performed personally by the employee; contractors may utilize others to perform job tasks and duties.

5. Supervision

Employees are supervised by a foreman or representative of the employer; contractors are not supervised on a daily basis.

6. Continuity

An employee typically works for the same employer for a lengthy period; contractors are often retained to complete one particular job for a shorter period.

7. Set Hours Of Work

An employee's hours and days are set by the employer; contractors dictate their own time.

8. Full Time Required

An employee typically works full time for an employer; contractors may have several jobs or work for others at the same time.

9. Doing Work On Employer's Premises

Employees work on the premises of an employer or on a route, or at a site designated by the employer; contractors typically work from their own premises and pay rent for their own premises.

10. Set Orders

An employee performs services in the order or sequence set by the employer; contractors often perform services at their own pace.

11. Submission Of Reports

Employees are often required to submit regular oral or written reports to the employer; contractors submit few or no reports.

12. Manner Of Payment

Employees are paid by the employer in regular amounts at stated intervals; contractors are paid upon the completion of the job or project, in a lump sum or other arrangement, such as on a commission basis.

13. Reimbursement Of Expenses

Employees are typically reimbursed for business and travel expenses directly related to the job; contractors pay their own expenses.

14. Furnishing Of Tools And Materials

Employees are usually furnished tools and materials by the employer at no cost; contractors typically furnish and pay for their own tools and materials.

15. Significant Investment

Employees typically have no significant financial investment in the facilities to perform services; contractors often have significant financial investment in an office, equipment, telephone, etc.

16. Realization Of Profit

Employees typically receive no direct profits from work performed; contractors often realize profit or loss as a result of their services or decisions.

17. Exclusivity

Employees typically work for one master; contractors may work for several persons or firms simultaneously.

18. Recognition

Employees are typically not known by the general public; contractors often have businesses known to the general public.

19. Job Security

Employees may be discharged at any time; contractors are typically discharged after a job is completed.

20. Right To Quit

Employees may quit their job at any time, often without incurring liability; contractors are usually legally obligated to complete a particular job to avoid liability.

Internal Revenue Service Guidelines Defining Employees vs. Independent Contractors

Facts

In each factual situation, an individual worker (Individual), pursuant to an arrangement between one person (Firm) and another person (Client), provides services for the Client as an engineer, designer, drafter, computer programmer, systems analyst, or other similarly skilled worker engaged in a similar line of work.

Situation 1: The Firm is engaged in the business of providing temporary technical services to its clients. The Firm maintains a roster of workers who are available to provide technical services to prospective clients. The Firm does not train the workers but determines the services that the workers are qualified to perform based on information submitted by the workers.

The Firm has entered into a contract with the Client. The contract states that the Firm is to provide the Client with workers to perform computer programming services meeting specified qualifications for a particular project. The Individual, a computer programmer, enters into a contract with the Firm to perform services as a computer programmer for the Client's project, which is expected to last less than one year. The Individual is one of several programmers provided by the Firm to the Client. The Individual has not been an employee of or performed services for the Client (or any predecessor or affiliated corporation of the Client) at any time preceding the time at which the Individual begins performing services for the Client. Also, the Individual has not been an employee of or performed services for or on behalf of the Firm at any time preceding the time at which the Individual begins performing services for the Client. The Individual's contract with the Firm states that the Individual is an independent contractor with respect to services performed on behalf of the Firm for the Client.

The Individual and the other programmers perform the services under the Firm's contract with the Client. During the time the Individual is performing services for other persons, substantially all of the Individual's working time is devoted to performing services for the Client. A significant portion of the services are performed on the Client's premises. The Individual reports to the Firm by accounting for time worked and describing the process of the work. The Firm pays the Individual and regularly charges the Client for the services performed by the Individual. The Firm generally does not pay individuals who perform services for the Client unless the Firm provided such individuals to the Client.

The work of the Individual and other programmers is regularly reviewed by the Firm. The review is based primarily on reports by the Client about the performance of these workers. Under the contract between the Individual and the Firm, the Firm may terminate its relationship with the Individual if the review shows that he or she is failing to perform the services contracted for by the Client. Also, the Firm will replace the Individual with another worker if the Individual's services are unacceptable to the Client. In such a case, however, the Individual will nevertheless receive his or her hourly pay for the work completed.

Finally, under the contract between the Individual and the Firm, the Individual is prohibited from performing services directly for the Client and, under the contract between the Firm and the Client, the Client is prohibited from receiving services from the Individual for a period of three months following the termination of services by the Individual for the Client on behalf of the Firm.

Situation 2: The Firm is a technical services firm that supplies clients with technical personnel. The Client requires the services of a systems analyst to complete a project and contacts the Firm to obtain such an analyst. The Firm maintains a roster of analysts and refers such an analyst, the Individual, to the Client. The Individual is not restricted by the Client or the Firm from providing services to the general public while performing services for the Client and in fact does perform substantial services for other persons during the period the Individual is working for the Client. Neither the Firm nor the Client has priority on the services of the Individual. The Individual does not report, directly or indirectly, to the Firm after the beginning of the assignment to the Client concerning (1) hours worked by the Individual, (2) progress on the job, or (3) expenses incurred by the Individual in performing services for the Client. No reports (including reports of time worked or progress on the job) made by the Individual to the Client are provided by the Client to the Firm.

If the Individual ceases providing services for the Client prior to completion of the project or if the Individual's work product is otherwise unsatisfactory, the Client may seek damages from the Individual. However, in such circumstances, the Client may not seek damages from the Firm, and the Firm is not required to place the Individual. The Firm may not terminate the services of the Individual while he or she is performing services for the Client and may not otherwise affect the relationship between the Client and the Individual. Neither the Individual nor the Client is prohibited for any period after termination of the Individual's services on this job from contracting directly with the other. For referring the Individual to the Client, the Firm receives a flat fee that is fixed prior to the Individual's commencement of services for the Client and is unrelated to the number of hours and quality of work performed by the Individual. The Individual is not paid by the Firm either directly or indirectly. No payment made by the client to the Individual reduces the amount of the fee that the Client is otherwise required to pay the Firm. The Individual is performing services that can be accomplished without the Individual's receiving direction or control as to hours, place of work, sequence, or details of work.

Situation 3: The Firm, a company engaged in furnishing client firms with technical personnel, is contacted by the Client, who is in need of the services of a drafter for a particular project, which is expected to last less than one year. The Firm recruits the Individual to perform the drafting services for the Client. The Individual performs substantially all of the services for the Client at the office of the Client, using materials and equipment of the Client. The services are performed under the supervision of employees of the Client. The Individual reports to the Client on a regular basis. The Individual is paid by the Firm based on the number of hours the Individual has worked for the Client, as reported to the Firm by the Client or as reported by the Individual and confirmed by the Client. The Firm has no obligation to pay the Individual if the Firm does not receive payment for the Individual's services from the Client. For recruiting the Individual for the Client, the Firm receives a flat fee that is fixed prior to the Individual's commencement of services for the Client and is unrelated to the number of hours and quality of work performed by the Individual. However, the Firm does receive a reasonable fee for performing the payroll function. The Firm may not direct the work of the Individual and has no responsibility for the work performed by the Individual. The Firm may not terminate the services of the Individual or the Firm. The Individual is permitted to work for another firm while performing services for the Client, but does in fact work for the Client on a substantial full-time basis.

Law And Analysis

This ruling provides guidance concerning the factors that are used to determine whether an employment relationship exists between the Individual and the Firm for federal employment tax purposes and applies those factors to the given factual situations to determine whether the Individual is an employee of the Firm for such purposes. The ruling does not reach any conclusions concerning whether an employment relationship for federal employment tax purposes exists between the Individual and the Client in any of the factual situations.

Analysis of the preceding three fact situations requires an examination of the common law rules for determining whether the Individual is an employee with respect to either the Firm or the Client, a determination of whether the Firm or the Client qualifies for employment tax relief under section 530(a) of the 1978 Act, and the determination of whether any such relief is denied the Firm under section 530(d) of the 1978 Act (added by section 1706 of the 1986 Act).

An individual is an employee for federal employment tax purposes if the individual has the status of an employee under the usual common law rules applicable in determining the employer-employee relationship. Guides for determining that status are found in the following three substantially similar sections of the Employment Tax Regulations: sections 31.3121(d)-1(c); 31.3306(i)-1; and 31.3401(c)-1.

These sections provide that generally the relationship of employer and employee exists when the person or persons for whom the services are performed have the right to control or direct the individual who performs the services, not only as to the result to be accomplished by the work but also as to the details and means by which that result is accomplished. That is, an employee is subject to the will and control of the employer not only as to what shall be done but as to how it shall be done. In this connection, it is not necessary that the employer actually direct or control the manner in which the services are performed; it is sufficient if the employer has the right to do so.

Conversely, these sections provide, in part, that individuals (such as physicians, lawyers, dentists, contractors, and subcontractors) who follow an independent trade, business, or profession, in which they offer their services to the public, generally are not employees.

Finally, if the relationship of employer and employee exists, the designation or description of the relationship by the parties as anything other than that of employer and employee is immaterial. Thus, if such a relationship exists, it is of no consequence that the employee is designated as a partner, coadventurer, agent, independent contractor, or the like.

As an aid to determining whether an individual is an employee under the common law rules, twenty factors or elements have been identified as indicating whether sufficient control is present to establish an employer-employee relationship. The twenty factors have been developed based on an examination of cases and rulings considering whether an individual is an employee. The degree of importance of each factor varies depending on the occupation and the factual context in which the services are performed. The twenty factors are designed only as guides for determining whether an individual is an employee; special scrutiny is required in applying the twenty factors to assure that formalistic aspects of an arrangement designed to achieve a particular status do not obscure the substance of the arrangement (that is, whether the person or persons for whom the services are performed exercise sufficient control over the individual for the individual to be classified as an employee). The twenty factors are described below:

1. Instructions. A worker who is required to comply with other persons' instructions about when, where, and how he or she is to work is ordinarily an employee. This control factor is present if the person or persons for whom the services are performed have the right to require compliance with instructions. See, for example, Rev. Rul. 68-598, 1968-2 C.B. 464, and Rev. Rul. 66-381, 1966-2 C.B. 449.

2. Training. Training a worker by requiring an experienced employee to work with the worker, by corresponding with the worker, by requiring the worker to attend meetings, or by using other methods, indicates that the person or persons for whom the services are performed want the services performed in a particular method or manner. See Rev. Rul. 70-630, 1970-2 C.B. 229.

3. Integration. Integration of the worker's services into the business operation generally shows that the worker is subject to direction and control. When the success or continuation of a business depends to an appreciable degree upon the performance of certain services, the workers who perform those services must necessarily be subject to a certain amount of control by the owner of the business. See United States v. Silk, 331 U.S. 704 (1947), 1947-2 C.B. 167.

4. Services Rendered Personally. If the services must be rendered personally presumably the person or persons for whom the services are performed are interested in the methods used to accomplish the work as well as in the result. See Rev. Rul. 55-695, 1955-2 C.B.H. 410

5. Hiring, Supervising, and Paying Assistants. If the person or persons for whom the services are performed hire, supervise, and pay assistants, that factor generally shows control over the workers on the job. However, if one worker hired supervises, and pays the other assistant pursuant to a contract under which the worker agrees to provide materials and labor and under which the worker is responsible only for the attainment of a result, this factor indicates an independent contractor status. Compare Rev. Rul 63-115, 1963-1 C.B. 178, with Rev. Rul. 55-593, 1955-2 C.B. 610.

6. Continuing Relationship. A continuing relationship between the worker and the person or persons for whom the services are performed indicates that an employer-employee relationship exists. A continuing relationship may exist where work is performed at frequently recurring although irregular intervals. See United States V. Silk.

7. Set Hours of Work. The establishment of set hours of work by the person or persons for whom the services are performed is a factor indicating control. See Rev. Rul. 73-591, 1973-2 C.B. 337.

8. Full Time Required. If the worker must devote substantially full time to the business of the person or persons for whom the services are performed, such person or persons have control over the amount of time the worker spends working and impliedly restrict the worker from doing other gainful work. An independent contractor, on the other hand, is free to work when and for whom he or she chooses. See Rev. Rul. 56-694, 1956-2 C.B. 694.

9. Doing Work on Employer's Premises. If the work is performed on the premises of the person or persons for whom the services are performed, that factor suggests control over the worker, especially if the work could be done elsewhere. Rev. Rul. 56-660, 1956-2 C.B. 693. Work done off the premises of the person or persons receiving the services, such as the office worker, indicates some freedom from control. However, this fact by itself does not mean that the worker is not an employee. The importance of this factor depends on the nature of the service involved and the extent to which an employer generally would require that employees perform such services on the employer's premises. Control over the place of work is indicated when the person or persons for whom the services are performed have the right to compel the worker to travel a designated route to canvass a territory within a certain time, or to work at specific places as required. See Rev. Rul. 56-694.

10. Order or Sequence Set. If a worker must perform services in the order or sequence set by the person or persons for whom the services are performed, that factor shows that the worker is not free to follow the worker's own pattern of work but must follow the established routines and schedules of the person or persons for whom the services are performed. Often, because of the nature of an occupation, the person or persons for whom the services are being performed do not set the order of the services or set the order infrequently. It is sufficient to show control, however, if such person or persons retain the right to do so. See Rev. Rul 56-694.

11. Oral or Written Reports. A requirement that the worker submit regular or written reports to the person or persons for whom the services are performed indicates a degree of control. See Rev. Rul 70-309, 1970-1 C.B. 199, and Rev. Rul. 68-248, 1968-1 C.B. 431.

12. Payment by Hour, Week, Month. Payment by the hour, week, or month generally points to an employer-employee relationship, provided that this method of payment is not just a convenient way of paying a lump sum agreed upon as the cost of a job. Payment made by the job or on a straight commission generally indicates that the worker is an independent contractor. See Rev. Rul. 74-389, 1974-2 C.B. 330.

13. Payment of Business and/or Traveling Expenses. If the person or persons for whom the services are performed ordinarily pay the worker's business and/or traveling expenses, the worker is ordinarily an employee. An employer, to be able to control expenses, generally retains the right to regulate and direct the worker's business activities. See Rev. Rul. 55-144, 1955-1 C.B. 483.

14. Furnishing of Tools and Materials. The fact that the person or persons for whom the services are performed furnish significant tools, materials, and other equipment tends to show the existence of an employer-employee relationship. See Rev. Rul 71-524, 1971-2 C.B. 346.

15. Significant Investment. If the worker invests in facilities that are used by the worker in performing services and are not typically maintained by employees (such as the maintenance of an office rented at fair value from an unrelated party), that factor tends to indicate that the worker is an independent contractor. On the other hand, lack of investment in facilities indicates dependence on the person or persons for whom the services are performed for such facilities and, accordingly, the existence of an employer-employee relationship. See Rev. Rul. 71-524. Special scrutiny is required with respect to certain types of facilities, such as home offices.

16. Realization of Profit or Loss. A worker who can realize a profit or suffer a loss as a result of the worker's services (in addition to the profit or loss ordinarily realized by employees) is generally an independent contractor, but the worker who cannot is an employee. See Rev. Rul 70-309. For example, if the worker is subject to a real risk of economic loss due to significant investments or a bona fide liability for expenses, such as salary payments to unrelated employees, that factor indicates that the worker is an independent contractor. The risk that a worker will not receive payment for his or her services, however, is common to both independent contractors and employees and thus does not constitute a sufficient economic risk to support treatment as an independent contractor.

17. Working for More Than One Firm at a Time. If a worker performs more than de minimis services for a multiple of unrelated persons or firms at the same time, that factor generally indicates that the worker is an independent contractor. See Rev. Rul 70-572, 1970-2 C.B. 221. However, a worker who performs services for more than one person may be an employee of each of the persons, especially where such persons are part of the same service arrangement.

18. Making Service Available to General Public. The fact that a worker makes his or her services available to the general public on a regular and consistent basis indicates an independent contractor relationship. See Re. Rul 56-660.

19. Right to Discharge. The right to discharge a worker is a factor indicating that the worker is an employee and the person possessing the right is an employer. An employer exercises control through the threat of dismissal, which causes the worker to obey the employer's instructions. An independent contractor, on the other hand, cannot be fired so long as the independent contractor produces a result that meets the contract specifications. Rev. Rul 75-41, 1975-1 C.B. 323.

20. Right to Terminate. If the worker has the right to end his or her relationship with the person for whom the services are performed at any time he or she wishes without incurring liability, that factor indicates an employer-employee relationship. See Rev. Rul. 70-309.

Under the facts of Situation 1, the legal relationship is between the Firm and the Individual, and the Firm retains the right of control to insure that the services are performed in a satisfactory fashion. The fact that the Client may also exercise some degree of control over the Individual does not indicate that the Individual is not an employee. Therefore, in Situation 1, the Individual is an employee of the Firm under the common law rules. The facts in Situation 1 involve an arrangement among the Individual, Firm, and Client, and the services provided by the Individual are technical services. Accordingly, the Firm is denied section 530 relief under section 530(d) of the 1978 Act (as added by section 1706 of the 1986 Act), and no relief is available with respect to any employment tax liability incurred in Situation 1. The analysis would not differ if the facts of Situation 1 were changed to state that the Individual provided the technical services through a personal service corporation owned by the Individual.

In Situation 2, the firm does not retain any right to control the performance of the services by the Individual, and thus no employment relationship exists between the Individual and the Firm.

In Situation 3, the Firm does not control the performance of the services of the Individual, and the Firm has no right to affect the relationship between the Client and the Individual. Consequently, no employment relationship exists between the Firm and the Individual.

Holdings

Situation 1: The Individual is an employee of the firm under the common law rules. Relief under section 530 of the 1978 Act is not available to the Firm because of the provisions of section 530(d).

Situation 2: The Individual is not an employee of the Firm under the common law rules.

Situation 3: The Individual is not an employee of the Firm under the common law rules.

Because of the application of section 530(b) of the 1978 Act, no inference should be drawn with respect to whether the Individual in Situations 2 and 3 is an employee of the Client for federal employment tax purposes.

EMPLOYMENT NEGOTIATING CHECKLIST

- ☐ Date Employment is to begin.
- ☐ Length of employment: Is employment for a definite term (e.g., one year) or at-will (e.g., terminable at any time with or without notice)? If employed for a definite term, is the contract renewable after the expiration of the original period? Can one or both parties terminate the agreement prior to the expiration of the term? If so, how much notice (if any) must be given before the termination is effective?
- ☐ Define the employee's title.
- ☐ Specify employment duties. Will the employee report to a superior?
- ☐ Number of required working hours, sick days, holidays and vacations. If the employee does not use sick days and holidays, can they be taken in the following year, are they lost, or will the employee be paid for them?
- ☐ Employment status: Is the individual considered an employee or independent contractor?
- ☐ Amount of base salary: When is it payable? Specify all deductions from the employee's paycheck.
- ☐ Are expenses reimbursable? What, when, how and to what extent?
- ☐ Are bonuses paid? How are they calculated and when are they paid? Are prorated bonuses given if the employee is fired or resigns prior to the natural expiration of his/her contract?
- ☐ Are commissions paid? If so, specify how they are earned. Is the commission a gross or net amount: If net, what deductions are included?
- ☐ Are there fringe benefits? For example, does the company offer use of an automobile, free parking, car insurance, gasoline allowances, death benefits, prepaid legal services, medical, dental and hospitalization costs, life insurance, company credit cards, stock options, pension and profit-sharing plans? Be sure to advise the employee of all of the ramifications of the benefit package (e.g., when does the pension or profit-sharing plan vest?).
- ☐ Possibility of job advancement. Are periodic raises given? What is the procedure for merit raises?
- ☐ What happens in the event of disability? Define the meaning of temporary and permanent disability.
- ☐ Discuss the company policy in terms of maternity and paternity leave.
- ☐ Is a physical examination necessary?
- ☐ Will relocation ever be required? If so, specify who will pay for it and the manner of reimbursement.
- ☐ Can the employee have side ventures in a non-competing business or must the employee work exclusively on a full-time basis?
- ☐ Will the company require the employee to sign an agreement containing a restrictive covenant prohibiting him/her from working for a competitor or setting up a competing business? If so, for how long will the restriction last and what territory will be involved?
- ☐ Who owns inventions and processes created by the employee during employment?
- ☐ How will formal notices be communicated by one party to the other?
- ☐ Can the contract be assigned?
- ☐ What happens if the company is sold, acquired or merged during the employee's employment?
- ☐ Will disputes be handled by litigation or binding arbitration?

It is also a good idea to discuss other matters which should be included in the company manual:

- ☐ Time clock regulations (if any)
- ☐ Rest periods
- ☐ Absences
- ☐ Safety and accident prevention
- ☐ Authorized use of telephone
- ☐ Reporting complaints
- ☐ Bereavement pay, jury duty, personal days
- ☐ Company policy regarding drugs and alcohol
- ☐ No solicitation or distribution rules
- ☐ Rules of conduct
- ☐ Code of ethics and confidential policies

SALES EMPLOYMENT CHECKLIST

Compensation

Salary (usually given to company-employed salespeople)

- ☐ What is the amount and when is it payable?

Draw (usually given to independent sales reps)

- ☐ Is it applied against commission?
- ☐ What is the amount and when is it payable?
- ☐ The draw can be stopped by the company any time without prior notice when commission earnings do not exceed draw.
- ☐ The sales rep is personally liable for repayment when draw exceeds commission earnings or when the rep is fired from his job.
- ☐ The company has the right to set off draw and reduce the amount of commission owed upon termination of the employment relationship.

Bonus (usually given to company-employed salespeople)

- ☐ Is the bonus gratuitous or enforceable by contract?
- ☐ What is the amount and when is it payable?
- ☐ Specify that prorated bonuses will not be given in the event the salesperson resigns or is fired prior to the date when the bonus will be paid. Avoid basing the bonus on a determination of profits because this may give the salesperson the right to inspect your company's books and records.

Commission

- ☐ Specify the commission rate and when it is payable.
- ☐ Avoid guaranteed shipping arrangements.
- ☐ Specify split commission policies if applicable.
- ☐ Specify all deductions from commission, how and when they are computed? e.g., returns, freight charges, unauthorized price concessions given by the salesperson, billing and advertising discounts, collection charges, failure of the customer to pay.
- ☐ Specify commission for large orders, special customers, off-price goods, and reorders.

Expenses (usually for company-employed salespeople)

- ☐ Specify the kind and amount of expenses that are reimbursable.
- ☐ Specify the kind of documentation the salesperson must supply in order to receive reimbursement.

Territory

- ☐ Are you giving exclusive or non-exclusive territorial rights? Define the particular territory and customers.
- ☐ Be sure to discuss all house accounts and document these in writing.
- ☐ What about products sold in one territory and shipped into another? Determine how this will affect your split commission policy.
- ☐ Can the salesperson sell in other territories not solicited by other salespeople, e.g., at trade shows?
- ☐ If exclusive territorial rights are not involved, insure that the salesperson will not receive commission for orders not actually solicited by him.

Duties

- ☐ Exercise best efforts in representing the company and its products or services.
- ☐ Make no representations, warranties, or commitments binding that company without the company's prior consent.
- ☐ The salesperson will be personally liable and required to reimburse the company in the event he exceeds his authority.
- ☐ Forward all field inquiries or complaints in the field to the company immediately.
- ☐ Must work full-time for the company without any sideline. Especially, must not represent or form a competing business.
- ☐ Must personally solicit the product and cannot hire an associate to represent the company without prior written approval.
- ☐ Maintain minimum general and automobile liability coverage in excess of $___ per occurrence.
- ☐ Attend sales meetings, both local and national.

- ☐ Call on accounts periodically, service accounts, and maintain accurate selling records and lead sheets.
- ☐ Assist in any collection efforts requested by the company.
- ☐ Promise to protect all trade secrets, customer lists, and other forms of confidential information acquired while working for the company.

Length Of Employment

- ☐ Date employment is to begin.
- ☐ Length of employment. Is employment at-will (the salesperson can be fired any time) or for a definite term, say two years?
- ☐ If employment is at-will, is notice required? If so, when must it be sent for the termination to be effective and how must it be sent (e.g., certified or regular mail?) *Never* give assurance of job security if you are hiring a salesperson at-will.
- ☐ If employment is for a definite term, is the contract renewed under the same terms and conditions after the expiration of the original agreement? Must notice be sent to confirm this?
- ☐ Peg employment to a minimum sales quota if applicable.

Termination

- ☐ Clarify when commissions stop: e.g., upon termination, upon shipment of an order, upon shipment with a final cut-off date, to eliminate the problem with reorders.
- ☐ Avoid severance compensation arrangements.
- ☐ Specify when a final accounting will be made.
- ☐ Limit the right of the salesperson to sue for commission within a specific period.
- ☐ Specify the prompt return of all samples, customer lists, orders, field information, with a penalty if not complied with.
- ☐ Include a restrictive covenant for additional protection in writing.

Note: The preceding two checklists may be used interchangeably if you desire; choose the negotiating points from both checklists for maximum advantage.

CHAPTER

2 Benefits And Financial Considerations

This chapter is devoted to discussing ways to avoid many problems regarding financial and non-financial employee benefits. Areas of discussion include an analysis of the important points of COBRA, ERISA, health insurance and related laws as well as employer provided perks such as meals, vacations and transportation benefits. Helpful suggestions are offered in areas where problems often occur and the strategies contained herein can often help you avoid such problems.

The complexity of employee benefits law is well established. New cases are constantly being decided and statutory developments implemented which have an impact on particular plans and practices. It is critical that you constantly update and evaluate the effect of these legal developments on your own health and benefits plans.

One area in particular—retiree health care benefits and successor benefits (when a person leaves a company to work in a new job)—has raised numerous problems. An employer's obligation to provide post-termination or retirement health benefits largely turns on whether those benefits are actually vested at the time of leaving. When workers change jobs, it is often unclear whether the old or new employer is obligated under COBRA to provide insurance to cover a pre-existing ailment. Current law has not definitely answered the variety of problems and questions that arise in this area—for example, which employer's plan provides primary insurance and which provides secondary insurance after the first pays off? What about workers who are not sure they have a pre-existing condition but still want to retain continuation coverage under COBRA? And, if the new plan doesn't address a condition the old plan covered, can the worker continue the old plan? These and other questions typify current confusion in many areas of employee benefits which can only be resolved over time.

Keeping abreast of changing laws and regulations can insure that your company is acting properly with respect to the administration and maintenance of employee benefits and plans. Claims for employee benefits are typically covered under federal Employee Retirement Income Security Act (ERISA) law; violations by company and/or plan administrators entrusted to deliver these benefits can be quite expensive.

FLEXIBILITY TO ALTER BENEFITS

Companies with written personnel policies should always reserve the right to alter or amend promises of benefits at any time, with or without notice, for maximum protection. Such a disclaimer should appear in bold, conspicuous language in all manuals and written policy statements.

The advantages of following this strategy can be great. In one recent case, a federal appeals court upheld the validity of a "reservation clause" in an employee handbook that allowed company-wide discretion to alter benefits without notice. A trial court had decided the case in the employee's favor, ruling that the company's change of a policy one day before it would have benefited a terminated worker violated ERISA. However, the appeals court reversed the decision in favor of the company, stating that although employees have the right to rely on statements concerning health benefits in company handbooks and manuals, nothing in ERISA prevents a company from changing such benefits, even suddenly, when the manual specifically reserves the right to do so.

Counsel Comments: *A petition was filed seeking a rehearing of the case and its application to your company depends on the unique facts of each situation. However, legal precedent suggests that employers may change benefits provided this is made clear beforehand in a company manual. Speak to competent legal counsel and review your company handbook or policy manual immediately before inserting useful language where necessary.*

What if no statement authorizing a change of company policy is actually contained in a manual, but the employer sends a letter to all employees altering or revising the manual, and specific language favoring the company is suddenly inserted into the manual? In one case, a long-term worker sued the company for breach of an express and implied contract. After a decade of employment, the worker felt twinges of job insecurity. He was aware that several superiors were questioning his job performance and he was not popular with his co-workers. Nevertheless, his long tenure and the fact that the company's employee handbook provided that an employee could only be discharged for cause, led him to feel self-confident. One day, however, the company suddenly amended its handbook's "for cause" provision to read "Employment is now at the will of the company and the company reserves the right to terminate its employees with or without notice or cause...and this section supersedes any previous statements to the contrary contained in earlier versions of the manual."

Three months later the worker was fired for poor work performance. At the trial he alleged that the earlier provision in the manual made it plain that an employee could not be fired peremptorily—but only for a proper cause, which had to be justified by management. The previous clause was a commitment which became a contractual obligation which the company could not cancel or amend without the consent of its employees. The worker also argued that he continued to work in reliance on that provision and that the "discharge at-will" provision which replaced it was an arbitrary and unenforceable alteration.

The company responded that none of its policy manual statements were immutable provisions but could be changed at the company's discretion. Furthermore, the worker had no contractual right to continue working at his job and when he was dismissed, his status was governed by the fire at-will provision. In reviewing the worker's charges, the Michigan Supreme Court ruled that: "It is one thing to expect that a discharge-for-cause policy will be uniformly applied while it is in effect; it is quite a different proposition to expect that a personnel policy having no fixed duration will be immutable unless the right to revoke the policy was expressly reserved...(a) policy is commonly understood to be a flexible framework for operational guidance, not a perpetually binding obligation." The court clinched its rejection of the worker's case by noting that many employers would be tied to anachronistic policies in perpetuity if they were barred from the right to make policy changes.

Counsel Comments: *To be on safer footing,* always *reserve the right to make policy changes in manuals before a change is announced. The more rights reserved in the manual, the better. For example, it is best to state that management reserves the right, in its sole discretion, to determine vacation time and employees must give advance notice, not less than one month, before vacations can be granted. However, avoid making any changes in bad faith (e.g., the temporary suspension of a discharge-for-cause policy to facilitate the firing of a particular employee in contravention of that policy) because the right to amend policies in bad faith or other non-justifiable situations may not be acceptable.*

EMPLOYER-PROVIDED MEALS, TRANSPORTATION AND RELATED BENEFITS

Employers often compensate their employees with various fringe benefits in addition to their regular salaries and retirement and health benefits. Two typical benefits are meals and transportation reimbursement for travel between home and work, paid directly or indirectly by the employer. Although the Internal Revenue Code now taxes many of these benefits, many employers do not fully understand applicable rules and the latest Treasury Department regulations. The following rules will simplify common areas of confusion.

Generally, reimbursement for meals, transportation and related expenses is includable in an employee's gross income. When such benefits are taxable, the benefits generally must be reported by the employer and are subject to federal income tax, Social Security and federal unemployment withholding. Non-taxable benefits need not be reported by an employer to the IRS. However, a benefit is excludable from the employee's gross income if the value of the benefit is so small as to make accounting for it administratively impractical (e.g., a company-provided auto for six hours per month). If the company has a computerized accounting system, the burden is on the employer to demonstrate why it is unreasonable to track the benefits provided.

Additionally, employer-provided meals, meal money and local transportation fare provided to employees irregularly are excluded if offered on an occasional (e.g., three or less times per month) basis as a result of overtime and to enable the employee to work overtime. So too are special "provided meals" paid by the employee with a company charge account or employer-given cash at the time of the meal for the convenience of the employer. (Note: This rule does *not* apply to actual meal money or cash reimbursements paid to employees.)

Other exclusions from taxation include the "limited transportation" rule. This applies to an employee (earning less than $124,690 in 1992 and not an officer or director) who commutes to and from work via employer-provided transportation due to unusual circumstances (such as being requested to come in at 4:00 a.m. on one early morning instead of the regular 8:00 a.m. reporting time) and because it is unsafe to use other available means of transportation (depending on the history of crime in the area). If such a test can be met, the employee is only required to report the first $1.50 per one-way commuting fare in his or her gross income.

> **Counsel Comments:** *To avoid exposing your company to an audit, only provide such compensation to those people who need to travel occasionally and not on a regular basis.*

Finally, pursuant to the "limited transportation hourly" rule, hourly paid employees earning not more than $62,345 in 1992 who are paid for overtime at one and a half times their general rate of pay and who use employer-provided transportation solely due to unsafe conditions may include in income only the first $1.50 per one-way commuting cost, provided there is a written company policy stating that transportation is not provided other than for unsafe conditions.

> **Counsel Comments:** *Since employers that provide workers with meal allowances and cash reimbursement for meals are usually required to report the value of such benefits, consider paying the meal vendor directly by charge account and be able to justify the exclusion based upon one of the above exceptions. When in doubt,* always *include the benefit as taxable income but consider paying your employees more taxable cash compensation to help offset an employee's higher tax burden.*
>
> *With respect to transportation benefits, analyze whether an employee fits into one of the special exclusion rules. If so, only include in gross income and withholding the first $1.50 of each one-way transportation trip.*
>
> *Be sure your benefits coordinator is aware of current IRS rules regarding the treatment of company automobiles for business and personal use. For example, employees must report as earned income the value of personal use of company automobiles using an annual lease value table available from the IRS. See IRS Publication 463 for details.*
>
> *Smart companies impose compliance rules for these items in company manuals and procedure books. Always have a written policy that sets forth recordkeeping re-*

quirements, reimbursement rules for company-related expenses, and penalties the worker may sustain for not following such policies.

Auto Use

Demand receipts or specific information before reimbursing parking and toll charges. Require employees who use personal cars for business to keep records of whom they went to see, when, for how long, for what purpose, and the mileage and related expenses that were incurred. Where a personal car is used for business, always require proof of insurance coverage; insist on receiving such information annually. Some companies acquire non-ownership automobile liability insurance policies as part of the company's insurance coverage to protect it against bodily injury and property damage claims, investigation and litigation costs from work-related accidents. Consider providing workers with written contracts which specifically authorize the individual to *indemnify and hold the company harmless* from any damages, claims, expenses or judgments arising from personal accidents incurred in company-provided autos.

Travel And Overtime

Travel time rules under the federal Fair Labor Standards Act and the Walsh-Healy Act are quite complicated and may cause your company to be liable for overtime pay for time spent by an employee during company-related travel (other than for normal commuting travel and time for eating and sleeping). Avoid violations or confusion with your employees in this area by disseminating written policies stating beforehand what time is paid for, at what rate, and clarify per diem arrangements, expense reimbursement and special allowances.

For non-exempt personnel away on overnight travel or who work away from a plant and outside regular working hours, one common method computes additional pay and overtime pay by adding total travel time and work time and deducting: (1) sleeping time up to a maximum of eight hours; (2) one-half hour each for breakfast and lunch; (3) one hour for dinner; and (4) some additional time each way for regular travel. Other companies pay for actual work time but add a per diem payment plus actual expenses for extended work away from the normal work site. Speak to a competent accountant or other professional for more details if applicable.

COMMON OVERTIME PROBLEMS

The federal Fair Labor Standards Act (FLSA), also known as the Federal Wage and Hour Law, requires that overtime in the amount of one and one half times an employee's regular pay rate be paid for hours worked in excess of 40 hours in a workweek. The act does *not* require that overtime be paid for hours worked in excess of eight hours per day or on weekends or holidays. In addition to common claims of employee entitlement and problems regarding the computation of overtime, other problems that frequently arise include whether an employee can waive the right to overtime pay, what rights employers have in requiring workers to work overtime, whether employers can equalize overtime on a day-to-day basis, problems with unauthorized overtime and the best way to settle disputes in this area.

Generally, employers cannot force workers to waive their entitlement to overtime pay. In one case, a union member was asked by the foreman if he wished to work the "sixth day" at straight time. The worker concealed his resentment for four years. He then quit his job and filed a wage claim before his state's labor commissioner for unpaid overtime. At an ensuing hearing, the company argued that it never required anyone to work overtime but in return for this accommodation, employees wishing to work a sixth day waived their rights to the usual time-and-a-half pay. The worker replied that the union contract required the payment of time and a half for overtime, that state and federal law imposed similar requirements and that he accepted the amount offered without protest by the company because he would have been barred from any Saturday work if he had insisted on his rights.

The hearing examiner ruled that the company violated its union contract when it paid straight time instead of overtime, and rejected the company's argument that the claim was barred when the worker "waived" his rights because the worker could not by himself, without the participation of the union, give the company an effective waiver.

Unless they work in such exempt capacities as executive, administrative or professional jobs and are excluded from overtime consideration or remuneration, employees may bring such claims before the U.S. Department of Labor or an equivalent state agency, or file a lawsuit in court. Department of Labor rulings typically disallow claims of employee "waivers" and the Fair Labor Standards Act specifically disclaims the right of employers to force workers into accepting a lower rate of pay for overtime or no overtime pay; court victory for an employee often means an award of his rightful pay together with expensive penalties and counsel fees.

Federal law requires employers who offer overtime to post signs outlining the federal minimum wage and overtime regulations conspicuously in places where workers enter and exit. In addition, most compensatory plans (also called comp plans) allowing workers time off without pay in the work period following one in which they worked excessive hours, or allowing them to work more than 40 hours one week to make up for working less than 40 hours in a previous week, are *illegal*. Each workweek must be considered separately in determining overtime hours, regardless of the length of the pay period, except for certain occupations (e.g., police officers or firefighters), and employers giving time off must compute the value of such benefits at one and one half the regular rate of pay.

Counsel Comments: *Contact a representative at your state's Department of Labor or the Wage and Hour Division of the U. S. Department of Labor for a formal opinion* before *implementing any company plan.*

Must an employer pay for overtime it has forbidden? If the company has no knowledge that an employee is working overtime, and has established a rule or policy prohibiting overtime work that is conspicuously posted on the employee bulletin board and distributed to workers in memos and work rules, an employee may not be entitled to overtime pay after making a claim. The statutes do not give an employee a right to work at-will in violation of instructions from the employer and then claim wages and penalties if the employer refuses to pay wages for the unauthorized work. Further, the Fair Labor Standards Act does not protect employees who deliberately underreport their overtime hours.

Counsel Comments: *The problem of unwanted overtime may be difficult to control at offices where there is an occasional need to work overtime. It is therefore incumbent on employers to watch out for the employee who hopes to build a nest egg out of a lump payment for a long stretch of concealed overtime. A written policy should be implemented informing every employee that if he or she feels entitled to overtime, he or she must report at the end of each week the number of additional hours worked. And, be sure to notify all employees in writing that the company has a firm rule forbidding any employee to work overtime without a signed okay from the employee's department head or a company officer.*

Can an employee refuse to work overtime? Generally, even under most union contracts, an employee may not refuse to work reasonable overtime; refusal to do so is good cause for discipline and even discharge *provided* advance warning of overtime requirements is given, overtime is distributed fairly among all workers, and progressive warnings were previously given to the worker or others. However, although the scheduling of hours is a management prerogative, adequate notice (i.e., before noon for occasional overtime, more than 24-hour notice for extended overtime) must be given if your company intends to prove misconduct and prevail at an unemployment compensation hearing.

When an employee deliberately refuses a reasonable request to work overtime for no justifiable reason, the company is in a strong position, particularly when it can be shown that the employee knew the company desperately needed the overtime performed and the employee's failure to work overtime on that shift caused the employer undue hardship.

Counsel Comments: *It is considered good employee relations to give the employee as much advance notice as possible so he or she can plan to stay late. Rotation of overtime is, of course, another widely accepted practice so that everyone can share in the monetary benefits, as well as the inconveniences. Overtime distribution is such a cause of controversy that union contracts often specify how it is to be allocated. To insure fairness, the wise supervisor will maintain a roster recording overtime worked by each employee, and will establish particular rules as to how the roster system will work.*

However, overtime work need not be distributed equally on a day-to-day or week-by-week basis. Arbitrators have usually held that companies merely have the obligation to equalize overtime as best as possible over the long run and, in particular, to avoid discriminating by offering more overtime to non-minority workers. To avoid poor communication in the workplace, supervisors should make it clear that overtime equalization does not mean day-to-day makeup for employees on the bottom of the list. Most arbitrators say that equalization should be effected "over a reasonable time." That could mean three months or even longer if the situation warrants.

Companies should also be careful when requesting participation in company-sponsored projects after-hours where compensation is expected. In one case a worker donating blood for a co-worker was delayed several hours beyond his normal quitting time. An arbitration was commenced by his union and the arbitrator said it was "absolutely clear" that employees were told they would be compensated for time spent while donating blood.

Counsel Comments: *Insist on a clause in a collective bargaining agreement or your policy manual giving the company sole discretion to determine whether to pay for after-hours mercy missions. Advise your supervisors that they cannot commit to overtime without written approval from the front office.*

Since the purpose of the Fair Labor Standards Act is to insure that employees are paid their full wages, employers should not make any deals to settle wage-hour claims for less than the full amount (even when a release is signed by the employee) to defeat the rights of the worker. Although usually courts are pleased when prospective litigants compromise their differences, no such compromise is accepted under the FLSA. An underpaid employee can be awarded damages equal to the amount of the underpayment (i.e., double damages). Thus, it may be wise for a company immediately to pay in full any claim for wages before the matter gets into the hands of a lawyer. Unless your company has a good defense against the claim, such as that the amount of hours calculated is incorrect, procrastinating could be very costly in this area.

EMPLOYEE SUGGESTIONS AND INVENTIONS

Companies frequently receive valuable suggestions, comments, ideas, designs, and inventions from skillful employees. Many of these suggestions can lead to money-saving and money-making devices. In such situations, is the company obligated to pay the employee for the use of the idea? Who owns the device or invention created?

In one case, a gifted supervisor confided to her immediate superior that she had "all by herself" created an improvement in the company's internal procedures for terminating service to delinquent subscribers, and recommended the adoption of her revamped procedure. The superior was impressed by the proposed change and, with the employee-creator's approval, conveyed the proposal to company officers. Her idea was soon put into practice, saving the company time and money, but all the employee received was warm praise. A month later, she demanded that the company pay her the fair value of her bright new idea. When her demand was rejected, she quit her job and sued the company for breach of a contract implied in law.

At the trial she insisted that the company encouraged employees to submit new ideas and inventions, and that her idea was a great money saver for which she should receive financial recognition. The company rebutted her claims by stating that she grossly exaggerated what her idea did for the company (i.e., at best it was a minor improvement in clerical work) and in any event no obligation was owed as a matter of law.

After a tough-fought trial and appeal, the New York Appellate Term agreed with the company and ruled that no money should be awarded to the employee. It held that the idea did contribute significantly to the company and noted that the employee did a substantial portion of the work while on the employer's premises, during working hours, and relied mainly on material provided by the employer. It also referred to an earlier New York case where the court declared: "To be accorded protection as a property right an idea need not reflect the flash of genius, but it must show a genuine novelty and invention, and not merely a clever or useful adaptation of existing knowledge."

The following pages provide strategies for avoiding litigation in this area. However, before you can implement them, the following basic concepts must be understood:

Work-for-hire. Generally, work-for-hire is defined as work prepared by an employee within the scope of his or her employment, or work specifically ordered or commissioned by the employer, which the employee creates in reliance upon an express agreement. Thus, for example, when an employee is specifically engaged to do something (e.g., solve a problem, or develop a new product, process or machine), and he/she is provided with the means and opportunity to resolve the problem or achieve the result, and is paid for that work, then the employer is entitled to the fruits of the employee's labors.

Shop-right concept. If an employee is not hired to invent or solve a particular problem, is the employee entitled to claim any rights to his/her discoveries outside of the work-for-hire doctrine? Maybe, depending upon the particular facts involved. For example, under the shop-right concept, when an employee makes an invention or discovery that is outside the scope of his/her employment, but utilizes the employer's resources (e.g., equipment, labor, materials and/or facilities) in making the invention, that invention may be owned by the employee subject to a "shop-right" on the part of the employer. This "shop-right," in certain instances, gives the employer a non-exclusive, irrevocable license to use the invention indefinitely, without having to pay a royalty.

Valuable ideas as opposed to patentable inventions. In a hypothetical case, an employee develops a manufacturing process during non-working hours which he/she thinks will save the company money. The employee tells the boss and the idea is incorporated into the company's production process. Not compensated for the idea, the employee resigns and sues to recover a percentage of the money saved by the idea's use. The employee's case is not as strong as it appears. The reason is that ideas, plans, methods and procedures for business operations cannot normally be copyrighted. This is also true with respect to certain ideas for intellectual property. The law generally states that ideas belong to no one and are there for the taking.

> **Counsel Comments:** *An idea is presumed to be a work-for-hire and property of the employer if an employee offers it voluntarily without contracting to receive additional compensation. Thus, for example, the hypothetical employee above would have a stronger case if it could be proven that the idea was an original, unique creation not requested or developed while working on company time or on the employer's premises, and it was furnished because of a specific promise and/or understanding that the employee would be promoted or compensated once it was implemented by the employer.*

To avoid misunderstandings in this area, companies are advised to follow these guidelines:

1. **Prepare written employment agreements with work-for-hire provisions.** Smart employers request all job applicants to sign agreements containing such clauses. The following is a good example:

> "Employee agrees that with respect to inventions (broadly defined as discoveries, improvements and ideas, whether or not shown or described in writing or reduced to practice) made, authored, or conceived by me, either solely or jointly with others, during my employment, whether or not during normal working hours or whether or not on the Company's premises or within one year after termination of my employment I will:
>
> "Keep accurate, complete and timely records of such inventions, which records shall be the property of the Company and retained on Company premises.
>
> "Promptly and fully disclose and describe such inventions in writing to the Company.
>
> "Assign and I do hereby assign, to the Company all of my rights to such inventions, and to applications for letters patent and copyright registrations in all countries and to letters patent and copyright registrations granted upon such inventions in all countries.
>
> "Acknowledge and deliver promptly to the Company (without charge) such written instruments and to do such other acts as may be necessary in the opinion of the Company to preserve property rights against forfeiture, abandonment, or loss, and to obtain, defend and maintain letters patent and copyright registrations and to vest the entire right and title thereto to the Company."

Clauses such as these will help document the parties' intentions that all inventions and ideas belong to the employer before the applicant accepts the job, and will reduce the employee's claim of entitlement for compensation.

2. **Avoid offering compensation when you receive a voluntary suggestion.** In one famous case, a homemaker mailed an unsolicited cheesecake recipe to a baking company. The recipe was used and became a popular money-maker. Although the woman sued the company for damages, she lost. The court ruled that no recovery was obtainable because the homemaker voluntarily gave her idea to the company.

> **Counsel Comments:** *The analogy of this case to your business practice should not go unnoticed. Make it clear to all employees with regard to voluntary suggestions that there is no obligation to pay anything if the idea is used, and that any payments made will be purely discretionary (e.g., not linked to any predetermined formula such as a percentage of specific company savings, revenue or profits generated from the idea).*

3. **Prepare an acknowledgment to document the employee's idea, invention or suggestion and which specifically *disclaims* any obligation for its use or compensation.** The document on the following page is a good example of this point.

> **Counsel Comments:** *Most employees submit ideas with the expectation of being recognized for their desire to play a role in the company's success. They are typically more interested in a raise or future promotion than direct personal gain. Do not be afraid to draft the type of acknowledgment contained on the following page for your protection. In most situations, the employee will sign such a document as presented.*

4. **Include a statement in your company's handbook indicating that although the company welcomes employee suggestions and ideas for improvements, all ideas must be made in writing, will not automatically be compensated (even if savings are generated), but that all suggestions will be treated as voluntary information which may be rewarded at the sole discretion of the company.**

COBRA DEVELOPMENTS

The Consolidated Omnibus Budget Reconciliation Act of 1985 (COBRA) affected the operation of employer-provided health care plans. IRS Code 4980B provides that a group health plan must offer continuation of coverage to those who would otherwise lose it. If an employer fails to offer such coverage, the law imposes penalties ranging from $100 to $200 per day for each day an individual is not covered. Thus, all employers are urged to review, understand and follow the technical complexities of this law with personnel supervisors, particularly because COBRA is an administrative compliance nightmare. Part of the problem for employers is that the Department of Labor, the agency responsible for protecting employees whose companies don't offer them their COBRA rights, has never issued guidelines or regulations. The only guidelines available are those proposed by the Internal Revenue Service in 1987, and an employer complying with this never-finalized IRS rule is not protected from a plaintiff's claim in court.

It isn't surprising that many companies run afoul of the law and fail to follow properly rules regarding notification requirements, conversion privileges, excluded individuals and time restrictions, because the law does not provide much guidance or instruction. In fact, good faith compliance may not be sufficient to protect the employer, as a recent California ruling demonstrates. The employer, a mental health residential treatment facility, offered its two health care plan options to a laid-off employee. When the plan chosen by the ex-employee went bankrupt, only the second plan—an HMO—remained. All current employees of the company were in the plan's geographic area and they signed up with the HMO. Since the ex-employee lived outside the area, she was left without any health continuation coverage. She sued her former employer for the health care coverage that was her right under COBRA and prevailed. Although the IRS regulations require only that COBRA coverage be the same as insurance offered "similarly situated beneficiaries"—as the employer argued, the U.S. District Court ruled that the employer had not satisfied its obligations.

Based on cases decided in this area, employers will have to assume burdens not always considered. The law is now being interpreted very broadly and the courts are ruling regularly that COBRA coverage be provided. Because the cases typically pit a former employee or an employee's dependent with substantial medical expenses

RECEIPT OF IDEA

On this day, received from (Employee's name) an idea concerning (specify) which was presented in the form of (specify: a note, letter, design, drawing, etc.)

The Company acknowledges the furnishing of this idea; however, it is specifically agreed to between the parties that no representations regarding compensation due for its use have been made to the Employee. Furthermore, the Employee agrees and understands that the Company is not obligated to pay any form of compensation to the Employee if the idea is eventually used or incorporated and that the Employee has voluntarily conveyed this idea to the Company on his/her own behalf, without fraud, coercion or duress.

It is understood and agreed to by the Employee that any monies that may be paid to him/her by the Company are not enforceable by contract but are gratuitous and that any such payment(s) and amounts are solely determined at the Company's discretion with no right of protest by the Employee.

Finally, the Employee agrees to assign all of his rights to such inventions, ideas etc. to the Company upon the signing of this acknowledgment and to sign all documents necessary to evidence same.

[NAME OF EMPLOYER]

By: ______________________________

[NAME OF EMPLOYEE]

Date ______________________________

against the employer or an insurance company, many courts are willing to interpret and apply COBRA with a view toward extending coverage wherever possible.

The result of a 1992 case demonstrates the difficulty employers face when trying to comply with COBRA. Here, an employee incapacitated by a series of strokes was maintained on her employer's group health insurance policy. After about a year the employee was taken off the company rolls. At that time she was in a coma and the COBRA continuation notice was sent to her husband. Misunderstanding the intent of the offer, and thinking his wife was still covered under the employer's group plan without premium payments, he waived his wife's insurance continuation rights. Later, as legal guardian, the ex-employee's husband tried to regain the option of COBRA coverage, but the insurance company refused. The husband sued and won; the court ruled that the employer should have included the Summary Plan Description with the COBRA notice sent to the husband and that without the Summary he was unable to make an informed decision.

Understanding the key elements of COBRA law will help your company avoid harsh penalties that arise when the rules are not followed. The following points highlight important compliance elements of the law.

Definition Of Group Health Plans

A group health plan is any plan maintained by an employer to provide for medical care to employees, former employees, or families of employees, whether that care is provided through insurance, reimbursement or a health maintenance organization. Typically, corporate wellness programs are excluded from being considered a group health plan, as are employee discount programs where any merchandise offered for discounted sale is not health related.

All group health plans are subject to the continuation provisions of COBRA, with the exception of private employers who normally employ less than 20 workers during the preceding calendar year. However, small employers must count all full-time and part-time employees together with other persons treated as employees under IRS Code definitions (i.e., sole proprietors, partners, agents, officers and directors who are eligible to participate in any of the company's group health plans) under this rule.

Definition Of A Qualified Beneficiary

A qualified beneficiary is any individual covered under a group health plan maintained by the employer. A new qualified beneficiary cannot be added after the day of termination by later birth, marriage or later-adopted children. Also, a qualified beneficiary who fails to elect COBRA continuation coverage stops being "qualified" at the end of the election period.

Definition of A Covered Employee

A covered employee is any individual who was provided benefits under a group health plan by virtue of either current or previous employment. Retirees and former employees covered by a group health plan may also be included in this definition, as well as agents, independent contractors, and directors of the company, provided they actually participated in the plan.

Definition Of A Qualifying Event

Upon the discharge of the employee as a result of a voluntary or involuntary termination, with the exception of gross misconduct, all terminated employees may choose to continue plan benefits currently in effect at their own cost. A person entitled to make a COBRA continuation election (a qualified beneficiary) must be permitted to make the election for at least 60 days commencing not later than the date on which the coverage terminates under the plan, and ending not earlier than 60 days after the date coverage terminates, or the date the qualified beneficiary receives notification of the qualifying event. However, the beneficiary must not be covered under Medicare or any other group health plan.

Other qualifying events occur upon the death, divorce or legal separation of a covered employee or upon a dependent child's arrival at the age at which he or she is no longer eligible to be covered by the plan. Once the covered employee or qualified beneficiary becomes eligible, that person is entitled to receive the same group health plan coverage that was in existence before the qualifying event.

Counsel Comments: *A company's hands may not be tied in the event that a group health plan is modified or eliminated; an employer may be permitted to* *change or eliminate a current plan provided all qualifying beneficiaries and covered employees are allowed to participate similarly under new plans.*

Length of Benefits

For termination of the covered employee, the extended coverage period is 18 months. However, if the terminated individual was considered disabled for Social Security purposes, the COBRA period is extended up to 29 months or the date the qualified beneficiary becomes covered by Medicare, whichever is earlier. Upon the death, divorce or legal separation of the covered employee, the benefit coverage period is 36 months to spouses and dependents.

Responsibility of Employers

The law requires that employers and/or plan administrators separately notify all employees and covered spouses and dependents of their rights to continued coverage. To avoid problems, this should be done by certified mail, return receipt requested to prove delivery and companies should periodically check for address and relocation changes and update employee files.

Employees and dependents whose insurance is protected under COBRA must also be provided with any conversion privileges otherwise available in the plan (if such coverage exists) within a six-month period preceding the end of the continuation period.

COBRA policies need not be complex; they should explain to employees in simple language that they may be entitled to continue their health insurance upon a qualifying event. One large company explains its compliance with the law in this straightforward statement:

> "According to the Consolidated Omnibus Budget Reconciliation Act of 1985 (COBRA), an employee and/or his/her dependents may be eligible to continue medical insurance coverage through the Company even though the employee and/or his/her dependents would otherwise be ineligible (i.e., termination of employment, death of a covered employee, etc.). If the employee and/or his/her dependents make the election to continue the coverage, they are responsible for the entire cost of the premiums.
>
> "Employees will be given information regarding their rights at orientation. Terminated employees will receive further information within 14 days. It is the employee's responsibility, however, to notify Personnel immediately in the case of a divorce, legal separation, or where a dependent child loses eligibility, so that insurance continuation can be offered."

> **Counsel Comments:** *Prudent employers and plan administrators should provide a timely notice of COBRA eligibility upon an employee's termination of employment or the occurrence of any qualifying event to insure the commencement of the continuation period, even if the employer intends to provide coverage at its expense for some portion of the COBRA continuation period. For protection, if you provide company-paid medical benefits to employees terminated for reductions in force and other "neutral" layoffs, obtain a signed waiver or acknowledgment from the employee documenting that the employer-provided health coverage is in satisfaction of the employer's COBRA obligation for that period. Be sure to compute the COBRA entitlement date for continuation of benefits so that the employee may make the election properly until 60 days after the employer-provided coverage expires.*

In one case the court upheld a $1 million judgment against a company which erred in informing an employee that he was eligible for COBRA coverage. The man had asked his employer if he would be able to continue medical coverage for himself and his wife, who was pregnant and expecting twins, even if he resigned to start his own business. Although the company said yes, it later attempted to revoke coverage after complications during childbirth created huge medical bills. The court ruled that the company could not revoke his COBRA coverage because he had been provided with erroneous information, even though he was not entitled to coverage at the onset!

> **Counsel Comments:** *Supervisors and human resources staff must examine all notice and benefits information carefully to understand, clarify and communicate COBRA exclusions and limitations. Al-*

ways be sure that your company provides correct information when denying COBRA coverage to an individual because of the existence of a secondary health plan or other factors.

An employer may not be required to offer insurance continuance under COBRA if gross misconduct can be shown, but proving this is often a problem. Who determines what constitutes gross misconduct? In the following case, a federal appeals court made that decision. As part of her job, an employee helped with the lunch service for the executive staff and their guests in the executive dining room. The employee had been informed by her supervisor, prior to beginning the waitressing, that any information overheard in the course of her work was to be held confidential and any disclosure of information would result in termination.

One day, she overheard two corporate officers talking about a manager who had befriended her. The employee felt she had a duty to that manager to pass on what had been said—and she did so. When this violation of confidentiality was discovered by her employer, the employee was fired for what the company called "gross misconduct." Accordingly, no COBRA notification was sent and when the ex-employee requested information from Human Resources about insurance continuation, her request was refused.

Because she felt her rights had been violated, the ex-employee took her complaint to federal district court. She argued that while what she did may not have been right, it was not gross misconduct. The company disagreed, stating that gross misconduct, as defined in its handbook, included breach of confidentiality.

The court ruled in favor of the employee. According to the definition used by California courts—the state in which the individual was employed—only a deliberate act performed maliciously to harm the employer can be considered gross misconduct. Although the plaintiff may have shown poor judgment, she was still entitled to COBRA notification upon termination, the court ruled.

Counsel Comments: *Gross misconduct is typically defined in each state's unemployment insurance code, which can be used as a guideline. Cases brought under COBRA are currently finding their way to the appeals level, so many COBRA questions still remain unanswered. At this point, employers should proceed with caution in this area.*

Here's a valuable tip: If you fire a worker for alleged misconduct or gross misconduct, always *contest the employee's application for unemployment benefits. Unless such a claim is contested by your company from the moment the application for benefits is filed, you run the risk that a favorable decision made on the employee's behalf will preclude your right to deny COBRA benefits under the gross misconduct exception. As the saying in personnel law goes, "No good deed out of kindness goes unpunished."*

HEALTH BENEFITS OF EMPLOYEES WITH AIDS

Companies must keep abreast of changing statutory and case law developments to insure they are acting properly in administering and maintaining employee health benefit plans. Claims for employee benefits are typically covered under federal Employee Retirement Income Security Act (ERISA) law, discussed in great detail in the next section of this chapter, and violations by employers and/or plan administrators can be quite expensive. However, a number of important recent cases have been decided which benefit companies; such cases may be able to guide you in the proper implementation and functioning of employee health plans.

Several cases deal with individuals inflicted with the AIDS virus. Although the recently enacted federal Americans With Disabilities Act specifically forbids private employers with more than 25 workers from firing, transferring or reassigning a worker who is HIV-positive, one area not yet resolved involves company obligations to provide and maintain health insurance coverage for workers with AIDS and related medical conditions. Some experts predict that, if legal precedent permits them to do so, companies will gradually reduce medical coverage and the lifetime cap for AIDS-related expenses for such individuals due to higher health insurance premiums. One recent federal Court of Appeals decision ruled that it *was* legal for a company to set a lifetime limit on the benefits payable under its group health insurance plan for AIDS. In that case, a company elected to set a small lifetime limit of $5,000 on benefits payable in connection with AIDS in order to avoid increasing its health insurance costs. This decision was made after it learned that one of its employees had tested positive for AIDS, although all other workers continued to receive a $1 million cap. Although the Texas Court found a connection between the benefits reduction and the worker's illness, it ruled that economic motivation was not, in itself, unlawful under the ADA and that the employer complied with a summary plan description that clearly reserved the right to amend or terminate the plan at any time.

In another case, an employee afflicted with the AIDS virus brought an injunctive proceeding challenging the employer's decision to suddenly reduce the lifetime maximum benefit from $1 million to $25,000. The employee's request was denied.

Counsel Comments: *All employers must review current company policies regarding limits and benefits to AIDS workers, since statistics indicate that one in 10 employers recently surveyed has one or more employees with AIDS, and many more currently have employees with the HIV virus. Seek comprehensive legal advice to take advantage of case developments, including a recent Supreme Court decision allowing a company to drastically reduce its health coverage of an employee with AIDS.*

However, recognize it is still difficult to predict with certainty the legality of reducing health coverage or benefits. Under the ADA, it is unlawful to refuse to hire any person afflicted with the HIV virus because you are concerned that it will have a negative impact on your insurance plan. It may be legal to establish, in a pre-existing plan, certain exclusions affecting AIDS sufferers generally, especially if you currently have no workers with AIDS or the HIV virus. All companies must also analyze the effect of your state's civil rights laws, which may be more strict than the federal ADA, before implementing any policy or changing existing coverage or benefits.

ERISA CONCERNS

The Employee Retirement Income Security Act of 1974 (ERISA) set up minimum standards for benefit plans, the vesting of benefits, and for communication to plan participants and their beneficiaries. It covers benefits an employee receives while on the payroll (welfare benefits) and benefits to be received upon retirement. The act covers six basic areas including communications (e.g., what must be disclosed to employees, how it must be disclosed and what reports must be filed with the federal government); eligibility (e.g., an employee's right to participate in a retirement benefit plan); vesting (e.g., rules regarding when and to what extent retirement benefits must be made non-forfeitable); funding (e.g., what employers must pay into a retirement plan to meet its normal costs and to amortize past service liabilities); fiduciary responsibility (e.g., how the investment of funds must be handled and the responsibilities of the plan administrators to oversee the plan and plan benefits as a fiduciary); and plan termination insurance to protect the payment of vested benefits.

Virtually all private employers are covered by ERISA in one form or another. For example, ERISA problems range from any plan, fund or program which provides medical, surgical or hospital care benefits, to retirement income or the deferral of income after retirement or termination (such as severance), to the handling of deferred compensation plans such as stock bonus and money purchase plans. The following rules discuss concerns you must be aware of to protect your company.

Communications To Employees

ERISA provides that all plan participants are entitled to:

- Examine without charge all plan documents, insurance contracts and copies of documents filed by the plan with the U.S. Department of Labor, such as detailed annual reports and plan descriptions;
- Obtain copies of all plan documents and other plan information upon written request to the plan administrator. (Note: The employer or administrator may impose a reasonable charge to cover the cost of the copies.);
- Receive a summary of each plan's annual financial report or summary annual report;
- Obtain a statement at least once a year at no cost telling the employee whether he/she has a right to receive a benefit at normal retirement age under the retirement plans and, if so, what benefit would be

paid at normal retirement age if the employee stops working under the retirement plans now. If there is no current benefit, the statement must tell the employee how many more years must be worked to earn the right to a benefit.

When an employee requests materials from a plan and does not receive them within 30 days, he/she may file a lawsuit in federal court. In such a case, the court may require the plan administrator to provide the materials and pay a penalty up to $100 a day until they are received, unless the materials were not sent because of reasons beyond the administrator's control.

Counsel Comments: *Most employers summarize various responsibilities in written communications to employees, such as statements in company handbooks. This practice is recommended to insure that companies adequately fulfill their responsibility of communicating ERISA rights to employees. Make sure the summary accurately depicts essential elements of the plan, because statements in a plan summary are usually binding. If such statements conflict with the plan itself, there is ample case law suggesting that the summary shall govern. In one case, a court ruled that "It is of no effect to publish and distribute a plan summary booklet designed to simplify and explain a voluminous and complex document and then proclaim that any inconsistencies will be governed only by the actual plan."*

Here's what federal ERISA law says about plan summaries: "A summary description must be written in a manner calculated to be understood by the average plan participant...sufficiently accurate and comprehensive to reasonably apprise such participants and beneficiaries of their rights and obligations under the plan."

Oral Pension Plan Modifications

A recent case illustrates several related problems of oral modifications of pension plans.

When an employee of a company agreed to work for a subsidiary, he was assured orally by officers of the parent company that, when he retired, his pension rights would be unaffected. Several years later, when the parent increased its pension formula, the subsidiary did not and the employee was not given the increase. Immediately after the parent company sold its interests to the subsidiary, the employee applied for his pension. He then brought suit against the parent company for not living up to its promise of maintaining the same pension for him as it did for its employees. The company argued that ERISA barred his claim for breach of contract and negligent misrepresentation because oral modifications cannot change the terms of a pension plan.

The Court ruled that no liability existed to the company for purported oral modifications of the terms of an employee benefit plan since all employee benefit plans must be established and maintained pursuant to a written instrument. The Court also stated that a central policy goal of ERISA is to protect the interests of employees and their beneficiaries in employee benefit plans. This goal would be undermined if courts permitted oral modifications of ERISA plans because employees would be unable to rely on these plans if their expected retirement benefits could be radically affected by funds dispersed to other employees pursuant to oral agreements. Exacerbating the problem is the fact that oral agreements are often made years before any attempt is taken to enforce them.

Responsibilities Of Plan Administrators

Plan administrators are considered fiduciaries with discretionary responsibility to act fairly. No one, including the employer, union or administrator, may fire or recommend the firing of a plan participant or beneficiary for seeking to obtain a benefit or exercise his/her rights under ERISA. If a claim for a benefit is denied in whole or in part, the employee must receive a written explanation of the reason for the denial and the individual must also have the right for the plan administrator to review and reconsider the claim. If an individual is discriminated against or has a claim for benefits which is denied or ignored, in whole or in part, a lawsuit may be filed in either state or federal court. If plan fiduciaries misuse a plan's money, or discriminate against an individual for asserting rights, the individual may seek assistance from the U.S. Department of Labor or file a lawsuit in federal court. The court may impose court costs and legal fees on the employer.

Plan administrators have discretion to construe the terms and effect of a plan, determine eligibility, authorize all disbursements, compute the amount of benefits, and to perform any such other duties as required by the plan. Thus, for example, if there is no contractual or statutory entitlement for workers to receive surplus funds, and such a surplus was not created by employee contributions, then the decision of the administrators not to distribute surplus funds to employees will be upheld.

Problems In Creating, Administering And Terminating Severance Plans

Severance plans, providing for compensation to employees in the event of separation or termination from employment, are covered under ERISA as an employee welfare benefit plan. Many lawsuits alleging violation of ERISA rights have recently been brought in situations where a division of a company with a large severance policy was sold and the division's employees terminated but immediately employed by the acquiring company with far less severance benefits. The newly hired employees were only retained for a short period and then fired.

Do the affected employees have rights under ERISA and may they collect the larger severance benefits from the previous employer? Typically, and as long as the employees were re-employed by the successor and not immediately subject to unemployment, employers have prevailed in such lawsuits.

In a severance context, courts often inquire whether the benefits were intended as a form of unemployment compensation (in which case immediate re-employment makes them unnecessary), or as a reward for past service (in which case immediate re-employment may not preclude receipt of benefits). The major factors courts look at when determining whether employers have ERISA obligations to pay severance include:

1. The employer's purpose in granting the benefit, determined in part from the employer's plan terms and past practice;

2. Consistent application of the plan (i.e., has the employer consistently granted or denied severance benefits to employees who suffered no period of unemployment?);

3. Industry practice;

4. Employer compliance with procedural requirements; and

5. Whether the decision-maker benefited from the denial of benefits. If so, the decision is analyzed closely.

Counsel Comments: *When workers are laid off, issues of severance and other post-termination benefits must always be scrutinized to avoid potential ERISA violations. As a business grows, informal pay policies are frequently relied upon by terminated workers as an economic expectation and contract right. When the business is sold, a buyer may view such payments as discretionary and gratuitous. This thinking differs from the view of terminated workers who consider such benefits guaranteed.*

Smart companies draft formal severance rules forbidding the payment of excessive severance and limiting the amount of severance to be paid if a company is sold. Currently, employers retain wide discretion in administering, modifying, and terminating severance plans. Reserving the right in writing to modify or terminate a severance policy at any time with or without notice may protect your company in this area, especially if language is conspicuously displayed in a company handbook and periodically disseminated to workers in a memo.

Standards Of Review In Granting And Disallowing Claims

Employee benefits law is quite complex. New cases are continually being decided which impact your company's plans and practices and evaluating the effect of these developments on your health and benefit plans is critical. When an individual claim is asserted, consider the following items before making a decision:

- Identify the specific benefits claimed.
- Identify the source of the right claimed (e.g., a written company plan, an informal promise or an ERISA right?).
- Is there a legal obligation to fulfill the claim?
- Did the company breach that obligation by refusing to fulfill the promise?
- If so, what are the potential consequences to the company?

- If not, how much will it potentially cost to defend a lawsuit and what other damages may possibly ensue?
- Are there any justifying legal arguments to defend the company's claim?
- Will settling the claim create a damaging precedent?
- Are there overriding moral concerns which support a settlement?
- Is there a statute of limitations defense?
- Will the possibility of failing to settle the case informally create the likelihood that other similarly situated employees act in concert once they learn about the lawsuit?

Obligations Owed To Departing Employees

New questions are constantly arising with respect to retiree health care benefits and successor benefits when a person leaves a company to work in a new job. An employer's obligation to provide post-retirement health benefits typically turns on whether those benefits are actually vested at the time of retirement. When workers change jobs, it is often unclear whether the old or new employer is obligated to provide insurance to cover a pre-existing ailment. Which employer's plan provides primary insurance and which provides secondary insurance after the first pays off? What about workers who are not sure they have a pre-existing condition but still want to retain coverage—if the new plan doesn't address a condition the old plan covered, can the worker continue on the old plan? These and other ERISA-related questions can only be answered after a thorough review by competent labor counsel and analysis of the particular facts of the matter.

Pension Benefit Concerns

To safeguard pension benefits, ERISA mandates that assets in a beneficiary's pension be virtually "untouchable." This is accomplished by requiring that plan administrators file numerous reports with the U.S. Department of Labor, the Internal Revenue Service and the Pension Benefit Guaranty Corporation, including plan descriptions (Form EBS-1), summary plan descriptions, material changes in the plan description or modifications of the terms of the plan, an annual report (Form 5500), an annual registration statement listing employees separated from service during the plan year, notification of change in status for plans subject to vesting, annual information reports for certain pension and deferred compensation plans, actuarial statements of valuation for other pensions and deferred compensation plans and numerous other reports for defined benefit plans covered by the termination insurance provisions with the Pension Benefit Guaranty Corporation.

Fiduciaries in charge of administering all plans must also diversify investments to minimize risks of large losses, cannot make secret profits, must act in good faith and exercise prudence and diligence, cannot deal with plan assets for their own account, and generally must act with the highest degree of skill, loyalty and care in the performance of their duties.

Complex problems frequently arise involving the effects of bankruptcy, domestic relations, criminal and creditor rights and the forfeiture of pension assets. In one case, for example, the court ruled that a retiree's landlord-creditor could garnish his pension money since the pension benefits had been paid to the employee. The court noted the distinction that ERISA's anti-garnishment protection ends when pension benefits are actually paid to an employee and that there was nothing to indicate that Congress intended to provide pension beneficiaries with a shield from legitimate claims made by creditors who provide shelter or food. (Note: The tribunal pointed out, however, that Social Security benefits are exempt from legal process under a section of the Social Security Act.)

> **Counsel Comments:** *Absent specific statutory directive, ERISA and its policies usually preserve pension funds from all types of external interference. However, the legality of forfeiture or alienation of pension benefits can only be answered by experienced labor or benefits counsel on a case by case basis.*

Waiver Of Pension Benefits

One older applicant was informed by management that if he wanted a job he would have to forego participation in the company's pension plan. This did not disturb the worker since he was already receiving a pension from his previous employer. Ten years later the employee retired and presented a claim for pension plan benefits to the plan administrator. When the claim was rejected, he instituted a lawsuit under ERISA, charging that he had been unfairly denied pension benefits. The court ruled that he was out of luck and noted that he had signed a pension waiver not under duress or coercion but of his own free will. He had executed the waiver a week after the hiring, so he had adequate time to contemplate the import of his decision and to consult an attorney.

The court ruled that excluding him from the company pension plan did not violate ERISA because "The plan in question is a defined benefit plan and therefore is expressly exempted from ERISA's bar against excluding employees who have reached a specified age. Nothing in ERISA indicates that Congress meant to prohibit employers from individually negotiating waiver agreements with older employees at the time of hiring." The federal tribunal also pointed out that ERISA contains no language either expressly prohibiting or limiting the use of waivers with respect to employee benefits. It does not even mandate that employers provide any particular benefits, nor does it require that every employee be covered in an existing plan.

Counsel Comments: *The effects of this and similar cases are quite interesting. If you wish to exclude a particular employee from receiving certain pension benefits, you may be able to do so. However, always consult counsel before implementing such a plan. Prepare a written comprehensive waiver confirming the employee's voluntary agreement to waive his/her claim to such benefits, and be sure the employee signs such a document in front of witnesses for additional protection.*

TUITION ASSISTANCE

Tuition assistance is an effective way of bolstering employee performance and morale while benefiting the company with better skilled workers. When considering a tuition reimbursement program for your company, be aware of:

- Company objectives in offering the program;
- Employee eligibility, such as who is qualified for reimbursement;
- Limits to the kinds of reimbursable items;
- Using company time to attend courses;
- Proper reporting, including procedures for turning in receipts and the kinds of receipts required for reimbursement;
- Situations when reimbursement is forfeited (e.g., not receiving a "C" grade or better, being fired for cause or receiving an unsatisfactory job performance evaluation before the course is completed).

Counsel Comments: *Include a sample education assistance program in a company handbook where applicable. Always state that the human resources department retains ultimate discretion to approve requests and specific items to be reimbursed and that the company may, without warning or notice, change the rules of reimbursement or deny reimbursement.*

Be aware that employers sometimes are legally obligated to pay employees for attending company classes. One employer conducted skill improvement classes for its staff. Classes were held once a week on company premises after working hours, from 5:30-7:30 p.m., and most employees were expected to attend. An employee left the company to take a job elsewhere. Soon afterward, he wrote a letter demanding payment for all the hours he had spent at company classes. He had methodically recorded his hours of attendance over a two-year period and sought time-and-a-half for overtime. When the company refused, he sued.

He argued in court that the "skill" classes were like any other form of work since they involved time and effort and were run for the benefit of the company. He stated that time-and-a-half was mandated since the sessions came after a full working day. The company responded that the classes were for the employees' benefit, to improve their skills and thereby their earning capacity. The fact that the classes were conducted after work hours had no effect on whether they should be considered compensated time. The court sided with the worker and ordered the company to pay the employee at time-and-a-half rates. A U.S. District Court remarked that the classes were conducted at the company's direction and that attending classes was part of an employee's duties. As a result, class time was compensable and, since the employee had already put in an eight-hour day at work, he was entitled to time-and-a-half under the wage law.

Counsel Comments: *Many companies encourage employees to take courses of study to improve their efficiency without paying extra wages. The employees typically attend schools which are neither controlled by nor on the premises of the* *employer. But remember one precaution above all: never make the employee's participation mandatory and never make attendance a condition of keeping the job or gaining a promotion.*

POTPOURRI OF CONCERNS

Several years ago, the author drafted a prototype employee manual for companies in the printing industry which covered most of the areas affecting employer-related benefits. The handbook focused on such issues as hours of work, company benefits, promotion criteria, and so forth and suggested rules for on-the-job behavior (i.e., reporting absences, authorized use of telephones, handling complaints, etc.). With well-drafted manuals, employers can create custom personnel policies and procedures governing standards of employee conduct, grounds for employee discipline and termination, internal complaint resolution procedures and other policies which are necessary and worth enforcing. This section, which is drawn from that manual, will briefly discuss important strategies and concerns in a variety of areas.

Disclaimers

Employment applications, personnel manuals, and written work rules are likely to be used by the employee in a termination-related lawsuit. Be sure they cannot be interpreted as providing employees with more rights than you intend to give. Look through existing manuals to see what they actually say. Remove anything that may be construed as a promise and substitute words such as, "In principle, we try to..." Place disclaimers in handbooks whenever possible.

Counsel Comments: *Although language may play a large part in defending against an unfair discharge case, some courts are not honoring disclaimers as a matter of public policy. Always consult with a lawyer experienced in labor matters before including disclaimers in your own company manual.*

Employee Status

Some companies establish a probationary period ranging from 30 to 120 days to evaluate an employee's performance. If you do so, be careful not to raise an employee's expectations of job security after the probationary period has expired. State that successful completion of a probationary period only guarantees a job *at-will,* which may still be terminated with or without cause or notice. And, when defining such an interval, instead of calling it a "probationary period," consider use of the term "introductory period," since that does not carry the same implication of permanency after completion.

For part-time workers, employers may not be required to provide any benefits other than those benefits covered under state and federal law (i.e., Social Security, Unemployment Insurance, and Workers' Compensation Insurance) during the probationary period. Speak to a representative at your state's Department of Labor regional office to get the facts.

Working Hours

Some states require coffee breaks, others do not. In addition, certain states require that employees receive a meal period a few hours after beginning work; other states require breakfast periods as well. Thus, check with the Department of Labor in your state for further details.

Must an employee be paid for on-call meal periods? In the collective bargaining agreement between one hospital and the union, the contract stated that: "If the employee is not relieved of his/her duties and is unable to leave the work area, the meal period...shall be paid at the rate of one and a half times the regular pay of the individual, including shift differential." A group of respiratory therapists who carried beepers and were told not to leave the premises to take a meal break because of constant emergencies were particularly affected by this clause. The workers filed a grievance when they were refused on-call payments taken during lunch hours. The hospital stated that no payments should be made because the beeper-carriers usually had their meals without interruption in the cafeteria. The workers argued that they were entitled to compensation while wearing the beepers since they were not released from duty and could not leave the work area.

An arbitrator ruled that since the workers were in a state of constant readiness and could not leave the hospital, they were still on duty, even when taking meals, and such status was primarily for the benefit of the hospital.

Counsel Comments: *Requests to eat in company facilities as a part of the job may constitute compensable work time. However, although a company may be liable to pay its workers when they are com-*

pelled to lunch at their workplace, there is little doubt that your company has the right to determine the timing of all breaks and how many workers must be present at a particular location at all times, if such a rule is established for a legitimate business reason.

Must you have the same pay policies for hourly and management personnel? As a general practice, most companies stick to "hours worked" in computing their hourly worker paychecks. Some employees are not paid for hours not worked even when absences from work are caused by factors such as hurricanes, blizzards, floods, riots and the like. On the other hand, management personnel are expected to accomplish their assigned tasks regardless of how many hours it requires and it is not typical to reduce their salaries for time not spent at work.

Time Card Procedures

Federal law requires that all companies keep an accurate record of an employee's work. Use of automatic time cards is a good way to comply in this area.

Counsel Comments: *Many companies consider it a serious work rule infraction, leading to dismissal, for a worker to punch in the time of another or falsify time card records. Make it clear in your company handbook that such action will not be tolerated.*

Pay Periods And Overtime

Some companies are supplied payroll checks by an outside service. If this is the case, you may wish to state that errors made by the company will be adjusted and paid the following pay period or that errors will be adjusted immediately. You may also wish to devise a company policy toward paying employees prior to the regular pay period—for example, in an emergency.

Can you put a stop to long-standing wage overpayments? In one case an arbitrator found that an erroneous pay differential of 16 cents per hour was premised upon meritorious work performance. When no "merit" was found to apply to a particular worker, the arbitrator ruled that the company's failure to continue paying the higher rate did not constitute a breach of the collective bargaining agreement and there was no obligation to continue the overpayments just because it was a long-standing mistake.

But what about past overpayments? In the case above, the employer agreed to waive its rights to recoup the money because recoupment "would be inequitable due to the likely hardship thereby created." A number of states have laws that prohibit deduction from an employee's salary, directly or indirectly, for losses resulting through no fault of the employee.

Counsel Comments: *Employers can take action for cash shortages caused by dishonesty or culpable negligence of an employee by firing any worker who does not notify the employer and offer to pay back any overpayments. This also applies to innocent mistakes if an employee's silence is intentional. However, it should be noted that federal wage-hour laws prohibit deductions from an employee's salary that would cause it to drop below the minimum wage.*

Draws And Advances

Sales reps are often advanced money designated as "draw" to be applied against and reimbursed by future commissions. These are designated in rep agreements as "draw against commission" or "advances against commission." When an oral agreement or written contract states that advances will be deducted from commissions to be earned in the future, a sales rep is *not* generally personally liable to return the unearned draw: in most states courts generally consider advances to be salary unless language in an agreement or the conduct of the parties expressly indicates that such advances were merely intended to be a loan. In most cases, the law considers the company to be in a superior bargaining position and therefore responsible for clearly indicating its right of repayment. Case law and experience reveal that most company lawsuits to recover excess advances are unsuccessful and that ambiguous language in a contract is almost always applied against the company which chose the language and drafted the document. Even leaving the company before the contract term has expired will not necessarily make the sales rep liable to return the excess. However, if he/she breached the agreement, courts may not permit the rep to profit from wrongful acts.

Counsel Comments: *To increase the chances of enforcing a claim and recover-*

ing excess draw, a company should take several steps. First, always indicate on each draw check the words "loan" in the bottom left corner of the check. When the rep endorses and cashes the check, this will document by implication the rep's agreement to accept the money as a loan. Second, prepare a promissory note or loan agreement, letter of indebtedness or financing statement and have the rep sign it each time he receives a draw advance. Finally, include the phrases "loan," "debt," or "charge" in all written contracts to make the sales rep liable. When reps sign written agreements which clearly specify that advances are considered a personal indebtedness to be paid from personal funds in the event the draw exceeds commission earnings, the chances of enforcing such agreements increase.

Overtime

Most states in addition to federal law require that overtime pay must be paid when a qualified employee works in excess of 40 hours per week. Special employees involved in government contracting or subcontracting work may also be required to be paid overtime if they work more than eight hours on any given day.

Counsel Comments: *Companies whose employees do extensive traveling on company business should implement specific programs for the payment of expenses and overtime. Travel status may be defined as commencing from the time of leaving the work station until reaching the geographical location of the work assignment and then returning. Exceptions to overtime, such as where an employee chooses to drive to a location rather than fly, should be discussed. Maximum payments (i.e., up to four hours of compensatory time per day) for layovers on weekends should also be regulated, as well as non-reimbursable situations.*

Attendance

Employee manuals should explain that continuous absences or tardiness may result in disciplinary action, including dismissal. Most companies specify the telephone number absent employees must call and by what time (e.g., no less than 30 minutes before starting time) to avoid problems.

Counsel Comments: *Some companies list a detailed schedule of company responses to repeated absences: for example, each person is allowed one unauthorized absence per year without a reprimand; the second absence results in a reprimand, the third results in a day's suspension without pay, culminating in termination of employment after the fourth absence. This kind of stated policy has both positive and negative features. Uniformly following such a stated policy may reduce charges of disparate treatment of workers (i.e., discrimination). For example, many discrimination charges arise when employees belonging to a minority group claim that their excessive absences result in firing while those of another group do not. On the other hand, a specific schedule can tie a company's hands by not allowing it to terminate a poor worker until the expiration of the stated policy. Thus a brief statement regarding a particular policy is preferred (i.e., "Failure to report an absence, or a series of unreported absences, may result in disciplinary action, up to and including dismissal.") And, if you apply your termination decisions fairly and uniformly by firing the most serious offenders first and documenting your decisions in writing, charges of discrimination can be reduced and/or defended far more effectively.*

Holidays

Some companies have a policy of allowing holiday pay for employees who have worked a minimum number of days (e.g., 30) in order to be eligible. Also, you may wish to state that if a holiday falls within a vacation period, the employee can extend his/her vacation period an additional day, or use that day of vacation at a later date.

Vacation Days

Each company has its own rules governing vacation days. Whatever plan you wish to implement, consider answering the following questions as a starting point:

- Must vacation days be used in the year they are granted, or can they be carried over to the next year? Can a pro-rated share, e.g., one-half of the days, be carried over?

- How long must an employee work in order to be qualified?
- Must vacation days be taken all at once, or can they be staggered? If so, in what amount?
- How much notice must an employee give before taking vacation time?
- Are there times (e.g., during peak seasonal demand) when requests may not be granted?
- If the employee leaves or is terminated, will he/she be paid for all unused vacation time? What if the employee is fired for cause?

Counsel Comments: *The last point must be considered carefully since some states require companies to pay accrued vacation pay in* all *circumstances, even resignations or terminations for cause, so check with counsel or your state's Department of Labor when in doubt. Whatever your vacation pay policy, be sure to draft it carefully, include it in your company's handbook and apply it consistently to avoid charges of discrimination and breach of contract.*

Personal Days

Some companies create a policy whereby no personal days may be carried over to the next year in the event they are unused or paid for if an employee resigns. Or, you may say no employee will be entitled to receive the monetary equivalent of a personal day if it is unused.

Voting

Most states require that employers allow workers up to two hours off from work for voting purposes. If you operate in such a state you cannot deny an employee the right to vote, even on paid company time.

Bereavement Pay

Some companies do not permit bereavement pay to extend beyond the day of the funeral service. But on this always touchy subject, most companies will not require any kind of proof before making funeral leave payments when a death in an employee's family occurs. Always specify the amount of leave that may be taken and the particular circumstances of entitlement to benefits. For example, a few companies state in handbooks that to be eligible for funeral leave pay, the employee must attend the funeral or funeral service and produce evidence of said death, in the form of a public notice or its equivalent, for a non-family death. They also specify that up to five days with pay will be granted for the death of an immediate family member but only up to one day (or specify) for the death of a mother-in-law, grandparent, etc.

Should a miscarriage be regarded as a bereavement? One arbitrator ruled that it was not. In arbitrations, grievances involving funeral or bereavement leave policies usually hover over interpretations of the appropriate clauses in the company's collective bargaining pact. Arbitrators usually lean toward strict construction of these clauses.

Counsel Comments: *Many companies request that the Personnel Department be notified as immediately as possible and state that since funeral leave pay is intended only to compensate an employee for wages lost due to absence to attend a funeral, if the funeral occurs during an employee's vacation or company-paid holiday, no additional compensation will be made.*

Also, be sure your company publishes accurate information regarding its death benefit policies. For example, is an estranged wife entitled to her husband's death benefits? In one case, a court ruled that she was because the couple had never legally separated or divorced, and the employee continued to maintain the family home during the brief period of voluntary separation before his death.

Jury Duty

Federal and most state laws prohibit companies from disciplining, terminating, or prohibiting employees from attending short-term jury duty. In other states, you may fire a worker who is required to attend a lengthy jury trial (e.g., more than a month) out of business necessity, but always check with counsel first.

Counsel Comments: *Some companies pay straight-time earnings less jury and witness fees received where permitted by law; you may be able to deduct such payments from regular pay where applicable,* *so check this point with your local Department of Labor for additional details.*

While jury duty is a protectable civic obligation, there is a difference when an employee is called as a witness rather than serving as a juror. Your company should also make the distinction of lost time arising when the employee is involved as the plaintiff or defendant in a civil legal action. Here, you may not wish to compensate the individual for time lost from work and are probably within your rights not to do so. Smart companies also specify rules governing efforts that should be made to try to get back to work when workers are excused from jury duty or witness duty during any half-day or more. Overtime considerations must also be explored (e.g., that time spent on jury duty or as a witness be counted as hours worked) for the purpose of computing overtime and that employees are permitted to work any overtime hours that normally would be scheduled for work if they were not on jury or witness duty.

Military Leave

Some companies pay the difference between a full-time employee's military pay and his/her salary up to a specific number of days. For example, you might state that the difference will be paid for 30 days if the employee has at least six months' service.

Personal Leaves

Unlimited personal absences or excessive absenteeism should not be allowed. A statement in the company handbook should say that employees who continue to be absent after a warning or counseling are subject to involuntary separation. On the other hand, always investigate with care the reasons for a person's absences. For example, some arbitrators and judges have ruled that personal-leave-related absences due to marital troubles, even if excessive, do not justify dismissals in limited situations. (Note: A detailed discussion of personal leaves is contained in Chapter 3.)

Disability Leaves

EEOC guidelines suggest that it is illegal to prohibit qualification for disability leave to workers who have not worked an extended period of time (e.g., 12 months) with one company. Thus, your employee manual should probably contain no more than a one- to three-month initial waiting period, which will probably be deemed legal as a matter of reasonable company policy.

Consider requiring all employees with disabilities to submit to examinations by company-designated physicians if the disability is particularly lengthy, or questionable. However, singling out one disability (e.g., pregnancy) for such treatment violates the law. If you insist on ordering a company exam, make the policy standard for *all* disabled workers and be sure the company physician is trained to avoid asking discriminatory questions before or during the exam.

Counsel Comments: *Acording to the recently enacted federal Family and Medical Leave Act, employees returning from disability are sometimes guaranteed job reinstatement. Many states, however, have more "worker friendly" laws, requiring that employees with a non-work disability be permitted to return to work as soon as they are physically able to resume their duties. Since state laws vary so, you should discuss the matter with legal counsel before implementing a policy in this area.*

A detailed discussion of maternity leave policies is included in the next chapter in the material about sex discrimination. Consult that section for further information.

Wage And Salary Laws

Under the federal Equal Pay Act, employers must be careful to avoid pay differentials based on sex for employees performing equal work on equal jobs in the same establishment. Thus, it is critical to review your payroll practices regularly to insure that wage and salary levels for all positions have been set fairly.

Reimbursement For Losses

This area includes the problem of whether a company must make good on a loss if an employee's belongings are stolen. In one case, several workers opened their lockers at work after returning from vacation and discovered that their tools and valuable personal items were missing. An arbitration was commenced after the company refused to reimburse the workers for their losses. At the hearing, management defended its position by stating that the company provided its workers with sturdy lockers and locks but couldn't put a security force on duty to watch the locker area because the cost would be prohibitive. Management also stated that the company could not reasonably be expected to guarantee the safety of every employee's personal belongings.

The union argued that, despite several previous incidents and complaints filed, the company had failed to do anything about the situation. Furthermore, the company could have made even a small effort to have the locker area patrolled. Instead, company neglect made the thieves bolder.

The arbitrator ruled that the company would have to reimburse the workers. "The contract between the company and the union states that the company will make reasonable provisions for the safety and health of the employees," noted the arbitrator. "Therefore, employees have the right to expect the company to respond in an appropriate manner to their complaints about the increased frequency of thefts. Having failed to respond to the complaints, the company violated the contract provisions on plant safety."

Counsel Comments: *If a firm permits its workers to leave tools and other personal belongings overnight on the premises solely as an accommodation, there probably is no legal obligation to reimburse the workers for stolen belongings, particularly if a company memo is prepared and distributed to all employees specifically disclaiming any obligation, in clear and conspicuous language. It is always a good idea to draft such a memo and disseminate it to the appropriate work force when applicable.*

However, if property used on the job is left at the plant for the mutual benefit of the employees and the company (often because the property is too big to take back and forth) then management must take reasonable steps to insure the safety of the property, particularly if incidents have occurred before and if the affected workers belong to a union and are protected by a collective bargaining agreement similar to the one in the above case.

Personal Liability For Debts And Wages

Can an executive inadvertently make himself personally liable for a company debt? Probably not, unless the executive was acting on his own, without corporate authority (such as personally promising to pay an employee's moving expenses without management's approval and which the company cannot afford to pay).

However, officers who are also shareholders in small, closely held corporations should also know that in some states, including Wisconsin and New York, they may be *personally* liable for unpaid corporate debts owed to employees and others. This even applies to shareholders who are not active in corporate management. For example, Section 630 of the New York Business Corporation Law makes the 10 largest shareholders of a closely held New York corporation personally liable for all debts, wages, salaries and many fringe benefits owed to any of the corporation's laborers, servants or employees. Similar laws may have been enacted in other states as the trend continues for management to be responsible for paying wages and other benefits owed, and not allowing a shareholder or *officer* to hide behind the corporate veil and avoid personal liability for taxes or related debts in the event the company has limited or no assets.

Transfer And Moving Expenses

Some companies have detailed policies regarding resettlement reimbursements. If you are interested in exploring or granting such a policy:

- Make sure all resettlement expenses are reasonable and the reimbursement covers expenses directly incurred by reason of the employee's change of residence at the request of the company.
- Be sure that all expenses are itemized by the employee and supported by appropriate invoices.
- Develop a resettlement policy for new employees covering reasonable moving, storage, enroute living and travel expenses of the new employee and immediate family, necessary to relocate at the initial point of assignment, with a *cap* on all expenses. Any other expenses must be documented in writing prior to extending an offer, approved by the company officer directly involved and submitted for consideration by the company's review board or senior management.

Counsel Comments: *Deviations from established policy should be kept to an absolute minimum. However, there are occasions where an employee may suffer an* *unusual financial hardship in connection with a transfer, especially if the employee has been transferred frequently. Should hardship cases arise which justify special consideration, discuss this with senior management before implementation.*

Pay special attention to situations where a relocated worker is terminated for cause shortly after moving. Is your company responsible to pay his/her relocation expenses? What about situations where a promise is made to pay relocation expenses to induce an employee from another company to jump to your firm but you then change your mind about continuing his/her employment shortly after the relocation occurs? Discuss these problems with counsel before making any final decision regarding the payment of relocation expenses to avoid legal claims of detrimental reliance and estoppel which are sometimes asserted by disgruntled ex-employees.

Bonuses

Many companies fail to understand the law regarding bonuses. Disputes often arise when an employee works a full year counting on a bonus, then doesn't receive it, or receives far less than was expected. But that is not the worst problem. Employers sometimes fire individuals after the bonus has technically been earned (at the end of the year) but before it is distributed (on February 15 of the following year). Lawsuits then ensue over whether the bonus should be paid or whether the person must be working at the time the bonus is paid as a condition of receiving it.

Other problems regarding bonuses can also arise. In one case, an employee accepted a promotion to a district manager's job and the employer promised him that his compensation would include a monthly base salary and certain benefits plus a 10 percent "bonus" of his district's "bonus income." "Bonus income" was defined as the district's net operating profit with certain adjustments. The bonus for a given calendar year was to be calculated after the calendar year and paid in February of the following year.

Nine years later the bonus formula was changed downwards—allowing the individual and other managers a diminished income from this source—but the employee did not challenge this change. Six years thereafter, in April, 1985, having learned that its district managers were being paid far more than comparable employees of its competitors, the company again drastically reduced its bonus schedule. The change was made effective in January, 1986. However, in that month, the employee and other district managers were informed that the 1985 bonus would be calculated not by the 1985 formula, but by the formula for 1986. In other words, the lower bonus was to be made *retroactive.* The employee received his 1985 bonus check, which reflected a reduction of $6,403.12, in February, 1986. He deposited the check and shortly afterward tendered his resignation, effective June 30th.

Shortly after quitting the company, the individual sued for full payment of the 1985 bonus. Among other claims, he charged that the bonus reduction was a violation of the Iowa Wage Payment Collection Laws. At the trial he related that the state's wage law describes wages as compensation owed for "labor or services by an employee, whether determined on a time, task, piece, commission or other basis of calculation" and that the retroactive reduction of the 1985 bonus was a violation of law since he had already worked a full year to earn it. The company responded that the state's wage law specifies that wages be paid in weekly, bi-weekly, semi-monthly or monthly installments and that the bonus did not meet the definition of wages because it was paid annually. Additionally, the company stated that all bonuses were gifts, anyway, and therefore not a legally enforceable obligation.

The court ruled in favor of the employee. The Iowa Supreme Court stated that the annual bonus was wages since it was clearly part of the compensation owed for the employee's labor and services, and its method of determination fell within the definition as an "other basis of calculation." The court also found that the bonus was not a gift because the company was contractually bound to pay it. Finally, the court decided that "...just because a given bonus is wages does not mean that it must be paid at least monthly; only wages due need to be paid at least monthly." (Note: The Iowa high court cited several other state courts which have similarly defined bonuses as wages, among them tribunals in Colorado, Idaho, and Delaware.)

A bonus is an additional sum of money paid to an employee in excess of his regular wage. There are generally two kinds—bonuses enforceable by contract and gratuitous bonuses—and they differ in several respects. In order to receive a bonus enforceable by contract, the following elements must be present:

1. A specific promise is made by the employer to pay a bonus;

2. The parties use an agreed-upon method to calculate the bonus;

3. The employee performs additional work, labor or services, or promises to refrain from doing something he is not obligated to do (e.g., to continue working and not resign for an additional year).

When all of these factors are present, an employee has a good chance of recovering a specified bonus from an employer if he is not paid. However, the law treats gratuitous bonuses differently. If an employer controls the timing, amount, and whether to pay a bonus at all, or states that the money is paid in appreciation for continuous, efficient, or satisfactory service, the employee probably does not have a valid claim in the event the bonus is not paid.

Counsel Comments: *Take the following steps to protect your company in this area, if applicable:*

Always treat bonuses as discretionary. Mention in a contract, periodic memos and employee handbooks that the company has the right to pay / not pay bonuses at its sole discretion, including the amount, if any, to be paid. By allowing the company arbitrarily to control and determine the timing, amount, and decision as to whether to pay a bonus at all, you are increasing the chances that such an arrangement will legally be considered a gratuitous bonus, not enforceable by contract.

Always condition the payment of bonuses, if any, on the employee's presence on the payroll on the date the bonus is paid.

State that pro rata bonuses will not be paid in the event an employee resigns or is fired for any reason prior to the bonus being issued.

Put all arrangements regarding bonuses in writing so there are no misunderstandings.

To avoid charges of discrimination, follow your bonus policy consistently and do not deviate from your policy for select individuals.

Avoid linking the bonus to some verifiable formula if possible. Such an arrangement (for example, bonuses linked to gross profits or sales volume) can create headaches and allow the employee the opportunity to commence a lawsuit seeking a formal accounting to verify the bonus from the company's books and records. Thus, resist basing bonuses on verifiable components because of your company's added vulnerability to a lawsuit in this area.

Finally, bonus payments are regulated by the federal Fair Labor Standards Act which, in some instances, may cause additional liability in the form of overtime pay to be computed when employees work longer hours to receive the bonus.

Wages And Raises

Questions or anxieties by workers over salary may be lessened if they are shown how their situation fits into a larger structure. The personnel director or other appropriate individual may evaluate the existing pay structure and recommend any necessary changes. Factors to consider in changing the pay structure include changes in the cost of living, competitive pay rates in other institutions and changes in job duties and responsibilities.

Counsel Comments: *Sometimes overlooked are discrepancies in pay rates based on gender. The Equal Pay Act of 1963 generally prohibits an employer from maintaining wage differentials based upon sex. The act makes it unlawful for an employer to pay different wages based upon sex to employees performing equal work within any establishment. Equal work encompasses work on jobs the performance of which requires equal skill, effort and responsibility, and which is performed under similar working conditions. For example, one major university was ordered to pay 117 women an award of $1.3 million after a federal court judge ruled that the university paid less money to women on the faculty than to men in com-*

parable posts. Note: Exceptions are permitted where the payment is made pursuant to a seniority system, a merit system which measures earnings by quantity or quality of production, or where the differential is based on any legitimate factor other than sex.

Furthermore, it is illegal for any company to discriminate against an employee in retaliation *for filing a complaint or giving testimony in an Equal Pay Act proceeding, or for instituting any proceeding under or related to the act.*

To avoid problems it is essential that you maintain accurate employee records concerning wages, hours, and other conditions of employment, and to make various reports as required. Since the EEOC has the legal authority to enter, inspect and investigate your company's premises and records and interview employees to determine if violations of the law have occurred, be sure the personnel administrator is familiar with the technical aspects of the Equal Pay Act.

Callback And Report-In Pay

Callback pay is defined as work paid when employees are requested to return to work because of need or emergency after they have completed their day's shift. Always pay employees for such work at normal base rates or applicable overtime, depending on the facts of each case. Note: there is no federal obligation requiring a company to pay for a guaranteed minimum number of hours when workers return, but this may be an obligation under an appropriate collective bargaining agreement.

Counsel Comments: *Avoid guaranteeing a minimum number of hours of work or pay for callback and report-ins, particularly in cases of emergencies beyond the control of the company. Put this in writing as stated company policy.*

Employees Acting As Headhunters

A few companies have programs that offer cash awards to employees if they recommend an applicant who is hired and retained beyond a minimum period. If so, be aware that nepotism rules may still apply.

Benefits Continuation Coverage

All companies should have a concise policy concerning continuing coverage rights for employees and/or their dependents. To avoid COBRA-related problems, make sure employees are aware of the circumstances that can change their status and their rights under the law. See the extensive discussion of COBRA earlier in this chapter.

Deferred Compensation And Wages Subject To Forfeiture

In most states, an executive, officer or employee is liable to return any compensation received during the period he/she was disloyal to the interests of the company. (Note: The concept of what constitutes disloyalty will be discussed in detail in the next chapter.) In some situations, employers may also not be responsible to pay deferred compensation due an employee, as the following case suggests.

Among the provisions in the contract between a hospital and its administrator was a deferred compensation plan. This plan provided for the hospital to make deposits in a savings account equal to 28 weeks' pay, and for subsequent annual deposits equal to two weeks' pay, during the term of the man's employment and/or until a total of 52 weeks' pay had been deposited. Six years later, the administrator's career came to an end when he was convicted of embezzling over $54,000 in hospital funds. The administrator confessed and ultimately made restitution of the stolen money. Thereafter, he demanded that the employer remit to him all the money in his deferred compensation account and sued for the funds when the hospital trustees rejected his demands.

In court, he argued that the addendum to his employment contract stated that, upon termination of employment for any reason, the money in the deferred compensation account was his and the plain language of the addendum obligated the hospital to pay that money, irrespective of any misconduct. Additionally, he argued that his ERISA rights had been violated by the employer's refusal to pay him the money.

The employer responded that such a provision was never intended to protect a corrupt or criminal employee; at most it was intended to provide funds for any employee who might have come to a parting of the ways with the hospital due to honest differences over job performance.

The court ruled that the employee forfeited any deferred compensation he earned during his period of unfaithfulness. The Ohio Court of Appeals stated that his contract of employment contained an implied and constructive condition that he would, in good faith, perform his duties as a hospital administrator. This condition required him to exercise the utmost degree of loyalty and fidelity in his dealing with the employer. "Once the employee's condition for payment of services is broken the employer has absolutely no obligation to uphold its end of the bargain, since consideration on the part of the employee does not exist."

Counsel Comments: *The Ohio tribunal applied the "faithless servant doctrine," which is the law in many other states. As described by the Kansas Supreme Court in another case, the doctrine holds that: "Dishonesty and disloyalty on the part of an employee which permeates his service to his employer will deprive him of his entire agreed compensation, due to the failure of such an employee to give the stipulated consideration for the agreed compensation. Further, as public policy mandates, an employee cannot be compensated for his own deceit or wrongdoing. However, an employee's compensation will be denied only during his period of unfaithfulness."*

It may be wise to consider not paying any employee money due when you believe the employee acted unfaithfully or improperly. Always *check with counsel before doing so because serious ramifications for denying earned wages under state and federal law can ensue if not handled properly.*

CHAPTER 3

On-The-Job Policies, Procedures And Problems

Once the decision to hire a particular applicant has been made and the job is accepted and confirmed in writing, companies should take a number of important steps to avoid wrongful discharge, breach of contract, invasions of privacy, discrimination and other causes of litigation stemming from alleged violations of rights during the employment relationship. This chapter will recommend practical ways to implement such strategies and avoid problems.

All companies must establish policies dealing with trade secrets, confidential information and other rules of conduct to protect their assets. This first section will cover applicable areas including code of ethics, avoiding anti-trust violations while working, training your staff to avoid violations of their fiduciary rights of loyalty and good faith, concerns regarding outside employment, the legality of competing with the company after discharge or resignation, and the enforcement of restrictive covenants and how to use such covenants to maximum advantage.

CONFIDENTIAL INFORMATION AND TRADE SECRETS

Employees often resign from a job or are lured away to a rival company to compete directly against their former employers. Sometimes, companies learn they are powerless to recover valuable customer lists, trade secrets and confidential information including prices and requirements of key customers. Such problems can be significantly reduced if management takes preventive steps that begin immediately after an employee is hired. The following strategies may decrease the chances that such problems will occur and increase the odds of a successful verdict for your company if litigation becomes necessary.

Definition Of A Trade Secret

A trade secret may consist of any formula, pattern, device or compilation of information used in business that gives a company an opportunity to obtain an advantage over competitors that do not use or know it. Although an exact definition is impossible, trade secrets are usually involved when:

- Your company takes precautions to guard the secrecy of the information (i.e., documents are kept under lock and key and only authorized personnel have access to them);
- Your company has expended significant money and effort in developing information;

- The information is difficult to acquire outside of the company (that is, it isn't generally known to outsiders);

- Employees are warned that trade secrets are involved, that they are obligated to act in a confidential manner and are tied to restrictive covenants which bar or limit them from working for competitors for a reasonable length of time after leaving the company, or have signed agreements not to disclose confidential information to prospective or new employers.

Company managers and executives frequently inquire whether their particular procedures and operating processes are considered trade secrets. Unfortunately, the answer is not always clearcut. All of the preceding four elements may have to be present to establish that a given process or procedure is a trade secret and to determine whether it has been illegally conveyed when an employee is discharged or departs. Recognize, however, that lawsuits and injunctions brought in this area are often quite complicated and costly, even for victorious companies, because each case must be decided and analyzed on its own particular facts and circumstances. Additionally, courts generally do not like to punish smart workers who learn on the job and try to better themselves thereafter using this acquired knowledge on a new job. Only when an employer will clearly be damaged and lose its competitive advantage will it likely be victorious in a lawsuit. And, this is only after it demonstrates that a trade secret or confidential information has been or will be conveyed.

In one case an employer lost an injunction action brought in an attempt to stop a competitor from using its customer lists. The situation arose when a former employee who had worked as a truck driver and occasional mechanic began working for a major competitor, to the company's detriment. However, the court noted that at least *three* copies of its customer list were on open display at different locations of the company's premises, and it was obvious that anyone could see the list. The Illinois Appellate Court stated that "...there was no evidence of any effort on the part of the company to insure that its customer lists should be considered secret or confidential. When one adds that a significant number of the names were publicly known the company forfeited any right to bar competitors from using the names... even though those lists were the product of years of hard work."

However, another injunction lawsuit brought by an Illinois company was granted in the company's favor. In this case, the company filed the lawsuit after one of its key employees formed a competing business. Here the Illinois Appellate Court conceded that the company's processes were available to the public but were acquired by the competing business when the ex-employee copied, rather than developed, valuable formulas. This amounted to a breach of trust and the pilfering of trade secrets by a former employee under circumstances entitling the victim to protection.

Counsel Comments: *Even though a trade secret can be learned by outsiders through legitimate channels such as trade publications and scientific reports, this does not mean it loses its character as a secret. If the idea is taken by an outsider or appropriated by an ex-employee, a company may be able to bar its use. The defense that the secret could have been obtained legitimately may not matter; if the employee got it improperly, he/she may not be able to use it. For example, an ex-employee's failure to show any independent research or experimentation may make it difficult to prove he did not resort to stealing the secrets he learned on-the-job.*

Can a company claim that an employee's expertise is a trade secret? An employee who leaves one job for another has a right to take with him all the skill and knowledge he has acquired, as long as nothing he takes is the property of the employer. Courts distinguish between the skills acquired by an employee in his/her work and the trade secrets, if any, of the employer. The former may be used by the employee in subsequent jobs, the latter may not. An employee's experience in executing a number of steps to produce a desired end is often not a trade secret. However, some cases in this area have been decided in the company's favor. When salespeople become friendly with customers in the course of their employment, they are allowed to call on these customers for new employers. But in some instances, they may be prohibited from using their knowledge of customer buying habits, requirements, or other special information when soliciting their former employer's accounts. For example, if a salesperson knows that a particular customer will be in short supply of a specific product at a certain time, he may not be able to use that confidential information acquired while working for the former employer.

Customer Lists

Perhaps the most frequently disputed issue concerning trade secrets involves customer lists. A "secret" list is not a list of companies or individuals that can be compiled from a telephone directory or other readily available source. A list becomes confidential when the names of customers can be learned by someone only through his/her employment—for example, when the salesperson secretly copies a list of customers that the company spent considerable time, effort, and money compiling and kept under lock and key.

Counsel Comments: *You must carefully consider all of the aspects of your case, both positive and negative, before bringing a lawsuit. First you must prove that trade secrets are involved; the next hurdle in any lawsuit often is proving that such trade secrets were stolen. When bringing a lawsuit based on misappropriation of trade secrets consisting of manufacturing methods or processes, most companies will face claims that the information is common public knowledge obtained by going through directories, trade journals, books and catalogs. Many times the question before a court is not how the ex-employees* could *have obtained the knowledge, but how* did *they? In one Texas case, a credible witness testified that he had seen a valuable customer list in the defendant's possession. Satisfied that this evidence sustained the company's case, the Texas court upheld a jury verdict which awarded the employer $400,000 in actual damages and $500,000 in punitive damages.*

Practical Strategies To Protect The Employer

Many companies include a comprehensive trade secrets and confidential information policy in a handbook or manual. All employers are advised to include such a statement in their manuals similar to the one beginning on the following page.

To convey to employees their obligation to protect the company's trade secrets when they are hired, many companies prominently display posters reminding workers of this obligation and publish such reminders on a continuing basis in company journals, work rules and policy manuals.

It is also wise to distribute memos, usually on an annual basis, reminding key employees of their continuing obligation to protect company trade secrets and requesting their written acknowledgment. The signed document should then be saved in their personnel files. A signed statement serves several purposes; it defines what constitutes a trade secret from the company's point of view and creates a climate of confidentiality when people are hired. Furthermore, it advises employees of the seriousness of the problem, warns employees that the company may take strong legal action if trade secrets or confidential information are conveyed to others during or after the employment relationship, and documents the employee's consent.

Counsel Comments: *Note that the sample statement beginning on the following page addresses many concerns. If you wish, you can incorporate your Conflicts of Interest, Ethics, Anti-Trust and other rules into the Trade Secrets section of your manual and cross reference these for additional emphasis.*

Some states have passed laws making theft of trade secrets a criminal offense. Legislation was enacted in New Jersey, for example, making it a high misdemeanor to steal company property, including written material. Other states such as Arkansas, California, Colorado, Maine, Michigan, Minnesota, Nebraska, New Hampshire, New Mexico, Ohio, Oklahoma, Pennsylvania, Tennessee, Texas and Wisconsin have similar laws. New York has gone even further in addressing this problem by declaring it a felony for anyone to steal company property consisting of secret scientific material.

When valuable written material is stolen and transported to another state, the Federal Bureau of Investigation and Justice Department can also assist you in apprehending the individual, because it is a federal crime to sell or receive stolen property worth more than $5,000 that has been transported across state lines. Thus, review the law in your state and inform new employees of the company's policy to prosecute criminal acts. Doing so both orally and in writing may play a significant role in reducing or eliminating potential problems.

Counsel Comments: *What files can an employee take with him when leaving a company? Generally, nothing that was*

SAMPLE STATEMENT ON TRADE SECRETS

The business of our Company involves valuable, confidential, and proprietary data and information of various kinds. Such data and information, called "Trade Secrets," concern:

* The names of Company customers and the nature of the Company's relationships (e.g., types and amounts of products acquired from the Company) with such customers;
* The Company's various computer systems and programs;
* Techniques, developments, improvements, inventions, and processes that are, or may be, produced in the course of the Company's operations; and
* Any other information not generally known concerning the Company or its operations, products, suppliers, markets, sales, costs, profits, customer needs and lists, or other information acquired, disclosed, or made known to Employees or agents while in the employ of the Company, which, if used or disclosed, could adversely affect the Company's business or give competitors an advantage.

Since it would harm our Company if any of our Trade Secrets were known to our competitors, it is the Company's policy that:

1. No Employee should, during or after his/her employment with the Company, use any Trade Secrets for his/her benefit, or disclose to any person, business, or corporation any Trade Secrets without the prior written consent of the Company.

2. Every Employee shall render exclusive and full-time services and devote his/her best efforts toward the performance of assigned duties and responsibilities (which may be changed at any time).

3. Every Employee should refrain from engaging directly or indirectly in any activity that may compete with, or result in a conflict of interest with, the Company, or that is not likely to be in the Company's best interests.

4. Every Employee should fully and completely disclose to the Company any inventions, ideas, works of authorship, and other Trade Secrets made, developed, and/or conceived by him/her alone or jointly with others, arising out of, or relating to, employment at the Company. All such inventions, ideas, works of authorship, copyrights, and other Trade Secrets shall be the sole property of the Company. The Employee agrees to execute and deliver to the Company such assignments, documents, agreements, or instruments which the Company may require from time to time to evidence its ownership of the results and proceeds of the Employee's services and creations.

5. The Employee understands that he/she owes the highest duty of loyalty with respect to his/her duties. This means that he/she will, among other things, maintain a constant vigil over Company property, never make secret profits at the Company's expense (e.g., service customers of the Company but bill them for personal benefit, or receive kickbacks or special favors from customers, etc.), dress in a proper fashion, not use drugs or alcohol while on the job, and maintain a personal or Company automobile in good condition, together with a valid driver's license.

6. Every Employee shall avoid discussing any matter of a confidential nature, or which constitutes a Trade Secret, with any competitor or its employees. This includes discussions regarding customers, pricing, and policies. The Employee is reminded that any such discussions may cause the Company and the Employee personally, to have violated anti-trust laws, including the Sherman and Clayton Acts. Sanctions of up to three (3) years imprisonment and fines up to $100,000 have been imposed on those who violate such laws.

7. Upon termination of employment, or at any time the Company may request, every Employee shall promptly return to the Company all memoranda, notes, records, reports, technical manuals, and other documents (and all copies thereof) in his/her possession, custody, or control relating to Trade Secrets, all of which written materials, and other things shall be and remain the sole

property of the Company. The failure to comply with this request shall be grounds for immediate dismissal. In addition, the Company shall not be obligated in any way to pay any severance upon termination to any Employee who fails to comply with the provisions of this paragraph specifically, and this memo generally.

8. Every Employee agrees to comply with the rules, regulations, policies, and procedures of the Company faithfully and to the best of his/her abilities. The Employee understands that the breach of any covenant contained herein may constitute substantial and irreparable harm to the Company, and the Company may seek injunctive relief and other relief which it deems necessary and appropriate under the circumstances to protect its rights and the Employee shall pay all reasonable attorney fees, costs, and expenses incurred by the Company in the enforcement of any such action.

I (name of Employee) have received and read a copy of this Trade Secrets and Confidential Information Policy statement, understand all of its terms and agree to be bound by the provisions contained therein.

_______________	_______________	_______________
[PRINTED NAME]	(Signature)	(Date)

developed while working for the company, including business-generated reports, letters, diagrams, photographs and all copies of such valuable materials which are necessary for the company's continued operations. Personal information can be retrieved, but should be scrutinized by a company official before it departs from the premises.

Outside Employment

Employers can take an active role to regulate outside employment. Most employers do not look favorably on moonlighting, but the worker who holds down several jobs is becoming more common. Companies have the right to place restrictions on their employees regarding outside employment. To do this effectively, we suggest that you publish a series of guidelines in your company handbook, defining the problem and outlining how such employment may be accepted or rejected by the company. One excellent set of guidelines includes the following:

> "Outside employment is employment engaged in by an employee of the Company in addition to employment within the Company. Such employment includes working for another person or self-employment, including business operations, or other interests or activities. No employee shall have conflicting employment while in the employment of the Company. Final determination of such conflict shall be made by the Personnel Department and it is the responsibility of an employee who wishes to engage in outside employment to submit in writing to his or her administrative supervisor *all requests* for approval of such employment. This request should include the nature and location of the outside employment and the specific hours to be worked.
>
> "After careful evaluation, based on whether or not this outside employment will interfere with the employee's assigned duties and/or cause controversy within the Company, the supervisor will notify the employee in writing of his or her recommendation. The request letter and the recommendation of the administrative supervisor will be sent through regular administrative channels for further recommendations. All material is then submitted to the Personnel Office.
>
> "Upon receipt of the employee's request and the recommendations of the supervisors, if it appears by appropriate administrative staff that a conflict does exist, the Personnel Administrator will make the final decision. Failure to notify the Company of any proposed outside job, or failure to abide by the decision of the Company in this regard, shall be grounds for discipline, up to and including immediate discharge."

Counsel Comments: *If your company allows employees to hold a second job after hours in non-competing areas, be sure that all employees notify the company in advance of their second jobs for permission, and that such jobs do not interfere with your company's needs for overtime service availability where required.*

DUTY OF LOYALTY AND GOOD FAITH

Courts generally impose a duty of loyalty and good faith upon employees in all industries. These duties exist throughout the worker's employment and are also present when the employee changes jobs and joins a new company. The following points explore such duties in greater detail.

Duty Not To Exceed Authority

A saleperson's or employee's authority is usually defined by the terms of his/her employment contract with the company. If the person exceeds this authority, he/she is responsible for the consequences of the unauthorized acts.

For instance, Jonathan, a manufacturer's representative, quoted a price for machine parts that was below the list price in order to obtain a large order. If his hopes materialize, Jonathan may be required to pay the difference between the list price and the price he quoted or risk being summarily fired. Thus, sales staff should never promise discounts that are lower than the quoted company rate unless specifically authorized to do so.

Counsel Comments: *The issue of whether the company is stuck and "must make good" on its salesperson's promises is not always clear cut. For example, if a customer is persuaded to buy a product* *because of a salesperson's promise that the goods can be returned, the company will not be liable if the buyer should have known that the salesperson had no authority to make this kind of "consignment contract." Whether a salesperson has such apparent authority to bind the employer depends on the particular facts of each case; for example, if from past dealings a customer knows that the salesperson has no authority to substantially vary the usual contract terms, and it is not customary in the industry for the manufacturer to accept returns except in the case of defective products, then the buyer will not prevail because it should have checked out the new terms with the company before going ahead. This is especially true when companies present customers with written agreements stating that "all sales must be confirmed at our home office" or words of similar effect.*

Duty Not To Work For A Competitor

A salesperson can inform his customers that he intends to leave his job and work for a competitor. However, an employee cannot work for a competitor while still employed by the present company (or maybe even thereafter if a valid restrictive covenant in an employment contract was signed). In one case a salesperson told customers that he intended to leave his company to work for a competitor. Although this was perfectly legal, he overstepped his authority by distributing the competitor's catalogs to these customers while still employed with the old firm. This, the court ruled, was improper; when he was terminated by his former company and sued, the individual was required to pay a considerable amount of money in damages for his disloyal actions, including repayment of wages and commissions received during the period in question.

An employee is under no obligation other than his duty to give loyal and conscientious service to an employer while in its employ. A salesperson's freedoms include the right to advise customers that he/she is going to quit and work for a competitor even while still working for his/her employer. In preparation for quitting a job, employees can look for another job without advising their employers, advise customers of the intention to leave and compete, and even take minor steps to organize a new company while still working. What they *cannot* do is to solicit business while on the employer's payroll, talk against the old employer and hurt its reputation or lie down on the job by not taking orders or working as diligently as before.

Counsel Comments: *To increase the chances that your employees will not work for a competitor while working for your company or thereafter, draft a noncompetition clause in all applicable employment contracts. The following clause illustrates this concern:*

"The Employee agrees to devote his entire time, skill, labor, and attention to this Company during the term of his employment and is forbidden from working for any other employer, specifically including any company or business that competes with the affairs of the Company, during this period. In the event the Employee breaches this obligation, he will be responsible to return any monies received from the Company during his disloyal period."

If your company hires independent sales reps, be sure they are forbidden from selling competing lines unless your company is aware of this and both parties sign an agreement acknowledging that the company does not object to this arrangement. (Note: Several comprehensive sales representative contracts are included at the end of the book for your edification.)

Duty Not To Make Secret Profits

An employee cannot make deals with customers in which he promises to perform favors in return for secret kickbacks involving money or vacations. Any employee engaging in such conduct without the company's knowledge and consent can be terminated and sued for damages, including disgorgement of all salary and other financial payments made during the disloyal period.

In one case a purchasing agent got greedy and decided to actively pursue the possibility of cash kickbacks from vendors. On his own, he set up a dummy corporation with a post office box and bank account. He began soliciting business from select vendors and arranged to have them forward a check for "consulting services" to his corporation. After being discovered, he was fired immediately for disloyalty and for violating the company's policy forbidding employees to accept gifts from suppliers. His use of the post office box also led to his indictment for mail fraud.

Although he argued that the purchases he arranged were always fair and competitive, the court was not impressed, stating that accepting secret kickbacks from suppliers is a breach of the employee's fiduciary duties, depriving his employer of loyal and honest service. "It isn't necessary to show that the company overpaid or received poor quality goods. The Purchasing Agent has a duty to disclose any conflict between his personal financial interests and the best interests of his employer. His receipt of secret kickbacks amounted to fraud."

> **Counsel Comments:** *The court emphasized the company's Conflict of Interest policy, which forbade employees from seeking or accepting "loans, services, payments, excessive entertainment, vacation or pleasure trips, or any gift of more than nominal value or money." Each year, employees were required to sign a card certifying that they understood and were complying with this policy. The fact that the individual signed the card while he was accepting kickbacks was further evidence of fraudulent conduct.*

Is it a crime for an executive to divert extra profits from his employer? In another case, an executive hatched a scheme to divert some of his company's profits his way by obtaining the board's approval to sell fertilizer to a "not-for-profit" association controlled by him and his friends. The "not-for-profit" association then resold the fertilizer at regular market prices, allowing the executive to pocket more than $100,000. After he was fired and indicted for mail fraud, his lawyer argued that no criminal behavior had occurred because the employer made money by selling the fertilizer to the "not-for-profit" association. Nevertheless, a jury found the executive guilty of mail fraud. The U.S. Court of Appeals noted that the former executive had used his fiduciary position to create a gain for his own company and had used the mails to order the fertilizer and resell it to other customers. Therefore, his employer was defrauded of the profit it could have obtained by selling the excess fertilizer directly to these customers at market prices.

> **Counsel Comments:** *The federal crackdown on so-called "white collar crimes" has produced many mail fraud and related indictments against executives who use their positions for personal gain at the expense of their employees. An executive owes a duty of undivided loyalty to the company. Any activity which creates a possible conflict of interest must be brought before the board of directors for approval before the individual proceeds with such possibly conflicting or harmful action. This even includes situations where an executive secretly promotes a product his company previously rejected.*
>
> *In one case, an executive had an undisclosed interest in a competing business while employed by another company. The court noted that he contributed substantial financial support to this business and aided in the development of the competing product.*
>
> *Time and time again, courts have ruled against the self-serving executive who acts for private gain. Even though his employer decides not to use a particular product, an executive does not have the right to lend assistance of any kind to a potentially competing business. Finally, as a general rule, a corporate officer has no authority to use corporate funds to pay personal debts. However, there have been instances where the courts have made exceptions because stockholders were aware of and condoned an officer's use of the money in the past, such as to help finance the purchase of a personal residence nearby the employer.*

Duties After Leaving The Company

After leaving a company, many sales employees either work for a competitor or compete directly against their former companies. Generally, they are free to do this as long as no restrictive covenant was contained in their contract. However, an ex-employee can still be sued for damages for revealing trade secrets or confidential information about his former company. (See the discussion of trade secrets at the beginning of this chapter.) However, labels mean nothing and calling something a trade secret does not necessarily make it so. As previously discussed, the information must be something not generally known outside the field which gives a company a competitive advantage. Most important, its secrecy must be safeguarded.

RESTRICTIVE COVENANTS AND COVENANTS NOT TO COMPETE

As discussed more completely in Chapter 1, reasonable, well-drafted restrictive covenants can go a long way toward protecting your company from disloyal ex-employees who attempt to steal trade secrets and confidential information. Even when clearly and reasonably drafted, however, restrictive covenants are not always enforceable. In a number of states, it is illegal for a company to restrain an independent contractor sales rep, agent, broker, and professional (e.g., physician) from working for a competitor after the contract has expired or been terminated. Further, if a company requires an employee to sign a contract containing a restrictive covenant after he/she has begun working, some state courts (including Oregon) will not enforce it unless the company gives a corresponding benefit such as an increase in salary, *bona fide* promotion or change in job status. If the employee does not receive additional consideration, the covenant may not be enforceable. However, other states do not require additional compensation since the offering of the present job is deemed ample consideration. Thus, always check the law in your state before considering any action in this area.

Obviously, restrictive covenants that are unreasonable in terms of geographic scope or time limitation (e.g., five years) will not be upheld. No precise definition exists that states what makes a restrictive covenant reasonable. The relevant considerations in court when deciding to enforce a covenant are:

1. The hardship to the employee if enforced;

2. Whether any special skills or training were involved;

3. Whether the employee had access to trade secrets;

4. Whether the employee had access to confidential information such as customer lists, specific business methods, established routes, and credit information;

5. Whether the covenant is confined only to the employer's actual business or includes a slew of allied activities;

6. Whether the covenant is confined only to those geographical areas where the company does substantial business; and

7. The bargaining power of the parties.

For example, unless a salesperson's services are special, unique, or extraordinary, some states will not enforce a written restrictive covenant. In one Texas case, the judge ruled that promotional material was publicly available and not a trade secret and that the skills of car salespeople did not qualify as special talents; therefore, the judge declined to enforce a one-year non-competition agreement.

If an employer is in breach of or violates an important contract term, then it lacks "clean hands" and may not be able to enforce the covenant. Thus, it is important that your company act accordingly and avoid any wrongdoing (such as not paying wages in a timely fashion or withholding commissions) that could justify a judge's decision not to enforce the covenant.

Counsel Comments: *If an employee fails to protest a company's change in benefits and later claims the company breached an obligation owed, that silence may be deemed a waiver of his right to object to the employer's alleged breach of contract.*

In some states, if the court finds the covenant to be overbroad in terms of geographic scope or time limitation, it has the ability to enforce the clause by merely reducing the time frame or territory; in other "all or nothing at all" states, the covenant will be stricken in its entirety without any modification. And when the employer prepares a restrictive covenant which is signed by the employee, the restrictions also apply to competing businesses conducted by the employee's family members (with background help from the employee) even though they did not sign any agreements.

Counsel Comments: *Most courts will grant injunctive relief rather than damages on a company's application. This means that the court issues an order (i.e., injunction) prohibiting the employee from working for the company's competitor. If* *the employee fails to comply with the court's order, he/she may be held in contempt. However, during the pendency of the action, if the employee believes he is right, his attorney may request court permission to post a bond for the damages the employer might be awarded so that the employee can continue to work for the competitor.*

STEALING AWAY EMPLOYEES

Generally, one company has the right to persuade another company's employees to join its ranks where the employees are not bound by a contract or restrictive covenant. A defecting company executive can, however, be successfully sued for luring away key employees. In one Massachusetts case a manager was offered a lucrative post with equity in a competing business. Before resigning his job, the manager secretly solicited four key employees to join him in defecting. After the four left, the company sued for damages caused by the manager's disloyalty.

At the trial the company stated that the defendant had been one of its major officers, bearing the title of Vice President and General Manager. While still performing these important functions, he enticed four key employees to leave with him. Their departures had a devastating impact on the company's productivity and sales. The manager responded that since he had never signed a covenant not to compete, he was free to leave the company and go to work for whomever he wished. Furthermore, since none of the other employees had signed covenants, he should not be held responsible for their acts since what he did was not illegal.

The court concluded that the defendant had violated his duty of loyalty and he *and the new employer* were required to pay damages. The Massachusetts Supreme Judicial Court reacted strongly, saying, "The defendants are liable for the breach of the manager's duty of loyalty by not protecting the plaintiff against the loss of key employees. As Vice President and General Manager, defendant was responsible for staffing and hiring necessary replacements and his duty to maintain adequate managerial personnel forbade him from seeking to draw key managers away to a competitor."

Counsel Comments: *The principle that a top managerial employee may not, before termination of employment, solicit employees to work for a competitor has been applied in many situations. The rule is most clearly applicable if the supervisor-manager, as a corporate pied piper, leads his company's employees away, thus destroying the employer's business.*

In addition to suing an individual on the basis of breach of the fiduciary duty of loyalty and good faith, some attorneys commence lawsuits against the new employer, based upon a legal theory called tortious interference with contractual relations, when they induce a valued employee to break a contract and go to work for them. Generally, if the key employee is under contract with a definite term and the employee breaks the contract before the expiration of the contract period, a lawsuit may be successful. However, when no formal written contract exists, and the employee is merely hired at-will (capable of being terminated or leaving at any time), such suits have less chance of success.

To increase the odds that your company will prevail, consider including the following language in all contracts signed by your key employees and executives:

"During the term of this Agreement and for a period of One (1) year thereafter, the Employee agrees that he will not hire or otherwise utilize the services of any employee or sales associate of the Company that was or is working while this Agreement is in effect. Both parties agree that the loss of any such employee or sales associate would result in irreparable harm to the Company and the Employee, therefore, grants the Company the right to seek damages, including reasonable attorney fees and costs, incurred in bringing an injunction action in a court of equity or other competent jurisdiction to enforce its rights hereunder."

Inserting a clause similar to the above in your employment agreements can increase the chances of success when a key employee or executive under contract leaves and takes other valued employees with him to compete against the interests of your organization.

CODE OF ETHICS

Some companies include a detailed section of policies relating to business ethics and conduct in a company handbook or manual. This can include, for example, a detailed discussion of anti-trust laws as they pertain to relations with competitors, suppliers, customers, distributors, and international transactions. *Ignorance of the law is no excuse* and companies must be aware that violations for breach of ethics can be substantial. For example, a violation of many of the anti-trust laws may constitute a criminal offense, subjecting the company to fines up to $1 million, and individual participants to jail sentences up to three years.

Counsel Comments: *One way to minimize potential problems is to include a section of general legal requirements in the handbook so that employees, particularly those in sales, will understand what they can and cannot do under the law (e.g., that they cannot accept secret gifts or discuss pricing policies with competitors). The following brief text is an example:*

"The Company has an excellent reputation. Throughout our growth, adherence to the strictest principles of business ethics and integrity has characterized our business dealings and firmly established the Company's reputation. There is one basic policy to which there will never be any exception made by anyone, anywhere, in any activity owned and operated by the Company. That policy is to play it straight, whether in contact with Customers, Suppliers, fellow Employees, or other individuals or groups. The only right way to deal with people is forthrightly and honestly. We are committed to compliance not only with the spirit and letter of the laws that apply to business, but also with the highest standards of ethics and morality. We expect and demand of every individual in the Company the same commitment. Any breach of this policy will, therefore, be cause for disciplinary action, which may include discharge."

It is a good idea to schedule an annual one day (or shorter) seminar on ethics for your key executives and managers. Some companies bring in private counsel to discuss recent developments in the laws and cover common areas of confusion.

COMMON ANTI-TRUST VIOLATIONS

Serious anti-trust overtones are present in many selling situations. For example, companies sometimes refuse to deal with a particular customer; distributors may be cut off from receiving future deliveries of product; salespeople may call a customer to verify a price; the list of examples is endless.

Unfortunately, anti-trust laws are complex, and management and staff often do not receive any preventive legal advice or guidelines. As a result, they do not know what types of conduct and speech are forbidden. Few people realize that individuals, including managers, field salespeople and company officers, may be *personally* liable for failing to act within the law. Penalties for such violations are severe: corporate officers have been subjected to criminal prosecution and punishment under the Sherman Act, even though they were acting for their corporation. Also, a corporate officer called before a grand jury investigating an anti-trust violation may be liable for damages in a private anti-trust action as well.

In any anti-trust action, protracted investigation and litigation inevitably are a heavy drain on a company's financial and personal resources, regardless of whether the employer ultimately wins or loses. Such suits typically last up to five years and require thousands of hours from operating personnel in preparing the defense and giving testimony, even for minor violations. For example, the Federal Trade Commission (FTC) is empowered to impose cease and desist orders and injunctions for common illegal practices. These hearings are mandatory once charges have been brought, so that even if the charges are eventually dropped, companies spend enormous amounts of time, paying heavy legal fees and enduring aggravation defending themselves at these proceedings. If the charges are proven, bad publicity ensues, not to mention civil liability up to $10,000 per day if the orders are subsequently violated.

A violation of the anti-trust and trade regulation laws by an employer results from the practices and internal policies of its managers, officers and sales personnel. Thus, a comprehensive corporate compliance program is essential, particularly since experts predict that companies will once again become targets of investigation as the Clinton Administration revives anti-trust enforcement. The following discussion centers on the key areas.

Deceptive Practices

The Federal Trade Commission Act declares unlawful "unfair methods of competition" and "unfair or deceptive acts or practices." Enforcement cannot be maintained by private lawsuits from individuals or companies. Rather, a claim must be made to the Anti-trust Division of the Justice Department or the Federal Trade Commission (FTC) for investigation and appropriate action. In many states, businesses and consumers may also contact the attorney general's office, which may file a suit on their behalf and enforce the state's own anti-trust and trade laws.

The definition of a violation is often subject to interpretation. However, under Section Five of the Act, the following practices are clearly illegal:

Orders: It is unfair for company salespeople to substitute goods different from those ordered, misrepresent a delivery date, fail to fill an order or not fill an order within a reasonable time after its acceptance.

Goods: It is illegal to ship unordered goods or ship larger amounts than ordered hoping the buyer will pay for them.

Terms of sale: Employees cannot misrepresent the terms and conditions of a sales offer, for example, by falsely stating important terms. Key terms have been identified as those pertaining to such things as warranties and guaranties of your product, the ability of the buyer to cancel a contract or obtain a refund, or the concealment of important facts in a credit or financing transaction.

Business descriptions: Employees are forbidden from misrepresenting their company's financial standing, reputation, length of time in business or facts concerning the company's plant, equipment or facilities. Personnel cannot be referred to as "experts" or "specialists" if they have no special training.

Product descriptions: Methods by which a product is produced cannot be misstated. For example, statements concerning the word "proven" cannot be used when no scientific or empirical evidence has been obtained to establish the truth of such a claim.

Customer coercion: It is unlawful to threaten a customer with legal action when you have no intent to carry out the threat. It is also unlawful to make fictitious inquiries which annoy a competitor, or pressure anyone into buying a product using coercion, intimidation, or scare tactics.

Secret rebates: Payment of confidential rebates by an employee is considered an unfair practice which suppresses competition. Thus, it is illegal to reward a dealer's sales staff for sales of your company's goods without the consent of the salespeople's employer.

Refusal-To-Deal Situations

Another common area of anti-trust violations involves "refusal-to-deal" situations. The Sherman Act prohibits "contracts, combinations, and conspiracies" in restraint of trade. The primary objective of this law is the preservation of competition. A determining factor in considering the legality of any business conduct is its competitive impact. Business conduct in the form of an unreasonable restraint of trade or an unfair method of competition that has, or probably will have, an adverse effect on competition is illegal. Anti-trust problems can arise in the initial selection of customers as well as in the refusal to deal with a current or former customer, by say, cancelling a distributorship, adjusting a selling policy to favor one customer over another, or not renewing a franchise. Since these practices abound in the marketplace, a customer cut off from a favorable source of supply is likely to quickly file a complaint alleging a violation.

The Sherman Act does not restrict the right of a businessperson to select customers. Generally, a company can cut off or refuse to deal with someone provided it has a good business reason that can be proved. The following reasons have been upheld by the courts:

- The dealer does not sell enough or cooperate in the seller's prices and programs;
- The dealer or customer fails to purchase an adequate volume of product or fails to promote and advertise the line adequately;
- The dealer does not adequately promote the seller's image (example: inadequate or sloppy display);

- The customer is responsible for excessive cancellations, order changes, or "cherry picking" of the line.

Any decision not to do business with an existing customer must be made by the company *alone* without discussions or consultations with the customer or any other party, particularly competing customers or distributors. The Sherman Act is violated when a group of competitors agrees not to deal with a certain party, or to deal only on certain terms. Even in the absence of an actual agreement among companies, substantially identical conduct among competitors may violate Section One of this law. This is sometimes referred to as "conscious parallelism."

Counsel Comments: *To avoid any appearance of impropriety and minimize a company's exposure in this area, a sales executive must be able to prove that a decision not to sell to a particular party was arrived at independently based on valid business reasons. The following strategies are recommended:*

1. Retain all correspondence and memorandums concerning customer accounts, particularly where bills are outstanding.

2. If a customer's order is refused, state the reasons in a letter to the customer and a private memo for the files.

3. Document your independence in reaching such a decision through the use of minutes of corporate meetings that cite facts evidencing a lack of discussion with the customer's competitors.

4. When dropping a dealer or distributor, advise field sales staff and reps never to discuss the decision with the dealer's competitors (or anyone else) before, during, or after the termination.

5. If you are contemplating a change in the terms of a contract with a customer in response to rumors circulating in the industry, confer with counsel to make certain that your company is not engaging in conscious parallelism or a group boycott.

6. If you do drop a customer, do not ask a competing dealer or distributor to buy more goods from you because you have recently terminated the competition. In addition, do not promise to terminate anyone's competitor on the basis of a promise to purchase more goods.

7. When terminating a customer, do not try to soften the blow by offering off-the-cuff excuses. Know what you are going to say ahead of time without offering formal reasons for the move, unless you have no choice. Then, be sure the reason you give is legally sufficient.

Resale Restrictions

The Sherman Act also requires that companies act properly with respect to resale restrictions. For example, someone who purchases a product generally has the right to do with it as he/she chooses, without restrictions by the seller. It is not permissible to agree with or require your customer or distributor to resell a product at a certain price or only within a specified market or geographical territory. Generally, however, it is legal to assign a distributor an area of primary responsibility for which his best efforts will be made to promote and sell the product in that area, and not to appoint any other distributor in that distributor's exclusive territory. Bear in mind that exclusive dealing arrangements, such as forbidding a distributor to handle competitive products, are usually vulnerable under the anti-trust laws. Thus marketers should never require an exclusive dealing arrangement, formally or informally, without careful consideration of the law such as coercing customers into ceasing to deal with your competitors and refusing to trade with them if they do.

A manufacturer is permitted to control original sales of its products through its agents. Only when the manufacturer restricts the *resale* of its products by others does a restraint of trade situation come into play. For example, the law allows a company to sell a product exclusively through independent sales reps by instructing them to sell that product only to ultimate consumers (as opposed to wholesalers or retailers) since the reps are not restricting the sale by consumers to others. However, if the company tells its dealers not to sell to a specific customer, that is usually illegal.

Tie-In And Other Restrictions

Some companies are also exposed to anti-trust violations by espousing combination sales and tie-in policies, which may unwittingly violate Section

Three of the Clayton Act. A tie-in arrangement typically requires the buyer to purchase two or more products. For example, a salesperson says, "Look, I know you only want to buy our B-10 model. But if you want it, you'll have to purchase six B-14's also. Otherwise, no deal." This foregoes the purchaser's ability and right of freedom in the marketplace.

Another illegal practice is the offering of requirements contracts. Here, purchasers are usually required to buy or lease all or a specified percentage of their requirements of a product from a given company, usually within a specific time. Thus, a salesperson may tell a customer, "If you want to buy our product, you must buy X amount or else no deal." Generally, this business arrangement is illegal because it forecloses to other sellers a significant portion of the market for that product. To avoid problems, companies should never enter into full-requirements contracts without careful analysis of the anti-trust issues.

> **Counsel Comments:** *Sales staff should never force a customer to purchase more of a product, or buy another product it does not need, as a condition to obtain a license, loan, another product or benefit. If this occurs, your company may have to respond to charges filed by the Justice Department or your local state attorney general's office—aggravation you can do without.*

Price Discrimination

A final area of concern is price discrimination. Federal enforcers can't tell you what to charge, but they'll jump all over you for price discrimination. Section 2 of the Clayton Act states that it is unlawful for a seller to discriminate in price among different customers when the discrimination has a proscribed competitive effect. It is also unlawful for a buyer knowingly to induce or receive a discriminatory price. Section 3 of the Robinson-Patman Act goes so far as to make it a criminal offense to be a party to or to assist in discriminations among competing purchasers.

Price discrimination typically occurs in two ways—through arrangements with competitors or through relations between customers and distributors. With respect to relations with competitors, it is unlawful per se to make any of the following arrangements, directly or indirectly, with competitors: "To agree to fix prices, stabilize prices, agree to a formula to determine prices, or enter into any agreement which may even have a remote or indirect effect on prices."

Examples of this include agreements to do the following:

- Divide or allocate markets, territories, or customers;
- Rig bids or submit bids knowing they will be unacceptable;
- Charge a maximum price;
- Limit production, set quotas, or discontinue a product;
- Boycott third parties;
- Depress the prices of raw materials with other raw materials purchasers;
- Establish uniform discounts or credit terms or eliminate discounts;
- Establish a system for determining delivered prices or a specific method of quoting prices.

> **Counsel Comments:** *These examples were all taken from actual cases where competitors were found to have committed per se anti-trust violations. As per se violations, they could not be defended or justified in any way, even though an employee's intentions may have been honorable, and even though the conduct was considered an industry-wide practice. Companies should also note that in many of these cases, the court did not have to prove the existence of a written agreement to find a conspiracy to manipulate price. Any understanding, whether oral or written, formal or informal, that gives the parties a basis for expecting that a business practice or decision adopted by one would be followed or unopposed by the other, is sufficient to incur the wrath of anti-trust enforcers. One court stated, "A knowing wink can mean more than words." And even if an employee attempts to regulate prices with a competitor, and that attempt fails, the employee is still liable for violating the law.*

With respect to relations with customers and distributors, under the Clayton Act, a seller may not charge one customer a higher price, or offer more favorable terms when the two customers should be treated equally, except in certain limited situations. All customers and distributors should be treated as equally as possible so as to not stifle competition by giving one unfair advantage over the other. Customer pricing, therefore, is not just a matter of individual price negotiation; anti-trust laws require that it be a carefully organized and documented business policy.

The law also covers discrimination in terms of sale other than price. Discrimination in terms of sale may permit favored customers to purchase at terms different from other customers—giving an advertising or freight allowance, cash discount, free merchandise, equipment, or a bonus to one customer and not another. This frequently occurs when employees and sales staff aggressively pursue accounts.

> **Counsel Comments:** *The giving of favored terms to certain similar customers and not others may violate anti-trust laws. Thus, it is recommended that employees be instructed to quote different prices, terms, and other incentives only* after *approval from management has been obtained, never before.*

In addition, sales staff must know the nature of the customer. For example, a company violates the law by granting a wholesaler's discount to a buyer who combines retail and wholesale functions, because the buyer may thereby gain an unfair price concession compared to the competition. Furthermore, if a manufacturer sells to a buyer who uses the product in his business operations and also resells the product to others, a user discount cannot be granted on the basis of total purchases if the buyer competes on product resale with other customers of the manufacturer that do not receive the user discount. In such a situation, the manufacturer must restrict the user discount only to those transactions that do not result in a resale.

Many of these prohibitions are, however, subject to a number of exceptions. Although all customers theoretically should be charged the same prices, the law does recognize situations in which customers are *not* entitled to the same price or in which one customer should be charged a lower price than another. A price differential or different terms of sale can be defended on either of the following grounds:

(a) If the price differential was given in good faith to *meet* (not beat) a price offered by a competitor; or

(b) If the price differential is based upon a *cost saving* reflecting a difference in the cost of manufacture, sale or delivery resulting from differing methods or quantities in which products are sold or delivered.

For example, price breaks are allowed when based on volume ordered, closeout sales, lower shipping and selling costs, good-faith meeting the competition, and lower commissions paid by the seller to its employee salespeople. All of these "costs defenses" may justify a difference in price or terms of sale.

> **Counsel Comments:** *Companies should establish proper accounting methods to reflect such cost variances. For example, if you are establishing affirmative pricing policies or granting advertising and promotional allowances and services, be sure your accounting methods and procedures reflect cost differences that permit you to reduce prices or terms of sale to selected customers. This can be done by maintaining a variety of records kept in the ordinary course of business that document and reflect company policies or reveal the nature of a business transaction or decision. For example, records of rejected orders and the reasons therefor may dispel the inference of a boycott. Cost accounting records may provide a defense to a price discrimination charge. Pricing records may refute a charge that prices were fixed by agreement rather than independently. Prices quoted to customers may afford to a seller the good faith meeting-of-competition defense to a price discrimination charge. Notices of promotional allowance plans may also show that such plans were made available to all customers, not just certain ones.*

Finally, since the exchange or communication of information regarding prices or terms is so carefully scrutinized, any perceived cooperation among competitors is suspect under anti-trust laws. More subject to suspicion than any other type of information exchange is the exchange of price information.

> **Counsel Comments:** *Be sure to instruct your employees and particularly sales staff to avoid, if possible, any contact with competitors, especially at trade shows and social gatherings. Although*

this sounds extreme, it is a good business practice, because many price-fixing situations occur at these sessions. Remember, any discussion of prices, warranties, uniform practices, or industry conditions between competitors is prohibited.

EMPLOYEE PRIVACY RIGHTS

Most workers are unaware that their privacy rights extend to the workplace where they are frequently violated by executives, security personnel, private investigators and informers. The law allows employees to recover damages when companies act improperly. For example, a court of appeals recently upheld a $350,000 jury award to a man who had been fired for insubordination after his employer discovered that he had surreptitiously tape-recorded a meeting during which he was demoted.

Workplace policies that attempt to monitor or regulate employees' habits and activities are increasingly subject to legal challenges. Legislatures and courts have demonstrated a growing desire to review and strike down policies that are directed at non-work-related employee behavior. On the other hand, employers successfully can defend many intrusive policies when they are linked sufficiently to legitimate workplace goals.

A growing number of employees are challenging employer practices in this area. The following pages explain recent developments with respect to employee privacy rights, including lie detector tests, drug, alcohol and AIDS testing, smoking in the workplace, employee searches, interrogations, wiretapping, eavesdropping and other forms of surveillance; rights of free speech; appearance rules; breaches of the confidentiality of employee records and related problems dealing with the disclosure of personnel files.

Lie Detector Tests

Prior to December 27, 1988, approximately 26 states did not regulate the use of polygraph tests. Following enactment of the federal Polygraph Protection Act of 1988, however, most of the millions of annual tests previously given have ceased.

The law is designed to protect employees in instances where abuse is most likely to occur (i.e., automatic lie detector tests for job applicants), and affects most companies in the areas of applicant screening, random testing of employees and lie detector use during investigations of suspected wrongdoing. Fines and penalties include back pay, job reinstatement and related damages, attorneys' fees and costs to successful litigants, plus civil penalties up to $10,000 and injunctive relief for actions brought by the U.S. Secretary of Labor within three years from the wrongful act.

Following is a thumbnail sketch of the Polygraph Protection Act:

Effect on state laws. In those states that currently have stronger laws prohibiting lie detector (defined as any mechanical or electrical device used to render a diagnostic opinion regarding honesty) tests, the state laws supersede the act. This is because the federal law sets minimum standards for private employers in each state to follow. Idaho law, for example, prohibits any employer from requiring as a condition of employment that an employee take a polygraph test, and violation of this law is a crime. Employers in states which had few restrictions, however, such as Florida, Illinois and New York, are required to follow the federal law.

Counsel Comments: *If your company has a more restrictive lie detector policy within an applicable collective bargaining agreement, that policy may supersede state or federal law.*

Prohibited uses. Generally, employers are prohibited from directly or indirectly requiring, requesting, suggesting or causing an applicant or employee to take any lie detector test. Tests can be administered in connection with an investigation, but only after reasonable suspicion has been established. Many procedural safeguards must be carefully followed: the individual must have an opportunity to obtain and consult with legal counsel before each phase of the test; be provided at least 48 hours' notice of the time and place of the test; be notified of the evidentiary basis for the test; be advised of the nature and characteristics of the test and instruments involved (i.e., two-way mirrors or recording devices); be provided an opportunity to review all questions to be asked at the examination; and be given a copy of the law, which mentions an employee's rights and remedies and which gives him/her the right to stop the test at any time.

Accepted uses. Although the federal law restricts the method under which the tests may be given, it does allow for lie detector use to investigate serious workplace improprieties. However, employees who submit to such a test must be given the results, together with a copy of the questions asked. Additionally, employers are forbidden from administering more than five tests per day, and each test must run no longer than 90 minutes. All persons administering such tests must be bonded with at least $50,000 of coverage, and are forbidden from recommending action regarding test results.

Counsel Comments: *Since employers must now have a reasonable basis for suspicion of wrongdoing to order the test, companies must be sure that such suspicions are well-founded lest they face liability. In addition, all exam results and action taken based on them must be guarded against careless dissemination to non-essential third parties to avoid charges of defamation. It is also interesting to note that the federal law forbids companies from allowing non-suspects to voluntarily take the test to "clear their own name."*

Psychological Tests

Can a union demand to see the results of psychological tests given to its members? When one company gave a test to help predict future work success, not one union member passed. The union demanded to look at the actual test results to see if the test was biased against workers with seniority. When the company refused, the union filed an unfair labor practice. At a hearing, the union contended that the company was bound to provide authorized union representatives with the information, and that without such an opportunity the union would be unable to determine whether the test was fair or biased. The company defended itself by saying that the test had been designed specially for the company at great expense, and that all involved had been guaranteed that the test results would be confidential. It also argued that the union was not qualified to determine whether the test was fair.

The National Labor Relations Board ordered the company to turn over the test results. When the company appealed in court, the U.S. Court of Appeals ruled that the union had the right to see the tests and how its members scored—whether the company liked it or not. It determined that the collective bargaining agreement provided for promotions based on seniority "whenever reasonable qualifications and abilities of employees are not significantly different." Therefore, the only way that the union could police the contract, since a legitimate question of fairness had been raised, was by examining actual copies of the tests. Note: In effect, the Court destroyed the value of the tests for future use since there was no way to prevent the contents from falling into unauthorized hands. A better approach might have been for the company to have discussed its intentions with the union *beforehand* and then deliver the tests to a neutral industrial psychologist for evaluation.

Counsel Comments: *All companies must be mindful of the restrictions imposed by the Polygraph Protection Act. Lie detector tests can no longer be given as part of a "fishing expedition" to uncover facts. Now, employers must use the test only as part of an ongoing investigation, must be able to demonstrate the suspected employee's involvement in the matter under investigation, and must be careful to follow all pre-test, test and post-test procedures, because failure to do so can lead to serious legal repercussions. All companies must think twice before requesting applicants or employees to submit to such tests; be sure to consult experienced legal counsel before acting in this area. Finally, please note that the federal law also prohibits use of "deceptographs, stress analyzers, psychological stress evaluators or any other similar device" to screen job applicants. It also restricts employers from taking action against incumbent employees who refuse to submit to such tests.*

Personnel Records

Generally, state law governs whether employees have the right to review their personnel records pertaining to employment decisions. In some states, including California, Connecticut, Delaware, Illinois, Maine, Michigan, Nevada, New Hampshire, Ohio, Oregon, Pennsylvania, Washington and Wisconsin, employees or their representatives do have this right. Even in these states, however, they generally cannot inspect confidential items such as letters of reference furnished by other employers, information about other employees, records of investigation, information about misconduct or crimes that have not been used adversely against them.

Counsel Comments: *Statutes are constantly changing so it is best to research current state law or speak with counsel for additional information.*

Rebuttal Statements. Do employees have the automatic right to include a rebuttal statement in their personnel file if incorrect information is discovered? Some states, including Connecticut, Delaware, Illinois, Michigan, New Hampshire, Washington and Wisconsin, permit workers to do this when the employer will not delete such comments. In fact, Connecticut, Delaware, Illinois, Michigan and New Hampshire have laws which *require* employers to send copies of rebuttal statements to prospective employers or other parties when information pertaining to a worker or his/her employment history is conveyed. Since each state treats the subject differently, review your state's law if applicable.

Off-Duty Surveillance. Some states (e.g., Illinois and Michigan) prohibit employers from gathering and maintaining information regarding an employee's off-premises political, religious and other non-business activities without the individual's written consent. In these states, employees and former employees can inspect their personnel file for the purpose of discovering whether any such information exists. If their file contains prohibited information, the employer may be liable for damages, court costs, attorney's fees and fines.

Credit Investigations. Employers are permitted to conduct a credit check if this serves a legitimate business purpose. However, the federal Fair Credit Reporting Act gives employees the right to know what's in their credit file and to challenge inaccurate information. If an applicant is rejected from a job because of a consumer report prepared by a retail credit bureau or similar agency, that applicant must be so informed and given the name and address of the agency. The person can then write or visit the agency directly to investigate the accuracy of the report. An employer requesting an investigative consumer report must notify an employee within three days that the report is being ordered and, upon request, provide a complete and accurate disclosure of the nature and scope of the investigation.

Medical Investigations. Employers routinely obtain medical information concerning their employees under many different circumstances, including when they collect health information for a group insurance plan, when an employee requests time off for a medical leave, and as part of a substance abuse assistance program. The law now recognizes that a duty of confidentiality can arise to protect this information and avoid dissemination to nonessential third parties. In addition, under emerging statutory state law and case decisions, employers who request medical information may be liable for the tort of intrusion and for the tort of public disclosure of private data. Some states have enacted legislation to limit an employer's disclosure of medical information in personnel files, and several courts have recognized a claim for negligent maintenance of personnel files when files containing inaccurate medical information are made available to third parties. For example, Connecticut has enacted a statute requiring employers to maintain medical records *separately* from personnel files and permitting employees to review all medical and insurance information in their individual files.

In California, employers are prohibited from using or disclosing employee medical information unless disclosure is compelled by law or the information is relevant to a lawsuit between the employer or employee, or is necessary to administer an employee benefit plan. The consequence of a recent case in Massachuetts indicates that employers in that state are even prevented from obtaining employee medical information directly from insurance providers without the employee's consent. Even though the information sought may be of significance to the employer, the employer may not be entitled to it under the Massachusetts privacy statute (which states in part that "a person shall have the right against unreasonable, substantial or serious interference with his privacy") when a physician-patient relationship exists, unless the information poses serious danger to the employer.

> **Counsel Comments:** *A series of state cases have decided, both pro and con, employees' invasion of privacy claims brought when company physicians disclose confidential medical information to the employer. Usually, if some of the information was previously contained in the employment records, and the issue presented was of legitimate concern to the employer, a court may rule that no breach of the confidential doctor-patient privilege took place if the information was conveyed for a valid purpose. However, since the outcome of each case depends on the particular facts, never make any decisions in this area without seeking advice from counsel. Certainly, it is best to carefully evaluate your company's need for medical information before requesting such data*

from an in-house physician, insurance company or other health provider and take steps to reduce the risk that such information will be disclosed to the employee's friends, family members and co-workers.

If employees ask to view such information, a personnel department representative should be present when the request is granted. Employees should not *be permitted to remove or alter their files in any way and no photocopies should be given; if copies are requested, the employee should be instructed to take notes instead.*

Searches

Employers use a variety of techniques when they suspect a worker of misconduct. These include:

- Searching the employee's office or locker without his/her knowledge or consent;
- Requesting the employee to open his/her briefcase or package upon leaving a company facility; and
- Conducting a "pat-down" search of the person.

The law regarding employee searches involves a careful balancing of the employer's right to manage a business with the privacy rights of employees. The Fourth Amendment to the United States Constitution protects all persons against unreasonable search and seizure of their persons, homes and personal property, and this doctrine applies when the employer is the government. Most private employers, however, are exempt from this doctrine (unless the private employer does extensive business with or is heavily regulated by the government) and generally are permitted to use a variety of techniques when suspecting a worker of misconduct. In fact, many arbitrators routinely uphold disciplinary actions against employees who refuse to permit a search of toolboxes or lockers on company premises, and even off the premises at a hotel or in a worker's garage. Although each case is decided on its own facts, the law generally states that searches are permissible if an employer has a reasonable basis for suspecting the employee of wrongdoing and the search is confined to non-personal areas of his/her office. The office and documents relevant to company business are considered property of the employer and can be searched anytime.

The legitimacy of any workplace search often depends on whether the employer provided advance notice, whether the search was justified under the circumstances, whether the search was done in a reasonable manner, and whether it was conducted in clearly designated company-owned property areas. One court employed a two-step balancing test in weighing the privacy rights of workers against the legitimate interests of employers. Under the court's analysis, a search is permitted provided (1) it is justified at its inception (i.e., if the employer has reasonable grounds for suspecting that the search will turn up evidence of work-related misconduct, theft, or suspected drug or alcohol use while on company premises, or that the search is necessary for a non-investigatory work-related purpose, such as to retrieve a file) and (2) if the search is reasonable in scope (i.e., if the measures adopted are related to the objectives of the search and not excessively intrusive in light of the nature of the misconduct being investigated).

Clearly visible personal items cannot be searched and employers cannot conduct a search if there is no reasonable ground for suspicion. Whether searches of an employee's briefcase, locker, or packages are legitimate depends upon whether the employee had a reasonable expectation of privacy.

Counsel Comments: *You can establish policies which make your employees' privacy expectations seem unreasonable. For example:*

* *Post signs throughout your plant reminding workers that personal property is subject to search;*
* *Distribute memos stating that surveillance measures will be taken on a regular basis;*
* *Prepare waivers to be* signed *by all employees notifying workers that lockers are subject to random, unannounced searches by authorized personnel and that failure to cooperate and consent to such searches may result in immediate discipline including discharge; and*
* *Disseminate handbooks stating that personal property is subject to search in company lockers.*

Such measures may reduce claims of illegal privacy invasions. For example, with such policies in place, one court found that packages could be searched. Another ruled that searching vehicles on company property was legal. One court even found a search valid on the basis that an employee had voluntarily accepted and continued employment notwithstanding the fact that the job subjected him to searches on a routine basis. This, the court concluded, demonstrated his willingness and implied consent to be searched, thereby waiving the claim that his privacy rights had been violated. However, when the employer does not have such policies in place, the lack of published work rules and regulations may actually *encourage* an expectation of privacy claim. For example, in one case the employer searched an employee's purse, which was stored in a company locker. The court ruled that this violated the employee's reasonable expectation of privacy since she was permitted to use a private lock on her locker and there was no regulation authorizing searches without employee consent.

Counsel Comments: *When searches are conducted they must be imposed on all employees, (not confined to one group of workers such as Afro-Americans), to avoid charges of discrimination; they also cannot violate constitutional or tort standards (e.g., by requiring employees to submit to unannounced body or strip searches).*

The expectation of privacy is greatest when a pat-down or other personal search of an employee is conducted and knowledgeable employers are reluctant to conduct personal searches, especially when random or done without specific, probable cause with respect to the individual involved.

In one case, an employer's security guards detained and searched a worker leaving a plant because he was suspected of stealing parts. According to testimony at the trial, the guards yelled at and shoved the employee. Although serious inventory shortages had been reported in the area where the employee was seen wandering shortly before leaving the plant, he was awarded $27,000 in damages after proving he had been singled out and treated unfairly by being subjected to the search; also, no stolen parts were found on his person and the search was conducted while many people were leaving the plant, causing him much emotional upset and embarrassment.

Counsel Comments: *Employees should be advised that their offices, desks, lockers and other company property may be searched at any time. After implementing such a policy, you should conduct regular random searches to demonstrate the company's commitment to enforcement. However, instruct staff not to open any mail marked "personal." If any employee refuses to consent to a search, prepare a statement acknowledging the refusal (signed by the employee if possible) and remind the worker that such conduct may jeopardize his job.*

Employees who believe they are victims of illegal searches are often asked the following questions by labor lawyers:

* *Have similar searches been conducted on you or your property before? If so, did you acquiesce in the search?*
* *Have similar searches been conducted on other employees?*
* *Were you given a warning that the employer intended to conduct a search?*
* *Was the object of the search company property?*
* *Did the search have an offensive impact?*
* *Were you forcefully grabbed, jostled, struck or held?*
* *Were you injured?*
* *Were you coerced, threatened physically or mentally abused in order to make you cooperate?*
* *Were you held against your will?*
* *Were you so intimidated by the experience that you were afraid to leave?*
* *Were you chosen at random for a pat-down search with no actual suspicion of wrongdoing?*

* *Did the employer search your belongings in an area that was truly private?*

* *Did the employer search you in front of non-essential third parties and, if no wrongdoing was discovered, was your business reputation harmed by such action?*

If the employee can answer yes to any of the last nine points, he/she may have a strong case, especially if the worker was fired, placed on probation, suspended or given an official reprimand after the search, even though he/she did nothing wrong. The tort actions most frequently alleged as a result of an improper employee search include assault, battery, defamation (in particular, slander per se), false imprisonment, invasion of privacy and abusive discharge. Since lawsuits related to searches frequently arise because of improper behavior, and since damages are routinely awarded by juries against companies in the six figures, review all of the foregoing strategies with counsel before implementation and be sure to act properly.

Interrogations

Generally, employers can question workers in an effort to discover illegal acts provided questioning is conducted during normal business hours, there are no threats or coercion forcing the employee to remain in the room, and the questioning serves a legitimate, reasonable purpose.

However, employees may have rights during these interviews. These include:

- The right to receive an explanation regarding the purpose of the interrogation (i.e., is the person a suspect?);
- The right to insist on the presence of a representative at the interview (particularly if the worker is a union member and has reason to suspect it may result in disciplinary action);
- The right to limit questions to relevant matters;
- The right to refuse to sign any written statements;
- The right to remain silent;
- The right to consult a lawyer before speaking; and
- The right to leave the room at any time.

All of the above points must be carefully considered before accusing a worker in an interrogation. If the company conducts the interrogation incorrectly, grave legal consequences may ensue, as the following cases demonstrate.

A checkout clerk was accused of failing to ring up merchandise purchases. The employee was interrogated by security personnel and told to accompany them to another location for additional questioning, where she remained uncomfortably for several hours. At the trial, the company proved that the woman failed to ring up purchases. However, a jury awarded the employee $27,500 on the grounds of false imprisonment, because the woman was never told she could leave the interrogation at any time.

In another case, three company representatives kept a supervisor in a manager's office for several hours until he finally signed a resignation notice and "admitted" his guilt concerning money given to him by a customer. The man sued the company for false imprisonment and won. Additionally, the court found that the facts supported the tort of intentional infliction of emotional distress.

Must a "suspect" employee be warned of her rights in an employment context before she confesses? One cashier accused of pocketing $36,000 in cash from COD deliveries was summoned and closeted with a company manager and private investigator hired to uncover the cause of the thefts. When the manager displayed the paid invoices taken from her desk, she burst into tears, admitted her guilt and signed a confession. She was then arrested and charged with embezzlement. At the trial, her defense was that she was framed. The D.A. offered her signed confession into evidence; her lawyer argued that her so-called confession was inadmissible because she was never advised of her constitutional right against self-incrimination, nor was she told that she need not make a statement.

The judge accepted the confession and the employee was convicted. She appealed the decision and was found guilty as charged. The Alabama Court of Criminal Appeals noted that the employee was not subject to a pending arrest, nor was any law enforcement officer present when she confessed. Thus, a confession made to a private citizen does not require a prior warning to the suspect of his or her rights.

Counsel Comments: *Employers must recognize that an employee's rights may be violated during an interrogation if he/she is restrained or confined by force or threat of force, thereby denying the worker's freedom of movement. A court will conduct a full-scale hearing as to the circumstances surrounding any interrogation or confession to make sure no undue pressure or third-degree methods were used. Interrogation of a suspect employee must always be handled with extreme care. Never lock the door; tell the employee that he or she can leave at any time. Know that it is no defense to detain the worker during normal office hours or provide breaks during the process, and that confinement for the purpose of extracting a confession is not permitted.*

Whenever you are questioning an employee, have another supervisor or manager present as a witness. Ask the employee to give his version of the facts. If the employee refuses, state that this constitutes insubordination and may lead to dismissal. Ask the employee to write down his version of the facts. Keep the facts regarding the affair confidential and only discuss them with essential personnel to reduce the risk of charges of defamation. Finally, obtain the opinion of counsel before proceeding with any interrogation.

Wiretapping And Eavesdropping

Because technological developments have enhanced employers' surveillance capabilities, electronic surveillance and monitoring devices are increasingly being used to keep tabs on employee conduct during the workday. Although these measures are primarily designed to combat employee theft, confidential information about an employee is also sometimes acquired.

Wiretapping and eavesdropping policies are generally regulated and, to some degree, prohibited by federal and state law. In liberal states such as Colorado, New York and Texas, it is perfectly legal for an individual to record his/her telephone or in-person conversation with another without first obtaining that other person's consent (since you need only one of the two parties' approval to tape). In such states, the recording may subsequently be used as evidence in a civil or criminal trial under proper circumstances (e.g., that the tape wasn't tampered with or altered and that the voices on the tape can be clearly identified).

Other states, however, are not permissive. California and Massachusetts, for example, forbid the interception of oral or wire communication unless both (or all) parties are advised and give their consent. These laws make it virtually impossible for employers to engage lawfully in surreptitious eavesdropping. Connecticut, for example, prohibits employers from operating any electronic surveillance device, including sound recording and closed circuit television cameras, in employee lounges, restrooms and locker rooms (but surveillance is *not* prohibited in work areas).

One Georgia company placed wiretaps on business telephones in certain stores. The court ruled that this was a violation under federal law and a violation of the employee's privacy rights under Georgia law. In another recent case, a supervisor monitoring the calls of one of its sales representatives overheard the sales representative say she was going to accept another employer's offer. Telling the employee what he had learned, the supervisor tried to dissuade her from leaving. The employee left anyway and sued the company for invasion of privacy. The court ruled that the employer had violated the law by listening to her personal calls, and awarded her damages.

Title III of the Omnibus Crime Control And Safe Streets Act. Those states which require that the other party be notified and consent to the taped telephone conversation, interview or interrogation, comply more closely with Title III of the Omnibus Crime Control and Safe Streets Act of 1968, the most important statute regulating the subject. This federal law prohibits deliberate and surreptitious eavesdropping, including the interception of employees' oral communications when uttered with an expectation that such communication is not subject to interception. This means, for example, that when employees speak confidentially in places where they can reasonably expect privacy (i.e., a bathroom), their employer cannot eavesdrop without violating the statute. Employers who fail to comply with this federal law are liable for actual and punitive damages and criminal liability for willful violations.

Counsel Comments: *Some companies maintain microphones between counter areas and a supervisor's office or instruct the office operator to listen in and monitor* *suspicious personal telephone calls by employees. In some situations, this is illegal and should be avoided. This kind of surveillance conflicts with Title III because the person eavesdropping or taping is not one of the two persons directly engaged in the conversation. However, if the conversation is between two employees on the job in a public area, both parties consent to the taping, and the employer has a genuine suspicion of wrongdoing, the act may be legal.*

A recent case illustrates the scope and limits of employee monitoring. An employer, accused of illegally eavesdropping, was sued for damages, even though the monitored conversation was purportedly business-related. Employees had previously been warned that the company monitored business calls. One day an employee received a call from a friend advising her that another job was available. When her company heard this, she was fired; whereupon the employee sued the ex-employer under federal law. The court rejected the company argument that the employee's knowledge of its monitoring policy constituted consent (since, arguably, the worker consented only to monitoring of business calls). Additionally, the court ruled that the company was required to hang up immediately when the employee received a personal call.

Despite this case, in certain instances "extension phone" monitoring (i.e., where microphones are placed over the customer service desk so a supervisor can get a better understanding of an employee's contacts with clients and the public, measure productivity, and help to detect non-business-related use of telephone resources) has been upheld as legal if it falls outside the scope of the federal statute or is considered exempt from this federal law.

For example, in one case, an employer installed a monitoring device to listen to conversations between customers and employees. An employee brought suit under federal law claiming illegal interception of her private conversations. The court ruled in favor of the employer, finding that the monitoring was done "for a legitimate business purpose" with the knowledge of the affected employees. Written notification of the monitoring program had been given to the employees, who were monitored for training purposes, and employees were required to sign waivers authorizing management to conduct surreptitious monitoring by use of electronic listening devices. The court was impressed by the fact that the employer only collected information needed for business purposes, established reasonable limits on the use of the data collected and refrained from monitoring private areas (i.e., restrooms, cafeteria, locker rooms or the employee's car).

Another recent case was ruled in favor of the employer. A supervisor used an extension phone to listen in on an employee he suspected of disclosing confidential information to a competitor. The court found the supervisor's conduct (which was spurred by a customer's tip) to be within the ordinary course of business and therefore exempt and legal under the language of the federal law. The court also found the employer to be open and above-board in its eavesdropping. All employees were informed of the policy when first hired, were given advance written notice of the monitoring, and no one protested the practice. Moreover, the policy served a valid business purpose.

Counsel Comments: *Although certain limited exceptions are set forth in Title III that allow an employer to eavesdrop on oral conversations or tap telephone conversations (e.g. where one of the parties consents), companies are advised to undertake an extensive analysis of the laws in their state before taking any action in this area. If the electronic surveillance law in their state imposes greater restrictions than Title III, you must comply with the requirements of both laws to be protected.*

Since lawyers representing companies in-house and in private firms have the ethical responsibility of obtaining the consent of all parties prior to recording a conversation, they should be reminded of this obligation on a continuing basis to avoid imposing liability both on themselves and their corporate clients. Also, photographing employees without their knowledge or consent for valid surveillance purposes has been held not to violate any federal or state laws regarding invasions of a worker's privacy rights. However, if the pictures are released to non-essential third parties and strongly suggest guilt which harms a person's reputation and is later proved to be untrue, the employee may have a valid cause of action for defamation.

Employee Testing

All forms of employee testing raise significant issues of potential violations of an employee's privacy rights. This includes honesty, psychological, and personality tests, genetic screening, substance abuse tests and polygraph examinations. This section will examine many of the problems involved and strategies that companies can use to act legally.

AIDS and Genetic Testing. Fear of AIDS is rampant in the workplace, but state legislatures and the courts are only beginning to define the rights of employees who have the disease. Before the enactment of the federal Americans With Disabilities Act, Section 504 of the Rehabilitation Act of 1973 prohibited businesses receiving federal money from discriminating against people afflicted with contagious diseases. Thus, firing an HIV-positive hospital worker would violate Section 504 of the act. In addition, most states have enacted laws protecting handicapped or disabled workers' rights of privacy and from on-the-job discrimination as long as they can perform their duties.

At present the law is not well settled in this area. AIDS testing of employees is mandated in some localities for food handlers, processors and waiters and most states, government agencies and the military mandate AIDS testing in blood donations. While civil liberties groups claim such tests unjustifiably discriminate and invade workers' rights of privacy, other groups argue that legislation should protect the safety of innocent members of society from exposure to the deadly AIDS virus.

The enactment of the ADA may significantly protect AIDS sufferers' privacy rights, since many pre-employment and on-the-job medical investigation practices and procedures that were once considered legal are now prohibited. For example, intrusions into a person's medical background and history are now substantially reduced. Application forms can no longer solicit answers to questions about whether the applicant is an individual with a disability, has a medical condition, or has ever been hospitalized or treated for a mental or emotional problem. Questions such as how many days was the applicant absent from other jobs and whether the applicant is currently taking medication are illegal. Pre-employment medical examinations cannot be conducted and employers are required to establish policies for staff and health providers regarding the disclosure and use of employee medical information.

Many employers are currently reviewing company handbooks and drafting statements protecting against the unnecessary dissemination of medical information, and are instituting policies requiring supervisors and health providers to consult with company lawyers before disclosing any medical information. Related problems that have emerged must be carefully addressed: for example, how can your company be sure that the results of any job-related medical tests will remain confidential so as to avoid charges of slander or libel and other invasions of privacy?

> **Counsel Comments:** *Due to the ADA and pertinent state laws, pre-hiring and on-the-job AIDS tests may not be legal. Since each case must be scrutinized on a factual basis, speak to a knowledgeable labor lawyer before implementing such tests.*

Even the issue of genetic testing is unsettled. Many major corporations are currently testing the relationship of inherited genetic traits to occupational disease to determine if there are certain predisposing risks to employees and job applicants. More and more companies are considering using such tests and the extent to which the ADA will curtail their use is now being studied by labor lawyers throughout the country.

Drug and Alcohol Testing. The sharp rise in company interest in drug testing has been fueled, in part, by high profile drug deaths. More companies are resorting to drug testing to identify drug users and reduce on-the-job accidents. Critics state that indiscriminate testing violates employees' rights of privacy, due process and freedom from unreasonable search and seizure. Proponents cite its success (e.g., the military's program has dramatically lowered drug use in the armed forces) and growing confidence in the reliability of current testing methods. Recent statistics reflect the magnitude of the problem within the applicant pool and existing workforce. For example:

- At least 20 million Americans use marijuana/hashish;
- At least six million Americans are cocaine users and 100 million are alcohol users;
- The typical recreational drug user in the workplace is three times as late as fellow employees and has 2.5 times as many absences of eight or more days;

- A recreational drug user is five times more likely to file a workers' compensation claim and is involved in accidents 3.6 times more frequently than other workers.

The following are some practical strategies, rules and guidelines for companies to consider and follow when implementing a drug or alcohol testing program.

Know the law: Some state and local governments have passed laws prohibiting testing of employees for drugs or alcohol. This includes a blanket prohibition in Florida and certain restrictions in San Francisco and Oregon. State law varies dramatically. For example, Utah generally permits employee testing with required procedural safeguards to insure that the testing is done in a reasonable and reliable manner with concern for an employee's rights of privacy. Connecticut only permits individual tests where a particular employee is suspected of being under the influence of drugs or alcohol and his impaired state adversely affects job performance. However, under Connecticut law, employees who test positive may not be fired if they consent to participate in and successfully complete a rehabilitation program.

Case decisions in other states such as California, New Jersey and Alaska seem to prohibit employee testing in positions that are not safety or security sensitive as a matter of public policy, particularly programs involving a large number of employees where there is no suspicion of individual wrongdoing. In New York, the State Division of Human Rights prohibits drug or alcohol testing of applicants before and after an offer of employment has been made unless the testing is based on a "bona fide occupational qualification."

> **Counsel Comments:** *Since the law differs so dramatically from state to state, is constantly changing, and may be even more stringent than the requirements of the Americans With Disabilities Act (discussed later in this section) it is critical that you obtain current advice from counsel before implementing any testing policy.*

Under current federal law, companies represented by unions cannot unilaterally implement a testing program without bargaining with the union over changes and conditions of employment. To do so would violate The National Labor Relations Act. However, the Supreme Court has upheld an employer's right to test employees for drugs and alcohol, rejecting a union's argument that testing is reasonable under the Fourth Amendment only when based upon individualized suspicion that an employee is impaired by drugs or alcohol on the job. In one case affecting railway employees, for example, the court ruled that the government's policy of testing all employees was important in assuring the safety of the railways and therefore outweighed the privacy rights of non-suspected workers en masse.

The Drug Free Workplace Act. The federal Drug Free Workplace Act of 1988, effective March 18, 1989, has had a major impact on federal contractors and grantees with federal contracts, requiring them to conduct anti-drug awareness programs and require workers to report any drug-related convictions as a condition of receiving federal funds. The law requires company-contractors ranging from weapons manufacturers to publishing companies and employee-grantees ranging from state governments to drug abuse treatment facilities to publish strict statements prohibiting drugs and educating employees on substance abuse. Employers must also report to the procuring agency any workers convicted of workplace-related drug activities and certify that they will not condone unlawful drug activity during the performance of the contract.

Under the Drug Free Workplace Act, to receive a federal contract for the procurement of any property or service in excess of $25,000 or for any employer or individual receiving any grants, regardless of the dollar amount, from the federal government, an employer must certify that it will provide a drug-free workplace. This includes publishing and distributing a statement advising employees that the unlawful manufacture, distribution, dispensation, possession or use of any controlled substance (including prescription drugs) is prohibited. The employer must institute a "drug-free awareness program" to inform employees about the dangers of drug abuse in the workplace, the employer's drug-free workplace policy, any drug counseling, rehabilitation, and employee assistance programs which are available and the penalties (e.g., discharge) that may be imposed upon employees for violations of the anti-drug policy.

Each employee working on the contract or grant must be given a copy of the above statement. The statement must indicate that the employee will abide by the terms of the statement and that he/she will notify the employer if convicted of a criminal drug statute within five days of conviction (employees must be hired pursuant to written contracts informing them of these requirements). The employer must then notify the contracting agency of such occurrence within ten days of receiving this notice. Contractors and grantees must make a "good-faith" effort to continue to maintain a drug-free workplace through implementation of the above.

Section 5152 (G)(b)(1) discusses penalties of suspension or termination from federal contracts for companies that violate the above conditions; these should be reviewed carefully. For example, each contract awarded by a federal agency is subject to the suspension of payments or termination of the contract if the agency determines that:

- The contractor made a false certification, failed to notify the agency within ten days of an employee's drug conviction, or failed to notify employees of the dangers of drug use (and/or failed to require them to sign a written contract to this effect).

Once notified of a problem, the contractor can defend his/her policies and actions in writing or at a hearing. However, if a final decision is entered against the contractor, it shall be ineligible for award of any contract by any federal agency and for participation in any future procurement by any federal agency, for a period specified in the decision, not to exceed five years.

> **Counsel Comments:** *Although the federal law creates a heightened drug-awareness policy, it does not mandate drug testing for company applicants or employees. Nor does the act explicitly sanction such testing as a way for a federal contractor to satisfy the requirements of the act. However, the existence of this law means that companies working for the federal government must conform to its more stringent guidelines rather than follow conflicting state laws.*
>
> *Also, be aware that the Department of Defense has issued regulations which require that a drug-free workplace clause be included in contracts with contractors involving access to classified information, and that certain drug tests become standard for workers involved in safety-sensitive positions. Although these regulations do not appear to relate directly to most companies, they may do so in the future.*

The Americans With Disabilities Act. Perhaps the most significant change affecting drug and alcohol testing involves the ADA. In reality, the ADA provides greater protections for individuals with disabilities than do many state laws, so all companies must reevaluate their policies.

The ADA specifically *excludes* from protection any employee or applicant who is *currently engaged* in the use of drugs. Although drug-testing processes are not specifically mentioned, the interpretive guidance to Section 1630.3 (a) through (c) states that "employers may discharge or deny employment to persons who illegally use drugs, on the basis of such use, without fear of being held liable for discrimination." Section 1630.16(b) allows employers to prohibit alcohol as well as illegal drug use at the workplace, and states that they may require that employees not be under the influence of alcohol or illegal drugs in the workplace, and may hold an employee who uses illegal drugs or is an alcoholic to the same qualification standards for employment or job performance as other employees.

However, an employer may not discriminate against an individual who is not currently engaged in illegal drug use but who has successfully completed a supervised drug rehabilitation program or is currently participating successfully in such a program.

> **Counsel Comments:** *Administration of drug tests is* not *considered to be a medical examination, so pre-hiring drug tests by employers do not violate the ADA's prohibition on medical examinations prior to an employment offer. In light of this, many companies are considering administering drug tests earlier in the applicant-screening process to eliminate drug users earlier in the process and save the company the expense of a post-hiring medical examination. Additionally, since the act neither prohibits nor encourages drug testing, employers probably have the right to conduct ongoing drug-testing programs with employees. Speak to competent labor counsel (and research the law in your state) for more details if applicable.*
>
> *Companies which administer pre-employment drug tests to applicants who test positive for drug use must be careful not to automatically disqualify them should the applicant apply for another chance of*

employment within a fixed period of time (such as six months thereafter). The reason is that such an individual may be deemed a "qualified individual with a disability" who may be able to prove successful completion of or who is in the midst of successfully participating in a rehabilitation program and is protectable under Section 104 of the ADA. Avoid inflexible drug policies with a fixed waiting period for future employment; rather, evaluate each case on its own merits.

Alcohol use and the ADA. The act makes a distinction between drug users and alcoholics. Individuals disabled by alcoholism are entitled to ADA protection. This includes applicants who would automatically not be considered for a job in the past as a result of testing positive for alcohol. Now, all employers with more than 25 employees must determine if that individual is capable of performing essential functions of the position offered with reasonable accommodation. Some experts have suggested that, in light of the inherent problems associated with pre-employment alcohol tests, employers should now consider eliminating such tests altogether.

Until enactment of the ADA the main federal law protecting handicapped individuals against discrimination was the Vocational Rehabilitation Act of 1973, which applied to government contractors and employers who received federal assistance. Today's numerous state and federal anti-discrimination laws, including the ADA, mean that all companies must follow strict procedures to insure that their treatment of alcoholic employees conforms to the law, since these workers are entitled to reasonable accommodation and protection from discrimination on the basis of their physical handicap of alcoholism. Employers may still prohibit the use of alcohol on the job and require that employees not be under the influence of alcohol when they report to work. Additionally, workers who behave or perform poorly or unsatisfactorily due to alcohol use may, like other workers, be fired or reprimanded. The ADA does not protect workers who drink on the job, or current abusers who cannot perform their jobs properly or who present a direct threat to the property or safety of others.

Reasonable accommodation of an alcoholic often consists of offering the employee rehabilitative assistance and allowing the opportunity to take sick leave for treatment before initiating disciplinary action. To be safe, even if the employee refuses treatment, documentation must show that repeated unsatisfactory performance took place before a termination decision is made.

In one recent case, for example, a company was found liable for not offering leave without pay for a *second* treatment in a rehabilitation program. The judge commented that one chance is not enough, since relapse is predictable in the treatment of alcoholics. In another case, the judge outlined a series of steps an employer must take to avoid violating the law. His guidelines are instructive:

- Offer counseling.
- If the employee refuses, offer a firm choice between treatment and discipline. If the employee chooses treatment, the employer cannot take any detrimental action during a bona fide rehabilitation program.
- In case of relapse, automatic termination is not appropriate, but some discipline short of discharge may be imposed.
- Before termination, determine if retention of the worker would impose an undue hardship on the company. If removal is the only feasible option, the company must still evaluate whether the alcoholic condition caused poor performance; if so, the company should counsel and offer leave without pay first.

Counsel Comments: *An employee assistance program can help your company prove that it is fulfilling its legal requirement of reasonable accommodation. Such programs can protect employers from discrimination complaints and should be implemented whenever possible. In some states, notably New York and Michigan, state laws require that an employer's group health plan include alcohol rehabilitation programs.*

Information pertaining to an employee's participation in a rehabilitative assistance program must be carefully protected to avoid violating a person's privacy rights. Above all, employers must be aware of how state and local laws, in addition to federal law, apply to their activities. Dealing with alcohol problems is difficult and complicated for any employer; yet, they must act professionally and sympathetically to avoid legal expo-

sure. To that end, documenting the problem and the help offered is essential in defending against all charges of disability discrimination and breach of an alcoholic's privacy rights.

Does the odor of alcohol prove an employee is drunk? One supervisor caught a whiff of what he thought was alcohol coming from a worker arriving at work. Telling the person, "You're drunk," he ordered the worker home. The next day the employee returned but was given a stern lecture on the dangers of alcoholism and was handed a copy of a reprimand which had been placed in his personnel files. The employee protested the reprimand through his union and sought its removal from his file. When the company refused, his union brought an arbitration grievance. At the hearing, he claimed that the supervisor jumped to a quick and erroneous conclusion on the day he staggered into work: instead of being drunk, he was actually feeling faint from having taken a strong medication which his doctor had prescribed for bursitis. He claimed the supervisor should have taken into account that he never was drunk on-the-job in the past and always performed his work carefully and competently.

The supervisor testified that the worker said nothing about being ill but definitely came to work with the smell of booze on his breath. However, the arbitrator ruled that the company must remove the reprimand. Evidence furnished by the worker's doctor showed that the medication was sufficiently potent to cause the employee to be sick and it was probable that his behavior was produced by the drugs. Thus, the arbitrator ruled, being sick is not a proper basis for a reprimand. He also stated that this was not a management problem that could or should be solved by discipline. Rather, the employee should have been referred to the company doctor, who had access to the employee's physician.

Counsel Comments: *Arbitrators have been considering an increasing number of alcohol and drug cases concerning use, possession or sale of drugs on or off the job; employer discipline or discharge methods have come under increased scrutiny. In those cases where company policies are unambiguous, consistently communicated and enforced, arbitrators generally have upheld disciplinary action for drug or alcohol involvement. But arbitrators have found discharge too severe a penalty for marijuana possession or use on company property, if the company had less severe rules for alcohol. In drug cases concerning off-premises situations, arbitrators are more likely to revoke discipline, especially if there is no connection between the activity and workplace performance.*

Typically, arbitrators consider the following factors when deciding any drug or alcohol related matter:

1. Whether possession or sale is involved;

2. The type of drug used;

3. If the alcohol or drug-related conduct or sale occurred on company premises;

4. The history of drug or alcohol use;

5. The impact on the reputation of the employer; and

6. The effect on the orderly operation of the employer's business.

Counsel Comments: *After considering test objectives (to screen applicants using drugs, to test employees suspected of using drugs/alcohol, etc.) companies should adopt a plan and record it in work rules, policy manuals, employment contracts, and/or collective bargaining agreements. This may reduce perceived privacy rights of employees and document company policy. For example, your manual might outline the steps management will take if they suspect that an employee is impaired on-the-job, including immediate testing, how the test will be administered and the consequences flowing from a positive result (such as immediate discharge with no severance or other benefits). If your policy is clearly stated, disseminated to all employees and is administered in a consistent, even-handed manner, the possibility of an employee challenge may decrease. However, failure to apply stated rules and regulations uniformly may result in charges of discrimination.*

Before adopting a formal plan, consider education and rehabilitation alternatives as well as all legal obligations.

Determine the scope of the testing program's coverage, which employees or applicants will be tested, under what conditions and the selection of testing facilities.

Inform workers that employees are not permitted to come to work under the influence of alcohol or drugs, even when consumed off the company's premises. Develop rules to cover off-premises conduct but be aware that invasion of privacy claims rise when off-premises conduct is monitored.

OSHA requires companies to take affirmative steps when alcohol or on-the-job drug use is suspected. Inform employees that testing for substance abuse may be required to avoid OSHA penalties for employer negligence.

Since random drug testing may create a legal problem, the same holds true for periodic unannounced searches of employee lockers, pat-down searches of individual employees, and use of undercover personnel to secure information regarding alcohol or substance abuse. Avoid conducting such searches until you have spoken to counsel.

Test Results

Companies must be careful of how they test. One worker filed a lawsuit in Louisiana after he was discharged for testing positive for marijuana. The main thrust of his lawsuit was that he had suffered great emotional distress when a company representative was required to stand by and watch as he urinated to provide a sample. He also alleged invasion of privacy under Louisiana law, wrongful discharge, intentional infliction of emotional distress and defamation. The company argued that having a supervisor stand by was the only way to insure that the test was not faked. However, the worker testified that he was taunted and insulted by the supervisor while taking the test. The jury agreed and awarded him $125,000, which was upheld on appeal based on the theory of negligent infliction of emotional distress.

Companies must also treat test results carefully and handle the results of drug/alcohol tests as they would any other confidential personnel information. Unwarranted disclosure of this information, even within your company, could result in expensive, time-consuming litigation for breach of privacy rights, including defamation, so be careful that the test results are not disclosed to non-essential third parties.

Counsel Comments: *Establish a separate employee file for testing information and results to minimize disclosure and safeguard employee privacy. Choose correct specimen collection procedures which balance privacy with authenticity. If possible, avoid direct observations of employee urination. A suitable alternative might be, for example, to take the temperature of the specimen immediately after it is provided, since this makes substitution difficult. Outline specimen identification procedures and establish a specific chain of custody to insure accurate testing. Understand the scientific ways the test could produce an erroneous result.*

Be aware that a termination based on a positive test which later proves inaccurate can lead to a multitude of legal causes of action, including wrongful discharge, slander and invasion of privacy. Thus, be sure to hire a reputable testing company, preferably one that carries an "errors and omissions" policy or other insurance protecting your firm from false test results.

Workplace Smoking

Most companies are aware of the growing number of federal, state and municipal regulations restricting an employee's right to smoke in the workplace. Coupled with Occupational Safety & Health Administration (OSHA) requirements to insure safety in many plants and warehouses, this is creating an additional need for all companies to reevaluate their smoking policies and implement either formal or voluntary rules, depending upon local laws.

Workplace regulations of smoking are divided into two categories: bans on smokers, under which employees are not permitted to smoke at any time (either on or off the job); and regulations of smoking, under which employees are forbidden from smoking in various parts or all of the workplace.

In December 1986, the United States Government concluded that environmental or secondary smoke posed a threat to non-smokers and ruled that federal agenices must take reasonable steps to permit smoking only in expressly designated areas. This federal legislation follows a national trend (passed in hundreds of localities and a majority of states) recognizing the rights of non-smokers to work in a smoke-free environment. Thus, knowing the law in the particular state, city and town where your company is located is critical. Additionally, many companies in states that do have formal laws are implementing informal policies to satisfy the requests and needs of their personnel.

> **Counsel Comments:** *Employers may be unable to unilaterally set a workplace smoking policy when employees are governed by contract because to do so would risk a charge of an unfair labor practice. Thus, where a collective bargaining agreement is in place, consult your labor unions before implementing any smoking policy.*

It is well established that employers have a common law obligation to provide a safe workplace for their employees. Under OSHA, management has the right to designate rules pertaining to work assignments to insure an employee's health and safety. Some companies, prompted by the discovery that materials used in their plants could be especially hazardous to smokers, are announcing that workers can be discharged unless they stop smoking in warehouses and factories. Others are refusing to hire smokers. One company introduced an absolute ban on smoking on-the-job after the company discovered that mineral fibers used in some if its acoustical-products plants could have adverse health effects on both smokers and non-smokers. To date, the policy has not been challenged by workers at the plant.

Thus, consider imposing tougher standards to comply with OSHA regulations because the failure *not* to impose a smoking ban may be grounds for a lawsuit against your company. For example, the Washington State Court of Appeals permitted a woman to sue her employer for negligence when she developed pulmonary disease following exposure to a co-worker's cigarette smoke. In another case, a female worker was awarded $20,000 in disability pay because she developed asthmatic bronchitis after being transferred to an office with several smokers. The court also ruled that unless the employer transferred her to a smoke-free office, she would be eligible for disability retirement benefits of $500 per month.

The following strategies may help reduce problems in this area:

1. **Speak to labor counsel before deciding to terminate or refusing to hire workers on the basis of smoking; such a decision may have serious legal consequences.** The law differs on a case-by-case and state-by-state basis. If you wish to adopt a policy that prohibits smoking on the job, avoid extending it beyond the workplace. To do so can create enforceability problems and may violate both an individual's right to privacy and state law. In 28 states, laws have recently been enacted to prevent employers (who typically justify such practices to keep the lid on rising health insurance costs) from refusing to hire or retain smokers. These states include Arizona, Connecticut, Colorado, Illinois, Indiana, Kentucky, Louisiana, Maine, Mississippi, Nevada, New Hampshire, New Jersey, New Mexico, North Dakota, Rhode Island, South Carolina, South Dakota, Tennessee, and Virginia. Some have gone even further by prohibiting employers from regulating employees' use of any "lawful product" or participation in any "lawful activity" during non-work hours. (Note: Consult the section "Engaging In Legal Activities Off Premises and After Working Hours" in Chapter 4 for more details.)

2. **Issue a formal written company policy when instituting on-the-job smoking bans.** This can reduce misunderstandings and confusion. Be sure to apply the policy in a consistent and uniform way to avoid discrimination claims. For example, while it may not be discriminatory to single out and discharge workers who violate company smoking rules, it is certainly discriminatory to fire female smokers but not male smokers who commit the same improprieties.

3. **Think twice before imposing a total on-the-job smoking ban.** Unreasonable smoking restrictions, such as an absolute ban on smoking throughout the premises, may lead to potential lawsuits on many different legal grounds. In addition to claims of violations of an individual's right to privacy, a total ban may create a possible "disparate impact" discrimination charge, since African-Americans and other minorities tend to smoke in greater numbers than their white counterparts and may be unduly affected by such a policy. Any policy must draw a rational connection between the non-smoking ban and on-the-job performance

(which is often hard to prove) to be legal. (Note: On the other hand, some restriction of on-the-job smoking is now required in light of the ADA's requirement for employers to reasonably accommodate employees who suffer from lung disorders and related medical problems.)

4. **Be responsive to non-smokers' complaints and seek to properly accommodate their needs.** All grievances should be considered and acted upon promptly. By separating smokers from non-smokers, rearranging desks, switching office assignments, moving non-smokers closer to windows or air vents, and erecting partitions, as well as considering other practical solutions, non-smokers may be reasonably accommodated without penalizing or affecting smokers. All such decisions should be made carefully on a case-by-case basis. A sympathetic management that understands and follows the needs of its workplace can go a long way toward protecting the company against formal litigation, OSHA investigations, union intervention or EEOC involvement.

5. **Finally, be sure that your company's policy complies with state law and local ordinances and understand the effects of such law before implementing any formal policy in this area.**

Constitutional Protections

Employers risk potential lawsuits based upon invasion of privacy, intentional infliction of emotional distress and wrongful discharge, among other causes of action, for violations stemming from unlawful interference into an employee's personal relationships and other off-duty conduct. This section will examine areas such as employers' attempts to regulate free speech, personal appearance, relationships with co-workers, and related subjects typically protected by the U. S. Constitution.

Free Speech. Beginning in the late 1960s, the United States Supreme Court ruled that government employees could not be fired in retaliation for the workers' exercise of free speech. In one leading case a teacher was fired for sending a letter to a local newspaper criticizing the school board. While acknowledging the government's need to conduct business efficiently, the court balanced the perceived harm to both parties and concluded that the basic right of free speech was more important (especially if government business was not disrupted). This and other cases came to allow public sector employees to speak out freely upon matters of public concern without fear of retaliatory dismissal. Later cases made a distinction in situations where government employees spoke out about matters of private interest (such as office morale, transfer policies within a particular department and creation of grievance committees) and ruled that the U. S. Constitution does not protect employees from dismissal on the basis of insubordination in these areas.

The notion of free speech, privacy, freedom from discharge as a result of whistleblowing and related constitutional rights has now been expanded to private employees, particularly in states which have enacted broad civil rights laws. Are there limits on freedom of expression? Can companies restrict employees' political affiliations? When does something stop being a political issue and become a rights issue? In many states, notably New Jersey, Connecticut and Massachusetts, a private employer cannot discipline, fail to promote or fire an employee because the company does not agree with the employee's comments on matters of public concern. Generally, even though the employer has the right to discharge employees at-will without cause or notice, the enactment of special civil rights laws in these and other states protects workers who speak out freely when this activity does not substantially or materially interfere with the employee's bona fide job performance or the parties' working relationship. In states having such laws, companies are liable for damages caused by discipline or discharge, including costs of bringing the lawsuit.

Can a company punish an employee for distributing inflammatory flyers? While walking through the employee parking lot one day, a supervisor spotted a worker handing out flyers to her co-workers as they entered the building. "Our employer," the circular read, "is firing people and forcing the rest of us to work faster to meet unfair quotas. We're taking terrible safety risks. There will be a rally downtown on Saturday to fight wage cuts and unfair production rates."

When the employee was suspended for causing disruption, she complained to the National Labor Relations Board, charging the company with an unfair labor practice. At the hearing she commented that she was communicating with co-workers on job-related matters—an activity protected by the labor laws. She also proved that she had distributed the flyers before the workday began and that her actions caused no disruption in normal company activity. Company counsel responded that the employer was responsible for maintaining safety and order at the workplace and that the employee's message was inflammatory and distributed on company property. Additionally, since her flyers lied about the company's actions and plans, they had the right to discipline her as a disloyal employee.

The NLRB ordered the company to reinstate the militant employee with backpay. Despite some hard language and misleading statements, the NLRB found that the flyer contained no statements encouraging disruption at the workplace, and there was no proof that the employee distributed it with a malicious intent to damage the company. Thus her efforts, though annoying to the employer, were a lawful organizing activity in connection with working conditions.

> **Counsel Comments:** *On the other hand, decisions made by the courts and the NLRB have made it plain that there is no legal protection for activities that are (1) unrelated to working conditions, (2) flagrantly disloyal, (3) damaging to the employer's property or reputation, or (4) materially disruptive.*
>
> *Employers should not take formal action against an employee without first researching the law of your state and speaking to counsel regarding the particular facts of each matter. Some companies overcome problems by proving the reason for a discharge was a result of legitimate business criteria such as poor performance and not bias. Avoid enunciating that the reason for discharge or discipline was annoyance with a worker's protest or comments on matters of public concern if you can demonstrate other "traditional" reasons for the action taken.*

Voting Rights. A majority of states have laws that prohibit employers from influencing how their employees vote. In some states (e.g., California, Louisiana and Ohio) private employers may not influence the political activities, affiliations or beliefs of their employees. New Mexico and South Carolina laws, for example, prohibit employers from discharging employees because of their political beliefs. State statutes differ markedly; thus never take action without first researching your state's appropriate law.

Rights Of Due Process. Generally, private employers do not have to give a hearing to employees accused of wrongdoing. However, if such a promise or right is contained in the company's policy handbook, written rules or procedures, or has been extended to others in the past, a company may have a legal obligation to allow an employee to grieve company action at an internal hearing.

> **Counsel Comments:** *The best way to overcome liability is to avoid making promises or giving such rights to employees in the first place. If promises have been given, be sure that they are followed accurately and uniformly to avoid charges of breach of contract or discrimination. For example, if a male employee was allowed to appeal a firing decision before a committee, be sure the same option is offered to a fired female worker.*

Asserting Union Rights. The National Labor Relations Act prohibits the firing of an employee because of his or her involvement in any union activity, because of filing charges, or because of testifying pursuant to the act. However, can a company fire a supervisor for attending union meetings? In one case a supervisor filed a complaint with the NLRB charging the company with unfair labor practices. He claimed he was treated unfairly when he was fired shortly after attending a number of union meetings, lending his support on behalf of the rank and file. The court ruled that at the time he attended the union meetings, the individual was part of management and his primary loyalty should have been to the company. The NLRB concluded that the company's action was legal since the law which protects employees engaged in organizational activities does not apply to supervisors. (Note: Should a supervisor be discharged for taking part in a union activity, his/her disloyalty may be used to bar that person from returning to employment.)

The law also protects employees who band together to protest wages, hours or unsafe working conditions. For example, under OSHA, if a group of non-union employees complain about contaminated drinking water, or about failure to receive minimum wages or overtime pay, your company may be prohibited from firing them under relevant state law.

Off-Duty Conduct. Attempts to regulate personal relationships and off-duty conduct of employees may subject employers to legal exposure. Disciplinary action in response to off-duty behavior that has no direct relationship to the workplace should be avoided or kept to a minimum. To protect themselves in this area, employers must:

(1) demonstrate a legitimate business need; (2) communicate reasonable policies in company handbooks, memos or other written documents; and (3) warn employees as to what constitutes objectionable conduct and the penalties for committing violations of stated company policy. Certainly, at a minimum, the regulations or policies enunciated must comply with your state's civil rights laws, must be consistent with other company policies, and cannot violate discrimination statutes in the process.

Does management have the right to actively enforce a non-fraternization rule aimed at curbing interoffice romances? One supervisor who was fired commenced a breach of contract action against a former employer. Apparently, the supervisor had given his live-in lover a promotion which placed her above several employees with more seniority, even though the company had an unwritten, traditional rule forbidding social relationships between management and lower-echelon employees. When questioned by the home office, the supervisor admitted that he and the co-worker were lovers; citing the non-fraternization rule, the company abruptly terminated him. He took the company to court and argued that his employment contract brought with it the company's implied covenant of good faith and fair dealing. He also stated that the non-fraternization rule was unfair, unreasonable and selectively enforced.

The company responded that its non-fraternization rule became reasonable and necessary after the company discovered that attachments between supervisory employees and their subordinates led to accusations of favoritism, which had a negative effect on morale. The company also argued that since the employee had no written contract guaranteeing job security, he could be fired at any time for any or no reason. The California Court of Appeals found that the company was legitimately concerned with appearances of favoritism, possible claims of sexual harassment, and employee dissension caused by romantic relationships. Given his actions, the terminated supervisor did not make a strong case that the company failed to act in good faith toward him.

Counsel Comments: *Other courts have similarly upheld the dismissal of employees romantically involved with co-workers. A Wisconsin court ruled that there were no constitutional or statutory rights barring such a dismissal. The court upheld an employer's decision to fire an employee whose relationship with a co-worker had created insubordination. Similarly, a U.S. District Court found no violation of public policy in dismissing an employee for his relationship with a subordinate. In another case, termination because of marriage to the employee of a competitor was found not to violate public policy and a terminated worker's abusive discharge lawsuit was rejected.*

Certainly, the chances of your company prevailing in this area are enhanced when employees are advised of a policy in writing and given advance warning of the possible consequences. A policy with a legitimate rationale, and applied uniformly, stands a better chance of a favorable court ruling.

For off-the-job *illegal* conduct, a company typically has the right to fire a worker if the illegal conduct harms the employer's reputation or has a negative impact on job performance. A more prudent course of action, however, may be to suspend the worker without pay pending a conviction on the criminal charges, just to be safe.

The law is not so clear regarding attempts to regulate *legal* off-the-job behavior. Some cases have given employers the right to bar employees from cohabiting with persons who work for a competitor. In one such case, a court upheld a company's written policy which stated that "The Company will not continue the employment of any person who lives in the immediate household of a person employed by a competitor." But in another case in a different state, an employer's rule prohibiting workers from dating employees of a competitor was found to be illegal.

Counsel Comments: *Before taking any action in this area, investigate the matter fully. Give the individual accused of a company policy violation the opportunity to explain the facts or to offer mitigating reasons justifying his/her acts or conduct. The employee's position in the company, the kind of acts committed, possible damage to the employer's reputation (an important concern if the company is located in a small community) and the* *justification to enforce such a policy are all factors that should be considered before making any final decision. Consult with counsel and research the application of your state's laws before making any decision.*

When discussing the matter with the individual involved, be sure to handle the investigation correctly to avoid potential problems associated with lawyer/client privilege. During any investigation, when an employee makes it clear that he/she is personally consulting a company lawyer, and the lawyer accepts the communication on that basis, the employee may be able to invoke the attorney-client privilege. Where there is a possible conflict of interest with the employer, house counsel should instruct the employee to seek outside legal advice to avoid problems with confidentiality and related breaches.

No Solicitation Or Distribution Rules. Many companies prohibit employees from soliciting or distributing literature or other items. Typically, such policies are legal provided the company enunciates the policy in writing and applies it consistently. One company handbook states its policy as follows:

"To prevent disruptions of Company business and harassment of Company personnel, Employees may not:

- Engage in soliciting donations or contributions;
- Sell chances, raffle tickets, services, or merchandise;
- Distribute merchandise or literature of any kind on company property during working hours. This includes soliciting or distributing literature to non-employees or visitors at any time.

"Under no circumstances may non-employees be allowed to distribute literature or solicit employees on company premises. Breaking any of these rules is considered serious misconduct and may be grounds for immediate discharge."

Counsel Comments: *A few companies allow employees to solicit or distribute literature during "non-working" hours—e.g., those periods, such as mealtimes, when they are not engaged in performing their work tasks and are away from designated working areas. In addition, you may wish to consider permitting certain select activities such as U.S. Savings Bonds or blood drives.*

Personal Appearance. Some companies prescribe standards in dress and personal appearance. At times, certain dress and personal appearance (e.g., no long hair) codes have been attacked as being either discriminatory or as violating a person's rights of privacy. Must an employee alter her appearance at her employer's request? One worker dyed her hair purple. She was given one week to change her hair color. When she rejected the boss's order, she was fired. The company was so incensed that it opposed her claim for unemployment compensation. At a hearing, it stated that her job involved dealing with customers, many of whom were revolted by her unconventional hair coloring. Keeping her aboard would have resulted in loss of business. Also, the company held that it was misconduct and insubordination for the worker to refuse its reasonable request that she drop her eccentric hair style.

The worker defended her position by stating that the company had no right to dictate her personal appearance and that there was no evidence that customers complained about her purple hair. She stated that since several customers complimented her for the new appearance, she was fired without good cause.

The New Mexico Supreme Court held that there was no evidence that the color of the worker's hair significantly affected the employer's business or caused customer complaints. "We do not question the employer's right to establish a grooming code for its employees, to revise its rules in response to unanticipated situations, and to make its hiring and firing decisions in conformity with this policy. However...it is possible for an employee to have been *properly* discharged without having acted in a manner as would justify a denial of unemployment benefits." But in another case, the opposite decision was reached. A Pennsylvania court ruled that an employee's refusal to report back to work was for good cause when the employer demanded he shave his beard. The court found no evidence supporting the employer's contention that a requested alteration in appearance was essential to performance of duties other than the employer's vague assertion that the employee's "modish" appearance might affect business.

In many situations, arbitrators and judges will uphold a company's personal appearance policy provided it is reasonable and justifiable. For example, requiring firefighters to be clean shaven has been upheld in some counties. However, one company's no-beard policy was held to be racially discriminatory. One worker, a bearded black man, impressed his interviewer and was hired. However, soon after he commenced working, he was summoned to the personnel office and notified that he would have to shave his beard. After being told about the company's no-beard policy, the worker explained that he wore the beard because he suffered from a skin condition peculiar to many black males which made him unable to shave. The company told him it made no exceptions and the man was eventually fired. He then filed a race discrimination charge with the federal Equal Employment Opportunity Commission. At the trial, the EEOC based its case largely on the evidence furnished by a dermatologist who testified that the worker suffered from pseudofolliculitis barbae (PFB), a skin disorder affecting almost half of all black males. The symptoms of PFB—skin irritation and scarring—are brought on by shaving, and in severe cases PFB sufferers must completely abstain from shaving. The dermatologist testified that to impose a shaving requirement on a black male employee who suffers from this condition is racially discriminatory.

The company responded that the no-beard policy had been enacted to maintain good relations with customers, and that the EEOC dermatologist relied too heavily on military studies. However, the company lost. The U.S. Court of Appeals held that the EEOC's evidence makes clear that the company's no-beard policy, as strictly enforced, had a discriminatory impact on black males. PFB prevents a sizeable segment of the black male population from appearing clean-shaven, but does not similarly affect white males. Thus, the company's policy, which made no exceptions for black males who medically are unable to shave because of a valid skin disorder, effectively operated to exclude those black males from employment. (Note: The court noted that the mere fact that a black male employee suffers from PFB is not sufficient to exempt him from the no-beard policy; only those who suffer greatly and cannot shave are protected.)

Can you bar male employees from wearing facial jewelry such as large earrings? In one case a court found that such a policy was not illegal since sex discrimination law prohibits only those discriminations which afford significant employment opportunities to one sex in favor of the other."The federal statute was never intended to prohibit sex-based distinctions inherent in a private employer's personal grooming code for employees which do not have a significant effect on employment and which can be changed easily in the workplace." Thus, the court ruled that the male employee could not establish impermissible sex discrimination unless every difference in dress or grooming requirements for men and women under an employer's rules was discriminatory.

Counsel Comments: *Good grooming regulations reflect a company's policy in highly competitive business environments.* Reasonable *requirements in furtherance of that policy are one aspect of managerial responsibility and may not constitute an invasion of a person's privacy if challenged, particularly if the company disseminated written rules advising workers of the consequences flowing from violations of such policies.*

One company writes in its handbook:

"Your personal appearance and hygiene are important to you and the Company. Always dress in a manner befitting your job, with due consideration to the needs of the Company, your fellow Employees, and your own safety."

Since the law varies by state and depends on each set of facts, do not impose personal appearance and dress standards without first obtaining counsel's blessing. While employers typically possess protection for dress and grooming codes, be careful that your company is not committing sex or sexual orientation discrimination in the process. For example, if a job applicant wearing an earring is rejected because the interviewer believes the applicant is gay, the applicant might have recourse in many states and cities, such as New York, which prohibits discrimination based on sexual orientation.

Private Phone Numbers. Typically, it is not an invasion of privacy for an employer to demand an employee's phone number, even if that number is unlisted since employees can be required to be accessible by telephone when away from work. In one case, an arbitrator upheld a company which suspended an employee for refusing to accept telephone calls directed to him at a vacation resort while he was on vacation.

Identification Cards. Does management have a right to compel its employees to carry identification cards? Although some workers have refused to do so, considering such a policy to be an infringement of a worker's right to privacy (particularly when the cards contain a worker's Social Security number and birth date for everyone to see), arbitrators have ruled that an I.D. card-policy can be necessary as a legitimate business interest when it is reasonably designed to meet the employer's needs for security and administrative purposes. In fact, the right to require employees to possess I.D. cards bearing confidential data does not have to be negotiated with a union since this is a right that a company generally possesses inherently. However, a distinction may be made if the company requires employees to wear their surnames on their outer clothing. Ruling against such a policy, an arbitrator in one case said, "The surname display constantly evidences itself even in those situations where personal identification is not required. It exposes the employee to those more dangerous situations when, in all common sense, the employee would not proffer his/her I.D. card."

Restroom Visits. Workers generally do not have rights of privacy to stay in restrooms for extended, unreasonable periods of time, particularly after being warned of such excessive respites and when the restroom visits are *not* medically related. However, if a medical condition justifies numerous trips to the bathroom (not for smoking or chatting), it may be wise to avoid disciplining or terminating a worker without further investigation and careful planning in light of the increased protections and reasonable accommodation requirements afforded to covered employees under the ADA.

Informants. Are company policies designed to encourage workers to inform on drug or alcohol abusers legal? One company strengthened its rules-of-conduct policy by declaring it to be an employee's duty to "report hazardous conditions which are caused by the use or possession of intoxicants, drugs or narcotics...If desired, the source of such information will be treated confidentially." The new rule sent a protesting union running to the National Labor Relations Board, which referred the matter to arbitration. At the hearing the union's representative stated that enforcement of rules against drug abuse was solely management's burden and to place such responsibility on employees would create an unfair "police state" atmosphere. The rule would also encourage unscrupulous employees to harass one another.

The company explained that the new rule was created in response to reports from front-line supervisors of the need to combat growing drug problems among the workers and the need to receive all the feedback it could get from employees to help in monitoring the safety of the work environment. To encourage employee cooperation, the company explained that it was willing to keep confidential any information supplied.

The NLRB ruled that the "informer" rule was valid. After noting that both management and the union agreed on the need to combat drug abuse, the referee decided that the basic premise of a drug-free atmosphere was vital and involved no violations of privacy.

> **Counsel Comments:** *Note, however, that an employee is under no ordinary obligation to divulge information on a co-worker.*

DEFAMATION AND RELATED CONCERNS

A defamatory statement arises when a communication (either oral or in writing) is made about someone which tends to so harm that person's reputation as to lower him or her in the estimation of the community or to deter others from associating or dealing with him/her. Defamatory statements in written form constitute libel; defamatory statements in oral form constitute slander. Defamation occurs when the statement is false, communicated to a third party, and no special privilege exists. Common on-the-job problems occurring in this area typically arise when employees inadvertently make disparaging remarks about competitors or when a company talks poorly about one of its employees.

Business Defamation

Often, during a sales presentation, a well-meaning salesperson will inadvertently make disparaging remarks about the competition. This type of sales tactic can leave your company wide open for a business defamation lawsuit. Just as individuals can sue each other for slanderous or libelous statements, a competing business can take your company to court for making statements damaging to its business reputation. Salespeople frequently compare the qualities and characteristics of their product or service with a competitor's during the sales presentation. Such comparisons are often inaccurate or misleading and sometimes tend to slander a company's business reputation and distort or disparage its products. Very definite rules govern what an employee can and cannot say about the competition. It is far better to restrain your staff and even lose an account or two than risk the much higher costs of having to defend your company in court. For example, suppose an employee has a plan for winning some of the competition's business and circulates among a number of customers a letter that, by-the-way, points out failures in the competition's products and services. This is fertile ground for a business defamation lawsuit.

Suppose a group of salespeople leave their company to form a competing partnership and many of their old customers follow. In an attempt to win them back, employees from the original company tell customers things like: the new company's equipment is faulty, it delivers substandard products, it bills irregularly and cheats its customers. As it comes out in court, these remarks are false, not to mention damaging. The final cost to the original company will be far higher than just the loss of a few clients.

Granted, these are both extreme examples, but similar real-life situations did make it to court with significant repercussions. In the first case, the company was forced to pay over $100,000 in damages for circulating the letter. In the second case, involving milk distributors, the original company paid a $25,000 defamation settlement, and probably $50,000 more in legal fees. Hundreds of companies have been sued by competitors for making slanderous statements. Economic injuries, including proof of lost contracts, employment, and sales have been redressed by legal actions for product disparagement, unfair competition, and trade defamation. In addition to private lawsuits, the Federal Trade Commission is empowered to impose a cease and desist order or injunction on companies that engage in unfair or deceptive trade practices through their employees. But that's not all. When a statement disparages the quality of a person's product and, at the same time, implies that the person is dishonest, fraudulent, or incompetent (thus affecting the individual's personal reputation), a private lawsuit for defamation may also be brought.

The following forms of wrongs fall under the heading of business defamation:

Business Slander: This arises when an unfair and untrue oral statement is made about a competitor. The statement becomes actionable when it is communicated to a third party and can be interpreted as either damaging the competitor's business reputation or the personal reputation of an individual in that business. Such a statement might call into question the honesty, skill, fitness, ethical standards, or financial capacity of the company or an employee.

Business Libel: This is the written form (i.e., advertising, product brochures, and letters sent to customers). Here, too, it is possible to damage reputations through statements that reflect on the conduct, management, or financial condition of the business.

Product Disparagement: This occurs when false or deceptive comparisons or distorted claims are made concerning a competitor's product, services, or property.

Unfair Competition: Injury to a business may also result from statements about your own product or service rather than a competitor's. Examples are false advertising of one's product, misrepresenting the qualities or characteristics of the product, or engaging in a related unfair or deceptive trade practice (regulated under the Federal Trade Commission Act). Unfair competition can arise in a variety of forms, including unlawful statements contained in newspaper or periodical advertisements, radio or TV commercials, direct mail pieces, advertising or sales brochures, catalogs, price lists, and "sales talk."

Counsel Comments: *Whether slanderous sales call comments are malicious or innocent in intent, they are illegal. It pays to let your employees know the rules about what they can and cannot say about a competitor and a competitor's product during the sales pitch. The following recommendations can help protect your company:*

1. Review your correspondence and promotional material before distribution. This will reduce the possibility that defamatory material is inadvertently distributed by your sales force. Companies often commit trade libel through their employees by disseminating false information that staff then pass along, intentionally or not, to their customers. It is a good idea for the sales manager to review all sales material before distribution by your employees. If any questions arise regarding accuracy, immediately consult with the appropriate department, such as advertising or legal.

2. Instruct employees to avoid repeating unconfirmed trade gossip, particularly about the financial condition of a competitor (i.e., that the competitor has discontinued its operations, is financially unstable or is going bankrupt). The law treats these statements as defamatory per se which means that a company or defamed individual does not have to prove actual damages to successfully recover a verdict. Money can be recovered against your company simply because the statement is untrue.

3. Tell employees to avoid statements that may be interpreted as impairing the reputation of a business or individual (i.e., that a principal in the competitor's business is incompetent, of poor moral character, unreliable or dishonest).

4. Insure that the staff avoids making unfair or inaccurate comparisons about a competitor's product. The law generally states that the mere "puffing" (sales talk) or offering of an opinion about your product or service which claims superiority over a competitor's product is not a disparagement as long as the comparison attempts primarily to enhance the quality of your product without being unfairly critical of the competitor's. But when you make a statement or pass along untrue or misleading information which influences a person not to buy, that's unlawful.

5. Advise employees of their obligation not to make slanderous statements or defamatory writings and conduct periodic training sessions to educate them in this area. In certain cases, companies were deemed not to be liable for the slanderous utterances of an employee acting within the scope of his/her employment unless it affirmatively appears that the employee was expressly directed or authorized to slander the plaintiff.

Employee Defamation

With respect to defamation committed in the workplace, courts have recognized valid causes of action by plaintiffs who suffered damage to their reputations from statements in discharge letters, office petitions, warning letters, performance evaluations, statements in management or employee meetings, and internal security meetings. Companies typically defend themselves in such actions by arguing that the statements communicated about the employee were true, or they had a qualified privilege to say such things, thereby insulating the company from prosecution. For example, a supervisor writes a memo stating that he had lost confidence in a particular employee's work and charging the worker with unsatisfactory performance and poor attitude. The worker is then fired, and sues the company for libel. The company will prevail if it can prove that the contents of the memo are the supervisor's honest opinion.

In one similar case the court ruled that such expressions, even if harsh, are protected and cannot be the basis of a libel suit. An employer has the right, without judicial interference, to assess an employee's performance on the job, since communication by one person to another upon a subject in which both have an interest is protected by a qualified privilege. Even extremely harsh opinions have found protection in the courts. Thus, a strong statement accusing a college professor of "lying, deceiving, making false statement...and ill advising" was upheld as a protected expression of opinion.

There are, however, occasions when "opinion" becomes slander. One stockbroker incurred the enmity of the company's vice president. A heated exchange between the two men culminated in the employee's termination. Shortly afterwards, two of his customers, who had learned of his dismissal, requested a meeting with the vice president to inquire about the status of their investments. At the meeting the vice president told them that the stockbroker was about to lose his stockbroker's license, was in big trouble with the Securities and Exchange Commission (SEC) and would "never work again." Told of these remarks, the stockbroker sued his ex-employer for slander. He argued that the company's qualified privilege was lost since the words were spoken with *malice,* designed to destroy his livelihood, and with knowledge that the statements were false.

The Texas Court of Appeals agreed and ruled that the vice president's words were not protected opinion. Viewed in the context in which they were communicated, the court found that the recipients of the statements could reasonably conclude that the comments were based upon undisclosed defamatory facts. The court also rejected the company's attempt to disclaim responsibility for the vice president's utterances since his status as a manager and an officer provided him with authority to speak for and bind the company. The vice president's loose "opinions" about the employee proved costly to his employer. The jury awarded him $212,875 for past and future damages to his reputation; $84,525 for lost damages; $19,791 for past mental anguish, humiliation and embarrassment; and $1 million for exemplary damages. This did not include the exorbitant legal fees paid by the company in its unsuccessful defense of the matter.

Companies must carefully guard comments made by upper management regarding an employee. When untrue statements are made which cause someone a great deal of embarrassment, humiliation and stress, damages for loss of reputation are available in an action for libel or slander because the loss of reputation is a foreseeable consequence of the publication of defamatory statements.

Counsel Comments: *Employers should establish policies regarding the disclosure of information. Potentially damaging communications in performance appraisals and comments made to prospective employers should be reviewed by a supervisor before dissemination and the contents should be disclosed to essential third parties only. Confine the evaluation to the subject. Make sure only those concerned in the matter are present or within earshot. Where possible, confidentiality should be maintained to avoid violations of privacy and defamatory implications. Avoid circulating damaging* written *materials because if the document is obtained by the plaintiff, proving his/her case will be easier.*

Always avoid disseminating written materials that are libelous per se or making statements that constitute slander per se. Defamation per se generally occurs when written or spoken communications impute commission of a criminal offense; impute infection with a loathsome communicable disease (such as AIDS); impute lack of integrity in the discharge of employment, profession, trade or business; or impute lack of chastity in a woman. A victim of libel or slander per se is not required to prove special damages at trial because damages are presumed from the harmful communication. For example, circulating an untrue memo around the office that someone is suspected of being a thief, drug abuser, drinks too much at lunch, is an emotionally unstable lunatic or is a whore are probably defamatory per se and should never be passed around. In a Virginia decision, a worker was awarded substantial compensatory and punitive damages against his former employer which had issued a memorandum accusing the employee of "mismanagement of funds." The Virginia court found that the employee had not committed fraud nor had he utilized funds for any purpose.

Employee References. Supervisory personnel should be instructed to avoid making excited and emotional remarks to employees, particularly those they are in the process of dismissing. Poor references can lead to expensive lawsuits so the best rule is to play it safe, whenever possible, by avoiding disparaging comments.

Is it libelous to inform a union, prospective employer, or other appropriate audience that a worker is dishonest? Not if the employer reasonably believes that the worker was guilty of dishonesty at the time the letters were sent. For example, if a collective bargaining agreement requires that communications be sent to a union, a company may not be guilty of malice or recklessness for sending letters to union personnel designated by the union contract as proper recipients of notices of dismissal, taking care to insure the confidentiality of the letter (for example, clearly marking the letter "confidential").

Counsel Comments: *Be sensitive about writing derogatory letters concerning ex-employees since they are fraught with danger. Imputations that an employee is lacking in competence, sobriety, honesty or chastity can lead to successful libel suits. Limit the dissemination of potentially damaging office rumors, gossip and scuttlebut conveyed as fact without any disclaimer or explanation.*

In the absence of a contract or other legal requirement that employee dismissals be given in writing, you may wish to avoid disclosing poor evaluations or comments about a worker or ex-worker. All too often, embittered ex-employees will harass companies and former supervisors with lawsuits if they can pin an action on a derogatory writing. Be cautious about committing your company in letters on the subject. The best policy for a company to follow, when an employee has left under a cloud and there has been no actual criminal action, is to avoid saying or writing anything imputing dishonesty or immorality to the ex-employee. Since a false statement by an employer that it discharged an employee for dishonesty may be libelous per se, why take chances? (Note: The implications of defamatory job references after a firing will be discussed in greater detail in Chapter 4.)

Public Disclosure Of Private Facts

A related concern for companies involves the public disclosure of truthful but private facts. One that publicizes a matter concerning the private life of another may be liable for invasion of privacy if the subject matter revealed is highly offensive to a reasonable person and is not of legitimate concern. While companies may legally discuss public facts, such as criminal records or information contained in official court documents, they may not generally publish information regarding an employee's or ex-employee's tax records or medical history (even an accurate diagnosis of AIDS) since the matters published are confidential and their dissemination is highly offensive to the reasonable person. Unlike defamation actions, truth is *not* a defense to an action for disclosure of private facts.

Counsel Comments: *Companies must be careful never to reveal or discuss private information with outsiders. In many states, including Connecticut, any dissemination of private employment data to prospective employers other than the dates of employment, position held and latest salary figures is illegal. Many states specifically prohibit the dissemination of confidential private medical information by statute. Since the laws in each state vary it is best to consult with counsel before disseminating any information regarding an employee that can even remotely be considered private.*

Freedom From Trespass And Other Rights

Employees have other rights, such as being protected from an employer's trespass. It is illegal to have a company investigator enter an employee's house when no one is home by forcing open a window in order to confiscate certain allegedly stolen property. Companies cannot appropriate the name or likeness of an employee—for example, as a model in a company advertisement or brochure—without first obtaining the employee's *written* consent or paying reasonable compensation or giving an additional benefit for such use. Also, it is illegal to place an employee before the public in a false light, such as by causing a letter that did not accurately reflect the employee's views to be published with the employee's name in a newspaper or magazine.

LIABILITY FOR ASSAULTS COMMITTED AGAINST EMPLOYEES AND CUSTOMERS

Cases in this area vary markedly depending upon the facts. First, many courts have held that the workers' compensation laws cover injury or death of an employee in the course of his employment arising from an attack, assault, or shooting by a fellow employee, customer, intruder or police officer. However, compensation is not always awarded to a worker who is assaulted at work when the assault arose out of a personal grievance (e.g., a lover's quarrel) unconnected with the worker's job even if it takes place during office hours. In such cases, when it merely provides a place where the assailant can find the victim, the role of employment in the assault is usually inconsequential. However, if an employee's job places him/her in a position of increased risk, compensation may be awarded even for a personally motivated assault. In one case, for example, an employee who worked as an outside salesperson was lured to an isolated house by her former husband—ostensibly on business—and was killed there by him. Since her solo job duties exposed her to increased risk of assault, her family was awarded benefits.

In cases where assaults are committed by supervisors and employees, the issue of determining employer liability typically leans on whether: (1) the assault occurs on or off company premises; (2) the assault occurs outside of or during work hours; (3) whether the assault was reasonably foreseeable knowing the history of the worker or supervisor; and (4) whether or not the assault was outside the scope of the worker's duties and employment.

Courts typically look at whether the assault was motivated by a personal grievance, harassment or threats, or whether it was job related. In cases of this nature, courts have generally held that an employer can be held liable for violence only where the aggressive employee holds a job which is likely to bring him into conflict with others. For example, employers have been held responsible for the acts of security guards, investigators, and assaults committed by employees whose functions are to guard or recapture company property.

Is the company liable if a supervisor attacks a discharged employee? In one case, a hotel kitchen steward fired a worker who arrived late for work on a regular basis. When informed of the immediate discharge, the worker refused to leave. He sulked around the kitchen, even though the steward told him several times to get out. While the steward was escorting the worker out the basement exit, a fight ensued. When the worker attacked the steward and tried to run away, the steward drew a knife and stabbed the ex-employee, seriously injuring him. While still in the hospital, the ex-employee brought a lawsuit against both the steward and the hotel, demanding heavy damages for his injuries.

The hotel attorney asked the court to dismiss the case as far as the hotel was concerned, arguing that this was a "personal grudge" fight between the parties and that since the worker was no longer employed at the time of the knifing, the employer was not liable. Nevertheless, the Louisiana Court of Appeals awarded him $16,500 from the hotel, ruling that the fight was reasonably incidental to the performance of the supervisor's duties in connection with firing the recalcitrant employee and causing him to leave the place of employment: it occurred on the employment premises and during the hours of employment. The court continued that since the assault was within the scope of the supervisor's employment, the employer was liable for the injuries. In another case, a discharged employee was assaulted by his foreman when he refused to let a supervisor examine his toolbox. The employee's claim for workers' compensation was upheld by the court even though the assault occurred after he was fired.

Counsel Comments: *Supervisors should be instructed that, if a discharged employee becomes rambunctious, they should contact the company security force or the local police and let them take over. If an assault occurs, even after the worker is let go, the company may be held liable for any damages to either the supervisor or worker.*

Always draft and include in your company handbook a statement prohibiting fighting or assaults on-the-job. State in the rules of conduct section that all employees must conduct themselves properly to insure an orderly and harmonious work environment and that assaults, unprovoked attacks, threats of bodily harm against anyone, horseplay, violations of company safety rules and unauthorized possession of weapons and firearms on company property will subject the employee to immediate disciplinary action, which may include discharge. Apply all discipline rules uniformly, making decisions on a case-by-case basis after careful planning and discussion with counsel.

With respect to accidental injuries caused by a co-worker on company premises (such as a car accident in the company parking lot), many factors are considered before determining employer liability. In one case the Illinois Appellate Court declared that an accidental injury to an employee while on the employer's premises, going to or from his employment by a customary or permitted route within a reasonable time before or after work, and which is received in the course of and arises out of the employment, cannot be sustained in a common lawsuit but must be redressed in a workers' compensation forum since accidental injuries received in parking lots maintained by employers for the use of their employees arise out of their employment.

Counsel Comments: *Most employees who are injured prefer to bring lawsuits based on common law theories rather than workers' compensation claims. This is because negligence suits against an insured driver or employer often produce larger awards for an accident victim than claims filed with a workers' compensation agency, especially where responsibility for the accident lies entirely with the co-worker. Always instruct litigation counsel to consider removing any lawsuit to a hearing before the appropriate workers' compensation tribunal where applicable.*

PRODUCT LIABILITY PITFALLS

Despite the proliferation of product liability lawsuits, few employers realize how important a knowledgeable staff can be in reducing exposure in this area. With the right training, an alert salesperson can help maintain the company's image, reduce litigation exposure, and increase the chances of a successful defense if a suit does occur. Claims in this area are soaring and the cost of insurance poses major problems for American businesses. More than 100,000 cases are filed each year. The average size of a product's liability verdict has risen from $169,197 in 1975 to more than $250,000 today and the number of recorded jury verdicts awarding $1 million or more to plaintiffs in personal injury suits has increased steadily each year. But perhaps the most alarming statistic is that the recovery rate for plaintiffs in all types of liability situations exceeds 65 percent.

The law has become very harsh against manufacturers and sellers of products because of the doctrine of strict liability. While interpretations vary from state to state, the doctrine generally means that a seller probably will be held responsible if it sells a product that is defective when it leaves the seller's hands and ultimately causes an injury. This precept has generally prevailed except in cases where the plaintiff misused or abused the product at the time of injury.

Supervisors and executives can create company policy to insure that employees adhere to adequate standards and controls; the following rules can help reduce exposure.

- **Make accurate statements regarding product warnings, characteristics, and use.** The law imposes an obligation upon the seller of a product to warn a user of any potential hazard, in language the user can understand. For example, sales personnel should be instructed not to say something like this: "Use of this equipment at improper voltage levels will result in damage to the product and concomitant operator hazard." A more appropriate message would be: "The equipment must be plugged into 120 volts only. If used at higher voltage, it can fly apart and injure or kill you."
- **Familiarize customers with a product's safety features and point out that these devices should be kept in place on the equipment or product at all times.** (That is, they should not be removed, circumvented, short-circuited, or bypassed.) All warnings about a product should be clear and conspicuous and state specific perils involved under both intended use and reasonable foreseeable misuse.
- **Avoid making exaggerated claims.** Salespeople should be informed of the dangers of exaggeration, particularly when describing the safety features of a product. Employees must be taught that statements that sound innocent, such as "This drug is non-addicting" or "Our wheel-guard safety feature eliminates the chance of accidents," can have legal consequences, because claims regarding a product's safety can be interpreted as statements of fact or warranties that can lead to liability. (Note: The issue of warranties and guaranties will be discussed in greater detail in the next section.) Employees have an obligation to carefully discuss the safety features of your product.
- **Review sales literature, warnings, and labels before distribution to be sure they are accurate and complete.** Since it is your employees' job to know what the material says and to interpret it properly, sales personnel should be instructed to review promotional materials for accuracy and to question ambiguous or misleading language. This may help them avoid parroting inaccurate claims during their sales presentations. If the literature is accurate and the employee understands what it says, the chances are reduced of statements being made during the sales pitch that differ from the labels or other written instructions.
- **Review all instructional materials that accompany the product.** If special training or instruction is required, the employee has a duty to inform the buyer about this, tell him/her how it can be obtained and whether there is an extra cost. If special training is required, the employee should play an active role in arranging it and follow up to be sure it actually took place. For example, sales staff and service people who visit plants subsequent to the sale and installation of machinery should examine the machinery to determine that all safety devices are properly functioning. If they are not, your employees should immediately

notify the purchaser in writing of the condition and suggest possible remedies. Annually, sales employees may wish to write their customers a standard form letter advising that it is the customer's obligation and responsibility to insure that safety equipment and devices are functioning properly at all times. The letter should also state that service people are available to repair or replace (at your standard cost) an improperly functioning safety device.

- **Be familiar with the technical specifications and limitations of the product.** Competent employees know how a product will be used, and under what conditions it is likely to fail.
- **Maintain proper selling and distribution records.** Retention of such records can decrease liability exposure and assist in the defense of a product liability lawsuit. Good product disposition records (i.e., when a product was purchased, who bought it and where), can enable your company to trace the handling of the product from the time it left the seller's hands. This can establish that the product was in perfect working order when it was sold by you or to you (assuming your company is involved in distribution). Ideally, a manufacturer should keep pertinent selling records for the life of the product including testing data, quality control, shipping records, receipts, and correspondence with customers. Such records will assist your insurance carrier and may even be a legal obligation as a condition of valid insurance coverage.
- **Become liability-conscious when handling customer complaints regarding defective goods.** Sales staff, for example, should be instructed *never* to admit fault, and avoid saying things like, "This is the third accident I've heard our product caused this month." Such statements may be admissible evidence pinning liability on the company.

Counsel Comments: *In the event of an accident, employees should never discuss the fact that the company carries liability insurance, who the insurance company is, the facts of the accident, or offer their opinion to anyone other than the company attorney or the insurance carrier. Some lawyers recommend that field staff be instructed to revisit the scene of the accident immediately to investigate the site and recover the defective product if possible. This may be a good idea but should never be done without the approval of counsel.*

All documentation relevant to the purported defective product should be collected for review by counsel as soon as possible. This is essential to any product liability defense. Request that all field salespeople file written reports informing company attorneys of any possible legal actions as soon as they are detected. Catching trouble spots early can neutralize legal complications. Direct that all reports be made and sent to the company attorney to maintain the protection of the lawyer/client privilege. Sending damaging memos to management may create problems since they can be obtained via a subpoena and used against your company at a trial.

A final word to management: Develop policies and enforce these rules for everyone involved. Since legislation related to sales and marketing is constantly being revised, schedule periodic product liability seminars to keep your employees abreast of changing rules.

WARRANTIES, GUARANTIES AND MISREPRESENTATION LAWSUITS

Employees often make warranty statements, in effect guaranteeing the performance of a product or service to prospective customers. Most companies, however, don't know where their employees should draw the line with well-intentioned sales talk, personal opinions, and promises, particularly with claims relating to safety features of a product, and do not know all the federal and state laws regulating such promises. Only written warranties are covered by the federal Magnuson-Moss Act, but all types are subject to various state regulations.

Magnuson-Moss requires that consumers be given a complete and understandable explanation of written product warranties before they buy a product. Nothing in the federal law requires a manufacturer to warrant a product; however, manufacturers that do provide a written warranty for consumer products costing $15 or more must comply with the disclosure provisions of the law.

Sales and marketing executives must familiarize themselves with the Uniform Commercial Code, which serves as a basis for state warranty law. Marketers who want to know their legal footing, however, should obtain copies of the fair-business laws adopted by most states. These generally are interpretations of the UCC with respect to warranties and servicing.

Express Warranties

Express warranties are created when certain statements are made by a seller to induce any customer, whether a wholesaler, retailer, or the ultimate consumer, to purchase a product or service. Such statements may be made in product literature, advertising, point-of-purchase displays, or by salespeople talking to buyers. For example, when an advertisement claims that a watch will operate underwater, the seller is liable for damage or replacement if the watch stops when the buyer goes swimming. If a salesperson tells the customer that the casing is strong enough to withstand pressure at great depths, another express warranty is created. Even if no statements are made but the ad depicts a diver wearing the watch underwater, the silent "statement" of the ad establishes a warranty.

> **Counsel Comments:** *Any affirmation of fact or promise creates an express warranty. When salespeople pass along the manufacturer's warranty, they should review the language with a supervisor to be certain that the elements aren't misleading; when they make their own warranties with respect to a product or service they're selling, they must adhere to specific guideline instructions.*

Implied Warranties

An implied warranty makes a promise about the condition of a product at the time it's sold. Employees should be familiar with two versions of this warranty, both of which are contained in the laws of most states. *Implied warranty of merchantability* is a promise that each product sold is in proper condition and that it will perform its intended function. Sometimes this is a called a "warranty of fitness for ordinary use." For example, a lawn mower should be capable of cutting grass without damaging the lawn or the lawn's appearance. If it fails to fulfill this minimal expectation, the buyer has the right to sue for breach of warranty, even if no express promise of the product's performance was made. *Fitness for a particular purpose* is another type of warranty that applies when the consumer relies on the seller's advice that a product can be used for a designated purpose. For instance, a lawn mower advertised for cutting tall grass or brush must be capable of doing so. Such a warranty is especially important in cases where the buyer is not well versed in using the product. When a naive purchaser is persuaded to buy a product designed for a specialized application, the seller may be liable if the device fails to accomplish the special tasks that the buyer had in mind when he made the transaction.

> **Counsel Comments:** *Implied warranties also cover used products. In such instances, the warranty reinforces the expectation that a product is still fit for its intended use and that it's in average condition for an item of its type and price.*

Companies can take many steps to reduce the risk of breach-of-warranty and misrepresentation lawsuits. Employees should be told that whenever a warranty is offered, they shouldn't promise coverage more complete than their companies can reliably provide.

To avoid confusion, put stated warranty terms and conditions in writing. Having the terms spelled out is especially important when it comes to disclaimers. Exceptions to, and exclusions from, the warranty or service contract should be spelled out prominently in bold type so that no buyer can claim he didn't see them. This can make a big difference in those states that permit sellers of products or services to disclaim implied warranties according to the Uniform Commercial Code. Disclaimers can severely limit damages that can be recovered by a customer, restrict the remedies available (stipulating that the customer receives a refund only of the purchase price), or waive the implied warranty altogether. A clause of this sort may be enforceable if it appears conspicuously in a written sales agreement. Employees should be reminded, however, that many courts won't permit disclaimers that are deemed unconscionable—that bar claims for personal injuries arising from the permitted use of the product.

When employees offer a warranty in the course of a sales call, they should be certain that it:

- Is concise and understandable;
- Avoids extravagant or deceptive terms;
- States specifically what is and, in some cases, is not promised;

- Promises only what the company intends to perform;
- Sets time or use limits, where applicable; and
- Limits the company's liability.

Misrepresentation And Breach Of Warranty Claims

When a customer relies on an employee's statements, purchases the product or service, and then it fails to perform as promised, the seller can also be sued for misrepresentation. Companies throughout the United States have paid millions of dollars in judgments for making such mistakes, particularly when staff sells high-ticket, hi-tech products or services. To avoid such problems, employees must be instructed regarding the law of misrepresentation and breaches of warranty relative to the selling function. They must understand the difference between "sales puff" (opinions) and statements of fact, and the legal ramifications of each.

Misrepresentation and breach of warranty are two legal theories on which an injured party seeks damages. While these two causes of action differ in terms of the kind of proof that is required and the type of damages that may be awarded by a judge or jury, both commonly arise in the selling context and typically arise when an employee makes erroneous statements or offers false promises or guaranties regarding a product's characteristics and capabilities.

Not all statements have legal consequences. When personnel loosely describe their product or service in glowing terms ("Our service can't be beat; it's the best around"), such statements are viewed as *opinions* and generally cannot be relied upon by a customer, supplier, or wholesaler. A standard defense used by company lawyers in misrepresentation and breach of warranty lawsuits is that a purchaser cannot rely on a salesperson's puffery because it's unreasonable to take these remarks at face value. But when an employee makes claims or promises of a *factual nature* regarding a product's or service's inherent capabilities (that is, the results, profits, or savings that will be achieved, what it will do for a customer, how it will perform, etc.) the law treats these comments as statements of fact and warranties.

The subtle difference between sales puffery and statements of fact is often difficult to distinguish. No particular phrasing is necessary; each case is analyzed according to its circumstances. Generally, the less knowledgeable the customer, the greater the chances the court will interpret a statement as actionable. The following strategies cover ways management and staff can work together to minimize exposure to costly misrepresentation and breach of warranty lawsuits. Instruct employees always to do the following:

- **Understand the distinction between general statements of praise and statements of fact made during the sales pitch, and the legal consequences.**
- **Thoroughly educate all customers before making a sale.** Employees should give as much information about the specific qualities of the product as possible, because when an employee makes statements about a product in a field in which the company is considered to have extensive experience, the law makes a defense that "it was just sales talk" difficult. This is especially true for highly specialized products or services sold to unsophisticated purchasers who rely entirely upon the technical expertise of an employee. However, if the salesperson deals with a customer experienced in the trade, courts are less likely to find an express warranty, since a knowledgeable buyer has a duty to look beyond the assertions of a salesperson and investigate the product on his own.
- **Be accurate when describing a product's capabilities.** Avoid making speculative claims, particularly with respect to predictions concerning what a product will do.
- **Know the technical specifications of the product.** Review all promotional material to be sure there are no exaggerated claims. Keep abreast of all design changes as well.
- **Avoid making exaggerated claims about product safety.** The law usually takes a dim view of such affirmative claims, and these remarks can be interpreted as warranties that lead to liability.
- **Be familiar with federal and state laws regarding warranties and guaranties.**
- **Know the capacities and characteristics of your products and services.**
- **Keep current with all design changes and revisions in your product's operating manual.**
- **Avoid offering opinions when the customer asks what results a product or ser-**

vice will accomplish unless the company has tested the product and has statistical evidence. If an employee doesn't know the answer to a customer's question, don't lead him on. Tell him you don't know the answer but will get back to him promptly with the information.

- **Remind employees never to overstep authority, especially when discussing prices or company policy.** Always remember that an employee's statement can bind the company with expensive consequences.

APPRAISALS AND PERFORMANCE REVIEWS

All companies can minimize the threat of wrongful discharge lawsuits through the use of accurate performance appraisals. Firing and/or disciplining unsatisfactory employees is not as simple as it used to be. Since the terminated individual may consult an attorney, it is *essential* to document problems in the employee's personnel file. Properly drafted performance appraisals can help protect your company by documenting employee problems; they also can improve performance. Therefore, appraisals should be prepared regularly, accurately and carefully.

Counsel Comments: *Too often, because supervisors are reluctant to hurt an employee's feelings, they inflate the appraisals and do not list the actual problems the worker has demonstrated. Never do this—when employers fail to note performance problems on appraisals, and lack sufficient documentation to prove inadequate job performance, they may not have a legal basis for firing an employee.*

One printing company did not follow this advice and suffered devastating results. The firm was sued by a former long-term worker who claimed he was terminated on the basis of age discrimination. Unfortunately, the company found itself with virtually no written documentation of the man's poor performance. The worst reviews were "satisfactory" (written favorably to build his confidence) and all warnings and reprimands he received were verbal (so there was no solid proof).

A jury found the company liable to the ex-employee and ordered it to pay $80,000 in damages over a three-year period, together with $40,000 in legal fees for the worker's lawyers. This sum was in addition to the approximate $90,000 the company had previously spent in legal fees for its defense and the work hours lost in preparing for the trial.

This actual case demonstrates the importance of issuing regular, accurate, carefully prepared—and never inflated—references and performance appraisals. Sparing a worker's feelings may lead to a weak legal position in the event of a firing.

Periodic Job Reviews

Is an employee entitled to periodic job reviews? Maybe in certain instances, particularly if language in a company handbook is specific enough to constitute a binding promise under the laws of some states. Although it is a good idea to state your performance appraisal policy in a company handbook as a statement of general company policy, *never* draft language which can be construed as an actual offer or commitment to regular job reviews.

Counsel Comments: *Be sure that language in your performance appraisal section refers to the company's employment-at-will policy and that the company reserves the right to make decisions related to employment in any manner other than as provided in the handbook.*

Companies often hesitate to implement a regular performance review program because of the time and effort needed to develop an effective one, and because supervisors have to spend valuable time completing review forms and communicating the results to employees. Managers often dislike doing periodic reviews because of the difficulty of summarizing someone's performance over a period of six months or a year on two or three sheets of paper, especially when the performance is not up to standard. However, skilled personnel may benefit from regular constructive feedback regarding their performance, especially when the employee helps to formulate his or her own performance goals.

Experts suggest that when employees are graded annually on job performance in specific areas, such as technical skills, problem-solving skills, management skills, and people skills, management will be better able to adjust to the individual's role in any change in company direction or emphasis. An effective review should include a discussion of past performance and should set goals for the future.

The following guidelines may help increase the effectiveness of performance appraisals and can protect your company:

1. **State your performance appraisal policy in the company handbook.** Employees are naturally suspicious of the performance review process, so it is up to the employer to explain the process in a way that minimizes such fears. The policy must also state the possible general outcomes (i.e., a final warning leading to discipline and/or discharge) to prevent surprises. It should also inform employees that extended absences or serious violations may result in a job review being rescheduled earlier than expected.

2. **Prepare the form correctly.** Performance appraisal forms should be designed so that exemplary as well as unsatisfactory work is noted. This can be done with a rating scale; i.e., "1-5" categories, or by using other numerical formulas. Leave sufficient space to note formal, objective problems in specific details. In addition, provide a space at the bottom of the document for both the supervisor's and employee's signatures indicating that both have read the evaluation and agree with it. (Note: Executive or management performance appraisal forms or guidelines for review may be different from those given to non-management employees.)

3. **Train supervisors to prepare appraisals correctly.** Instruct them to draft their remarks clearly and objectively and avoid stating conclusions rather than facts. For example, a sleeping incident should be reported like this: "Employee was observed with his head resting on his desk and his eyes closed for ten minutes; he did not respond to me when his name was spoken in a normal tone of voice," rather than: "The employee was observed sleeping on the job." If contested in an arbitration or litigation, the first example would be less likely to be construed as a biased, subjective remark.

> **Counsel Comments:** *All reviews should be supported by documentation where available since it is always helpful to back up your general assessment of performance with specific examples. It's much more meaningful to talk about the details of the employee's performance on a specific project than to simply say the work was generally good or poor. Also, think about the review as a tool for helping the person improve already acceptable performance.*

4. **Avoid playing favorites.** Supervisors must apply the same standards to all employees, regardless of race, color, age, sex or national origin. If an Asian or female employee, for example, is warned about excessive tardiness, while white, male employees with the same record are not, a charge of race or sex discrimination may materialize.

5. **Discuss all problems with higher level supervisors before discussing the performance appraisal with the employee.** Employers should monitor the implementation of the performance appraisal system. One way of doing this is to have each appraisal reviewed by a higher level supervisory employee before it is presented to the employee.

6. **Familiarize the employee with the appraisal process before formal discussion.** Good supervisors provide employees with copies of an employee's job description, goals and standards previously established for the performance period before the meeting. The employee should be requested to evaluate his/her own performance prior to the review. Then, employee and management should sit down and compare evaluations. This will stimulate discussion and the process can help the employee identify any gaps in expectations.

7. **Develop uniform policies with respect to employees who are given unsatisfactory reviews.** For example, if performance is unsatisfactory (as defined by your company in a specific manner), an employee should be given written notice of the need to improve performance, including specific steps to correct all problems. During that time you may wish to place the notified worker on 30 or 60 days' probation. If at the end of the probation period the employee's performance has not improved to the satisfaction of the supervisor, then other corrective action may be taken, including suspension without pay or termination.

8. **Always respond to criticisms of the appraisal by the employee.** If the employee refuses to sign the appraisal, this should be noted. If the employee attaches a statement which disagrees with the supervisor's remarks, upper management should be alerted and a response prepared *immediately*.

Counsel Comments: *Unless a response is formulated, dated, attached to the appraisal, and a copy given to the employee, the company might be construed as agreeing with the contents of such remarks.*

9. **Keep the contents of all appraisals confidential.** Only executives and supervisors who need information about employees when considering them for promotions, transfers, progressive discipline and/or discharge should be allowed to view employee performance records. For example, if it is later proved that key information contained in an appraisal was false (e.g., "It appears that the employee has a drinking problem") and it was read by non-essential third parties, the company could be subjected to a lawsuit based on defamation, and be liable for a significant amount of damages.

Counsel Comments: *A clear, concise statement on company policy regarding the disclosure of the contents of personnel files may reduce employee fears on the subject. Although not legally obligated in many states, some companies permit employees to see copies of material in their personnel files and draft corrections of any disputed information in their files, including performance appraisals. If this is permitted, allow the worker to view his/her file* only *in the presence of a supervisor. Additionally, note that it may not be a good idea to allow workers to make copies of all materials since damaging evidence may be introduced against the company in the event of a lawsuit.*

The same degree of care with appraisals should be applied to all interoffice correspondence since the circulation of confidential memoranda within a company has given rise to lawsuits, particularly where the employer did not take adequate precautions to determine whether derogatory information was accurate. In one recent case, a terminated employee sued his former boss for defamation when memos and performance appraisals describing the employee's poor job performance were distributed and read by several executives. The employee was awarded $90,000 after proving that the information was false. You can avoid similar problems by limiting information in personnel files, applicant information, credit references, etc. to key personnel who require access, and it is a good idea to establish controls about the kinds of documents that are contained in such files. Always maintain tight control over such information for additional protection.

COMMUNICATION AND COMPLAINTS

When judging performance, remember that not all jobs can be rated the same way. Often, an employee will be upset with his/her performance evaluation or some other non-related concern. Open lines of communication are important in any organization. One way to anticipate and prepare for a disgruntled employee's termination lawsuit is to be aware of his/her perceived problem *before* legal action is contemplated. Thus, workers should be encouraged to present their complaints to management either during their employment or at the time they decide to resign. Many complaints can be resolved before the situation gets out of control and your company should establish an effective procedure for receiving and acting upon all employee complaints. In addition, when juries hear testimony regarding a company's alleged callous treatment of a terminated worker, they are often impressed by additional testimony offered from the other side which establishes good-faith efforts by the company to correct problems before they become unmanageable.

Some companies establish internal complaint mechanisms for handling problems. If an employer has established a credible internal complaint resolution procedure, problems can be detected before a request for termination is made. Employees who feel they are being mistreated can appeal a poor performance appraisal or memo which they believe is unfair; this gives the employer an opportunity to review the situation and determine if a remedy is necessary.

Counsel Comments: *Some companies have stated policies, for example, where complaints are first addressed with the immediate supervisor. If the problem is still unresolved, or the worker feels uncomfortable discussing it with his/her immediate supervisor, the complainant is instructed to contact the plant manager. As a final resort, if the matter is still un-*

resolved, the complainant may discuss it with the president of the company.

The following is an example of an *informal* policy:

"The Company maintains a Bulletin Board to keep you advised of all items that are of interest. You should check the Bulletin Board every day to be sure you are aware of what is going on. From time to time, the Company may also distribute memos which you are required to read and sign.

"If something is troubling you, or if you feel you are not being treated fairly, you should discuss the matter with your Supervisor. If you ever think of leaving the Company, we would be interested in knowing why. An Employee's dissatisfaction may be caused by some condition or situation which can be corrected, so please discuss this with your Supervisor before you decide to resign.

"All complaints received by you will be given full consideration and treated in a confidential manner. Be assured that there will be no discrimination or retaliation against any Employee who presents Management with a complaint."

An informal internal complaint resolution procedure similar to the above offers the following advantages:

- It may give the company warning of an employee's grievance, and possibly of a developing type of grievance.
- It may give employers the opportunity to correct poor managerial decisions before an employee is discharged or resigns.
- It may permit disputes to be settled quickly, at minimum cost.
- It may give the company a defense in the event that the employee failed to exhaust internal administrative procedures before bringing a lawsuit.
- It may demonstrate the company's good faith to a jury.
- It may build employee morale by opening lines of communication.

There are, however, disadvantages to a *formal* internal complaint resolution policy, particularly one that is poorly designed or administered. Such a policy contained in a company handbook may enumerate strict rules and methods of handling disputes. For example, some company policies give workers the right to be represented by an attorney at a formal hearing, receive a written response from a committee within a specified number of days after the complaint is received, and allow the employee the right to challenge the formal decision by an appeal process which eliminates the possibility of the worker's termination during the process. Other policies specifically state that all company decisions must be based on concrete facts supported by proper evidence.

Although well intentioned, such formal policies can create problems for your company. For example:

- They may give rise to discrimination liability if the procedures are not applied uniformly.
- They may cause companies to lose flexibility and create an incentive for some employees to delay discharge by appealing their dismissals.
- They may cause antagonism in the workforce.
- They may be viewed by employees as a mere "rubber stamp" of previous management decisions.
- They may supply the employee with valuable information for use against the company in the event of litigation.

An actual case illustrates this last point. The author recently represented an employee who had been discharged. At his termination interview, the company stated one reason for his dismissal; at a complaint resolution hearing after discharge, a completely different reason was offered. Both reasons were factually incorrect and legally insufficient in his particular case. The second false reason given at the grievance hearing confirmed the employee's belief that he had been dismissed unfairly and the author was able to negotiate a substantial out-of-court settlement as a result.

Counsel Comments: *Informal internal complaint resolution procedures can help companies evaluate termination decisions and correct mistakes (such as inadequate raises or promotions) before they wind up in court or before a federal or state agency. However, all procedures should be applied uniformly to prevent discriminatory treatment. Finally, your company may wish to avoid establishing formal procedures for the foregoing reasons.*

Open Door Policies

Is an employee entitled to a chance to improve her job performance after bringing a complaint as suggested in a company's open door policy? One bank teller was suspended after committing several errors. She attempted to resolve the problem through the company's open door policy but was refused the opportunity and was summarily discharged. She sued the company for breach of contract, citing violation of the company's policy manual. At the trial she argued that the contents of the policy manual constituted a contract and she accepted employment with the company in reliance on that contract. She claimed the company had a legal obligation to discuss and attempt to correct her inadequate performance before firing her and breached that obligation by denying her the opportunity.

The company responded that the open door policy contained in the manual was merely a general statement of personnel policies, and that the manual clearly stated it was not to be considered a contract or obligation granting job security and related protections. Arguing that it had the right to hire and fire its workers at will, the company requested that the lawsuit be dismissed.

The Minnesota Court of Appeals agreed with the company. It cited the disclaimer in the policy manual which read, in part: "The policies described here are not conditions of employment and the language is not intended to create a contract between the company and its employees." The Court pointed out that, in this case, the company had no formal legal obligation to honor its open door policy or give the worker a chance to improve her job performance.

Counsel Comments: *Many courts, including those in Minnesota, recognize that a company's policy manual or handbook can modify an employment-at-will relationship. If language in the handbook constitutes a firm offer and the offer has been communicated by dissemination of the handbook to the employee, the next question to be considered is whether the offer has been accepted and consideration furnished for its enforceability. In the case of unilateral employment contracts, be aware that where an at-will employee continues employment with knowledge of new or changed conditions, the new or changed conditions may become a contractual obligation.*

PROMOTIONS, DEMOTIONS AND RELATED CONCERNS

Generally, private employers are free to decide when to give promotions and raises. A common obstacle appears to be in situations where a union member believes he/she was not promoted in violation of pertinent provisions contained in a collective bargaining agreement. Even here, arbitrators will not overrule management unless it can be proven that the employer violated a union pact or acted in an arbitrary manner. For example, some union contracts specifically bar discrimination against any employee because of union membership or non-membership. If a supervisor refused to recommend a worker to a higher position solely because of a union affiliation, this would violate the agreement.

When there is no contract provision at all limiting the company's rights in selecting employees for promotion, a company's rights are unlimited and it may be free to ignore seniority even on the basis of skill, ability and physical fitness. (Note: This is not recommended though as will be discussed below.) And, absent limitations in union contracts, companies are generally free to change job classifications, job duties, eliminate jobs and create new job classifications.

Counsel Comments: *Your company may be violating federal and state discrimination laws if a member of a protected class, such as a worker over 40 with more seniority and ability, is denied the same promotions and raise opportunities given to a (younger) non-minority member.*

To minimize breach of contract claims, avoid making specific promises in company handbooks, job interviews and employment contracts which guarantee or commit your company to pay specified bonuses and promotions, unless this is your intention.

Can an employee enforce promises of promotion? One young research chemist was offered a job with a competitor. When approached with an offer to work for the company, he startled the president with the size of the requested starting salary. The president offered a more modest figure but indicated that if he helped develop a marketable product, he'd get handsome bonuses. After accepting the position and doing a good job, the man failed to receive promised raises. He complained bitterly, was fired, and commenced a lawsuit against the ex-employer charging breach of employment contract and failure to deliver on promotion-oriented promises.

Although sympathetic to his plight, the court ruled in favor of the company. The U.S. District Court stated that the disappointed chemist could not sue on a promise of promotion unless it was more definite than this one, since all the worker received was "hopeful encouragement, sounding only in prophecy." The employee had received only the same rosy promises usually given to professional and executive aspirants to urge them on in their efforts. The court noted that these statements lacked the specific details so essential to a contract.

Counsel Comments: *If, upon hiring, the president had declared: "On such-and-such a date you will be promoted to head of your research division at $85,000 yearly and receive a guaranteed minimum yearly bonus of $10,000," the chemist may have won. Even then, he might have had trouble proving such a promise was made without written documentation evidencing the promise.*

As for bonuses, the sum must be ascertainable and courts will not guess at amounts. Thus, all personnel in charge of hiring must be instructed not to make specific promises regarding the timing or amount of bonuses or raises and to understand the distinction between discretionary bonuses, advances and promotions and the types of promises that may be specific and definite enough to be enforceable by contract. (Note: Consult Chapter 2 for a more detailed discussion about bonuses.)

Non-Monetary Promotions

Experts recommend several effective employee retention strategies when promotions or salary leaps are not possible for an employee. In such instances, you may wish to:

- Heighten the employee's stature in the company by widening the area of responsibility. This is a "promotion" without the title.
- Assign new projects that involve more creativity.
- Eliminate menial parts of the job; for example, have the paperwork done by an assistant.
- Involve employees in enhanced decision-making, not just window dressing.

Pay Increases Enforceable By Contract

When do additional job duties justify a pay increase? Typically, unions file grievances on behalf of members seeking extra pay when extra work is imposed on union members. In one case an arbitrator ruled that three additional tasks imposed were at a lower skill level than required for the next classification of worker. All three were *de minimus* with respect to the time required for their performance so the union failed to demonstrate that it was entitled to extra compensation on behalf of the workers.

When a company adds tasks to a job classification under a collective bargaining agreement, arbitrators generally consider two issues when asked to increase the workers' compensation: (1) whether the tasks require a higher level of skill than the work already performed; and (2) whether these new tasks require a significant percentage of the employee's time to perform. If the answer to both questions is "yes," additional compensation may be warranted.

Demotions

In directing the work force, an employer generally has the right to demote workers at will. A worker is responsible for keeping up his standard of performance no matter how long he has been with the company. Demotion for sub-par performance is not so much discipline as it is a transfer to a job more suitable to an employee's ability and companies can force an unwilling employee to accept a new job or risk discharge.

Counsel Comments: *An exception to this rule may depend on the existence of a collective bargaining agreement. Even so, unions do not have the upper hand in prohibiting employers from changing or issuing new rules, although they can request that an employer justify the reasonableness of its demotion rules.*

Downgrading or abolishing a job will often be upheld by arbitrators where genuine changes at a company, including a business downturn, increased mechanization or a shortage of materials, account for such a move. Also, depending on the facts, a reduction in pay may not be a compelling reason to refuse work and employees who have been laid off for a period of time cannot require that they return to jobs that pay exactly what they received previously. However, a New York court held that a bricklayer recalled to a lower-paying menial laborer's slot had the right to turn down the job and still collect unemployment benefits because the job was not within his experience, rather than because of the lower stipend.

PROGRESSIVE DISCIPLINE

Performance appraisals are a useful tool in a well-administered progressive discipline system. Such a system can help an employer to change an employee's performance and, if successful, salvage an employee who has not been performing up to standard. Progressive discipline can also be used to build a file against an employee and convince him/her that protesting a dismissal in court would be futile. By placing the employee on notice of a performance problem and providing an opportunity to correct the problem, your company can establish a record to support your position that the employee was fired for a valid reason.

Counsel Comments: *In too many cases, supervisors recommend dismissals of individuals, without having supporting documentation to back up their decisions. Many can verbally describe a worker's performance problems, but do not have* written proof *(unsatisfactory performance appraisals, written memos to the employee, records of lateness or excessive absences, etc.). Often, the individual's personnel file does not support a firing decision because of the favorable appraisals it contains. This must be avoided at all times.*

However, by utilizing a system of progressive discipline and disciplining the worst offenders first, post-termination litigation can be discouraged, and the record of progressive discipline can establish to a jury that the reason given by an employer for the firing was real and not a pretext.

Consider implementing the following strategies:

1. **Specify in your company's handbook or employee manual the kinds of conduct that are serious enough to justify immediate termination without a warning.** Many companies have a discipline structure that includes a series of oral and written warnings and suspension before an employee can be terminated for breaking company rules of conduct. But for some offenses, dismissal should be automatic. By listing the kinds of infractions which can lead to immediate discharge in a Rules of Conduct section, you place employees on notice and offer less ammunition to complain of a firing if they commit serious acts.

These acts may include: theft or dishonesty; falsifying records or information; punching another employee's time card; leaving the job or company premises without prior approval from a supervisor; insubordination, or disrespect of company work rules and policies; willful refusal to follow the directions of a supervisor (unless to do so would endanger health or safety); assault, unprovoked attack or threats of bodily harm against others; use of drugs/possession of alcoholic beverages on company premises or during company paid time while away from the premises; reporting to work under the influence of drugs or alcohol; breach of ethics; disclosing confidential and proprietary information to unauthorized third parties; unauthorized possession of weapons and firearms on company property; intentionally making errors in work; negligently performing duties or willfully hindering or limiting production; wasting materials; sleeping on the job; excessive lateness or irregular attendance at work; failing to report absences; sexually harassing or abusing others; and serious violations of state or federal laws while on company property.

This list is not meant to be all-inclusive. Rather, its intention is to communicate the kinds of conduct that may lead to immediate firing rather than progressive discipline and should be prohibited under any circumstances.

2. **State your progressive discipline policy in the supervisor's manual rather than in the employee handbook.** In many states, courts are ruling that employees have the right to rely on statements contained in employee handbooks. Thus, for example, if the handbook states that all employees must first be orally warned, then warned in writing, then suspended without pay before being fired, a company might have to follow this policy before termi-

nating an unsatisfactory worker or be liable in a lawsuit for breach of contract. Although this is useful as a policy in general, the company might desire to terminate a particular worker suddenly rather than bind itself to the lengthy process of notification, review and then discharge. Offering specific policies in the supervisor's manual only may minimize this potential problem.

3. **Prepare a system of progressive discipline suitable for your company.** The steps might include:

- Informal meetings and oral reprimands (followed by a memo of such a meeting placed in the employee's file);
- Written deficiency notices with a statement in the memo spelling out the consequences of failure to correct performance problems. (An example might be: "If immediate improvement is not demonstrated by (specify what must be achieved and by when), further disciplinary action up to and including termination may be taken.");
- Unsatisfactory performance evaluations;
- Suspension without pay and/or termination.

> **Counsel Comments:** *Each company should implement its own system using the above as a guide. However, each step must be applied uniformly and consistently. Once established, do not deviate from these procedures for anyone. For example, during discharge, be sure to discipline or terminate the worst offenders first: do not use any other basis. Remember that you invite a lawsuit based on sex, race or age discrimination if you have several people with a chronic problem, such as absenteeism, but choose to fire the older (or minority or female) employee first. However, if those with the worst absenteeism records are discharged first, especially after warnings, a claim of discrimination may never materialize or if it does, be deflated.*

4. **Prepare written deficiency notices properly.** The written deficiency notice should state facts (i.e., dates and times of incidents, and specific details of violations or rules). In the event of a lawsuit, a comprehensive memo can refresh the supervisor's memory and its accuracy will less likely be questioned. Additionally, the memo should establish a reasonable timetable for correction which provides the employee with a fair opportunity to improve. For example, if the company gives an employee a period of one week to correct deficient performance, this may create the impression that the employee is being "set up" for a firing. It may also be wise to include a statement regarding a reasonable amount of time that a warning shall remain in effect—for example, not more than 12 months from date of issue.

> **Counsel Comments:** *All warnings given to the employee should be signed by both the supervisor and employee and dated. If the employee refuses to sign, the supervisor should note this on the form.*

5. **Give ample opportunity to hear the employee's version of the story before taking further action.** This will make your company appear fair, and may give you the opportunity to decide if the facts are accurate. In addition, knowing the employee's version will help you to prepare a defense in the event the matter is litigated in the future.

> **Counsel Comments:** *Some companies allow disciplined workers the right to grieve or appeal disciplinary decisions. Rules or procedures are established and publicized in personnel manuals providing workers with specified procedures (i.e., written notice of the appeal must be given to the company or an employee appeals board within a specified number of days after the decision, etc.). Although such appeals processes may work in theory, in practice they can become an administrative nightmare for companies and should be* avoided *unless absolutely necessary—as in a collective bargaining agreement with union workers, where they may serve the positive function of reducing protracted arbitrations.*

6. **While applying disciplinary measures uniformly is important, remember that exceptions to any company policy may arise when considering the nature of the job and the circumstances of each case.** For example, the higher the job in the corporate chain of command, the greater the right to disagree, argue, question and even disobey. What is seen as insubordination in a clerk, justifying disciplinary procedures, may very well *not* be

so in an executive because courts allow executives to exercise more discretion. Thus, apply a discipline policy uniformly but note special problems inherent in trying too hard to be consistent.

Counsel Comments: *A time-honored rule in labor relations, typically upheld by labor arbitrators, holds that if an employee believes a supervisor's orders are in any way improper, the employee must first obey them and then file a grievance except where the work involved may endanger the employee's health, safety or well-being. In most cases, a worker's refusal to perform requested tasks is viewed as insubordination, justifying discipline. Thus, try to use the same punishment for similar infractions but be mindful of limited exceptions. Exercise all decisions in this area with care.*

7. **Instruct company supervisors to avoid confrontations at disciplinary conferences.** All meetings should be conducted in a low-key fashion. Other rules to follow include:

- Avoid shouting.
- Inform the employee of the reasons for the meeting.
- Listen to the employee's version of the facts.
- Establish realistic goals and timetables.
- Always be authoritative.
- Never apologize for the decision because this may be construed as a sign of weakness.

8. **Use a supervisory pecking order effectively.** Some experts recommend involving the direct supervisor at the initial phase of the discipline process. Then, if the issue remains unresolved, the next phase can include the supervisor's manager. Disputes that go beyond this point should be referred to a person not involved in the circumstances (such as a vice president) to avoid charges of bias or subjectivity.

9. **Consider suspensions without pay as a final recourse before firing.** A suspension without pay may get the employee's attention by notifying him/her of the seriousness of the problem. Also, it may demonstrate fairness to a judge, arbitrator or jury, since the company gave the employee one last chance to correct deficient performance before discharge.

Supervisor Manuals

Some employers issue a "confidential" supervisors' manual which discusses rules and policies to be followed regarding appraisals, progressive discipline policies and other internal matters. The problem with supervisors' manuals is that their instructions and directives often differ from promises made to employees in company handbooks and manuals.

Counsel Comments: *When lawyers representing terminated workers review such manuals, they may gain additional negotiating strength after discovering numerous inconsistencies. To avoid confusion and varying practices within a company, consider eliminating supervisor manuals. If you do use them, be sure all copies are kept under lock and key and that none can be obtained by non-essential employees since you don't want your supervisors' manuals floating around where they can be read or used by disgruntled employees.*

PROBATIONARY PERIODS

Any employee who is new at a particular job, whether recently hired, promoted, or transferred, should go through a short-term (i.e., one to three months) probationary period for evaluation purposes. Especially with respect to initial hires, the first month or so is considered an introductory training period. The supervisor should evaluate the individual's suitability for the position and ask the employee to consider whether the position meets expectations and/or personal needs. A carefully structured introductory period is an important factor in establishing attitudes and work habits.

Counsel Comments: *The problem with probationary periods is that they are often construed by applicants, new hires and employees as* minimum *periods of job security during which they may not be fired (i.e., "until the end of the probationary period."). To minimize this potential problem, advise all transferees and newly hired employees that the company is free to terminate the worker* before *the expiration of any probationary period. Better still, always classify and refer to this as* *an "introductory period" to minimize reliance on job security expectations.*

MILITARY LEAVE

Military leave policies often impact smaller companies quite severely. Small employers must deal with the loss of key employees, executives and supervisors for extended periods of time and many companies are unsure of the legal ramifications concerning job vacancies, benefits and related issues. The Military Selective Service Act, originally enacted June 24, 1948, and amended several times, delineates reservists' rights and must be followed by companies with reservist status employees. It requires that public and private employers grant a leave of absence to reservists and members of the National and Air National Guard who were permanent employees for weekly and weekend drills, summer camps, and other types of training duty and emergencies.

Extended Reserve Duty

Reservists are not required to give the employer any advance notice of call-up, nor are they required to provide the exact date when they will return. However, under normal circumstances, if asked, employees may be able to furnish employers with the approximate beginning and ending dates of the training and the appropriate travel time involved to allow an employer to adjust work schedules and meet the needs of the reservist and the company.

An important aspect of the law is that companies are not required to pay employees who are on military leave. Although optional, some employers voluntarily make up the difference between typically lower military pay and the civilian salary on a short-term basis depending on the company's commitment to civic duty and ability to compensate.

Counsel Comments: *A company is prohibited from forcing an employee to use vacation time for military training.*

Protected Jobs

Employers must assist reservists when they return and cannot deny promotions, seniority or other benefits because of reserve obligations. For example, if an employee was promoted right before the call-up or promised a raise, he or she should receive a job in line with the promised promotion and raise upon return. Additionally, upon the reservist's return, the company must reinstate all benefits plus offer those benefits (e.g., additional pay) that would have been earned if the reservist had continued actively at work.

The Military Selective Service Act provides that employees who are in military service are regarded as being on an unpaid leave of absence from their civilian employment. Even if they are in military service for a period up to four years or if they are called up for short-term emergency duty merely to serve in a motor pool across town rather than in a distant location, they must be offered a job with the same pay, rank, and seniority upon their return. This federal law does not require a company to give the reservist back the *same* job, but one that is similar in pay, rank and seniority.

A reservist must apply for reinstatement to his or her employer in a timely fashion. Following release from duty, reservists may take as much as 90 days of unpaid leave time to be with their families or become reaccustomed to civilian life, if they wish. However, if they want to return to work immediately (even the day after they come home), the employer must take them back immediately. These re-employment obligations extend to new owners of a company and companies previously or presently in bankruptcy, as long as the company maintains a payroll.

Counsel Comments: *The only exception is for reservists with dishonorable discharges. In these rare cases, employers may not have to re-hire the individuals and employ them for at least one year, but speak to counsel because the rules are tricky.*

Any company not following the above guidelines is subject to investigation and action by the local U.S. Attorney's office. Charges can also be brought under The Veteran's Benefits Improvement and Health Care Authorization Act of 1986 and The Veteran's Re-employment Rights Act. These laws prohibit discrimination in all aspects of employment, including hiring, promotions and discharge, on the basis of membership in the military reserve or National Guard.

Counsel Comments: *Companies which receive job applications from reservists and don't hire them must fully document the reasons for denial. Be sure to verify that adverse employment selection decisions are based on factors other than the applicant's belonging to the military, such* *as that another candidate had more experience or training and was better qualified. This may reduce charges of potential violations which are often the target of investigations.*

Legal Remedies

Any individual denied the benefits to which he or she is entitled under these laws may file a motion, petition, or other appropriate pleading in the federal district court sitting in any district where the employer maintains a place of business. Companies with operating subsidiaries or sales offices in different cities can be served from legal authorities in any of these locations. An individual may also apply for the aid of the U.S. Attorney or a comparable official who, if reasonably satisfied that the person is entitled to the benefits or was denied employment because of military status, shall act on the complainant's behalf in seeking a settlement of the claim or in representing the individual in any judicial proceeding.

AVOIDING ON-THE-JOB DISCRIMINATION

Enactment of the Civil Rights Act of 1991 has thrust the issue of discrimination into the national spotlight. Various forms of discrimination, including sex harassment cases punctuated by the Judge Clarence Thomas-Anita Hill confrontation, and the enactment of the Americans With Disabilities Act underscore the concern employers are now feeling in this area. This section will examine many current discrimination laws pertaining to on-the-job rights and offer numerous ways employers can avoid tough new penalties for non-compliance.

The Civil Rights Act Of 1991

The Civil Rights Act of 1991, which took effect on November 21, 1991, implemented a series of sweeping changes to federal anti-discrimination laws. The legislation expands procedural options and remedies available to employees and overruled a series of important U.S. Supreme Court decisions that limited employees' legal recourse. In doing so, Congress amended six different statutes that together prohibit discrimination based on race, color, religion, sex, national origin, disability and age. Those statutes are Title VII of the Civil Rights Act of 1964, the Americans with Disabilities Act of 1990, the Vocational Rehabilitation Act of 1973, the Age Discrimination in Employment Act of 1967, the Civil Rights Act of 1866 and the Civil Rights Attorney's Fees Awards Act of 1976. Virtually all employers are touched by the legislation.

The act prohibits racial discrimination in all aspects of the contractual process, including demotions, transfers, promotions, wages and working conditions, as well as hiring and discharges. Retaliation and on-the-job harassment are also protected. Now, both the act and the Civil Rights Act of 1866, commonly called Section 1981, which prohibits racial discrimination with respect to the management and enforcement of employment contracts, obligate all private employers, regardless of size, to act legally.

In the Supreme Court's 1989 *Patterson v. McLean Credit Union* decision, the Court ruled that Section 1981 did not extend to conduct occurring after the establishment of a contract, so claims of racial harassment on the job, denials of promotions, demotions and discharge decisions could not be brought. Until this decision was handed down, Section 1981 had been an attractive remedy for race and national origin claimants because it allowed for jury trials and unlimited compensatory and punitive damages. The act reverses this Supreme Court case and Section 1981 once again applies to race and national origin claims alleging harassment and other "postformation conduct" such as discipline, demotions, transfers, all promotions and discharges.

Prior to the act, claimants typically could only receive their jobs back, together with retroactive job pay and restoration of seniority benefits. Now, in cases where intentional race, color, sex (including pregnancy), national origin, religion or handicap discrimination can be proved by one or more complainants, the act authorizes jury trials, reasonable witness and attorney fees paid to the individual harmed, together with compensatory and punitive damages depending upon the size of the employer.

> **Counsel Comments:** *Compensatory and punitive damages are available only for* intentional *discrimination and* unlawful *harassment, and do not apply where a job practice is not intended to be discriminatory but nonetheless has an unlawful disparate impact on persons within a protected class.*

Employers with more than 14 but less than 101 employees are liable for compensatory and punitive damages totaling no more than $50,000 per claimant; between 100 and fewer than 201 employees their exposure is $100,000; for employers with more than 200 but fewer than 501 employees, the cap is $200,000 and for larger employers, claimants may receive up to $300,000. Compensatory damages are defined as money for future pecuniary losses, emotional pain, suffering, inconvenience, mental anguish, loss of enjoyment of life and other non-pecuniary losses. Punitive damages are damages paid if the employer acted with malice or reckless indifference to the federally protected rights of an aggrieved individual.

Counsel Comments: *These damages are not the only exposure your company can face. Job reinstatement, back pay, interest and restoration of lost seniority benefits may also be awarded in addition to the above mentioned caps. Thus, it now becomes critical to avoid committing intentional discrimination because your company may be exposed to huge potential damages.*

Burdens Of Proof. The law changes the burdens of proof required for a complainant to prevail in any discrimination litigation and demonstrates the significance of the distinction between disparate *treatment* cases and disparate *impact* cases under the act. Disparate treatment claims, for which the above damages flow, require proof of intentional discrimination. Disparate impact cases involve employment practices such as hiring and promotion tests, educational requirements, and height or weight standards that are essentially neutral but allegedly discriminate against minorities or women in actual practice.

The act substantially shifts the burden of proof to employers in cases alleging disparate impact by now requiring employers to demonstrate that any particular practice is job related for the position in question and consistent with business necessity. In mixed motive cases, where the evidence shows that both permissible and impermissible factors were present in the challenged practice (for example, where a female is denied advancement both on account of her gender and also because of job performance problems and her inability to get along with co-workers), it is sufficient for the employee to show that the subject consideration was a *motivating* factor.

Counsel Comments: *This is an easier test for the plaintiff to meet. And, even though an employment practice with a disparate impact is job related and supported by business necessity, the employment practice may nonetheless be unlawful if the complaining party proves that a different employment practice with less disparate impact exists and the employer failed to adopt the alternative employment practice.*

The act also expands employees' rights to challenge allegedly discriminatory seniority systems by allowing people to attack such systems at a later date without worrying that the statute of limitations has run out. It also affects all U.S. citizens employed overseas by American companies and bans test norming—the procedure by which the scores of tests administered for employment or promotion are adjusted on the basis of race, sex, or other characteristics of the person taking the test.

Strategies To Reduce Problems. Experts suggest that the act will increase compliance burdens and the cost of doing business. Since the law facilitates access to the courts and juries, reduces plaintiffs' problems in proving discrimination and exposes your company to significantly greater damages, it is important to be mindful of the technical aspects of this law and act properly.

According to Eric J. Wallach, an employment lawyer and partner in the New York City law firm of Rosenman & Colin, the following rules must be followed:

1. **All employers must review hiring, promotion and compensation criteria to ascertain whether they are validly job-related and consistent with business necessity.** This requires an analysis not only of these standards themselves—and whether they are specific to the relevant personnel objectives—but also of the consequences that result from these standards. For example, are there statistical imbalances in the workforce that are directly or indirectly traceable to such standards?

2. **Proper documentation including employment forms, job descriptions and performance evaluations must be prepared to adequately support any personnel decisions regarding hiring, promotions, and compensation.**

3. **Appropriate procedures must be consistently applied in every case and such decisions must never be made on the basis of sex, race or religion.**

4. **Employers with overseas operations must be attentive to whether their managers abroad are**

enforcing the anti-discrimination laws to all employees who are U.S. nationals.

5. **All employment strategies must take into account the demographics of the workplace.** Companies must avoid statistical personnel imbalances with regard to women and minorities.

Although no employer is likely to avoid the expected increase in employment-related litigation, Attorney Wallach recommends that management should consult with counsel and human resource experts in regard to these complex issues to minimize the likelihood of such problems and your legal liability in the event of lawsuits.

There are many other concerns that companies can follow to reduce potential problems. These include the following:

6. **Ban the practice of "race norming" and other practices used to alter or adjust in any way the scores of job applicants or employment-related tests on the basis of race, color, religion, sex or national origin.**

7. **Review all current and considered affirmative action policies.** For example, under the act, the law restricts the ability of government personnel directors to hire anyone but top-ranking applicants from civil service tests. If the law is deemed retroactive, hiring and promotion based on factors other than strict rankings might be subject to legal challenge, particularly by non-minorities arguing reverse discrimination.

> **Counsel Comments:** *Speak to counsel about the legality of continuing programs that favor women and minority members in hiring and promotion because there appears to be confusion regarding whether the new law impacts court-ordered remedies, affirmative action, and conciliation agreements.*

8. **Instruct management to train all employees to avoid any on-the-job behavior that could be interpreted as sexually harassing or racially discriminatory.** One bus driver's supervisor called him "nigger," told racist jokes, gave him inferior equipment, and took runs away from him and gave them to junior drivers. He complained, to no avail. Under extreme stress, the worker experienced a rapid decline in health and eventually became completely disabled. He brought suit and a jury awarded him $12.1 million, including $10.7 million in punitive damages.

9. **Consider hiring additional qualified minorities such as females or non-whites to avoid charges of discrimination.**

10. **Analyze the law of the foreign country where you are operating.** An important exception to the act is that U.S. employers doing business abroad are exempted from following the act where compliance would violate the law of the country in which the employer's foreign workplace is located. Also, while foreign corporations controlled by U.S. employers must obey the rules of the act, the law does not apply to foreign businesses not controlled by a U.S. employer (analyzed under facts such as common ownership and financial control).

11. **Prepare and include in your company's handbook a definitive equal employment opportunity policy.** The following is an example:

"Our company is committed to providing all employees and applicants for employment equal opportunity, without regard to race, religion, color, national origin, sex, age, marital status, disability (where disability is unrelated to job requirements), veteran status, or membership or nonmembership in a labor organization or any lawful organization. All company policies, practices, and procedures covering recruitment, hiring, assignment, conditions of employment, compensation, training, promotion, transfer, and termination are to be administered equally and in accordance with state and federal laws and regulations, and are based solely on merit. It is the company's policy that an individual's rights shall not be infringed upon by another employee. All employees are required to notify their supervisor or other appropriate officer immediately if they believe they are being subjected to such conduct, or are aware that such actions are taking place. A prompt, confidential investigation will then be taken by the company without any direct or indirect reprisal to the complainant."

> **Counsel Comments:** *Since most discrimination laws state that a company is liable for the acts of its supervisors and employees unless it can prove it took* immediate *and* appropriate *corrective action, preparing and distributing to all employees an equal employment opportunity policy similar to the above is an important first step.*

12. Review the law in your own state. Each state has its own particular anti-discrimination laws, which are often stronger than federal law. All policies aimed at curbing and eliminating potential on-the-job discrimination must be thoroughly analyzed with counsel before implementation to create safeguards in this area.

13. Review all employment contracts and consider drafting broad arbitration clauses for additional protection. In one New York case, the Appellate Division, First Department, ruled that employees who have agreed to arbitrate all disputes with their employers cannot bring lawsuits claiming race discrimination in open court. In the case, an employee signed a U-4 form in which he agreed that all disputes with his employer be arbitrated. He resigned because of a pay dispute and brought an action for race discrimination under New York State's Human Rights Law which gave him potentially greater rights. He lost and was ordered to proceed to arbitration instead.

> **Counsel Comments:** *The ruling was a significant victory for the company because the employee had sought $25 million in punitive damages; under New York arbitration laws punitive damages cannot be awarded. Since the law is quite confusing in this area and varies from state to state, always discuss the applicability of this strategy with experienced counsel before implementation.*

The Age Discrimination In Employment Act

A recent development concerns the enactment of a federal law called the Older Workers Benefit Protection Act. The act is designed to protect older workers from voluntary early retirement programs, written waivers and releases and their effect upon Age Discrimination in Employment (ADEA) claims, and deductions from severance pay and disability benefits to those eligible for retirement. Another development concerns a recent Second U.S. Circuit Court of Appeal case prohibiting employers from refusing to hire anyone over 40 because they are "overqualified."

Until 1990, confusion reigned over the enforceability of releases and waivers signed by older workers. Now, enactment of the Older Workers Benefit Protection Act has eliminated much confusion when its provisions are properly followed.

The act makes clear that in relation to a firing or resignation of a worker over 40, a company can protect itself from potential violations of ADEA claims by utilizing waivers *provided* the following factors are met:

1. The waiver is part of an agreement which specifically states the worker is waiving his/her ADEA rights and is not merely a general release;
2. The agreement containing the waiver does not disclaim any rights or claims arising after the date of its execution;
3. The worker receives value (such as an extra month of severance) in return for signing the agreement;
4. The worker is advised in writing of the right to consult an attorney of his/her choosing before signing the agreement;
5. The worker is advised in writing of his/her right to consider the agreement for a period of 21 days before it is effective; and
6. The worker is given at least seven days following the execution of the agreement to revoke it.

Where employers request the signing of releases or waivers in connection with mass termination programs and large-scale voluntary retirement programs, the act is even more strict. For example, all individuals included in the program must be given at least 45 days to consider the agreement and each employee must also be provided with numerous facts including the class, unit or group of individuals covered by the program, any eligibility factors for such program, time limits applicable to the program, the job titles and ages of all individuals selected for the program and the ages of all individuals not eligible for the program.

> **Counsel Comments:** *These revised waiver and disclosure requirements make it important that individual and group terminations now be communicated properly to potential ex-employees over 40.*
>
> *If your company is considering preparing releases in connection with the firing of any older worker, be sure that the agreement is written in clear and simple language, and unambiguously releases all claims relating to the worker's termination of employment. This will reduce the chances that ill-informed employees can successfully assert they were coerced into signing a waiver, and that such a document should not be enforced because of a*

lack of negotiation, ambiguity of language in the release, or evidence that the employee had not signed the document voluntarily.

The releases included at the end of this chapter are examples of the kinds of documents some companies are preparing to reduce problems. These documents are included for illustrative purposes only. Always consult counsel before drafting and implementing any waiver or release.

Finally, for maximum protection, designate and train select company personnel to assist in termination decisions, review the law and answer older workers' questions in this area.

Voluntary Early Retirement Offers. In view of recent changes in the law, all voluntary early retirement programs must now be scrutinized closely so there is no chance of threat, intimidation or coercion of the worker to whom the benefit is offered. All older employees must now be given sufficient time to consider the options, and receive accurate and complete information regarding benefits.

Don't forget to examine special rules regarding the kinds of "voluntary" benefits that may be offered under the act before contemplating making an offer. Although the federal legislation validates many company developed plans, it must be followed precisely so as to not backfire against employers.

"Overqualified" Job Applicants. Employers should be aware that a refusal to hire overqualified applicants may constitute age discrimination. In one recent case, a production manager with more than 30 years experience in the printing industry was unable to find a job with the parent company after its subsidiary company fired him due to financial cutbacks. The parent company notified the worker that he was overqualified for some of the positions he had applied for. The employee argued that the real reason he was denied employment was his age, since at least three younger applicants were hired by the parent company in positions for which he had applied.

The employee sued the company in federal court alleging age discrimination. Although the employer won the case at the trial court level (it was dismissed), the appellate court reversed the trial court and ruled that a genuine issue of material fact existed. It also stated that characterizing an applicant in an age discrimination case as overqualified has a connotation that defies common sense. The court stated: "How can a person overqualified by experience and training be turned down for a position given to a younger person deemed better qualified? Denying employment to an older job applicant because he or she has too much experience, training or education is simply to employ a euphemism to mask the real reason for refusal, namely, in the eyes of the employer the applicant is too old."

Counsel Comments: *In this litigious age, companies must take special care not to violate stringent age discrimination laws. Therefore, when considering the application of an experienced older worker, never admit that the reason you are refusing to hire that person (to the benefit of a younger worker) is that the worker was overqualified. Consider carefully all the potential ramifications and speak to experienced counsel before making any decisions or comments to the rejected older applicant to avoid problems.*

Americans With Disabilities Act

Until recently, the main federal law protecting handicapped individuals against discrimination was The Rehabilitation Act of 1973, which applied mainly to government contractors and employers who received federal assistance. To remedy its limited applicability, Congress enacted the ADA to widen the scope of protection available to disabled workers. As we have stated, the main object of this law is to protect any person with a physical or mental impairment that substantially limits "one or more life activities." This covers a broad range of disabilities, including deafness, cancer, heart disease, epilepsy, paralysis, hearing or visual impairments, organic brain syndrome, mental retardation, depression, AIDS and learning disabilities. In addition, the ADA protects persons who have a history of a disability or who are perceived as having a disability; it even covers alcohol or drug use for workers who rehabilitate themselves.

Counsel Comments: *By contrast, the term disability does not include physical characteristics within a normal range and not the result of a physiological disorder, such as baldness, bisexuality or compulsive gambling.*

Despite the fact that employers with 25 or more workers may not discriminate against any qualified individual with a disability in regard to job application procedures, hiring or discharge of employees, employee compensation, terms and privileges (including job classifications, fringe benefits, promotion and training opportunities, advancement, job training and other conditions of employment), many companies are still not following this new federal law. It is reported that some employers are still asking about disabilities at the hiring interview, are requesting that applicants take medical examinations *before* they receive a job offer, and are still using outdated employment applications with improper language.

Although the ADA does not require an employer to give preferential consideration to persons with disabilities, a person with a disability cannot be excluded from consideration for a raise, promotion or on-the-job opportunity because of an inability to perform a marginal function. For example, an employer may not classify disabled applicants or employees in a way which limits their opportunities or status because of their disability. Different pay scales may not be adopted for workers with developmental disabilities if the job duties of such individuals are the same as for other workers. It is also impermissible to exclude or deny equal jobs or benefits to an individual because of that person's relationship or association with a disabled person. For example, an employer cannot fire an individual because that person does volunteer work with AIDS victims.

Examples Of Reasonable Accommodation. Under the ADA, the employer must make decisions without regard to an individual's disability, provided that he or she is able to perform the essential functions of a job, with the employer providing reasonable accommodation. On-the-job accommodations that must be provided to employees include:

- Restructuring or modifying work schedules;
- Offering part-time work;
- Permitting the employee to work at home;
- Reassigning an individual to a vacant position;
- Providing readers or interpreters for blind or deaf persons;
- Acquiring or altering equipment or devices;
- Making existing facilities readily accessible to the disabled;
- Adjusting or modifying examinations, training materials and policies;
- Adjusting marginal job requirements; and
- Allowing flexibility in arrival and departure times for people who require special vehicles for transportation or who are confined to wheelchairs.

Counsel Comments: *Fortunately, employers are only required to make such accommodations if the disability is known, if the accommodation requested is reasonable, and if the employee is truly disabled. An employer is relieved of responsibility to accommodate a disabled employee when to do so would impose an undue hardship. Factors considered in determining whether undue hardship exists include the nature and the costs of the accommodation to the employer, the overall financial resources of the employer (i.e., number of employees, overall size of the business, etc.) and other related factors. Courts will look at the type of operation, overall size, budget, profitability of the employer and the financial impact of the suggested accommodation in determining whether undue hardship exists.*

The facts concerning what constitutes undue hardship vary from case to case. For example, a small company may not be required to hire two employees (a blind accounts receivable clerk and a reader) if the company has an opening for only one clerk. Essentially, however, if the employer can afford to accommodate, it must do so.

Employers are permitted to suggest voluntarily the kind of accommodations that may be made. This can be done, for example, to raise desks a couple of inches to accommodate wheelchairs by inserting blocks under the desk legs. Or, a parking garage may be required to modify a rule barring all vans with raised roofs, including those that are wheelchair accessible, if a wheelchair-user driving such a van wishes to park in the facility and overhead structures are high enough to accommodate the height of the van. However, if complete remodeling of the location is required, such as removing architectural barriers, widening doors, installing ramps, and providing braille, large print documents and closed captioned decoders, the employer will have to determine whether remodeling is affordable or whether it would impose undue hardship on the business.

Counsel Comments: *The ADA imposes strict requirements and accessibility guidelines on new buildings with respect to windows, doors, stairs, entrances, drinking fountains, sinks, toilets, telephones, elevator controls, alarms and signs, access to conference rooms, exits and maneuverability in hallways.*

The ADA also specifies that reasonable accommodation includes job restructuring, part-time or modified work schedules, and reassignment to vacant positions. Under ADA, an employer may not reduce the number of hours an employee with a disability works because of transportation difficulties and employees must be given consideration for a flexible schedule as long as that employee maintains the same number of working hours as are required of other workers in that position. In situations where, because of a disability, an employee is no longer able to perform the essential functions of his/her current job, a transfer to another vacant job for which the person is qualified is considered a reasonable accommodation; if such a position is available within the company an employer must make every effort to transfer the employee to that vacant position.

Counsel Comments: *Undue hardship has many interpretations under the ADA. Larger, more profitable companies may have greater difficulty maintaining that the cost of an accommodation constitutes undue hardship than will smaller, less profitable businesses. Experts suggest that less than half of the persons with disabilities currently employed need job accommodations requiring expenditures by the employer and that less than 15 percent need job accommodations that cost more than $500.*

With respect to promotions and training, employers cannot use standards, criteria or other administrative methods that discriminate on the basis of disability. Employers can, however, refuse to assign or reassign an individual with an infectious or communicable disease to a food-handling job. An employer may also state as a defense the fact that an employee poses a direct threat to the health or safety of other employees.

Acquired Disabilities While Working. Under the ADA, employers now have enhanced obligations to current employees who develop disabilities while on the job. Wrongful discharge of such persons could result in severe penalties, particularly for workers who contract the AIDS virus, become drug users off the premises or who develop alcohol problems affecting their attendance or performance.

AIDS and AIDS-Related Diseases. More than 1 million Americans—one in 250—are now thought to be infected with the HIV virus. Most people infected are young adults between the ages of 25 and 44, the age category that contains half the nation's workers. AIDS and AIDS-related diseases are protected "handicaps" within the meaning of the Rehabilitation Act and are considered covered disabilities under the ADA. However, to be regarded as an impairment, the employee's HIV status must be known by the company. For example, one plaintiff was unable to prove that he had been discharged solely because of a perceived disability where the company did not know he was HIV-positive.

Counsel Comments: *Employment and educational records, in addition to medical records, often contain information indicating than an individual has a disability.*

Although a person who poses a significant risk of communicating an infectious disease to others in the workplace will not be otherwise qualified for his or her job if reasonable accommodation will not eliminate that risk, case decisions indicate this does *not* extend to decisions excluding workers who are asymptomatic HIV carriers, those experiencing AIDS-related complex and those AIDS patients who are still physically capable of working. Thus, employers should not base employment decisions on the fact that an individual has AIDS or other contagious diseases or infections, unless there is no reasonable accommodation that will prevent the risk of transmission and enable the infected individual to perform the essential functions of the job.

Counsel Comments: *All companies should develop and follow comprehensive AIDS policies so that people with AIDS or HIV infection receive the same rights and opportunities as workers with other serious illnesses. Such policies must comply* *with all relevant state and federal laws and regulations and be based on the scientific fact that the HIV virus cannot be transmitted through ordinary workplace contact. All policies should be communicated by supervisors and upper management but all medical information concerning employees should be screened to maximize confidentiality considerations.*

As previously stated, HIV screening should not be required as part of pre-employment or routine workplace medical examinations. Companies must also establish education and training programs to reduce potential workplace problems, especially in places such as hospitals where there is a higher risk of HIV exposure.

Finally, as discussed on page 64 in Chapter 2 in the section entitled "Health Benefits Of Employees With AIDS," the U.S. Supreme Court has left undisturbed a ruling from the U.S. Court of Appeals for the Fifth Circuit, approving a medical plan that capped at $5,000 the amount of coverage for HIV-related illnesses.

However, the Equal Employment Opportunity Commission (EEOC) recently ruled that companies may not exclude AIDS coverage from their medical plans altogether because such an exclusion violates the ADA. Some smaller companies that established self-insured plans were excluding coverage for pre-existing conditions for a period of time (typically up to a year) after a person became employed. As a result of this ruling, companies must now proceed with caution and seek competent legal advice before implementing any self-insured plan which seeks to preclude coverage for HIV and AIDS sufferers. Additionally, any plan previously established which excludes persons with AIDS may now have to be modified.

Drug Use. Post-employment drug tests are permitted and employees who are currently illegal drug users are not protected from adverse action. However, if an individual has successfully completed a supervised drug rehabilitation program or has otherwise been rehabilitated successfully and no longer uses drugs, or is presently participating in a supervised drug rehabilitation program and no longer uses drugs, that person cannot be penalized.

Alcohol Use. Although American society and the workplace has suffered greatly from the proliferation of illegal drug use, the most widely abused drug—alcohol—is legal. The amount of alcohol-related lost time and non-productivity is staggering. To minimize the dangers of alcohol abuse, employers must remain vigilant and be aware of how problems are manifested. However, due to the enactment of numerous state and federal anti-discrimination laws, including the ADA, all companies must follow strict policies and procedures to insure that their treatment of alcoholic employees, particularly those workers who are entitled to reasonable accommodation and protection from discrimination on the basis of their physical handicap of alcoholism, conforms to the law.

How can an employer determine whether the physical condition of a worker who drinks only outside of work hours constitutes an alcoholic condition protectable by law? What sanctions can be imposed on workers drinking on the job? Is a company obligated to allow a worker time off to attend AA meetings and clinics without terminating that individual? All employers must know answers to these questions and establish policies and practices affecting alcoholic workers to avoid running afoul of the law in this area.

Employers are permitted to prohibit the use of alcohol on the job and require that employees not be under the influence of alcohol when they report to work. In addition, workers who behave or perform unsatisfactorily due to alcohol use may be fired or treated in the same way as other workers. This is because workers who drink on the job or alcoholics who are incapable of performing their jobs properly or who present a direct threat to property or the safety of others are not protected under the law.

However, all companies must be especially careful before making any adverse decision affecting an alcoholic worker and analyze each case on its particular facts.

Reasonable accommodation of an alcoholic often consists of offering the employee rehabilitative assistance and allowing him/her the opportunity to take sick leave for treatment before initiating disciplinary action. Even if the employee refuses treatment, documentation which clearly demonstrates repeated unsatisfactory performance must be in place before a termination decision is effectuated. In one recent case, for example, a company was found liable for not offering leave without pay for a *second* treatment in a rehabilitation program! The judge commented that one chance is not enough, since it is recognized that relapse is predictable in the treatment of alcoholics.

Counsel Comments: *In another case, the judge outlined a series of steps an employer must take to avoid violating the law which is worth repeating:*

* *First, offer counseling.*

* *If the employee refuses, offer a firm choice between treatment and discipline. If the employee chooses treatment, the employer cannot take any detrimental action during the period of the rehabilitation program.*

In case of relapse, do not automatically terminate, but some discipline short of discharge can be imposed.

* *Before termination, determine if retention of the worker would impose an undue hardship on the employer. If removal is the only feasible option, the company still must evaluate whether the alcoholic condition caused poor performance; if so, the company should counsel and offer leave without pay first.*

By establishing and offering an employee assistance program, your company can help provide the required reasonable accommodation and not violate the law. Such programs may protect employers from discrimination complaints and should be implemented whenever possible. In some states, notably New York and Michigan, state laws require that an employee's group health plans cover alcoholic rehabilitation programs.

When firing alcoholic workers covered under union collective bargaining agreements, an employer's position is strongest when the company can prove that all employees were notified of rules regarding disciplinary misconduct *before* accepting employment; that those rules were reasonable; that the company conducted a fair and objective investigation; that the employer first sought or encouraged the employee to receive treatment; that if the employee refused, he/she was given additional warnings before termination; and that the final penalty imposed fit the seriousness of the act(s).

Counsel Comments: *Employers must face the alcoholism problem in a sympathetic yet professional way. Documentation of the problem and the help offered is essential in defending any charge of disability discrimination. Information pertaining to an employee's participation in a rehabilitation assistance program must be carefully protected to avoid violating the individual's privacy rights.*

Above all, employers must be knowledgeable of the applicability of state and local laws to their activities, in addition to federal law, and be sure to follow such laws. It is essential to consult experienced labor counsel before taking action on these complex issues because although the ADA provides a minimum level of protection for disabled individuals, many states, such as New York and California, have stronger laws favoring employees. In states which previously allowed medical examinations and drug testing, the ADA has curtailed the effect of such statutes, further eroding an employer's power.

Damages for ADA violations are substantial. When a court has found an illegality, it can order injunctive relief and impose civil fines and other monetary assessments. Individuals may sue and recover monetary remedies in the form of back pay, accrued benefits, reasonable attorney fees and even be awarded a previously denied job. If the Department of Justice chooses to prosecute a company, the employer may be required to pay compensatory damages to any aggrieved persons, plus the cost of the reasonable accommodation, and may be fined as much as $30,000 for an initial violation and up to $100,000 for any subsequent violation.

SEX DISCRIMINATION

The body of sex discrimination law has many facets. To avoid exposure to charges of sex discrimination, the law requires equal pay for equal work and equal treatment, policies, standards and practices for males and females in all phases of the employment relationship. This includes hiring, placement, job promotion, working conditions, wages and benefits, layoffs and discharge. For example, it is discriminatory in virtually all states to:

- Refuse to hire women with preschool-age children while hiring men with such children;
- Require females to resign from jobs upon marriage when there is no similar requirement for males;
- Include spouses of male employees in benefit plans while denying the same benefits to spouses of female employees;
- Restrict certain jobs to men without offering women a reasonable opportunity to demonstrate their ability to perform the same job adequately;
- Refuse to hire, train, assign or promote pregnant or married women, or women of child-bearing age, merely on the basis of sex;
- Deny unemployment benefits, seniority, or layoff credit to pregnant women, or deny granting a leave of absence for pregnancy if similar leaves of absence are granted for illness;
- Institute compulsory retirement plans with lower retirement ages for women than for men.

The Equal Pay Act Of 1963

One common form of illegal activity pertains to unequal pay for equal work. For example, one major university was ordered to pay 117 women an award of $1.3 million after a Federal Court judge ruled that the university paid less money to women on the faculty than to men in comparable posts.

The Equal Pay Act (EPA) prohibits covered employers with two or more employees from paying unequal wages to male and female employees who perform substantially the same jobs. While the EPA and the Civil Rights Act of 1964 both prohibit sex discrimination in the workplace, the EPA has limited application since it applies only to wage inequities between the sexes. When equal skill, effort and responsibility for the same job are required, equal pay must be given. Further, an employer may not retaliate against a female worker, such as by firing her, because an EPA charge was initiated or her testimony was given. A female worker may seek damages in federal or state court or through the EEOC, and may obtain a trial by jury. Successful litigants are entitled to recover retroactive backpay, liquidated damages, reasonable attorney fees and costs.

Employers *may* pay differential wages if there is a bona fide pre-established seniority system, a merit system or a system which measures earnings by quantity or quality of production or if the differential is based on a legitimate factor other than sex. However, the EEOC is empowered to investigate carefully all charges made pursuant to the EPA within two years after the cause of action accrued to determine whether the company-offered exclusions are valid.

Key provisions of this law are:

- Employers are obligated to maintain and save records documenting wages paid to each employee.
- Once a plaintiff shows that she performs work in a position requiring equal skill, effort, and responsibility under *similar* working conditions, and that she was paid less than employees of the opposite sex, the burden shifts to the employer to show an affirmative defense that any wage differential is justified by a permitted exception. Practices that perpetuate past sex discrimination are not accepted as valid affirmative defenses.
- If willful violations (defined as reckless disregard of the law) are found, double backpay may be awarded.
- Fringe benefits are included in the definition of wages under the law. Thus, employers cannot differentiate with items such as bonuses, expense accounts, profit-sharing plans, leave benefits, etc.
- Under the EPA, it is not a defense to a charge of sex discrimination in benefits that the costs of such benefits are greater with respect to one sex than the other.

Counsel Comments: *To avoid charges of EPA violations, always prepare* precise *job descriptions that demonstrate different duties and responsibilities for different pay. When offering jobs with different salaries and benefits, try to give those with extra duties to applicants on the basis of additional education and work experience, rather than sex. Investigate all charges of unequal pay immediately and* *without bias. It is also a good idea to perform audits periodically within each unit or department of the company to insure that no EPA violations have occurred.*

Pregnancy Discrimination

A significant problem facing employers is the impact that pregnancy discrimination and related leaves, child care and disabilities play in their financial bottom line. Many companies are being sued by employees claiming sex discrimination based on preferential treatment. And, due to the enactment of numerous state laws and the federal Family and Medical Leave Act, larger companies are required to provide increased maternity and paternity leaves for their employees.

This section clarifies what constitutes pregnancy discrimination and related areas, including maternity and parental leave, disability pay during pregnancy and a woman's right to reinstatement when she is able to return to work.

Generally, a company cannot treat pregnancy-related disability or maternity leave differently from the way it treats other forms of disability or leaves of absence. To do so violates both federal and state discrimination laws. The Pregnancy Discrimination Act of 1978, an amendment to Title VII of the federal Civil Rights Act of 1964, prohibits discrimination on the basis of pregnancy, childbirth and related medical conditions. The law requires employers to review their leave, benefit, job reinstatement and seniority policies to insure that they treat pregnancy-related disability and maternity-leaves of absence the same as other temporary absences for physical disabilities.

The law also demands equality in health coverage for pregnant workers. Most state laws say that disabilities caused, or contributed to, by pregnancy, miscarriage, abortion, childbirth and subsequent recovery are, for all job-related purposes, temporary disabilities, and should be treated as such under any health or temporary disability insurance or sick leave plan available in connection with employment—a position affirmed by federal law under the Pregnancy Disability Act of 1978. Although companies are not required to provide any health care benefits, when they do, pregnancy must be treated the same way as any other medical condition.

Counsel Comments: *This means that sick leave and disability benefits have to be paid only on the same terms that apply to other employees who are granted leave for temporary disabilities. If company health care is provided, maternity care must be included and coverage must be the same for spouses of males and females. Limitations on maternity coverage for pre-existing conditions must be similar to limits on other disabilities. If extended benefits are given for other disabilities, so too must extended benefits be given for pregnancies occurring during a covered period.*

In one recent case, employees were granted basic hospital, surgical and major medical benefits under a company's health insurance plan. Employees and their dependents were reimbursed for 100 percent of the charges for basic medical care with the exception that wives of male employees were reimbursed for pregnancy-related charges at the rate of only 80 percent of the actual charges. In addition, the plan provided that an employee could not continue coverage more than three months following termination. Benefits for dependents terminated at the same time as those for employees, except for pregnancy benefits for dependent spouses. The spouse of a male employee was covered for maternity expenses throughout her pregnancy, even if it extended for more than three months after her husband's termination.

A female worker, terminated because of a business slowdown, became aware of her pregnancy a few weeks after her dismissal. Her baby was born more than three months after the termination. She participated in the three-month continuation of the medical plan and then requested medical benefits for her pregnancy from the company equal to those provided to wives of male employees under the company's health insurance plan. The company rejected her claim.

Thereupon, she brought a lawsuit charging the company with illegal sex discrimination. In court, she argued that the package of benefits received by the company's male employees was superior to the package received by females employees, since a terminated male employee's pregnant wife received pregnancy benefits beyond the three-month continuance of the health plan, whereas a terminated female employee could not.

The company argued that benefits to a female employee could be different from those granted to the spouse of a male employee, and that her claim confused discrimination between employees (which the law forbids) with discrimination between an employee and a non-employee spouse (which the law allowed).

The court found that the company was guilty of sex discrimination and that the ex-employee was entitled to the same maternity coverage as the wives of male employees. Said the Oregon Court of Appeals: "The company plan explicitly treats pregnancy of the male employee's spouse differently from all other medical risks, including the risk of the female employee's pregnancy, which is covered only for three months after discharge. The employer's plan, therefore, gives married male employees a package of medical benefits that is more favorable than the package of medical benefits provided to married female employees. It singles out pregnancy as a covered risk in a manner that adversely affects female employees as against male employees and, therefore, discriminates against female employees because of sex."

> **Counsel Comments:** *An EEOC regulation strongly supports the Oregon court's decision: "It shall be an unlawful employment practice for an employer to make available benefits for the wives and families of male employees where the same benefits are not made available for the husbands and families of female employees; or to make available benefits for the wives of male employees which are not made available for female employees."*

Pregnant Workers and Pregnancy Leave: Even before the enactment of the Family and Medical Leave Act, the rights of pregnant workers changed dramatically over the past few years since approximately 30 states, the District of Columbia and Puerto Rico have adopted some form of family or medical leave. Those states include Alaska, California, Connecticut, Delaware, Florida, Georgia, Hawaii, Illinois, Iowa, Kansas, Kentucky, Louisiana, Maine, Massachusetts, Minnesota, Montana, New Hampshire, New Jersey, North Carolina, North Dakota, Oklahoma, Oregon, Rhode Island, Tennessee, Vermont, Washington, West Virginia, and Wisconsin. The laws give female workers either job security (i.e., the right to have her job back within a certain period of time after giving birth) or the ability to enforce the right to take a maternity leave. Also, some states, including California, New York, New Jersey, Rhode Island and Hawaii, provide paid maternity leave (one-third to one-half of the regular salary) under Workers' Compensation laws, for a period usually up to 26 weeks, and include pregnant women in their temporary-disability insurance coverage. Other states, such as Minnesota, Oregon and Connecticut, are granting workers, both male and female, the right to care for their newborn and adopted children for a period of time after birth.

In 1992, the number of pregnancy discrimination lawsuits filed with the EEOC exceeded 3,000. An article which ran in early 1993 in *The New York Times* stated that more than 57 percent of women age 16 or older are in the workforce and more than 2 million have babies each year. The article reported that more than 80 percent of employed pregnant women have full-time jobs and of the approximately 57 million women in the workforce, 85 percent of working women are likely to become pregnant during their careers. Citing a study by the Families and Work Institute, the article also stated that 84 percent of women expecting children work into the final month of the pregnancy; approximately one-third return to work within eight weeks, half return within three months and more than two-thirds return to work within six months after giving birth.

Due to the sheer numbers of employees involved and increased legal scrutiny and activity in this area, it is essential to operate properly.

The following rules will simplify what employers must generally do to comply with the law in this area:

- Pregnancy is a disability that must be treated the same as any other disability.
- Although employers may require workers to give notice of a pregnancy, such a requirement must serve a legitimate business purpose and must not be used to restrict a worker's job opportunities.
- Employers are prohibited from discriminating in hiring, promotion and firing decisions on the basis of pregnancy or because of an abortion.
- Employers cannot require pregnant workers to exhaust vacation benefits before receiving sick pay or disability benefits unless all temporarily disabled workers are required to do the same.
- The decision as to whether payment for pregnancy disability leave will be given must be in accord with policies governing other forms of disability leave; if paid leave is provided for workers with other disabilities, the employer must provide pregnant

workers with paid leave for their actual disability due to pregnancy and related childbirth.

- Time restrictions placed on pregnancy-related leaves (i.e., that pregnancy leaves not exceed four months) must be reasonable and job related; if not, they may be illegal.
- It is illegal to place pregnant workers on involuntary sick leave if the company has no policy of placing workers with other forms of disability on involuntary leave; if a worker is physically able to work, the company cannot force her to leave merely because she is pregnant.

Counsel Comments: *To minimize wrongdoing, distinguish between leaves of absence for pregnancy and leaves for post-natal care. This should be clearly explained in a company handbook. Many well-run companies provide pregnant employees with paid leave for their actual disability due to pregnancy, followed by a personal leave for purposes of child care, which may or may not be paid, depending on the company's policy for personal leave, and federal and state law.*

In designing a company manual, it is wise to organize your "leave of absence" policy into three categories: (1) Disability/Sick leave; (2) Personal leave; and (3) Military leave, with the specific procedures and other provisions explaining each type of leave. Jury duty and personal day provisions should be treated in a section on attendance or absenteeism, since these kinds of paid absences are usually of shorter duration than leaves of absence.

Most importantly, think ahead before firing any worker after being informed that she is pregnant. Many such workers automatically assume that pregnancy was the reason of the discharge and file a claim alleging pregnancy discrimination with the EEOC or appropriate state agency. It may be a better idea to continue the person's employment until she voluntarily leaves to give birth, rather than fire her several months before the birth, to avoid the added costs and burdens of contesting such a charge. If you must fire a pregnant female worker, be sure that her file supports the decision (i.e., unfavorable job performance appraisals and repeated written warnings are present in the file and were presented to the female employee before your company was notified about her pregnancy). If you are concerned about the potential adverse ramifications in a particular situation, always seek the advice of competent legal counsel before making any final decisions in this area.

The Family And Medical Leave Act

A major concern faced by pregnant workers is the ability to get their jobs back after giving birth. Up to now, only some states had laws requiring companies to hold jobs open for pregnant workers. The signing of the FMLA by President Clinton will certainly impact millions of employees working for companies with 50 or more employees who desire job-protected leave. This section will analyze pertinent details of the legislation and offer strategies for companies to follow.

The act, which was signed into law on February 4, 1993, affects private and non-profit employers as well as federal, state and local government employees. It applies to companies who employed 50 or more employees within a 75-mile radius for each working day for each of 20 or more calendar workweeks in the current or preceding calendar year (about half of the nation's workforce) and takes effect on or about August 4, 1993. Part-time employees and employees on leaves of absence are counted in this calculation provided they are on the employee's payroll for each day of the workweek. Conversely, employees who began employment after the beginning of a workweek, were terminated prior to the end of a workweek or who worked part-time on weekends, are not included in the equation.

Counsel Comments: *Since companies with less than 50 employees are exempt, analyzing the number of employees who must be counted becomes an important consideration for organizations close to the "magic" 50 number. Experts predict that some companies who employ approximately 50 workers might terminate a few one way or another to avoid the law's requirements and burdens. However, it is possible to maintain a sufficient work-*

force and still be exempt from the law's impact by hiring temporary, contract employees or part-time workers who work 25 or fewer hours a week.

An eligible employee, defined as someone who has been employed for at least 12 months *and* worked for the employer at least 1,250 hours during the 12-month period immediately preceding the commencement of the leave, is allowed to take up to 12 weeks of unpaid leave in any 12-month period for:

- The birth of a child;
- The adoption of a child;
- To care for a child, dependent son or daughter over the age of 18, spouse or parent with a serious health condition; or
- To convalesce from a serious health condition that makes it impossible for him/her to work.

The 12 months of employment rule need not have been consecutive and the number of hours needed to satisfy the 1,250-hour requirement will be computed liberally according to guidelines promulgated under the Fair Labor Standards Act (FLSA). Additionally, some employees who require continuing medical supervision (i.e., workers with early stage cancer or who had major heart surgery) who must undergo frequent medical examinations or treatment but are nonetheless capable of working part-time still fit into the category of suffering from a "serious health condition" and qualify for leave time. Those workers who qualify are required to give 30 days advance notice unless advance notice was not anticipated or not practical, such as in a premature birth or sudden, unexpected illness.

The law applies equally to both male and female employees. Thus a father, as well as a mother, can take family leave and at the same time or sequentially, depending upon the family's preferences and economic considerations. However, if both spouses are employed by the same company, the law limits the total amount of leave to 12 weeks for both in most situations.

For those workers claiming serious health situations, the law permits an employer to obtain medical opinions and certifications regarding the need for a leave. The certification must state the date on which the serious health condition began, its probable duration, the appropriate medical facts within the knowledge of the health care provider regarding the condition, and an estimate of the amount of time the employee needs to care for a family member or himself. If an employer has doubts about the certification, it may require a second opinion from a different health care provider chosen by the employer. If both opinions differ, a third opinion from a provider jointly designated or approved by the employer and employee will be final and binding.

A key element of the law allows a person taking leave to be restored to his or her position or to an *equivalent* position, with *equivalent* benefits, pay, and other terms and conditions of employment, upon returning from the leave. The burden is on the employer to give the worker back the same or equivalent job. This differs from a comparable or similar job wherever possible. Also, no employer may deprive an employee of benefits accrued before the date on which the leave commenced. On the other hand, if the employer was about to lay off the worker just before being notified of the leave, the employee's right of reinstatement is no greater than what it was when the layoff occurred.

During the time the worker is on leave, an employer is not required to pay the worker but is required to maintain health insurance benefits at the level and under the conditions coverage would have been if the employee had continued in employment.

Counsel Comments: *Nothing requires an employer to provide health benefits if it does not do so at the time the employee commences leave. However, if the employer was considering establishing a health plan during the employee's leave, the worker on leave is entitled to receive the same benefits other workers still on-the-job receive. But, an employer has the authority to demand repayment for the group health-care premiums paid by the employer during the leave if the employee fails to return after the period of leave to which the employee is entitled has expired and the reason was not caused by a recurrence or onset of a serious health condition or other circumstances beyond the employee's control. Also, the law prohibits a worker on leave from collecting unemployment or other government compensation.*

Important Exceptions. There are numerous exceptions employers should be aware of. First, an eligible employee may elect, or an employer is permitted, to substitute any accrued paid vacation leave, personal leave or family leave of the employee under pre-established policies in handbooks or employee manuals for any part of the 12-week period of family leave. As a result, many companies will not be seriously impacted by the new law by transferring existing personnel, hiring temporary workers and working out job-sharing arrangements to fill vacancies since they previously implemented effective leave policies and gave time off. Those companies need now only provide both paid and unpaid leave up to a total of 12 weeks. Also, the act gives employers the right to count time off against paid vacation days or other accrued personal leave.

The leave requested may not generally be intermittent or on a reduced schedule without the employer's permission or except when medically necessary; employers are permitted to require an employee taking intermittent leave as a result of planned medical treatments to prove the medical necessity for the leave and to transfer temporarily to an equivalent alternative position. This provision gives employers greater staffing flexibility by enabling them temporarily to transfer employees who need intermittent leave or leave on a reduced schedule to positions that are more suitable for recurring periods of leave.

Finally, employers can exempt highly compensated employees in the highest paid 10 percent of the workforce (within 75 miles of the facility at which the employee works) provided granting the leave would cause substantial and grievous economic harm to the employer. As reported in the legislative history of the Senate version of the bill, "In measuring grievious economic harm, a factor to be considered is the cost of losing a key employee if the employee chooses to take the leave, notwithstanding the determination that restoration will be denied."

Counsel Comments: *Note however that a key employee who takes leave is still eligible for continuation of health benefits, even if the employee has been notified that reinstatement will be denied. Under such circumstances, no recovery of premiums may be made by the employer if such employee has chosen to take or continue leave after receiving such notice.*

Enforcement Concerns. The Secretary of Labor has the authority to investigate alleged violations of the FMLA. This includes requesting employers to submit their books and records for inspection. Violations are punishable by injunctive and monetary relief. For employers who violate the law, monetary damages include an amount equal to the wages, salary, employment benefits, or other compensation denied or lost to an employee. In cases where no compensation or wages is lost, the law imposes other forms of damages, such as the actual amount of out-of-pocket money incurred in paying someone else to provide care. Interest on any judgment is permitted. In the event a willful violation is proved, employers are liable for additional damages equal to the amount of the award.

Counsel Comments: *A court has the discretion to award no liquidated damages when an employer proves any act or omission was made in good faith and the employer had reasonable grounds to believe it was not acting improperly. This might occur, for example, after receiving a lawyer's written opinion that the company was not violating the law after being notified by an employee that a violation was, in fact, being committed. Thus, it is important to request and save all favorable written opinions from counsel for this purpose.*

The law also imposes reasonable attorney fees, expert witness fees and other costs and disbursements.

At the time of this book's publication, no interim rules or cases have been published to help simplify the act's provisions. Therefore, employers must proceed cautiously in this area and speak to legal counsel for pertinent information. Employers are forbidden from discriminating against workers who attempt to utilize the act or who protest alleged violations. Similarly, it is unlawful to retaliate against any worker by discharge or reduced benefits because an employee has filed a charge or instituted a proceeding concerning the law or is about to give (or has given) testimony regarding the act.

Most importantly, in the event your state law is more comprehensive or offers greater benefits to workers than the federal law, the state law is not pre-empted by the federal legislation. Thus, for example, state or local laws that provide greater employee protection, longer leave periods, or paid leave will predominate. For exam-

ple, in Oregon, 12 weeks of parental leave is provided to workers in companies with 25 or more employees; thus, Oregon's law would apply to smaller companies. Finally, the FMLA cannot take away rights granted to employees in collective bargaining agreements, pension plans, ERISA rights, or rights granted as a result of the Americans With Disabilities Act and other discrimination laws.

Hazardous Jobs

Recently, the U.S. Supreme Court stated that employers cannot ban women from certain hazardous jobs, even if the motive is preventing birth defects in fetuses those female workers may be carrying. In the case in question, the Supreme Court ruled that a manufacturer acted illegally by prohibiting women capable of bearing children from holding jobs involving exposure to lead during the manufacture of batteries. The court ruled that such a policy forces some women to choose between having a child and keeping a job, and thus violated federal laws against sex discrimination.

Counsel Comments: *Despite the ruling of this case, women who insist on remaining in such jobs still have the right to sue their employers for damages on behalf of a child born with prenatal injuries caused by workplace conditions, even years after being exposed to such hazardous conditions. To minimize liability, employers should educate workers about any dangers they may face on the job. Employees should be encouraged to ask for reassignment from hazardous jobs in the event they become pregnant. However, to meet Supreme Court guidelines, such reassignments must be* voluntary, *and there can be no reduction in a worker's compensation benefits or seniority rights. If no alternative position is available, consider offering the worker leave with full pay during the pregnancy to reduce potential problems.*

Some companies require female workers to execute releases which state that the worker has been advised of the potential hazards to her and her fetus. When such releases are signed knowingly and voluntarily, a company's exposure may be reduced since it demonstrates the employee's awareness and consent to the risks.

Pregnancy And ADA

The ability of pregnant workers to succeed in demanding special accommodations has been strengthened by the passage of state and local laws. For example, a recent decision by New York City's Commission on Human Rights cited pregnancy as a "per se disability" requiring a company to make reasonable accommodation if asked to do so by an employee. Under many of these new laws the physical demands of pregnancy may require companies to allow pregnant workers to work at home or rearrange their work schedules. This means that when a woman seeks reasonable accommodation during pregnancy, an employer may now be required to be responsive to the particular physical limitation which the employee brings forward on a case-by-case basis. Employers unwilling to comply with such a request are required to justify their decisions by demonstrating that compliance would create an undue hardship.

Under the ADA, the issue of whether pregnancy is considered a covered disability has not been tested, but regulations published by the EEOC, which enforces the ADA, suggest it will not be since the regulations state that "temporary non-chronic impairments that do not last for a long time and that have little or no long-term impact usually are not disabilities."

Counsel Comments: *Be sure your company understands the impact state and local laws may play on the treatment of pregnancy-related accommodations to avoid violating the law.*

Maternity Leave

The following rules should govern your company's policies in this area:

- Employees who are on maternity leave are entitled to accrue seniority, automatic pay increases and vacation time on the same basis as other employees on medical leave.
- Employers may require a physical examination and doctor's certification of ability to return to work only if such is required of all temporarily disabled employees.
- After the birth, an employer cannot prohibit a woman from returning to work sooner than the company policy dictates.

- The law requires the granting of maternity leave of absence if leaves of absence are granted for other reasons.
- It is illegal to place a time restriction on the duration of maternity leaves unless the same restrictions are applied to leaves for other temporary disabilities.

Counsel Comments: *To avoid common maternity leave problems, do not place time restrictions on the duration of maternity leaves unless the same restrictions are applied to leaves for other temporary disabilities. Post-disability care should be treated as personal leave and the rules governing this should be established in a company policy manual. For example, the manual can state that two weeks personal leave is given upon written request, and that this may be extended at the company's discretion in unusual circumstances, but for no more than* X *weeks.*

Require all pregnant women, like other disabled employees, to submit a doctor's certificate stating the length of time they will be unable to perform their duties due to pregnancy. Usually, such a certificate states disability for two weeks before and six weeks after the birth. If the employee requests additional time for post-disability child care, you would then consider such a written request pursuant to company policy on unpaid personal leaves of absence, and federal and state law.

Can pregnancy bar an employee's recall from layoff? Of 200 employees in a particular department, only four were women. One of the women was laid off due to a reduction in force in December 1989. In June 1990, the company recalled 18 workers, including the plaintiff. Because she had become pregnant in March 1990, her physical state was carefully reviewed by the company's medical department. The company doctor rejected her request for recall on the ground that she "lacked apparent ability to do the work." In doing so, the doctor overruled a finding of the employee's own doctor that she was fully capable of resuming work.

The conflict in medical opinion led the plaintiff to file an immediate grievance demanding a return to her occupation and back pay for all losses suffered. At the arbitration hearing, she set forth that the company employed close to 1,000 women, many of whom go through much of their pregnancies without being placed on leave. She argued that there was no valid reason why the same right could not be extended to her, especially when her own doctor okayed her return to work. The company responded that the job was far too strenuous for a pregnant employee and that the other women employees mentioned by the plaintiff were employed in other departments where the work was lighter.

The arbitrator ruled that the continued layoff was entirely justified. The plaintiff failed to prove that the company doctor's decision was unreasonable, arbitrary or discriminatory since the company doctor was a specialist in occupational medicine (while the plaintiff's doctor was not). However, the arbitrator stated it was not advisable to place a "standard" restriction on a pregnant employee.

In keeping with the medical literature on this point, employers should evaluate each case on an individual basis, taking into account the physiological changes that occur in the various stages of pregnancy.

Since it has been reported that more than two of every three new employees entering the workforce is a female, it becomes increasingly important to spell out a sound maternity-leave policy in your company manual. One large company established the following leave of absence for expectant mothers:

"All employees who become pregnant should notify management. The date to which a pregnant employee may work prior to delivery must be determined by the employee's doctor based upon the employee's type of work and her physical condition. However, the Company reserves the right to initiate a pregnancy leave if the employee's work habits, quality, or quantity of work are adversely affected by her pregnancy.

"A pregnancy leave shall not normally extend for more than four months, and it should normally start one month prior to and extend no more than three months past the expected date of delivery. The pregnant employee must notify management at least two weeks prior to the last day of her leave that she will return to work. The intent of this policy is to give the new mother sufficient time to determine if she will be able to return to work and also give the Company sufficient notification to plan its staffing."

Counsel Comments: *Even with the FMLA, your company can advise an employee that you cannot guarantee a return to her job after her maternity leave for postnatal care if it exceeds a certain number of weeks (e.g., 12), but be sure that your policy treats all other personal leaves in the same way.*

When formulating policy on disability leaves, consider imposing a flat time limit on all such leaves (i.e., four months) which includes pregnancy-related disability leave. Your other option is not to specify a time limit, relying instead upon the duration of actual disability substantiated by required medical proof.

If an employee is out on leave for a pregnancy-related medical disability that actually continues (by complications substantiated by required medical proof) for more than three to four months, many state laws say that you must allow her to return to work when she is physically able to resume her duties.

Paternity Leave

Paternity leave is typically defined as personal leave for child care without pay which occurs after the physical disability from pregnancy and/or birth has been removed.

Parental leaves for postnatal care differ from disability leaves in that they are typically given without pay and are considered personal leaves of absence for the purposes of company policy, as opposed to money given for an absence from work caused by a physical disability.

More and more employers are recognizing the need to provide paid and unpaid time off for employees to take care of newborn and aging relatives. This trend is not altruistic since studies show that workers with child care problems are likely to quit their jobs and allowing parental leave is often cheaper than replacing employees permanently.

As previously stated, the law varies markedly from state to state. In some states, for example, the law only extends to parents who wish to care for their natural newborn or adopted children (parental leave) as opposed to time off caring for elderly parents or attending to family-related medical problems (defined as family leave). In addition to the kinds of leaves that are permitted, each state differs on the duration of the leave (from six weeks per year up to a maximum of 24 weeks over a two-year period), whether a job will be held open while the employee is out on leave, whether both spouses who work for the same company may be allowed to take leaves at the same time, and the extent to which all or part of the leave is unpaid.

Counsel Comments: *It is essential to research the law in your state regarding family leaves. This is especially true since states with tougher sanctions and penalties than the FMLA must be followed. Since the majority of states are currently considering similar laws, do not feel secure if your particular state currently has no legislation in this area, because laws are rapidly changing. In fact, all employers should conduct a periodic yearly review to keep current in this area.*

More than 25 percent of all companies in the United States provide some form of parental or family leave for employees. In those states not requiring such policies, your company must now follow the federal FMLA law. Publish benefits in a company handbook or policy manual so that employees will have advance notification of what is available.

One company publishes the following parental leave rules:

"The Company will provide leave time to employees experiencing the birth or adoption of a child under the following terms and conditions:

"1. All employees who have completed at least nine (9) months of continuous service are eligible to request Parental Leave Time.

"2. Parental Leave Time can be requested for the period beginning no earlier than one month prior to the birth or adoption of a child and/or for the period beginning no longer than three months after the birth or adoption of a child.

"3. Parental Leave Time can extend no longer than sixteen (16) weeks in total, including time before, during, and after the birth or adoption of a child. Employees may elect to use accrued sick time (or sick bank time) for any portion of this leave time. Employees may be required to use some or all of accrued vacation time during a parental leave.

"4. All salary and benefits will terminate during the entire period of which leave is unpaid with the exception of company paid health benefits.

"5. Management will guarantee a return to the employee's job after a parental leave which does not exceed sixteen (16) weeks in total. However, for a parental leave request in excess of sixteen (16) weeks, the Company is under no obligation to assure the employee that his/her position will be available upon his/her return.

"6. If the employee fails to return to work on the date set at the time of the approved leave request, he/she will be terminated and the termination date will be the date of which any paid leave elected has been exhausted or the actual date on which the leave began if no paid leave was used, unless an extension was agreed upon. The maximum allowable extension is six (6) weeks.

"7. Each request will be considered with regard to the Company's operational needs, the personal needs of the employee, and other disability leave time requested concurrently by the employee. Additionally, requests for other leave time during the year could be affected by requests for parental leave."

To avoid charges of discrimination, guidelines promulgated by the EEOC require that male and female employees receive the same benefits. If unpaid leaves of absence are provided by your company, fathers as well as mothers of newborn or adopted children must be given such personal leave. Also, if the company permits extended child-care leave to mothers, employee-fathers must receive the same benefits.

Counsel Comments: *It is essential that your company be consistent in its benefits and leaves policies, showing no favoritism to one sex over another. The following practices violate federal and state discrimination laws in the administration of fringe benefits and entitlement to continue pension, profit-sharing plans, bonuses and other financial benefits while on leaves, as well as vacations, holidays, and paid leaves:*

* *Conditioning benefits available to employees and their spouses and families on a particular status such as "head of household" or "principal wage earner";*
* *Making certain benefits available to wives of male employees but denying them to husbands of female employees;*
* *Denying a job or benefit to pregnant employees or job applicants.*

Sex Harassment

Another prohibited form of sex discrimination is harassment. Several years ago, the U.S. Supreme Court ruled that sexual harassment was actionable under Title VII of the Civil Rights Act of 1964. The importance of this development is that companies may now be held strictly liable for the acts of their supervisors and employees who engage in on-the-job sexual harassment, even if management is not aware of the problem. Due in part to the Judge Clarence Thomas-Anita Hill hearings, legal actions involving sexual harassment are on the rise, since many more women now possess the confidence to step forward with their own experiences of harassment. In fact, the EEOC has seen a jump of more than 50 percent in the number of harassment complaints filed nationwide since the hearings and more than 8,000 formal complaints were filed with the agency in 1992. Studies indicate that the vast majority of working women (more than 85 percent) believe they have been sexually harassed on the job at one time or another.

To cite just one example, one former airline employee was recently awarded $7.1 million in punitive and compensatory damages for a sex discrimination-harassment charge. With the enactment of the Civil Rights Act of 1991, employers can now face as much as $300,000 in punitive and compensatory damages (such as for pain and suffering) in a jury trial for charges of sexual harassment. Previously, monetary damages under federal law were limited to back pay and other forms of equitable relief.

Sexual harassment cases are on the rise in a variety of non-traditional areas. For example, if a person is passed over for a promotion or denied benefits in favor of an individual who submitted to sexual advances, the passed-over person is considered to be a victim of sexual harassment under federal and state guidelines. Additionally, if a worker initially participates in social or sexual contact, but then rejects continued unwelcome advances, that constitutes sexual harassment in most instances. The fact that the person who is being subjected to the conduct does not communicate to the perpetrator his or her negative reaction often may not exculpate the company from liability.

The EEOC has published guidelines stating that "Where employment opportunities or benefits are granted because of an individual's submission to the employer's sexual advances or request for sexual favors, the employer may be held liable for unlawful sex discrimination against other persons who were qualified but denied that employment opportunity or benefit."

The same is true, for example, where a complainant's job application was denied and the person chosen for the position had been granting sexual favors to the supervisor.

The harassment can come from any source, not just fellow employees. For example, sexual harassment was found in one case when female employees were required to wear revealing uniforms and suffer derogatory comments from passersby. And, claims of sexual harassment are not limited to women. In one case that received nationwide coverage, a jury awarded $196,500 in damages to a man who claimed his supervisor demoted him because he refused her sexual advances. According to court testimony, the employee and his supervisor met one night in a hotel room, but the man refused to continue the relationship. The man proved he was demoted and passed over for a promotion as a result. In another case, the termination of a male employee for rejecting the advances of his homosexual male supervisor proved costly to a company.

Imaginative lawyers representing claimants in sexual harassment suits are also asserting other non-traditional causes of action in federal and state courts. These include wrongful discharge, fraud, intentional infliction of emotional distress for outrageous conduct, invasion of privacy, and assault and civil battery if the harassment involved unwanted touching. Awards from these suits often include large sums for mental anguish, back pay, reinstatement and punitive damages by a jury and insurance coverage for the defense of these charges may not be available. Damages incurred by employers also include hefty legal bills from lengthy courtroom litigation and adverse media attention.

The Doctrine Of Strict Liability

In many states, courts are ruling that companies are responsible for the acts of their supervisory employees regardless of whether the company knew about the incident. In some cases, the courts are ruling against companies on the basis that they should have known. When no prompt action is taken to end the harassment, employers often become strictly liable for the incident(s).

Title VII of the Civil Rights Act of 1964 granted employees protection from sexual discrimination, including harassment, but it is the EEOC guidelines which are employed to carry out the provisions of the act and define the concept of harassment.

The EEOC has stated that an employer is responsible for the acts of its agents, regardless of whether the acts are forbidden by the employer. In other instances—for example, when an employee harasses a fellow employee or when a non-employee, such as a client or customer, harasses an employee—the company is responsible if it knows or should have known unless the employer takes immediate and appropriate corrective action.

Definition Of Sex Harassment

Unwelcome sexual advances, requests for sexual favors, and verbal or physical conduct of a sexual nature all constitute sexual harassment when:

- The person must submit to such activity in order to be hired;
- The person's consent or refusal is used in making an employment decision (e.g., to offer a raise or promotion); or
- Such conduct unreasonably interferes with the person's work performance or creates an intimidating, hostile, or offensive working environment (e.g., humiliating comments are repeatedly addressed to the complainant).

Defining what constitutes sexual harassment depends upon the facts of each particular case. In instances when employees of either sex are propositioned for sexual favors in order to receive a promotion or raise (these are referred to as "quid pro quo" cases), the issue may be clearcut. In other situations (e.g., the "hostile, intimidating, work environment case") the issue is less clear. Typically, to establish a prima facie case, the employee must prove that (1) he or she was subjected to unwelcome sexual conduct; (2) the unwelcome sexual conduct was based on his or her gender; (3) the unwelcome sexual conduct was sufficiently pervasive or severe to alter the terms or conditions of the employee's employment and create an abusive or hostile working environment; and (4) the employer knew or should have known of the harassment and failed to take prompt and reasonable remedial action.

Courts have ruled the following to constitute sexual harassment with respect to hostile, intimidating work environment cases:

- Extremely vulgar and sexually related epithets, jokes or crusty language, provided the language is not isolated and is continuously stated to the complainant;
- Sexually suggestive comments about an employee's attire or body;
- Sexually degrading words describing an employee;
- Repeated touching of the employee's anatomy, provided the touching is unsolicited and unwelcome;
- Showing lewd photographs or objects of a sexual nature to employees at the workplace;
- Requiring females to wear revealing uniforms and suffer sexual comments from non-employee passers-by;
- Offensive, repeated requests for dates, even if the calls are made to the complainant after work;
- Continued advances of a sexual nature which the employee rejects, even after the parties break off a consensual sexual relationship.

Protecting The Company From Sex Harassment Claims. How your company investigates and acts on complaints can determine whether it will end up in court and incur substantial damages.

In one recent case, for example, after a company investigated a sexual harassment charge and found that it had merit, the employer did nothing further but to warn the supervisor. When the supervisor continued his unlawful conduct (by showing lewd pictures to the complainant), the female worker quit her job and filed a complaint with the EEOC. She was awarded $48,000 when the court ruled that the company had failed to act on its investigation.

EEOC guidelines specify preventive affirmative steps which may create immunity from liability for employers. In determining whether an employer is liable, some courts look to see if a comprehensive policy against sexual harassment was in place at the time the incident(s) occurred and whether the employer acted promptly and properly. In one case, the fact that the defendant-employer's policy on sexual harassment was vague and ineffective in protecting the victims of alleged harassment was crucial to a finding of employer liability. In that case, the court was dismayed by the company's inadequate investigation (the investigation assumed the supervisor was not the harasser, there was no documentation of the investigation in the personnel file and the supervisor had previously harassed other women in the company unhampered).

Basically, a prevention program—the best tool for eliminating sexual harassment—should include a comprehensive written policy advising workers about the dangers of sexual harassment and that sexual harassment may result from conduct by co-workers as well as supervisors. Also, employees need to be advised that not all complaints must be addressed to the employee's supervisor, especially when the supervisor is responsible for the harassment.

The following is a set of rules and strategies to assist your company in this area:

1. **Issue a specific policy in work rules, company manuals and employment agreements defining sexual harassment and prohibiting it in the workplace.** Any policy on harassment (sexual or otherwise) on the job should not only state the company's position, but also state procedures to follow should an employee feel he/she is a victim of such harassment. The following is an example:

"It is our policy to maintain a work environment free from all forms of harassment directed toward the race, ethnicity, sex, age or handicapping condition of an individual. Therefore, the use of disparaging terms, derogatory remarks and displays of insensitive treatment directly or indirectly related to race, ethnicity, age, sex, or handicapping condition will not be tolerated.

"This policy pertains to every aspect of an individual's work relationship with the Company including recruitment, selection, compensation, benefits, training and development, continuing education, social and recreational programs, promotion, transfer, demotion, relocation, corrective action, termination, and all other terms and conditions of employment.

"Any employee who believes there has been a violation of this policy has the right and responsibility to report the perceived violation as soon as possible, either to his/her supervisor, the Personnel Manager, or the President. Any complaint received by a supervisor must be reported to the President.

"The President will investigate all allegations promptly, objectively, and confidentially. The complainant has the right to invite a colleague to be present at any proceedings regarding the complainant. The Company will take no adverse action against an employee, who, in good faith, complains of harassment or reports the harassment, and will, to the fullest extent possible, protect such an employee against reprisal from other employees.

"Disciplinary action, including dismissal, where appropriate, will be taken where it is determined that harassment did take place, or where a supervisor has failed to report violations of this policy to the Personnel Manager or the President.

"The Company recognizes that the question of whether a particular course of action or conduct constitutes harassment requires a factual determination. The Company recognizes also that false accusations of harassment can cause serious harm to innocent persons. Therefore, a thorough investigation will be conducted in each case. Malicious accusations will be subject to appropriate sanctions."

Periodic reminders in policy manuals, journals and letters to employees may not only clearly define what constitutes sexual harassment, but state that any related action will not be tolerated and could lead to immediate discipline, including discharge. Additionally, employees should be notified regularly that anyone experiencing or observing such treatment is *required* to report this to management immediately, and that all communications will be held in strict confidence with no direct or indirect reprisals to the informant and/or complainant.

2. **Educate supervisors as to what constitutes sexual harassment and ways to handle any problems that may arise.** Management must be trained to address itself promptly and properly to all complaints in an objective and responsive fashion.

3. **Develop an internal complaint procedure that directs employees to "seek out" a neutral manager.**

4. **Create, through employee education, an atmosphere that encourages complainants to come forward if they have been harassed.**

5. **Take speedy action to investigate and resolve complaints.** Employees should be reminded that all complaints will be promptly and confidentially investigated. Supervisors and management should be instructed to investigate all charges, no matter how slight. The investigation would include:

- What exactly was said or done that constituted sexual harassment;
- The circumstances under which the event occurred (e.g., at a meeting, luncheon, or sales call);
- Where it happened (in the office, someone's home, etc.);
- The name of the party who allegedly caused the harassment; and
- Names of any witnesses.

All the details of the incident(s) must be documented including how the complainant acted, whether the incident was isolated or part of a series, and whether the complainant has spoken to anyone else about the incident.

Counsel Comments: *When interviewing the alleged perpetrator(s), the company, if possible, may wish to use two investigators to conduct the interviews. By using two investigators, each can check on the other's conduct to insure that neither gets too zealous or aggressive during an interview. According to James J. Oh, a lawyer with the law firm of Connelly, Sheehan and Moran in Chicago, and author of "Internal Sexual Harassment Complaints: Investigating To Win" which appeared in the Autumn 1992 issue of* Employee Relations In Action, *Volume 18, No. 2, if either the victim or perpetrator sues the company, the two investigators can corroborate each other's testimony at trial and the corroborated testimony may be more persuasive to a judge or jury. Using two investigators is a more reliable way to gather the facts because it is often difficult to ask questions and take notes at the same time. The collective decision of two investigators is often more sound than the unilateral decision of one.*

Attorney Oh recommends that neither of the investigators should be susceptible to accusations of bias due to past dealings with either the victim or perpetrator. In his excellent article, he writes that in one case, a former supervisor who was discharged after charges of sexual harassment were made against him brought suit against the company, claiming that the company had not conducted a fair and unbiased investigation as was mandated by the company's own policies. The super-

visor claimed that the person who conducted the investigation had a grudge against him because the supervisor had embarrassed the investigator by proving him wrong on two previous occasions. Although the court was troubled by the plaintiff's allegations, the defendant ultimately prevailed because the plaintiff, an at-will employee, failed to prove his discharge violated public policy.

6. **Train supervisors to remain unbiased.** Instruct the supervisor never to reach any conclusion until after he/she gathers all the evidence (e.g., by speaking to witnesses, if any). A manager investigating harassment charges should treat the incident as an accusation with serious consequences. Harassment charges must never be dismissed without full investigation. The company's policy and the investigation must recognize that either sex can be guilty of harassing and that harassment can be heterosexual or homosexual. All charges must be treated with equal concern and managers must be made to understand that harassment can occur even without physical touching.

Counsel Comments: *Since written materials may end up in court, be accurate with any notes written during the investigation. Take notes during interviews, but don't prepare a formal report which draws a conclusion. In fact, it may be better to brief superiors orally.*

If multiple incidents are reported, investigate each separately, preparing a detailed factual chronology of each.

7. **When interviewing witnesses, conduct the interview to insure privacy, such as in a room without windows, so non-essential company personnel will not see or hear what is going on.** Phrase questions so that you do not disclose any information you have already learned. Instead of asking "Did you see X touch Y?" put the question in an open-ended fashion, so that it is not an allegation: "Did you see anyone touch Y in a way that made Y uncomfortable?" Merely ask the person to report what he/she saw or heard. Avoid asking for opinions (e.g., "Did the worker ask for it?").

8. **Make all decisions in an objective manner.** Weigh all the evidence to determine the truth. Do not assume that either party is right. Avoid making definitive statements or conclusions about what occurred. In the initial investigation, stick to relevant facts only—not either party's family or sex life. Investigate the employment history of all parties involved. Does the accused person have a history of similar acts or poor work performance? Is there a reason that the complainant might have fabricated the story?

9. **Determine whether the alleged act(s) really happened and, if so, whether they legally constitute sexual harassment.** Be sure you can document your decision with concrete evidence. Draft a written report for the file; consult with and have the report reviewed by upper management before a final decision is made. Do not disparage the accused's character, job performance, or family life, as this can contribute to a finding of libel or slander, should the accused sue for defamation.

10. **Be consistent in the decision.** Determine the appropriate disciplinary action to be imposed. To avoid charges of race, age or sex discrimination, be sure that whatever action is taken is consistent with previous related forms of discipline. Consider transferring the complainant or the accused to a different department, especially if one of the parties has already agreed to move. If a transfer seems the appropriate solution, offer it but do not *force* the complainant to transfer since that might be interpreted as illegal retaliatory action for making the complaint.

11. **Implement a course of action immediately after your company is notified of a problem.** Never treat complaints lightly, particularly when they are in writing.

12. **Seek legal advice.** Speaking to a labor lawyer when you receive a written complaint is a good idea, because in addition to obtaining practical advice on how to properly investigate and act on the charge, the lawyer may assist you in drafting a written response. If a charge is then filed with your state's Human Rights Commission or the EEOC, the document can serve as a first step in demonstrating that an adequate response was taken in a timely fashion.

The checklist on page 161 may be consulted to be sure all the bases are covered.

Counsel Comments: *Keep all investigations strictly confidential. Impress the need for confidentiality on all involved. Never use actual case information in training others.*

Finally, all employees should be reminded periodically that any person who violates company policy concerning harassment will be subject to disciplinary action and possible discharge. This can go a long way toward reducing harassment within your plant or office.

Non-Sexual Harassment. All employers must take adequate steps so that no harassment, even if it is not sexual in nature, occurs within the company. Can an employee charge her psychiatric injuries to a supervisor's harassment? In one case, an employee experienced constant "run-ins" with her supervisor. Matters between them took a bad turn one day when the worker, having completed all of her work, was chatting with her co-workers. When the supervisor ordered her back to work, she told him that she had nothing to do because the computer which generated the assignments was not operating. Nevertheless, the supervisor demanded that she begin working. When the employee insisted that there was no work, the supervisor suspended her for the remainder of the working day and the following day too.

When the employee returned, the supervisor personally began giving her work orders despite the fact that all of her co-workers received their work orders from a dispatcher. When she questioned this procedure, she was again suspended. The worker became hysterical and was rushed to a hospital, where she was given a tranquilizer. Thereafter, she remained under a doctor's care for over two months. Shortly after she returned to work, she was warned about munching on some food while working. When she told the supervisor not to interrupt her work, she was again suspended.

This time, the employee did not return for three months, during which time she was treated by a psychiatrist. She filed a claim for Workers' Compensation, seeking benefits for the two periods during which she was away from work. The company opposed her claim. During a hearing, the company argued that her case for benefits was built upon malingering and exaggeration and that her job experiences involved only the normal give-and-take between employees and supervisors; a bit of criticism about not working should have been insufficient to produce the reaction the employee claimed she endured. The company also argued that the worker was blaming it for mental difficulties having nothing to do with the job.

The employee stated that even before the day when the supervisor accused her of not working, he had repeatedly singled her out for criticism and had taken an intense, irrational hatred to her. In fact, she argued that she was treated by a psychiatrist for anxiety and depression caused by the supervisor's harassment.

The Pennsylvania Commonwealth Court ruled that the employee's mental injuries were job related and ordered that she receive Workers' Compensation. It stated that the employee's testimony was not limited to her belief that she felt she was being harassed; she also described the actual events—that her supervisor accused her of not working when she was performing her duties and that she was singled out by her supervisor and told to go back to work when her duties had been completed to the same extent as those of co-workers in the same vicinity. These events constituted abnormal working conditions as a matter of law. With the addition of medical evidence establishing that the abnormal working conditions caused the psychiatric injuries, the court found that the employee had established her case for benefits.

Counsel Comments: *Similarly, the court awarded Workers' Compensation to an employee whose mental troubles arose because he was singled out for public criticism by his supervisor when co-workers were not subjected to this treatment. The employee eventually developed a fear of going to work, which led to a disabling "panic disorder."*

To avoid similar legal problems, supervisors and management should be cognizant of the potential causes of action arising from mental distress claims and be instructed how to avoid these potential problems.

Final Points About Sex Discrimination

Sex discrimination in the workplace exists in many forms. In case after case, courts and anti-discrimination agencies have hacked away at the long-time stereotype of the "weak female" who must be barred from strenuous "men's work" and restricted to gentler employment. For example, a federal court ordered a public utility to consider women for switchmen's jobs; another employer was forbidden to

CHECKLIST FOR SEXUAL HARASSMENT INVESTIGATIONS

I. PRELIMINARY CONSIDERATIONS

A. Use two investigators, if possible.

B. Create a confidential file.

C. Conduct interviews in a private room.

II. GATHERING THE FACTS

A. Review relevant personnel files and company policies.

B. Interview the victim.

1. Take her complaint seriously.
2. Explain the investigation but don't promise complete confidentiality.
3. Find out what happened: GET SPECIFICS.
4. Find out the effect of the harassment on the victim.
5. Find out names of witnesses.
6. Ask the victim what she wants.
7. Assess her credibility.
8. Take a statement, if warranted.
9. Type the notes of the interview.

C. Interview the perpetrator.

1. Explain the purpose of the interview but state that no decision has been made on the truthfulness of the allegations.
2. Identify the victim and the specific basis of the sexual harassment complaint.
3. Ask him to respond to the charges.
4. Find out names of witness.
5. Assess his credibility.
6. Take a statement, if warranted.
7. Type the notes of the interview.

D. Interview corroboration witnesses.

1. Try to elicit identity of victim and perpetrator from the witness as opposed to identifying the victim and perpetrator to the witness at the beginning of the interview.
2. Find out what he or she knows: GET SPECIFICS.
3. Distinguish between firsthand and secondhand knowledge.
4. Assess the credibility of the witness.
5. Take a statement, if warranted.
6. Type the notes of the interview.

III. EVALUATING THE FACTS AND MAKING THE DECISION

A. Evaluate the facts from a reasonable woman's perspective.

B. Distinguish between "unwelcome" and "voluntary" sexual conduct.

C. Draft a thorough, even handed report.

1. Make the report chronological.
2. Describe when first learned of the complaint.
3. Provide exact details of the complaint.
4. Note the documents reviewed.
5. Describe the interviews.
6. For all witnesses, distinguish between firsthand knowledge and rumor.
7. State conclusion as to whether sexual harassment occurred and provide specific justification.
8. Recommend corrective action if sexual harassment occurred. The corrective action should:
   a. be reasonably calculated to prevent further harassment.
   b. not punish the victim.
   c. be consistent with the discipline imposed in the past in similar situations.

D. Submit the report to the decision-making official. That official should:

1. not be a rubber stamp.
2. point out deficiencies in the report.
3. ask follow-up questions.
4. conduct interviews him or herself if necessary.
5. document his or her actions.

E. Follow up with the victim and perpetrator after the decision has been made.

impose a 35-pound weight-lifting limit on women employees. Since these stereotypes are vanishing rapidly, management must take steps to insure that supervisors are trained to act properly in all areas potentially affecting women. Finally, remember that parenthood is a neutral status that an employer may not treat differently for female applicants and employees.

Sexual Bias Discrimination. In some states, the law forbids employers from discriminating in all phases of the job on the basis of an individual's sexual preferences. To avoid problems in this area, we suggest that you speak with competent counsel for more information about relevant state and local ordinances and rulings. It is best not to fire or deny employment opportunities to a known homosexual or lesbian merely on the basis of that person's sexual preference or lifestyle.

RELIGIOUS DISCRIMINATION

The Civil Rights Act of 1964 prohibits religious discrimination and requires employers to reasonably accommodate the religious practices of employees and prospective employees. This law covers employers of 15 or more persons. Various state laws also prohibit discrimination on the basis of creed (i.e., because of a person's observance of a certain day as a Sabbath or holy day). In New York, for example, employers may not require attendance at work on such a day, including travel time, except in emergencies or in situations in which the employee's presence is indispensable. Absences for these observances must be made up at some mutually agreeable time, or can be charged against accumulated leave time.

A recent Supreme Court case illustrates just how costly a lack of knowledge in this area can be. A terminated worker sued after she was fired for refusing to work overtime on Saturdays due to her religious beliefs. In this particular case, an auto manufacturer hired a woman to work on an assembly line. Initially, the job did not conflict with her religious beliefs, which required that she not work from sunset Friday to sunset Saturday, because the assembly line operated only from Monday through Friday. However, when the company began requiring mandatory overtime on Saturdays, the worker refused on religious grounds, and was fired after missing a series of Saturday work shifts.

The employee brought suit in federal court, alleging the company violated Title VII of the Civil Rights Act that makes it unlawful to fire or discriminate against an employee on the basis of "race, color, religion, sex or national origin," and that a 1972 amendment to the law requires employers to prove they are unable to accommodate an employee's religious practice without "undue hardship."

The primary issue before the trial court was whether the company had made a bona fide attempt to meet the needs of the employee. The court ruled that the woman's absence did not injure the company and that her request was not unreasonable. The worker was awarded $73,911 in back pay and benefits, despite the employer's argument that the proper running of the business would be affected by high absenteeism rates on Saturday, numerous complaints from co-workers that the employee should not receive special privileges (i.e., that it was unfair to require them to work on Saturday while allowing the woman to take time off) and waiting lists of more senior employees requesting transfers to departments with no Saturday work.

However, the Supreme Court let the lower ruling stand, commenting that the company could have acted on the employee's request without undue hardship through the use of people employed specifically for absentee relief.

The following summarizes what companies can do in this area to avoid civil rights suits:

- Employers have an obligation to make reasonable accommodations to the religious needs of employees and prospective employees;
- Employers must give time off for the Sabbath or holy days except in an emergency;
- If employees don't come to work, employers may give them leave without pay, may require equivalent time to be made up, or may allow the employee to charge the time against any other leave with pay, except sick pay.

Employers may *not* be required to give time off to employees who work in key health and safety occupations or to any employee whose presence is critical to the company on any given day. Also, employers are *not* required to take steps inconsistent with a valid seniority system to accommodate an employee's religious practices and are *not* required to incur overtime costs to replace an employee who will not work on Saturday.

Employers have no responsibility to appease fellow employees who complain they are suffering undue hardship when a co-worker is allowed not to work on a Saturday or Sabbath due to a religious belief, while they are required to do so. Finally, employers are *not* required to choose the option the employee prefers, as long as the accommodation offered is reasonable. However, penalizing an employee for refusing to work on Christmas or Good Friday most likely constitutes religious discrimination, depending on the facts.

Counsel Comments: *With each request by an employee or prospective employee for time off for religious practices, document the date and nature of the request and the alternatives considered by your company in meeting that request. When an employee's request is denied because of an undue hardship, a full record of the nature of the hardship should be kept on file.*

The definition of a "religious belief" is quite liberal under the law. If a worker's belief is demonstrably sincere, the belief can be considered religious even though not an essential tenet of the religion of which the employee is a member. The applicant's or employee's knowledge that a position would involve a conflict does not relieve the employer of its duty to reasonably accommodate, absent undue hardship.

In most cases, the court weighs the facts to determine whether the employer offered a reasonable accommodation or that undue hardship existed; the plaintiff will attempt to show that the hardship was not severe or that the accommodation offered was not reasonable.

What constitutes undue hardship varies on a case-by-case basis. Generally, undue hardship results when more than a de minimis cost (i.e., overtime premium pay or a collective bargaining agreement is breached) is imposed on the employer.

The "undue hardship" defense is an exception that companies may use successfully to circumvent current law in this area. Speak to legal counsel to fully explore your options and document such a defense in the most appropriate manner.

RACIAL DISCRIMINATION

Statistics indicate that more than 29 million Afro-Americans, 17 million Hispanic Americans, 6 million Jews, 2.5 million people of Arab descent and 1.1 million Native Americans will enter the U.S. workforce during the next 20 years. Although such minorities were discriminated against in the past, the enactment of various federal laws, including Title VII of the Civil Rights Act and 42 USC Sections 1981 and 1982, prohibits intentional discrimination based upon ancestry or ethnicity. Some companies practice blatant forms of minority discrimination by paying lower salary and other compensation to blacks, Hispanics, Asians, Pacific Islanders, American Indian and Alaskan natives (Native Americans), and other persons having origins in Europe, North America and the Middle East. Others engage in quota systems by denying promotions and jobs to individuals on the basis of race and color. Still other employers utilize more sophisticated and subtle forms of race discrimination. In fact, of the more than 70,000 complaints filed with the EEOC in 1992 alleging job discrimination, complaints based on race accounted for more than 40 percent, the most of any category.

Federal laws prohibit employers of 15 or more employees from discriminating on the basis of race or color. Specifically, federal law applies to companies with a minimum of 15 employees on each working day in at least 20 weeks in the current or preceding calendar year; federal laws do not apply to employers with 14 or fewer employees, private membership clubs, religious organizations and Indian tribes. Virtually all states, however, have even *stronger* anti-discrimination laws directed to fighting job-related race and minority discrimination. In many states, for example, companies with fewer than eight employees can be found guilty of discrimination.

Both federal and state laws generally forbid private employers, labor unions, and state and local government agencies from:

- Denying an applicant a job on the basis of race or color;
- Denying promotions, transfer or assignments on the basis of race or color;
- Penalizing workers with reduced privileges, reduced employment opportunities and reduced compensation on the basis of race or color;
- Firing a worker on the basis of race or color.

Discrimination can occur during any of the following employment stages: recruiting, interviewing and hiring, promotion, training, transfer and assignment, discipline, layoffs, and discharge procedures. Also, an illegal act can be committed by any member of the employer's staff, from the president down to the supervisor, interviewer or receptionist. It can even occur through outside independent contractors (such as surveillance teams hired by the company). In one case, for example, a black supervisor was confined to an office and interrogated by private investigators hired by the company to obtain a confession regarding missing warehouse stock. Despite his claims of innocence, the employee was questioned for two hours; later he was fired by the company. At the trial it was determined that the reason given for the firing was pretextual and that the company was out to discharge him because he was black. Although the company claimed it was not responsible for the incident since it had hired an outside service to investigate and make recommendations regarding the matter, the individual was awarded a large settlement for mental anguish, even though he obtained a better-paying job within one month after his discharge.

Proving Allegations. Typically, the EEOC or relevant state agency will investigate charges of race discrimination or related retaliation. The EEOC has broad power to secure information and company records via subpoena, field investigations, audits, and interviewing witnesses, both employees and outsiders. Statistical data may be presented to demonstrate a pattern or practice of discriminatory conduct. Often, contents of an individual's personnel files and files of others in similar situations are examined and presented. Data on workforce composition may reveal a pattern or practice of exclusion or channeling. Regional or national data may shed light on whether a decision locally made was, in fact, racially discriminatory.

In cases where circumstantial evidence is presented to prove race discrimination, the burden is on the plaintiff to raise an inference of discrimination. This is often done through the use of statistics, computer records, payroll records, and so forth.

Counsel Comments: *For more information on the Civil Rights Act of 1991 and its impact on race and color discrimination claims, consult a previous section in this chapter.*

Affirmative Action

Today the trend in the corporate community is to attract and cultivate a diverse workforce. Affirmative action involves making a specific effort to recruit individuals on the basis of classifications (personal characteristics) such as race, sex, religion, and veteran status, when the number of such individuals within the company is greatly below the number of such individuals within the community where the company is located. Affirmative action also involves taking positive steps to insure that such individuals, when employed, have an equal opportunity for benefits and promotions within the company.

Initially, affirmative action programs were begun in compliance with federal regulations imposed upon employers having government contracts or subcontracts worth in excess of $10,000. Recent Supreme Court decisions have modified the rules so that an employer's voluntary affirmative action plan will be legal if there is a "manifest imbalance" in the makeup of the employer's workforce for a particular job category, the plan has a limited duration, and the legitimate expectations of other workers are not trampled upon. Thus, voluntary reasonable affirmative action programs established by employers will not be found to constitute reverse discrimination provided company plans have flexible goals and not rigid quotas which exclude a whole class of applicant (e.g., white males). Additionally, a company must be able to justify, statistically or otherwise, the need for an affirmative action plan and the plan must be capable of being eliminated or altered when certain goals are met.

In the Equal Employment Opportunity Commission's view, by enacting Title VII, Congress clearly intended to encourage voluntary race, sex or national origin-conscious affirmative action plans or programs in order to attain equal employment opportunity.

The "backlash" from non-minorities over the legality of such plans has diminished since the late 1970s when the first cases were announced; today, recruiters and experts agree that more employers are implementing such plans out of a desire to increase the number of minorities within their companies.

Counsel Comments: *There is no private duty for companies hiring minority employees to institute affirmative action policies. In today's job market, companies are looking for the best possible candi-*

date. If it happens that a company would prefer choosing the minority candidate with equal credentials over the non-minority applicant, so much the better. Although the laws have not changed dramatically during the past few years regarding the legality of affirmative action plans, the current economic climate is making it far more difficult for minority applicants to utilize such plans because fewer companies are hiring employees, minority or otherwise.

AGE DISCRIMINATION

Age discrimination complaints have increased markedly with older workers feeling the impact of company restructurings. This is especially true in industries such as advertising, sales and fashion where image sometimes counts as much as skill and experience. In fact, the EEOC recently reported a large increase in the number of age discrimination charges being filed from approximately 23,000 in 1990 to more than 30,000 claims in 1992.

Federal and state discrimination laws are designed to promote employment of older persons based upon their abilities, irrespective of age. They also seek to prohibit arbitrary discrimination and to help employers and workers find ways of addressing problems arising from the impact of age upon employment. The following thumbnail sketch outlines what employers *can* do under federal and state discrimination laws pertaining to age:

- Fire older workers for inadequate job performance and good cause (e.g., tardiness or intoxication);
- Entice older workers into early retirement by offering additional benefits (e.g., bigger pensions, extended health insurance, substantial bonuses, etc.), which are voluntarily accepted;
- Lay off older workers, provided younger employees are treated similarly;
- Discriminate against older applicants when successful job performance absolutely requires that a younger person be hired for the job (e.g., in the case of a flight controller).

The following actions, however, are prohibited by law:

- Denying an older applicant a job on the basis of age;
- Imposing compulsory retirement before age 70;
- Coercing older employees into retirement by threatening them with termination, loss of benefits, etc.;
- Firing older persons because of age;
- Denying promotions, transfers, or assignments because of age;
- Penalizing older employees with reduced privileges, employment opportunities or compensation because of age.

Proving Allegations. It is illegal to terminate anyone on the basis of age. Whenever an older employee (over 40) is fired and claims discrimination, the issue is basically whether the company's decision was made because of age or was the result of a reasonable, non-discriminatory, rational business decision. Typically, an older worker must use circumstantial evidence to prove that the employer's motive was improper—for example, by demonstrating that he or she was between 40 and 70 years of age, was doing satisfactory work, and vacated a position that was subsequently filled by a substantially younger employee under 40.

But, discrimination is sometimes proved by age-related statements made to the claimant (such as "You are too old, why don't you retire?" "The employee is burned out and forgetful," "You are stupid and old."). Age bias suits have been upheld when brought by senior employees who were subjected to demeaning jokes and adverse remarks about their age. To prevail however, such comments must be shown to constitute direct evidence within the context of an age discrimination case.

Statistics may also be used to prove discrimination (showing, for example, that a company fired five older workers in the past year and replaced them all with employees under 40). In a "pattern or practice" case brought under the ADEA, the plaintiffs must prove that age discrimination is the defendant's standard operating procedure or the systematic result of an employer's intentionally discriminatory practices. Direct evidence may be used to establish such an illegal pattern or practice (e.g., where an older applicant for a job at a spa is told directly by two employees that they have a policy of not hiring older workers because they want to maintain a "macho image"). In addition to direct evidence, a pattern or practice of intentional age discrimination may also be shown by an accumulation of evidence including statistics, patterns, practices, general policies and specific instances of discrimination.

> **Counsel Comments:** *When employers can support firing decisions with documentation of poor work performance such as written warnings, an older worker's chances of proving age discrimination often diminish. Additionally, if staff avoids making liability-sensitive statements, remarks or threats with respect to age and the employee is unable to obtain statistical proof that the company had a practice of firing older workers and replacing them with younger ones, the chances of provng a claim may be reduced. To head off such claims, use every form of employee communication to caution employees and supervisors against making discriminatory chatter.*

A major problem area concerning age discrimination is on-the-job discipline and warnings. Progressive discipline is useful in reducing the risk of wrongful termination lawsuits: by documenting employee disciplinary incidents through precise records of conferences, warnings, probation notices, remedial efforts and other steps, companies sometimes demonstrate that an eventual termination was not motivated by discrimination but stemmed from a good-faith business decision.

> **Counsel Comments:** *The danger here is that many companies apply their system of discipline and warnings in a haphazard fashion and fail to use the same punishment across the board for similar infractions. You invite an age discrimination lawsuit (or other discrimination charge) if several employees have a chronic problem (such as absenteeism) and the older employee is the first to be fired for that reason, while workers under 40 are only given warnings.*

On-the-job discrimination is regularly practiced in many areas. For example, companies must be able to offer strong proof that diplomas or other academic achievements are *essential* qualifications for a particular job. Otherwise, they may be subject to attack by older workers on the basis that limiting job promotions to recent college graduates at the company is a mere ploy designed to bar older workers from desired jobs or promotions.

Vacation Time. Is it age bias to place a cap on vacation time? One company fell into dire financial straits. When a new management team took control, it quickly ordered drastic employment economies. Various employee compensation and fringe benefits were cut, including the amount of vacation time employees could earn within a year. Regardless of how much time an older worker had put in at the company (older workers with 30 years or more of service were allowed to take up to 35 days of vacation each year under the old plan), no worker could take more than 20 days under the revised plan.

A group of older workers protested the vacation cap. They contended that the plan constituted illegal age discrimination because the original program was calculated on the basis of seniority which, as a general rule, correlates with age, so that the company's alteration of its program had a disparate effect on the oldest workers. By cutting benefits, such a policy also was calculated to force older workers to resign under the company's "voluntary" termination program.

The company responded that the vacation reductions were a cost-saving measure to keep the company afloat. Not only did the company cut vacations, but it instituted a hiring freeze, eliminated floating and birthday holidays and reduced medical and dental insurance benefits. Thus, the company argued that the decision was not influenced by age but rather the need to cut costs.

The U. S. District Court agreed with the employer. It noted that nothing in the federal laws barring age discrimination prohibits employers from altering the terms of a benefit seniority system so long as the new system is not a subterfuge for engaging in arbitrary age discrimination. The court added, "While it is mere common sense to assert that employees immediately affected by the four-week cap were upset by the loss, to claim that their jobs were made intolerable as a result does not begin to approach the objective standard necessary to constitute an act of constructive discharge." The court also noted that the ADEA permits age-based reductions in employee benefit plans where justified by significant cost considerations but places the burden of proof on the employer to demonstrate that its actions are lawful.

Seniority Rights. Do the age bias laws protect an employee's seniority rights? In one case a company eliminated 75 jobs by modifying a collective bargaining pact in such areas as early retirement, recall rights and "bumping" based on seniority. One 53-year-old worker filed a lawsuit accusing the company of terminating his employment on the basis of age. He argued that workers disparately affected by the company's action were seniors since by and large, workers with high seniority are generally older than individuals with low seniority. When the union and company eliminated recall rights based on seniority, older workers were thus discriminated against. The company responded that seniority rights are not necessarily a matter of age, since they are based on the result of years of service with the company. Thus, many younger workers have more seniority at the company than their older co-workers. It also claimed that the workers who were retained or rehired were chosen on the basis of what they could contribute to the company, not on the basis of age or seniority.

The court was impressed with the evidence forwarded by the company that merit and competence had played important roles in determining which employees were retained or rehired, and ruled in favor of the company. It stated, "Because seniority as a function of age is dependent upon the age at which an employee began to work for the company, employees with greater seniority are not necessarily older than employees with less...Elimination or derogation of seniority rights is not sufficient by itself to raise an inference of age discrimination in violation of the ADEA. Therefore, there was no failure to refuse to hire or discharge any individual or otherwise deny any individual with respect to his compensation, terms, conditions or privileges of employment because of such individual's age."

Retirement Plans. Another related area is forced retirement. This occurs when companies exert pressure on older workers to opt for early retirement or face firing, demotion or a cut in pay. Some also threaten workers with poor references unless they accept an offer of early retirement.

Companies contemplating a large layoff or seeking to reduce payroll through early retirement incentives must do so carefully to avoid charges of age discrimination. Under the ADEA, it is illegal to impose compulsory retirement before age 70 unless the employee is a "bona fide executive" receiving an annual company-paid retirement benefit of at least $27,000 per year after reaching 65, or is in a "high policy-making position" during a two-year period prior to reaching age 65. Some states have passed similar laws which protect older employees from being victimized by forced retirement and mandatory retirement plans. For example, under a law recently enacted in New York, most public employees cannot be forced to retire no matter how old they get. Private sector employees (with limited exceptions for some executives and tenured college faculty members) are also protected.

Can early retirement plans violate age discrimination laws? That depends on several factors. The employer will have to show that the plan is "bona fide" (e.g., plan benefits are based on an employee's length of service), that the employee's decision to accept early retirement is voluntary and that the reasons for the plan are non-discriminatory (i.e., not based on age).

Counsel Comments: *To avoid charges that a person was not given sufficient time to reflect and weigh the options of an early retirement offer and thus was constructively discharged,* always *prepare clearly written releases and documents which give retirees time to consider the offer, seek advice from an attorney and even repudiate the decision after signing the document. For maximum protection and due to the recent enactment of the Older Workers Benefit Protection Act, discussed earlier in this chapter, all early retirement offers should be documented in writing so that your company can specifically include detailed provisions waiving any potential liability to age discrimination charges. Consult that section for more details and be sure to draft all releases and waivers properly.*

Is the demotion of an older employee equivalent to a constructive discharge? One man who had worked for 33 years with a company was suddenly urged to consider accepting early retirement. His immediate supervisor told him that the company was in the process of reorganizing and that his position was being eliminated. The alternative to early retirement was a less prestigious job at lower pay. The employee took the early retirement package. Shortly afterwards, he learned that his duties had been divided among two younger employees, aged 38 and 40. He filed an age discrimination case, stating that he was pushed out because he was 52 and the company wanted to hire younger workers at less pay for his position. He also stated that the alternatives offered to him were demotions and to accept the demotions would have been equivalent to constructive discharge.

The company stated that he was pushed out not because of age but rather because the job was being eliminated. It also argued that no constructive discharge took place because the other jobs offered were well paying.

The court ruled that no constructive discharge took place because the jobs offered were reasonable and not demeaning. (Note: Constructive discharge is defined as a situation where working conditions are so difficult and unpleasant that a "reasonable person" in the employee's position would feel compelled to leave. An employee could validly claim that he had been victimized if, for example, he were an executive offered a menial, low-paying position.)

> **Counsel Comments:** *The ADEA does not forbid employers from adopting policies against "underemploying" persons in certain positions rather than forcing retirement so long as those policies are applied evenhandedly. However, there is danger that such policies may serve to mask age discrimination. Thus, when elimination of a job is imminent, rather than terminating the individual or discussing a forced retirement package, consider an older senior worker's request to be offered a lower paying job, inferior in status to the post you are about to terminate. Automatically refusing such a request may leave your company open to charges of age bias.*

Specific Benefits. Due to recent legal developments, companies are required to provide more information on retiree coverage, including its lump sum value to each employee, so retired employees or employees offered retirement incentives appreciate the value of retiree benefits. Also, while ERISA-governed pension plans must meet narrow vesting, funding and participation requirements, the same rules do not apply to health care programs.

> **Counsel Comments:** *Employers should explicitly* reserve *the right to modify the terms of their welfare plans in plan documents and related materials, so that they can change such plans at their discretion. Companies whose plans do not state that they can and may be changed without notice at the company's discretion should amend them as soon as possible to reflect that policy.*
>
> *Design all retirement plans to support corporate and human resource objectives. For example, if the company anticipates a shortage of skilled workers within ten years, it should not offer a package which encourages early retirement of experienced, skilled employees.*

Litigation Avoidance Measures. To avoid charges of age discrimination, consider the following before terminating an older worker:

- Did the older worker request a transfer to another position before the firing? Was it refused? If so, were similar requests granted to younger workers?
- How was the older worker terminated? Was he/she given false reasons for the termination? Did he/she consent to the decision and has your company received a letter protesting the discharge?
- Was the older worker immediately replaced by a younger worker? Were younger workers merely laid off and not fired?

Positive answers to questions like these may prove age discrimination. For example, 143 persons were forced to retire prematurely from an insurance company at the age of 62. The large number of employees made it difficult for the company to overcome charges of age discrimination, and the workers collectively received more than $6 million in back wages. In another case, a company denied job training to two older employees and then fired them. The company claimed the men were unskilled and not qualified to continue employment. The workers filed timely claims and recovered $79,200 in lost wages, benefits and legal fees.

All of these concerns must be properly addressed to avoid liability in this area.

DISABILITY DISCRIMINATION

The past decade has seen a tremendous increase in litigation and legislative activity, at both state and federal levels, structured to protect handicapped individuals from job discrimination. There is good reason for this: the number of Americans having disabilities has been estimated to be from 37 million to 43 million people, half of whom fall within the prime working ages of 16 to 64. In addition, although more than two-thirds of Americans who have disabilities would like to be gainfully employed if given the chance, their unemployment as a group is above 60 percent.

Before the enactment of the ADA, the main federal law protecting handicapped individuals against discrimination was the Rehabilitation Act of 1973, which applied to government contractors and employers who receive federal assistance. This law prohibits denying an otherwise qualified applicant or employee a job or opportunity, including fringe benefits, promotion opportunities and special training, solely on the basis of a handicap. Employers who have government contracts or subcontracts worth over $2,500 must take affirmative steps to employ and promote handicapped workers and must not discriminate against them. For example, a recent Justice Department opinion declared that HIV-infected people are considered "handicapped" within the meaning of sections 503 and 504 of the Rehabilitation Act of 1973, protecting them from discrimination in the workplace.

To remedy the limited applicability of the Rehabilitation Act of 1973, the ADA was enacted effective July 26, 1992. The Equal Employment Opportunity Commission has jurisdiction over and enforcement responsibility for Title I of the ADA, prohibiting employment discrimination against anyone with a disability. Experts suggest that this federal law will go a long way toward making existing facilities accessible to handicapped employees, restructuring certain jobs to provide for reasonable accommodation of persons with handicaps, and offering more part-time or modified work schedules for persons with disabilities.

For a comprehensive discussion of the ADA, see "The Americans With Disabilities Act," earlier in this chapter. The following summarizes many of the important aspects of this law for your business. Now companies are required to:

- Eliminate any inquiries about medical examinations or forms designed to identify an applicant's disabilities.
- Avoid adverse classifications of job applicants or employees because of disability.
- Avoid participating in a contractual relationship, including a collective bargaining agreement, that has the effect of discriminating against job applicants or employees with disabilities.
- Avoid discriminating against an applicant or employee because of that individual's relationship or association with another who has a disability.
- Make reasonable accommodations to the known physical or mental limitations of an applicant or employee, unless doing so would impose an undue hardship on the employer.
- Avoid denying employment opportunities to an applicant or employee solely to avoid making reasonable accommodation because of a disability.
- Avoid employment tests or selection criteria that have a disparate impact on individuals with disabilities unless the test or criterion is shown to be job-related and supported by business necessity.
- Administer employment tests in the manner most likely to reflect accurately the job-related skills of an applicant or employee who is disabled.

Any decisions not to hire an applicant because of physical defects or a mental condition will now be scrutinized closely. The Equal Employment Opportunity Commission has released regulations defining and commenting on the ADA. Officials at the Society for Human Resource Management commented that the major areas of importance clarified in the regulations include:

1. Determining whether an individual's current physical or mental condition is a "direct threat" to the health or safety of the individual or others may be a relevant job criterion.

2. Additional medical costs or increased workers' compensation premiums is not a legitimate basis for the employer to deny a qualified individual with a disability a job opportunity.

3. Determining whether a particular job function is or is not "essential" is clarified somewhat by saying that a collective bargaining agreement may be consulted.

4. Employers are permitted to provide state workers' compensation offices with medical information about employees for purposes of administering second-injury funds without violating the confidentiality provisions of the ADA. However, an employer may not inquire about an applicant's workers' compensation history.

5. Defining "reasonable accommodation" may include providing personal assistants to help a qualified individual with a disability perform an essential job function. However, providing a per-

sonal assistant to help with daily attendance care does not appear to be required.

Counsel Comments: *Even though the law prohibits and curtails numerous activities and actions, it was not meant to penalize your business. For example, employers are generally permitted to terminate workers who are physically unable to perform their duties due to a physical or mental impairment. But the employer must demonstrate present inability to do the work required, not future or past inability. Employers can deny jobs to handicapped workers if they can demonstrate that the position poses a danger to the individual's health and welfare. Jobs may also be denied if the employer can demonstrate that the job generally cannot be performed by such a class of individuals (for example, the job of an airline pilot or firefighter). Employers may also deny jobs to handicapped workers if they can demonstrate that the hiring would interfere with productivity or create dangers in the workplace.*

Special Comments Concerning AIDS and HIV. Must an employee reveal that he is HIV positive? Probably not, provided the employee's actions do not evince a willful and wanton disregard of the employer's interests. If the deception (e.g., one day a month absences for "personal" reasons) is designed to protect the person's privacy and not to harm or be disloyal to the employer, notifying the employer of such a condition may not be required. Along with the ADA, most states have now enacted laws protecting workers with AIDS, AIDS-related complex or the HIV virus as being handicapped persons and thus protected under the law.

Can you compel an employee to be examined for AIDS? Probably not, for the same reason.

RETALIATION DISCRIMINATION

Employees who legitimately assert discrimination rights by filing charges in federal court with the EEOC or state agencies, are protected from adverse action in retaliation by any employer. If the individual reasonably believes that a Title VII violation was committed, the employer should not take any action adverse to the rights of the employee, such as failing to promote, discharging, or unduly criticizing the employee, as a direct result of that action.

Acts taken by the employer as a direct result of the employee's filing charges or threatening to go to the EEOC, or bringing a lawsuit are viewed by the courts as retaliatory. Types of acts that fall into this category include:

- Transfer or reassignment that is undesired (even with no loss in pay or benefits);
- A transfer out of the country;
- Threats, when repeatedly made and when disruptive to the worker's job performance;
- Harassment on the job;
- Giving unfavorable references to a prospective employer, or otherwise interfering with the employee's efforts to obtain a new job;
- Interfering with an employment contract;
- Attempting to persuade a current employer to discharge a former employee;
- Firing the employee or forcing retirement by eliminating the position and offering only lesser alternative positions;
- Denying or suspending severance payments;
- Retroactively downgrading an employee's performance appraisals and placing derogatory memos in the employee's personnel file;
- Refusing to promote or reassign an employee or adding preconditions for a requested reassignment;
- Transferring the employee to a job with poorer working conditions;
- Increasing the workload without good reason;
- Adversely changing the company vacation policy;
- Delaying the distribution of tax and social security forms.

Counsel Comments: *Many employers who are accused of discrimination have valid defenses and can overcome such charges. However, they foolishly take steps deemed to be in retaliation against the individual's freedom to pursue such claims, and eventually suffer damages resulting from the retaliatory actions,* not *the alleged discrimination! Therefore, instruct management and supervisors never to take adverse action against an em-*

ployee or former employee when a formal discrimination charge has been filed.

JOB SAFETY

On the average, more than a dozen U.S. workers die each day from injuries in the workplace and another 10,000 are hurt seriously enough to lose work time or be placed on restricted duty. Even so, numerous changes benefiting workers have occurred in the area of health and safety. Federal and state laws give employees the right to refuse dangerous work and receive accurate reports concerning toxic substances in their working environment. Increased activity by representatives of the federal Occupational Safety and Health Administration (OSHA) has also played a large role in protecting employees from unsafe working conditions.

How OSHA Affects Employers

The 1970 Occupational Safety and Health Act requires employers to provide a safe and healthful workplace. This federal law applies to every private employer who is involved in interstate commerce, regardless of size. Furthermore, most states have passed occupational safety and health plans approved by federal OSHA. Some of these laws are even stricter in their compliance and enforcement standards than the federal law. For example, in one recent case, the Supreme Court of Illinois ruled that the federal Occupational Safety and Health Act does not prohibit state officials from enforcing criminal penalties against employers who violate OSHA regulations.

In that case, an Illinois company coated wires with toxic compounds. This practice continued despite knowledge by the company's supervisors that such manufacturing processes were harmful to workers. The company and several of its officers were indicted on criminal charges of aggravated battery and reckless conduct under state law. When the company appealed, the Supreme Court ruled that the state of Illinois was allowed to proceed with its own prosecution, notwithstanding the existence of the federal OSHA law, since "prosecutions of employers who violate state criminal law by failing to maintain safe working conditions for their employees will surely further OSHA's stated goal of assuring, so far as possible, every working man and woman in the nation safe and healthful working conditions."

The Occupational Safety and Health Administration, created to enforce this law, issues regulations on worker safety that employers must follow. OSHA inspectors visit work sites to insure compliance and penalties can be imposed, including significant fines and/or imprisonment for employers and key personnel who willfully or repeatedly violate OSHA laws or fail to correct hazards within fixed time limits. The law includes an extremely broad general duty clause requiring all employers to furnish a workplace that is free from recognized hazards. This means that employers are required to comply with safety rules, are subject to inspections without notice (with an employee representative present) and that no employee who makes a complaint can be subject to retaliation, loss of work or benefits, or demotion.

Under OSHA, workers are allowed:

- To refuse to perform work in a dangerous environment (e.g., in the presence of toxic substances, fumes or radioactive materials);
- To strike to protest unsafe conditions;
- To initiate an OSHA inspection of dangerous working conditions by filing a safety complaint;
- To participate in OSHA inspections, prehearing conferences and review inspection hearings;
- To assist the OSHA compliance officer in determining that violations have occurred;
- To petition that employers provide adequate emergency exits, environmental control devices (e.g., ventilation, noise elimination devices, radiation detection tags, signs and protective equipment) and the ready availability of medical personnel;
- To request time off with pay to seek medical treatment during working hours;
- To request eating facilities in areas which have not been exposed to toxic substances;
- To request investigations when they are punished for asserting their rights.

Every aspect of plant safety is governed by OSHA, which is a part of the U.S. Department of Labor, and is responsible for promulgating and enforcing job safety and health regulations. OSHA personnel inspect workplaces to monitor compliance with the Act and issue citations against employers when the agency discovers unsafe workplace conditions.

For example, OSHA has issued guidelines for the agency's response to workplace catastrophes resulting in multiple fatalities, extensive injuries, massive toxic exposures, or extensive property damage. Every company should study the OSHA instruction to update its own emergency response plan to interact with OSHA's investigation.

Often OSHA may offer technical support and will send a monitor to the site. Upon arrival at the accident scene, the OSHA representative will notify the employer and the person in charge of supervising response to the incident—unless the employer is preoccupied with rescue or emergency response activity. The OSHA representative may record with a video camera all characteristics of the event to help in determining the cause of the accident. An OSHA team member may provide voice-over narrative to the recording. If the inspection site is a large one, an employer contact will be asked to accompany the inspection team on a walkaround. This person must be familiar with the operation and be able to contact appropriate union personnel as needed.

If the employer refuses OSHA access to the accident site, the compliance officer will immediately contact the area director. The compliance officer will continue off-site inspection activities such as taking photos, videotaping, and interviewing witnesses from a public area while a warrant is being prepared. If records and documents are refused by the employer, these and other physical evidence may be subpoened. In extreme cases where OSHA representatives fear that evidence may be disturbed, the team leader may go so far as to place the site under 24-hour observation.

Penalties For Non-Compliance. House and Senate committees with labor jurisdiction are holding hearings on bills designed to strengthen OSHA. Key provisions of suggested legislation would require employers to create joint labor-management health and safety committees at the work site, strengthen criminal penalties against corporations and their executives in cases of death or serious injury, and extend coverage to the more than 7 million state and local government employees who have no OSHA protection. Under the current statute, OSHA may seek criminal penalties whenever a willful violation of a specific standard causes the death of an employee. Punishment is by fine of up to $10,000 or by imprisonment up to six months; punishment doubles for subsequent violations. In addition, state officials are increasingly bringing criminal actions against employers, corporate officials and supervisors for employee deaths resulting from safety violations. Among the kinds of criminal actions being sustained are aggravated battery, reckless conduct and manslaughter prosecutions of supervisors. Penalties for civil violations have now risen to a maximum of $7,000 per incident and for repeated violations, up to $70,000 per incident.

> **Counsel Comments:** *Health and safety violations are becoming more expensive for companies to defend and more prevalent in terms of the number of charges filed. Since the trend is to add more teeth to penalties arising from such violations, including increased fines and jail time for company officers, supervisors and managers, be certain that your company hires an individual or team of people knowledgeable about specific state and OSHA regulations and requirements, or train selected individuals to supervise and oversee problems in this area.*

Protection From Retaliation. An important aspect of the federal OSHA law is that it protects workers from retaliation after they assert their rights. In one case, a number of workers walked off the job, claiming it was too cold to work. The company fired them, stating that they violated established work rules by stopping work without notifying their supervisor. The workers filed a complaint alleging an unfair labor practice. The U.S. Supreme Court ruled that since the workers were within their constitutional rights to strike over health and safety conditions, the firing was illegal. As a result, the workers were given their jobs back, together with lost pay. In subsequent cases the Supreme Court has affirmed the right of an employee's good faith refusal to work in the face of hazardous conditions which might lead to death or serious injury when the employee has no reasonable alternative.

> **Counsel Comments:** *There is also an increasing trend in many states to prohibit the discharge of or discrimination against any employee who files an occupational health and safety complaint. Protection against whistleblower activities pertaining to health and safety in the workplace are becoming the norm and your company should avoid terminating workers who take action in this area. Also illegal are reprisals such as demotions, transfers, or reduced hours against workers who gripe to OSHA. Please consult the section in the next chapter entitled "Whistleblowing Statutes" for more information on this subject.*

Safety Equipment. Must an employer foot the bill for safety equipment demanded by the union? There is no set obligation under OSHA for employers to bear the cost of safety equipment. Instead, management and labor usually negotiate the bottom-line battle at the collective bargaining table. The haggling may not stop there, however, if contract language leaves any room for maneuvering, and unless the labor contract very specifically says otherwise. Where the collective bargaining agreement is silent on the subject, management has the right to promulgate reasonable safety and health rules—even to insist that employees furnish their own safety gear as a condition of employment. In practice, however, most agreements do contain detailed safety and health provisions, with the union insisting that the company foot the bill for the gear.

With respect to ordinary safety decisions, if there are no safety hazards involved and the company is not bound by a contract clause or a longtime past practice, then it alone may have discretion to decide what conveniences, such as fans or air conditioners, will be provided to employees.

Counsel Comments: *Maintaining a safe workplace begins with the orientation of new workers. Set the stage from the beginning by letting the new employee know that safety is a very important focus at your workplace. While job descriptions and work environment will determine what specific safety training must be given an employee, all new workers should receive an overall safety orientation.*

Management's commitment to accident and injury prevention must always be conveyed. Make clear that employee participation is needed to prevent accidents. Request that workers notify management without penalty, of any unsafe condition or potential hazard. Constantly remind supervisors to maintain safe and productive work operations. Advise workers not to undertake a task before learning the safe method of doing it and being authorized by a supervisor to proceed. Remind new employees about hazard recognition and that any injury, even a slight one, must be reported and treated immediately.

Workers' Compensation

Protecting your company from worker injuries, claims and lawsuits is a demanding job. Each state has enacted its own peculiar rules with respect to workers' compensation, which provides aid for employees who suffer job-related injuries. In most cases, the issue becomes one of determining whether the injuries suffered were job related. What was originally designed largely for the protection of industrial workers has now come to affect white collar employees as more courts and administrative agencies liberalize traditional interpretations of job-related injuries. The workers' compensation bill for the nation comes to around $50 billion annually. This section will briefly summarize important concerns in this area.

Injuries Suffered During Work-Related Travel. Is an employee injured while traveling to or from work entitled to benefits? Generally, the answer is no. However, when the employer agrees to provide the worker with the means of transportation, pay the employee's cost of commuting, or if travel is required while performing his/her duties, the scope of employment may include the employee's transportation. For example, if the employee regularly dictates office memos into a dictating machine within the vehicle, the car may be deemed part of his/her workplace.

Workers'compensation benefits are sometimes provided when the employee is injured while returning from company-sponsored education classes. An employee may also be entitled to benefits if he or she is on a special mission for the employer; if the employer derives a special benefit from the employee's activity at the time of the injury; if the travel comprised a dual purpose, such as combining employment-related business needs with the personal activity of the employee; if the employment subjected the employee to excessive exposure to traffic risks; or if the travel took place as a result of a split-shift working schedule.

If a worker leaves the employer's premises to do a personal errand, no compensation should ensue. However, if an injury is sustained when an employee goes to the restroom, visits the cafeteria, has a coffee break, or steps out of a non-smoking office to smoke a cigarette, workers' comp boards and courts typically recognize that employers benefit from these "non-business" employee conveniences and often award compensation.

Horseplay. Not every on-the-job injury is covered under workers' compensation. State courts seem to be divided on whether an injured employee can recover for horseplay: a company may be liable where it failed to select qualified supervisors, failed to supervise work areas, failed to enforce safety regulations and contributed to the injury by requiring an employee to work among employees with a propensity for horseplay. In one case, while conceding that an employer is not ordinarily responsible for the intentional misconduct of an employee who ignited someone's clothing, the court added that management was remiss in failing to stop the horseplay after a worker complained about it. The company was found liable since it should have, "in the exercise of reasonable supervision, taken steps to prevent or reduce the likelihood of dangerous sport by the members of its staff."

Compensable Injuries. The following list summarizes the kinds of injuries that *are* compensable:

- Pre-existing conditions that the workplace accelerates or aggravates, such as a bad back, even if pain from the injury is delayed until a later time;
- Injuries caused during breaks, lunch hours and work-sponsored recreational activities such as a company-paid New Year's Eve party, and on-the-job injuries caused by company facilities, such as a shower located on premises;
- Ordinary diseases such as lung cancer, if contracted by asbestos exposure at work as a result of the usual conditions to which the worker was exposed by his/her employment;
- Injuries resulting from mental and physical strain brought on by increased work duties or the stress caused by a requirement that the employee make decisions on other employee dismissals. In some states, this includes employees who develop a disabling psychosis because they cannot keep up with the demands of the job and a supervisor's constant harassment.

Intoxication. Intoxication injuries sustained by a traveling salesperson on company business who goes on a drinking spree and gets involved in an auto accident or is injured in a barroom brawl are not usually legally compensable. However, intoxication may not be a per se bar to compensation benefits. For compensation to be denied, the evidence must show that the employee was so intoxicated that a court can say as a matter of law that the injury arose out of his/her drunken condition and not out of his/her employment. Intoxication which does not incapacitate the employee from doing his job may be insufficient to defeat the recovery of workers' compensation, even though on-the-job intoxication may have been a contributing cause of the injury.

Obligations Of Employers. Company exposure to lawsuits in this area often arise when employers do not carry adequate workers' compensation insurance despite their promises, fail to post signs or required notices under state laws indicating that employees are covered by workers' compensation, or furnish negligent or improper medical care to injured workers. In addition, most states prohibit companies from firing, demoting or otherwise punishing an employee for filing or pursuing a workers' compensation claim. However, a false representation on an employment application could enable your company to terminate an individual, provided the employee knowingly and willingly made a false representation after the hire as to his/her physical condition, the employer relied on the false representation and there was a causal connection between the false representation and the injury.

Counsel Comments: *Note, however, that under the ADA a company may not inquire whether an applicant has filed for workers' compensation in a former job.*

To reduce high workers' compensation bills and increasing legal exposure, companies are advised to engage the services of a competent physician to review the medical care an injured worker is receiving. Such a person may be able to determine, for example, whether less expensive home care is more appropriate than hospital care. A medical consultant can also evaluate claims from the employee's doctor to see if they are self-serving.

Under compensation laws in most states, each employer must promptly provide medical, surgical, optometric or other treatment for injured employees as well as provide hospital care, crutches, eyeglasses, false teeth, and other appliances (and repairs of such items) necessary to replace, relieve or support a part of the body. Your company's medical team may eliminate unnecessary treatment but an injured employee may select his/her own physician for authorized treatment, provided that physician is authorized by the state's workers' compensation board.

Self-Insurance. Consider self-insuring and other alternatives to lower insurance premiums. While each state has its own rules, employers may be able to choose between a state or private insurer, where applicable. Several states are working on 24-hour plans which merge workers' comp and group health coverage. These plans probably will include employee deductibles and co-payments, which workers' compensation per se does not allow. The first such law, a 1990 statute passed in Florida, encourages employers to offer a 24-hour program.

Other states have set up state workers' compensation funds, intended either to be competitive with the private insurers (approximately 13 states as of this writing) or monopolistic (six states). Some funds operate simply as assigned risk plans, taking the burden from private insurers. In some states insurers are marketing a new type of coverage that is a cross between insurance and self-insurance, with plans that offer deductibles ranging from $100,000 to $1 million. Under these programs, the insurers pay all claims up front and are later reimbursed by the employer for claims falling within the deductible. Unlike a self-insurance plan, this offers a cash-flow advantage to the employers.

Counsel Comments: *Since workers' compensation plans are subject to state mandate, each company must study the law of the state or states in which it operates to see where cost-cutting may be permissible and available. For instance, does the state allow the employer to name which providers can treat an employee?*

The bottom line on minimizing workers' compensation charges is to keep the workplace safe and train employees in safety on an ongoing basis. All companies should take a preventive approach to avoiding worker injuries and to insure a clean and healthful working environment. Take steps to reduce worker stress, exposure to hazardous substances, vision impairment, repetitive motion injuries and exposure to computer terminal-caused injuries from video display terminals. Management should work closely with its employees and request regular employee suggestions to reduce potential safety violations. You may also hire safety consultants who will visit the work site and make suggestions. Many insurance companies provide this service at no cost.

Since safety training is mandated by federal regulation, regular training sessions for management and supervisors should be conducted to insure that employees know of company policies and abide by the law. Follow-up field inspections may also be helpful to monitor compliance.

All companies should publicize specific, strict rules regarding employee safety and related matters in company handbooks. A statement on safety should include a list of prohibited forms of conduct (such as horseplay, assault, unprovoked attack, or threats of bodily harm against anyone, drinking on the job, carrying firearms, etc.) and the consequences of committing such acts (i.e., suspension or immediate discharge). There should also be a stated policy reminding workers how to report accidents, seek medical attention, and so forth. The following is an example:

"If you become ill, or are injured while working, notify your Supervisor immediately. First aid treatment and transportation to your home or to a hospital will be arranged as needed. If you require a doctor, the Company will contact a physician for emergency treatment until you reach your own personal physician. If you are injured on the job, you may be entitled to Workers' Compensation. Any injury or illness must be reported to your immediate supervisor at once, so that proper reports can be filed. Failure to do so may jeopardize your compensation.

"When the company conducts monthly safety meetings, you are required to attend all paid company and/or regulatory meetings on safety. You will be disciplined accordingly for failure to comply with this rule."

Many companies conspicuously post weekly or monthly safety concerns and tips on a bulletin board which addresses problems of current interest. Brief weekly safety meetings may also be scheduled to bring employees up to date on safety concerns.

Finally, since the outcome of each workers' compensation case varies depending on the particular facts and unique state law, always seek the legal advice of a competent workers' compensation specialist. Issues such as how long an employee may delay in filing a claim, whether coverage is available for stress-related injuries, and what kinds of injuries are covered, can become complicated and typically require a lawyer's advice.

Form A
GENERAL RELEASE
(specifically waiving an age discrimination claim)

KNOW ALL MEN BY THESE PRESENTS THAT I, for and in consideration of the payment to me of $_X_, do for myself, my heirs, executors, administrators, successors and assigns, in addition to all the promises made herein, hereby release and forever discharge (name of Employer) and its parents, divisions, successors, predecessors, subsidiaries, affiliates, assigns, and the directors, officers, servants, agents and employees of each of them, and each of their heirs, executors and administrators, and all of them (hereinafter collectively "Releasees") from any and all actions and causes of action, claims and demands, suits, damages, costs, attorneys' fees, expenses, debts due, contracts, agreements, and claims for any compensation or benefits whatsoever, in law or in equity, which I or anyone claiming by, through or under me in any way might have or could have against Employer and Releases, including, *but not limited to,* any claims whatsoever which arose out of, or which could be claimed to have arisen out of, my employment with, or the separation of my employment from, Employer that I ever had or now have against Employer or Releasees from the beginning of the world to the date of this Release.

This Release includes, but is not limited to, claims under the Age Discrimination In Employment Act of 1967, as amended ("ADEA").

I expressly acknowledge that I have read this Release and have had at least twenty-one (21) days to discuss it with legal counsel of my choice before signing and that I realize and understand that it applies to and covers all claims, demands, and causes of action, including those under ADEA, against Employer or Releasees or any of them, whether or not I know or suspect them to exist at the present time. I further understand that this Release will not be accepted by Employer if I sign it prior to the expiration of 21 days from the date I received it.

I further acknowledge that this Release is not part of a program being offered to a group or class of employees and that my execution of this Release is made voluntarily without coercion in any way.

I understand that I shall have a period of seven (7) days from the date I sign this Release to revoke it. If I decide to revoke this Release, the revocation must be in writing signed by me and received by Employer before the expiration of the seventh (7th) calendar day following the date I sign this Release. Consequently, this Release shall have no force and effect until the expiration of seven (7) calendar days following the day on which I sign it, and Employer shall likewise have no obligation hereunder until after that time.

I understand that nothing herein waives any rights or claims I may have arising under ADEA after the date on which I sign this Release.

I will not apply for or otherwise seek re-employment with Employer at any time.

I will keep the terms, amount and fact of this Release and the payment hereunder confidential and will not hereafter state the facts or terms of this Release to anyone (except my attorney and spouse), including, but not limited to, any past, present or prospective employee or applicant for employment with Employer.

Nothing herein nor the payment hereunder shall be construed as an admission of any liability on the part of anyone for any matter, all liability being denied.

I have not relied on any representation, expressed or implied, made by Employer or any of its representatives.

This Release constitutes the entire understanding between myself and Employer and cannot be modified except in writing signed by both myself and Employer.

I intend that this Release shall not be subject to any claim of fraud, duress, deception, or mistake of fact, and that it expresses a full and complete settlement of any claims whatsoever I ever had or may have against (Employer) or any Releasee.

I will not file any complaint, suit, claim or charge against Employer or any Releasee with any local, state or federal agency or court. If any agency or court assumes jurisdiction of any complaint, suit, claim or charge against Employer or any Releasee on my behalf, I will request such agency or court to dismiss the matter.

I understand this Release is contractual and based on my representation that I will comply with the terms set forth herein. Should I breach any of the terms of this Release, I shall repay to Employer all sums paid to me hereunder, plus reasonable attorneys' fees incurred in connection with the enforcement of the terms of this Release, in addition to any other damages caused by my breach of any of the terms of this Release. Nothing herein shall be construed to limit any other remedies Employer or Releasees may have under law or in equity.

I, intending to be legally bound, hereby apply my signature voluntarily with full understanding of the contents of this Release.

________________________ ___________________________

Witness NAME OF EMPLOYEE

DATE____________________

I, STEVEN SACK, am an attorney licensed to practice law in the State of New York. I represent , I have explained to him the consequences of signing this Release and he has indicated to me an understanding thereof and that he is signing this Release of his own free will.

____

STEVEN SACK, ESQUIRE

Form B
COVER LETTER AND RELEASE
(specifically waiving an age discrimination claim)

TO: Severed Employee

FROM: The Company ("The Employer")

RE: Older Workers Benefit Protection Act

This communication apprises you of your rights under the Older Workers Benefit Protection Act ("OWBPA") which amends the Age Discrimination in Employment Act ("ADEA"), that Congress recently passed. The OWBPA establishes certain standards as regards waivers that the Employer obtains from its Employees.

The OWBPA amends the ADEA by adding a new section which establishes standards for a "knowing and voluntary" waiver. The OWBPA sets forth seven basic requirements for a knowing and voluntary waiver:

(1) The waiver has to be part of an agreement between the Employee and the Employer and it has to be written in understandable English;

(2) The waiver must refer specifically to rights or claims arising under the ADEA;

(3) The waiver cannot cover rights or claims that may arise after the date on which it is signed;

(4) The waiver must be exchanged for consideration, and the consideration must be in addition to anything of value to which the employee is already entitled;

(5) The Employee must be advised in writing to consult with an attorney before signing the agreement;

(6) The Employee has to be given a period of at least 21 days to decide whether to sign the waiver; and

(7) The Employee is entitled to revoke the waiver within seven days after signing it, and the waiver does not become effective or enforceable until the revocation period has expired.

GENERAL RELEASE

FOR GOOD AND VALUABLE CONSIDERATION, the adequacy of which is hereby acknowledged, in the form of payment to Employee of a severance benefit in the amount of ($XX) salary less withholding for federal and state taxes, FICA and any other amounts required to be withheld, Employee agrees that he/she, or any person acting by, through or under Employee, RELEASES AND FOREVER DISCHARGES [Name of Employer], and its parent company and its subsidiaries, affiliates, predecessors, successors, and assigns, as well as the officers, employees, representatives, agents and fiduciaries, *de facto* or *de jure* (hereinafter collectively referred to as "Released Parties"), and covenants and agrees not to institute any action or actions, causes or causes of action (in law unknown) in state or federal court, based upon or arising by reason of any damage, loss, or in any way related to Employee's employment with any of the Released Parties or the termination of said employment. The foregoing includes, but not by way of limitation, all claims which could have been raised under common law, including retaliatory discharge and breach of contract, or statute, including, without limitation, the Age Discrimination in Employment Act of 1967, 42 U.S.C. Sections 621-634, as amended by the Older Workers Benefit Protection Act of 1990, Title VII of the Civil Rights Act of 1964, 42 U.S.C. Sections 2000e *et. seq.* and the Employee Retirement Income Security Act of 1974, 29 U.S.C. Sections 1001 *et. seq.* or any other Federal or State Law; except that this General Release is not intended to cover any claim arising from computational or clerical errors in the calculation of the severance benefit provided to Employee, or retirement benefit to which Employee may be entitled from any plan or other benefits to which Employee may be entitled under any plan maintained by any of the Released Parties.

Employee covenants and agrees to forever refrain from instituting, pursuing, or in any way whatsoever aiding any claim, demand, action or cause of action or other matter released and discharged herein by Employee arising out of or in any way related to Employee's employment with any of the Released Parties and the rights to recovery for any damages or compensation awarded as a result of any lawsuit brought by any third party or governmental agency on Employee's behalf.

Employee further agrees to indemnify all Released Parties from any and all loss, liability, damages, claims, suits, judgments, attorneys' fees and other costs and expenses of whatsoever kind or individually, Employee may sustain or incur as a result of or in connection with the matters hereinabove released and discharged by Employee. Employee warrants that he/she has not filed any lawsuits, charges, complaints, petitions, or accusatory pleadings against any of the Released Parties with any governmental agency or in any court, based upon, arising out of or related in any way to any event or events occurring prior to the signing of this General Release, including, without limitation, his/her employment with any of the Released Parties or the termination thereof.

Employee acknowledges, understands and affirms that: (a) This General Release is a binding legal document; (b) Released Parties advised him/her to consult with an attorney before signing this General Release, (ii) he/she had the right to consult with an attorney about and before signing this General Release, (iii) he/she was given a period of at least 21 calendar days in which to consider this General Release prior to signing, and (iv) he/she voluntarily signs and enters into this General Release without reservation after having given the matter full and careful consideration; and (c) (i) Employee has a period of seven days after signing this General Release in which he/she may revoke this General Release, (ii) this General Release does not become effective or enforceable and no payment shall be made hereunder until this seven-day-revocation period has elapsed, and (iii) any revocation must be in writing by Employee and delivered to (specify), Human Resources within the seven-day-revocation period.

IN WITNESS WHEREOF, the Employee signs this General Release this ___________ day of ___________________, 1993.

____
Employee's Name (please print)

WITNESS:

____

____
Signature

Date:_________________________

ACKNOWLEDGMENT

I HEREBY ACKNOWLEDGE that [Name of Employer] in accordance with the Age Discrimination in Employment Act, as amended by the Older Workers Benefit Protection Act, informed me in writing: 1) to consult with an attorney before signing this General Release; 2) to review this General Release for a period of 21 days prior to signing; 3) that for a period of seven days following the signing of this General Release, I may revoke this General Release, and this General Release, will not become effective or enforceable until the seven-day-revocation period has elapsed; and 4) that no payment shall be made until the seven-day-revocation period has elapsed.

I HEREBY FURTHER ACKNOWLEDGE receipt of this General Release for my review on the ____ day of ______________, 199 .

Witness: Employee:____________________________

(Print or Type Name)

______________________ ____________________________

Signature of Employee

CHAPTER 4

Firing And Termination Decisions

Statistics indicate that 3.8 of every 100 employees are fired or resign from their jobs each month. Experts suggest that more than 250,000 workers each year are terminated illegally or unjustly. Until recently, employees had few options when they received a "pink slip," because a legal principle called the employment-at-will doctrine was generally applied throughout the United States. Under this rule of law, employers hired workers at will and were free to fire them at any time with or without cause and with or without notice. Beginning in the 1960s however, courts and legislatures began handing down rulings and enacting legislation to safeguard the rights of non-unionized employees. Congress passed laws specifically pertaining to occupational health and safety, civil rights and freedom to complain about unsafe working conditions.

Thirty years later, there has been a gradual erosion of the employment-at-will doctrine. Many states, for example, have enacted public policy exceptions that make it illegal to fire workers who take time off to serve as a witness in a criminal proceeding, participate as a juror, disclose or threaten to disclose an employer's alleged violation of public safety or health laws, or participate in military service. Some courts have ruled that statements in company manuals and handbooks constitute implied contracts which employers are bound to follow. Other states now recognize the obligation of companies to deal in fairness and good faith with long time workers—for example, prohibiting employers from terminating workers in retaliation when they report on abuses of authority, or denying individuals an economic benefit (a pension that is vested or about to vest, commissions, bonus, etc.) that has been earned or is about to become due.

A few states even allow wrongfully terminated workers to sue in tort (as opposed to asserting claims based in contract) and recover punitive damages and money for pain and suffering arising from the firing. Employees who have sued under tort theories for wrongful discharge have recovered large jury verdicts. Innovative lawyers are asserting federal racketeering (RICO) claims, seeking criminal sanctions and treble damages against companies, in addition to fraud and misrepresentation claims against individuals responsible for making wrongful termination decisions.

Firing an employee, especially a long time worker, can be hard. Besides the emotional difficulties which sometimes arise, companies must be aware of and prepare for the possibility that the terminated employee will seek legal advice and action. Thus, you must prepare properly for the firing decision *before* taking action. This chapter will recommend a series of strategies to reduce company exposure from termination litigation, including ways of minimizing legal exposure from breach of contract, wrongful discharge, and discrimination lawsuits.

TERMS OF EMPLOYMENT

In most states, in the absence of an agreement establishing a fixed duration (e.g., a two-year contract), an employment relationship is presumed to be a hiring at will, terminable at any time by either the company or the employee. While courts in most states have carved out exceptions to this general rule (e.g., allegations that the hiring constitutes an express or implied promise to terminate the employee only for cause; that the firing violates important public policy such as whistleblowing or discrimination protection; or that the firing violates an implied obligation to deal fairly and in good faith), some states still allow an employer the unfettered right to discharge an employee for a good reason, a bad reason, or no reason at all.

Companies should avoid making representations to the employee regarding job security (e.g., "No one ever gets fired around here except for a good reason"). The better way is to state orally at the hiring interview and confirm in writing in the employment application, company handbook distributed to employees, and in the employment contract signed by the employee before beginning work, that employment is at will (e.g., "Either party may terminate this agreement at any time, with or without cause and with or without notice.").

Avoid hiring employees for a definite period of time (e.g., one year). By hiring someone at will, you may be able to fire without providing a legitimate reason or cause, depending upon the law in your particular state and provided there are no exceptions (such as discrimination).

When you hire an employee for a fixed term of employment, you increase his/her chances of recovering damages in a lawsuit because the burden of proof falls on the employer; the company may find itself having to demonstrate the actions which gave it a legitimate reason to fire before the expiration of the fixed term. This is often difficult to do. By hiring at will, the company can eliminate this problem.

If, however, you need a for-cause justification because you have given a worker job security, such as a definite one-year contract in writing, the following are examples of causes which justify job terminations notwithstanding such an offer:

- Habitual lateness or excessive absences;
- Failing to report absences;
- Disrespect or unprofessional conduct;
- Insubordination or disobeying company work rules, regulations and policies;
- Exceeding authority;
- Negligence or neglect of duty;
- Dishonesty or unfaithfulness, such as making secret profits, stealing, misusing trade secrets, customer lists and other confidential information;
- Theft of company or a co-worker's property;
- Falsifying records or information;
- Punching another employee's time card without approval from management;
- Leaving the job or company premises without prior approval from a supervisor;
- Willful refusal to follow the directions of a supervisor (unless doing so would endanger health or safety);
- Assault, unprovoked attack or threats of bodily harm against others;
- Sexually harassing or abusing others;
- Use of drugs or possession of alcoholic beverages on company premises or during company-paid time while away from the premises;
- Disclosing confidential and proprietary information to unauthorized third parties;
- Unauthorized possession of weapons and firearms on company property;
- Intentionally making errors in work, negligently performing duties, or willfully hindering or limiting production.

PERSONNEL RECORDS

Carefully review an employee's personnel records and files before making the firing decision and informing the employee. Some states permit terminated workers to review and copy the contents of their personnel files. For example, California law provides that an employee is to be given access to personnel files used to determine his or her qualifications, promotions, pay raises, discipline and discharge. Other states which allow both current and terminated employees to inspect personnel files maintained by employers include Connecticut, Delaware, Illinois, Maine, Michigan, Nevada, New Hampshire, Ohio, Oregon, Pennsylvania, Washington and Wisconsin. Some of these states also permit inspection by a representative designated by the employee.

Most states also give employees the right to review information supplied to an employer by a credit reporting agency under the Fair Credit Reporting Act of 1971, as well as to review all medical and insurance information in the file. However, confidential items such as letters of reference, records of internal investigations regarding theft, misconduct or crimes not pertaining to the employee, and confidential information about other employees can generally be denied to the employee.

Counsel Comments: *Sometimes, these files do not support firing decisions because they contain favorable recommendations and comments. For example, if the employee was hired for a definite term and can be fired only for cause, or the company gives a terminated individual specific reasons why he/she was fired, the file may contradict these reasons as factually incorrect and/or legally insufficient.*

All employee records must be reviewed for "smoking guns." We have already suggested that company supervisors avoid inflating employee appraisals wherever possible (see "Appraisals and Performance Reviews" in Chapter 3). Obviously, if you tell an employee that he/she is doing well and include favorable written comments in the personnel records, then suddenly fire the worker, you are asking for trouble. The following actual case illustrates this problem:

An employee of a prestigious financial institution was part of a four-member team responsible for devising and selling syndications on behalf of the employer. He had worked for approximately nine and a half years and was earning an annual base salary of $125,000. Each year he had consistently received large year-end bonuses (the pevious year's bonus had been $50,000). The employee was suddenly fired in late November, the company claiming that his work performance was not satisfactory and that he did "not fit the image of an investment banker." The employee, who believed his job performance was excellent, hired the author of this book to represent him. He also felt cheated since the company offered no severance benefits, would not allow him to receive a pension which was due to vest within six months, and refused to pay him a bonus for the substantial portion of the current year he had worked.

After investigating the matter, the author asked the client if he had collected copies of pertinent information from his personnel file. The client produced a number of excellent reviews. In addition, he was able to locate a memo, which had been circulated throughout the company and delivered to the company's president, congratulating each member of his group by name for placing a large deal that year and citing each member (including the client) for outstanding work.

During negotiations, the author informed management of the existence of this memo and argued that in view of the client's history of receiving large raises and year-end bonuses, excellent performance evaluations and the favorable memo, the firing was unjustified and probably done to save the company a large sum of money. The company was also advised that a jury would probably take a dim view of what had transpired.

After extensive meetings, the client obtained an out-of-court settlement that included a year-end bonus, severance pay representing one month's salary for every year of employment, the company's agreement to qualify the man for a substantial pension, continuation of employer-paid medical insurance for six months at the company's expense, up to $7,500 worth of benefits for an outplacement employment search by a reputable firm, and a letter of recommendation. On reflection, it is doubtful that the client would have obtained such a favorable settlement with-

out a copy of the congratulatory memo collected and saved by him.

Never underestimate the importance of reviewing all personnel files of which the employee may also have copies in order to anticipate problems. Where possible, try to limit the employee's access to personnel files and related documents. Smart employees who suspect they may be fired typically plan ahead by gathering copies of all pertinent materials and handbooks before they are asked to leave. Instruct staff in your personnel relations department only to allow the inspection and copying of such records with the approval of management. Further, instruct staff that they are required always to be present when an employee is reviewing such documents. Some companies allow an employee to take notes from a document but not to make copies. Also, since employees sometimes gain access to these materials via a friend in the personnel department, advise staff that providing employees or ex-employees with access to such information or making copies secretly on their behalf may lead to immediate dismissal.

Employee Access To Records

Employees may have access to their personnel files as part of the discovery process during a lawsuit even in those states which do not ordinarily compel access. And, in many instances, employment data (such as memos placed in an employee's file) which was not subject to employee inspection or received by the employee during his/her employment may not be introduced and used against the employee in a lawsuit.

In some states, such as Illinois and Michigan, an employee can bring a legal proceeding to expunge false information contained in the personnel file and known by the employer to be false. These states allow people to collect attorney fees, fines, court costs and damages in the event an employee discovers false information or errors regarding off-premises activities (e.g., political, associational, etc.) which do not interfere with work duties.

PROGRESSIVE DISCIPLINE GUIDELINES

Follow precisely your company's progressive discipline guidelines. Some supervisors are reluctant to follow progressive discipline when dealing with inadequate performance by salespeople or higher level personnel, but management must insist on even-handed application of the rules. Employers must meet with employees early, discuss their performance problems frankly, and set written goals or objectives, which are acknowledged and signed by both. Doing so will help defend against termination litigation.

Counsel Comments: *Avoid firing individuals, especially longtime employees, without following progressive discipline unless the employee is such a disruptive element or menace that it is imperative to fire suddenly. Most lawsuits are commenced by angry individuals. When a company appears to have been fair—to have met with the employee, discussed the problems regarding performance, and given the worker sufficient opportunity to correct these problems—the worker will have less cause to be angry when eventually fired and will be less likely to sue.*

It is imperative that the company apply its system of progressive discipline to all workers equally, and not on any other basis. For more information, see "Progressive Discipline" in Chapter 3.

EMPLOYEE MANUALS

Language in company policy manuals is sometimes viewed as containing promises that employees may rely upon. As previously discussed, courts in some states are ruling that provisions in personnel manuals and handbooks distributed to employees are enforceable against employers. The fewer rights and protections companies give to employees in their handbooks, the less chance they will violate such promises and be liable for damages.

In the 1970s, employers began to use their employee handbooks to dress up their image as a good place to work by promising job terminations only "for cause" or under specified procedures. A number of state courts began to view these promises as enforceable "implied contracts," even though they may not have been read by the employee until after accepting employment and were not signed by either party, as is customarily required to enhance contract enforceability. Some state courts have ruled that the promises in employee handbooks may be legally enforceable as implied contracts.

Actual cases demonstrate the kinds of problems and questions that exist in this area. For example, what if the employer makes a promise, then makes a disclaimer equivalent to taking back the promise? Can an employer change the handbook after a hiring, taking back some of the promises contained in the version which the employee relied upon when he/she was hired? For how long are the promises effective?

To play it safe, avoid making any promises in company manuals that you have no desire to keep. Remember, if a company fails to act in accord with published work rules or handbooks, it may be construed as violating an important contract obligation.

Types of promises to avoid in handbooks, which give unnecessary rights to employees during and after a firing, include:

- Allowing the employee to appeal or mediate the decision through an internal non-binding grievance procedure;
- Stating that the employer must give reasonable notice before the firing;
- Stating that the employee can only be fired for cause after internal steps toward rehabilitation have been taken and have failed;
- Guaranteeing the employee the right to be presented with specific, factual reasons for the discharge before the firing can be effective.

Counsel Comments: *In the area of severance, however, specific promises can help the company. For example, by stating that all workers terminated due to a business reorganization or job elimination will receive modest severance of X weeks in total or a small amount of severance computed at the rate of* one *week per year of service, you can minimize claims by ex-employees that they should receive larger severance packages. If you include such a provision in your handbook, be sure it is followed in all instances: do not grant additional severance packages to select employees, because your company may commit sex, race or age discrimination in the process.*

For example, by offering a male employee under 40 years of age with four years service a severance package of eight weeks, you may be committing sex or age discrimination if your company offers a female employee over 40 with the same amount of service only four weeks' severance. Keeping severance offers to a minimum and sticking to such a policy can save your company plenty of money and exposure in the event a terminated worker contests the firing. Even with such a policy, always state in the manual that no severance will be paid for workers who are terminated for cause, poor performance after a series of warnings, or who resign.

EMPLOYMENT CONTRACTS

If a contract exists, always review the employee's contract before firing that person. Examine whether notice of termination (e.g., 30 days) is required. If so, the failure to send timely notice, or sending no notice, may place the company in breach of contract. Never give employees more rights than necessary in written agreements.

Counsel Comments: *Remember that failure to give timely notice as required by a contract, or failure to follow the requirements of notice as set forth in the contract, may expose the company to a breach of contract claim. In some instances, it can even cause the agreement to be extended for an additional period.*

For example, many companies have written employment contracts with their executives. Some of these agreements run for a period of one year and state that if timely notice of termination is not given at least 30 days prior to the expiration of the one-year term, the contract will automatically be extended and renewed under the same terms and conditions for an additional year. If the company fires the executive two weeks before the end of the year, or forgets to send timely written notice via certified mail (as called for by the contract), the employee could have a legal basis to insist on working for an addi-

tional year. He/she would at least have a stronger basis to negotiate for additional severance before filing a lawsuit.

In order to map out an effective action plan, be sure you know what your contract says about notice and other requirements. By precisely following the contract's requirements, you can eliminate some of an employee's potential claims and legal causes of action after discharge.

STATUTORY CONSIDERATIONS

Consider whether statutory or public policy considerations prohibit a firing. A variety of federal and state statutes restrict an employer's freedom to discharge employees and protect workers from being fired, even in an at-will firing state; many of these laws probably apply in your state. For example, dismissals are illegal when they are based on age, sex, race, national origin or religion, union membership or participation in union or political activity, group activity to protest unsafe work conditions, refusal to commit an unlawful act on the employer's behalf (e.g., commit perjury or fix prices), reporting alleged violations of the law (whistleblowing), performing a public obligation, or being sued for nonpayment of a debt or wage garnishment.

The most comprehensive and significant federal legislation is Title VII of the Civil Rights Act of 1964, as amended by the Equal Employment Opportunity Act of 1972 and the Civil Rights Act of 1990. Under these laws, employers cannot fire workers based upon personal characteristics of sex, age, race, color, religion, national origin, and non-disqualifying physical or mental impairments unrelated to job qualifications. The previous chapter explored these subjects in great depth. The law also protects from reprisals workers who exercise their First Amendment and other rights, including refusals to take a lie detector test or speaking out about health and safety conditions. A discussion of other factors that may enter into the legality of a firing follows.

Credit Problems

The Consumer Credit Protection Act of 1973 forbids employers from firing workers whose earnings have been subjected to a wage garnishment arising from a single debt. However, employees may presumably be fired after being hit with other garnishments. Some states have enacted laws which give workers additional protection; check the applicable law in your state.

Severance And Retirement Benefits

The Employee Retirement Income Security Act of 1974 (ERISA) prohibits the discharge of any employee who is prevented thereby from attaining immediate vested pension rights, or who was exercising rights under ERISA and was fired as a result. ERISA also entitles employees to certain rights as participants in an employer's pension and/or profit-sharing plans. ERISA provides that plan participants are entitled to examine without charge all plan documents, including insurance contracts, annual reports, plan descriptions and copies of documents filed by the plan with the U. S. Department of Labor. If a worker requests materials from a plan (including summaries of each plan's annual financial report) and does not receive them within 30 days, he/she may file a suit in federal court. In such a case, the court may require the plan administrator to provide the materials and pay the worker up to $100 a day until he/she receives them (unless the materials were not sent for reasons beyond the administrator's control).

Asserting Union Rights

The National Labor Relations Act prohibits the firing of any employee because of his or her involvement in union activity, because of filing charges, or because of testifying pursuant to the act. Workers who believe they have been fired for similar reasons typically file charges with a regional office of the National Labor Relations Board.

The law also protects employees who band together to protest about wages, hours or other working conditions. For example, if a group of non-union employees complain about contaminated drinking water, or about failure to receive minimum wages or overtime pay, their employer could be prohibited from firing them if their charges are proven.

Attending Jury Duty

The Jury System Improvements Act of 1978 forbids employers from firing employees who are empaneled to serve on federal grand juries or petit juries. Most states have enacted similar laws. For example, in New York, any person who is summoned to serve as a juror and notifies the company prior to serving, may not be discharged or penalized. While an employer may withhold wages during the period of service, the job must be held open for the employee's return and any retaliation taken against the employee is considered criminal contempt of court. The same protection also applies to employees who are victims of crimes, or who are subpoened as witnesses in criminal proceedings.

Reporting Railroad Accidents

Two federal laws govern here. The Federal Railroad Safety Act prohibits companies from firing workers who file complaints or testify about railroad accidents; the Federal Employer's Liability Act makes it a crime to fire an employee who furnishes facts regarding a railroad accident.

Engaging In Legal Activities Off-Premises And After Working Hours

It may also be illegal to discharge a worker who participates in legally permissible political activities, recreational activities, or the legal use of consumable products before or after working hours. Political activities include running for public office, campaigning for a candidate or participating in fund-raising activities for a candidate or political party. Those activities may be protected if they are legal and occur on the employee's own time, off company premises and without the use of employer property or equipment.

Recreational activities are defined as any lawful leisure-time activities for which the employee receives no compensation and which are generally engaged in for recreational purposes. The definition of consumable products even protects the rights of people who smoke or drink alcohol before and after working hours and off the company's premises.

The right not to be fired for exercising these legally-permitted activities generally depends on applicable state law; to date, 28 states have passed some form of legislation in this area and the trend is for more states to follow. In New York, for example, employers cannot discriminate in hiring, promotion and other terms of employment due to off-duty activities in four specific categories: political activities, use of a "consumable product," recreational activities and union membership or exercise of any rights granted under federal or state labor law. Employers who violate the law are subject to a lawsuit by the State Attorney General seeking to restrain or enjoin the continuance of the alleged unlawful conduct. Penalties are provided ranging from $300 for initial wrongdoing to $500 fines for subsequent acts. Additionally, aggrieved individuals may commence their own lawsuits and recover monetary damages and other forms of relief.

According to Barbara Franklin, in an article which appeared in the December 17, 1992 issue of the *New York Law Journal*, most state laws do not protect workers who moonlight, violate their employers' conflict-of-interest policies or engage in non-work activities proscribed in collective bargaining agreements. New York's statute, and others, does not apply to public employees who violate existing rules against unethical conduct and journalists who engage in political activities. Additionally, according to Lewis Maltby, director of the American Civil Liberties Union National Task Force on Civil Liberties in the Workplace, with the exception of New York, Colorado and North Dakota (which have broader laws in place), most state laws only cover the rights of people who smoke off-premises, making it a violation of law for employers to refuse to hire (and sometimes fire them.)

Counsel Comments: *In the vast majority of states with such laws, it is illegal to refuse to hire smokers. It may also be illegal to discriminate against smokers by charging higher insurance premiums unless the company can demonstrate a valid business reason, such as higher costs. However, people who smoke off-duty must still comply with existing laws and ordinances prohibiting smoking on-premises, such as only in designated areas.*

All employers should review company policies pertaining to substance abuse and think twice before taking adverse action against workers who extensively drink alcohol off-premises. Review existing insurance policies and coverage for gaps. Minimize the regulation of employees' conduct outside of the workplace, such as those who engage in dangerous activities off-hours including smoking, sky-diving, bunji-jumping, scuba-diving, or even employees who over-eat.

Be wary of making, adopting, or enforcing any rule which prevents employees from participating in political activities, affiliations or political action. This means threatening to fire workers who organize to protest better working conditions. In one recent California case, a group of individuals organized to promote equal rights for homosexuals at a large communications company via a class action lawsuit. The California Court ruled that such activity was protected by state law.

Since some states do not have specific laws protecting employees from engaging in political activity, and the laws vary so, always consult with counsel and review applicable state law before taking action in this area.

PUBLIC POLICY EXCEPTIONS

Courts and state legislatures have carved out other exceptions to the employment-at-will doctrine based on public policy considerations. For example, in some states, workers may be protected from discharge who:

- Refuse to violate criminal laws by committing perjury on the employer's behalf, participating in illegal schemes (e.g., price-fixing or other anti-trust violations), mislabeling packaged goods, giving false testimony before a legislative committee, altering pollution control reports, or engaging in practices abroad which violate foreign, federal and state laws.
- Perform a public obligation, exercise a public duty (e.g., attend jury duty, vote, supply information to the police about a fellow employee, file workers' compensation claims) or observe the general public policy of the state (e.g., refuse to perform unethical research).

A detailed analysis of some of these important subjects follows.

Whistleblowing

The law generally protects workers who expose abuses of authority through "whistleblower" statutes, which are in force in many states, including California, Connecticut, Hawaii, Louisiana, Maine, Michigan, Minnesota, New Hampshire, New Jersey, New York, Ohio, Rhode Island, Tennessee and Wisconsin. Michigan, for example, has enacted a Whistleblower's Protection Act which protects employees from retaliation (defined as discharge, threats, or discrimination against an employee regarding the employee's compensation, terms, conditions, locations, or privileges of employment) after they report suspected violations of laws or regulations. This statute provides specific remedies, including injunctive relief or actual damages or both, reinstatement, back wages, fringe benefits, seniority rights, or any combinations of these remedies. Costs of litigation, including reasonable attorney fees and witness fees, are also mandated under the law. Some other states have even stricter laws with greater penalty provisions.

People who work for federal agencies are also protected from being fired for whistleblowing. In one case, a nurse was dismissed after reporting abuses of patients at a Veterans Administration Medical Center. She sought reinstatement and damages before a federal review panel, which ordered that she be reinstated and awarded her $7,500 in back pay.

The following actual cases illustrate examples of firings that were found to be illegal in this area:

- A quality control director was fired for his efforts to correct false and misleading food labeling by his employer.
- A bank discharged a consumer credit manager who notified his supervisors that the employer's loan practices violated state law.
- A financial vice president was fired after reporting to the company's president his suspicions regarding the embezzlement of corporate funds.

For an employee's conduct to constitute protected activity, the majority of whistleblower statutes require that the employee have a reasonable belief that the employer's conduct violated a law, regulation or ordinance. Most statutes also require some proof that the employee intended to, or did, report the violation.

Counsel Comments: *The biggest potential for violations in this area occurs with safety-related claims made by disgruntled employees. Under numerous federal laws, including The Clean Air Act, Safe Drinking Water Act, Solid Waste Disposal Act, Toxic Substances Control Act, Water Pollution Control Act, Occupational Safety and Health Act, Asbestos School Hazard Detection and Control Act, and most federal discrimination laws, employees are permitted to come forward and report alleged violations affecting public safety. In addition, more than half the states protect reporting of actions that* *are contrary to the health, safety, welfare and environmental laws.*

To protect your company in this area, all employers should remember the following:

1. **Avoid committing safety violations.**

2. **Know the law in your state regarding whistleblower protection.**

3. **Require workers to report violations first to a supervisor within the company, rather than going outside.** Such a statement in your work rules or policy manual may be helpful since not all whistleblowing activity is protected under this public policy exception. Some companies have *successfully* fired workers who "blew the whistle" without properly investigating the facts, who bypassed management or tattled in bad faith. In some states, employers must be given a reasonable period of time to remedy any violations before the employee has the right to report the violation to a public body. However, the employee may not be required to report the violation first to his or her employer when the report would not result in the prompt resolution of the problem.

Counsel Comments: *Remind workers in writing that problems sometimes arise and that the company should* always *be notified and given a reasonable period of time to correct its mistakes before news of a violation is leaked to an outside agency. Such a strategy can help your company defend itself from charges that it fired a worker illegally and that it violated a public safety law or ruling.*

4. **Recognize that some state whistleblower laws do not protect workers who question internal management systems.** Michigan's statute, for example, does not protect workers who report an employer's violation of internal rules, regulations or policies. It only protects workers who report safety, health and environmental violations. Many other states also restrict what workers may legally report. Be aware of this and act accordingly, because each case is decided on its own particular facts.

5. **Speak to an experienced labor lawyer before you decide to fire the suspected employee.** Huge damages can be assessed against companies who fire workers illegally. Such lawsuits may carry large punitive damage awards and damages for emotional distress. In a recent case, for example, $8 million was paid to settle a whistleblowing claim pursued by the Justice Department under the Federal False Claims Act.

Most courts assign to the employee the initial burden of proof of establishing that he or she was unlawfully discharged in retaliation for reporting an employer's unlawful conduct. Companies can defeat such a claim by demonstrating that the company did nothing wrong or that the individual was fired for a legitimate reason, such as poor work performance or a business reorganization.

Counsel Comments: *A competent labor attorney can analyze potential damages and determine the best way to avoid exposure in this area. When an employer learns that one of its employees has reported alleged improprieties concerning the employer, the first reaction might be that such disloyal and damaging conduct warrants immediate discipline, up to and including termination. Always control such an impulse until after you have spoken at length with counsel and have received the green light. For the best result, confer with counsel before the decision to fire has been made, not after.*

Implied Covenants Of Good Faith and Fair Dealing

Courts in California, Montana, New Hampshire, Massachusetts and Wisconsin, among other states, have further eroded the "at-will" doctrine by imposing a duty of good faith and fair dealing on long-term employment relationships. This applies especially in situations where longtime workers are fired before receiving anticipated benefits such as accrued pension, profit-sharing or commissions. Workers with seniority sometimes receive large monetary damages after proving this covenant was violated. For example, one man with 40 years of service claimed he was fired so his company could avoid paying commissions otherwise due on a $5 million sale. A Massachusetts court agreed and awarded him substantial money (lost compensation for predictable policy renewals), even though he had been hired at will. Another employee was fired after working 13 years without a written contract or job security guarantee. However, the court ruled that the company had fired him merely to deprive him of the vesting of valuable pension and other benefits (e.g., stock options) in his fifteenth year of service. The employee was awarded $75,000 in damages.

Typically, the employer's duty to act in good faith and fair dealing applies only to cases where an employee has been working for the company for many years or where the person is fired just before he or she is due to receive anticipated financial benefits. In one recent case, however, the Montana Supreme Court reasoned that the covenant of good faith and fair dealing is imposed by law. The court upheld a $50,000 jury award of punitive damages (more than 25 times the compensatory damage award) because the employer had promised to write a favorable letter of recommendation in exchange for the employee's resignation. Despite this promise, the employer delivered a letter of recommendation merely stating the complainant's dates of employment. In addition, the employer only returned a copy of the letter of resignation despite the employee's request for the original. These actions, the court found, justified the jury's finding of "fraud, oppression, and malice."

Counsel Comments: *Actual cases such as these support the right of employees to receive the fruits of their labors. Recognize, therefore, that if you fire someone just before he/she is due to receive anticipated benefits, and the firing is not justified (for cause), the person may be entitled to damages.*

However, not all longtime workers are entitled to such protection; each case varies depending upon the facts. If a company fires someone for a valid reason, the fact that he/she has been with the company for a substantial period of time or is eligible for a substantial benefit may not make the firing illegal under a covenant of good faith and fair dealing theory.

Sales Rep Protection Statutes

Even if the firing is legal, it is important always to pay earned compensation (wages, accrued vacation, commissions, etc.) to avoid wrongdoing. For example, most companies are unaware of the growing trend in many states to require prompt payment of commissions to independent sales representatives (also called agents or brokers) who are fired. Failure to pay promptly may leave companies liable for penalties typically up to three times the commission amount, plus reasonable attorney fees and court costs if the case is eventually litigated. States with laws protecting reps include Alabama, Arizona, Arkansas, California, Florida, Georgia, Iowa, Kansas, Kentucky, Louisiana, Illinois, Indiana, Maryland, Massachusetts, Michigan, Minnesota, Mississippi, New Hampshire, New Jersey, New York, North Carolina, Ohio, Oklahoma, Pennsylvania, South Carolina, Tennessee, Texas and Washington; specific details about such laws are provided in Appendix Z.

Some statutes even require that a formal written contract be issued and executed with each person selling products or services on an independent-commission basis. These agreements must specify the method by which commissions are computed and paid, and a signed copy must be given to each salesperson upon hiring.

Do not overlook the significance of these laws. Since exemplary damages and counsel fees are now being awarded regularly to successful sales reps who do not receive earned commissions within *days* after the commissions are due or they resign or are terminated, companies must be careful to pay commissions on a timely basis to avoid such penalties. Furthermore, it is essential to maintain proper books and records and give reps a proper accounting of commissions owed. Now companies must be aware of these laws (which govern in the state where the rep, not the company, is located) to avoid litigation in this area.

Counsel Comments: *Companies can employ several strategies to reduce the harsh effects of such laws by:*

1. Being mindful of demands received for commissions owed. All claims for commissions (particularly demands received in writing), should be investigated and responded to immediately by the company to avoid additional liability. This must always be done, especially if no money or a lesser sum is owed. Send the response via certified mail, return receipt requested, to prove delivery. This will help demonstrate your company's good faith and can minimize the imposition of additional damages and penalties by proving there was no willful intent to deny earned commissions to the salesperson.

2. Executing written contracts with all of your reps, even if the law in your state does not require them. Written agreements reduce confusion and clauses can be drafted to favor the company in many areas. An example of several comprehensive agreements setting forth these points is contained in the Appendix.

3. Considering including an arbitration clause in all of your rep agreements. Specify that all controversies will be settled in the city where the company is located, rather than where the rep resides or does business. This may force out-of-state reps who wish to sue in a distant locale to come to your state to proceed with their claims. In addition, the contract should state that a rep can only recover the amount of unpaid commissions plus interest in the event of arbitration. This provision may be enforced by the arbitrator(s), notwithstanding state law to the contrary.

4. Consulting a knowledgeable labor lawyer whenever you have a problem. Obtaining sound legal advice is essential to formulating strategies and protecting your company in this area.

Other Exceptions To The Employment-At-Will Rule

Each state has its own laws regulating firings due to absences from work caused by disability, maternity leave, jury duty, voting, bereavement and other factors beyond an employee's control. You must know the particular law in your state to be sure that you are not in violation when firing someone. Further, be careful to apply firing policies consistently throughout the company.

Implied Contract Exceptions

In addition to federal and state statutory restrictions on an employer's freedom to discharge employees and the public policy exceptions outlined above, newer protections may restrict the at-will authority of companies to terminate employment without having to state a reason. This protection is in the form of "implied contract" terms created by representations and promises published by employers in their employee handbooks.

A number of state courts began this legal trend by ruling that company retirement, sick leave, and fringe-benefit plans described in employee manuals were enforceable promises of compensation. Later, such rights were incorporated into federal ERISA law, but ERISA did not affect an employer's right to terminate a person's job "at will." As previously stated, many states have now ruled that promises in employee handbooks may be legally enforceable as implied contracts.

The first step in determining a company's liability in such cases is to determine if the words relied upon were sufficiently definite to constitute a promise. Courts often rule that statements in employee handbooks are not legal promises but merely puffery aimed at enhancing morale, and the existence of disclaimers may be legally sufficient to void the enforceability of such promises. The company may also protect itself by reserving the right to print revisions to the manual which eliminate promises contained in earlier editions that were previously given to the worker.

The implied contract exception to the employment-at-will doctrine may extend to oral promises made at the hiring interview. For example, if a company president tells an employee at the hiring interview, "Don't worry, we never fire anyone around here except for a good reason," a legitimate case might be made to fight the firing, provided the employee could prove that the words were spoken and that it was reasonable to rely upon them (i.e., that they were spoken seriously and not in jest).

This recently occurred in a case decided in Alaska. At the hiring, an employer stated that an applicant could have the job until reaching retirement age so long as he performed his duties properly. When the employee was fired suddenly, he argued that his job performance was excellent and that he had relied upon the promise of job security in deciding to accept the job. He won the case after proving the words were spoken. Several witnesses had overheard the promise at the job interview and testified to this fact at the trial.

A New Jersey employee complained that, relying on an employer's oral promise that he could be fired only for cause, he turned down a position offered by a competitor. Several months later he was summarily fired. The court, noting that promises were made inducing him to remain in the company's employ, ruled that the employer had made representations which transformed the employment-at-will relationship into employment with termination for cause only. After finding that the employee's decision not to accept the competitor's offer was significant, binding the employer, the court ruled in the employee's favor.

Counsel Comments: *Not all oral promises are enforceable against a com-*

pany, particularly when an employee is promised "a job for life." Promises of lifetime employment are rarely upheld due to a legal principle referred to as the Statute of Frauds. Under this law, recognized in most states, all contracts with a job term exceeding one year must be in writing to be enforceable. As a result, courts are generally reluctant to view oral contracts as creating permanent or lifetime employment. Usually, such contracts are viewed as being terminable at will by either party. Thus, a "lifetime contract" may theoretically be terminated after one day!

Some states have laws that limit the duration of an employment contract to a specified number of years (e.g., seven). Nevertheless, we recommend that your company never extend such offers, even in jest, to avoid potential problems, unless following through on the offer is your company's intent.

Discrimination Laws

Significant damages are recoverable when an individual receives unfair treatment because of a personal characteristic such as age, sex, race, religion or handicap. This may include job reinstatement in the event of a firing, wage adjustments, back pay and double back pay, promotions, recovery of legal fees, expert fees and filing costs, compensatory and punitive damages. Recourse can also include the institution of an affirmative action program on behalf of fellow employees. Thus, *always* consider whether the firing violates discrimination laws.

When a recently fired employee or salesperson enters a labor lawyer's office, one of the first points the attorney considers is whether he or she has a valid claim of unfair termination based upon discrimination, one of the exceptions to the employment-at-will rule.

For example, assuming equal work, did the company pay the same salary to women as to men? Were elderly salespeople let go first because of slipping sales quotas? Were minority technicians with excessive absences the first to be fired, while white workers in similar positions with the same attendance records were only given final warnings?

Discrimination claims pose a serious problem to all companies these days. Tens of thousands of formal complaints are filed each year with appropriate agencies and thousands of discrimination lawsuits are tried in court annually. These actions cost businesses millions of dollars in legal fees, lost workers' time and bad publicity. However, by recognizing the kinds of conduct that constitute discrimination during hiring, training and firing of employees, executives and owners can minimize or avoid litigation exposure. Any member of the employer's staff, from the president down to a supervisor or receptionist, can act in a way that will trigger a discrimination suit.

As discussed in Chapter 3, it is illegal to terminate anyone on the basis of age. Whenever an older employee (over 40) is fired and claims discrimination, the issue is basically whether the company's decision was made because of age or was the result of a reasonable, non-discriminatory business decision. Typically, the older worker must provide evidence that the employer's motive was improper. This is sometimes done by demonstrating that he/she was between 40 and 70 years of age, was doing satisfactory work, and was forced to leave a position that was then filled by a younger employee under 40. Age-related statements made to the claimant (e.g., "You are too old; why don't you retire?) and statistics (e.g., the company fired five older workers in the past year and replaced them with employees under 40) may also be used as proof. The following thumbnail sketch generally outlines what employers can do under discrimination laws pertaining to age:

- Fire older workers for inadequate job performance and good cause, provided younger employees are similarly treated.
- Entice older workers into early retirement by offering additional benefits (e.g., bigger pensions, extended health insurance, substantial bonuses, etc.) which are voluntarily accepted.
- Lay off older workers, provided younger employees are similarly treated.
- Choose younger rather than older applicants when successful job performance absolutely requires that a younger person be hired for the job.

However, the following actions are prohibited by law:

- Denying an older applicant a job solely on the basis of age.
- Imposing compulsory retirement before age 70.

- Threatening termination, loss of benefits, etc.
- Firing older persons because of age.
- Penalizing older employees with reduced privileges, employment opportunities or compensation, because of age.

Counsel Comments: *Early retirement programs are legal and do not violate federal age discrimination laws so long as participation is voluntary. If your company offers a financial package containing early retirement inducements, be sure it really contains worthwhile incentives such as additional pension benefits (extra years of age and service for pension calculations), lump sum severance payments (e.g., an extra month's pay), cash inducements and retirement health programs. Take the proper steps to reduce the risks of age discrimination litigation arising from "forced retirement." Never exert pressure on older workers to opt for early retirement by threatening firing, demotions, poor recommendations or references, or a cut in pay.*

Back up all firing decisions with proper documentation of poor work performance or "for cause" factors. Instruct staff to avoid making liability-sensitive statements, remarks, or threats with respect to age. It is also a good idea to study carefully and continually the company's statistical hiring and firing patterns. This may enable you to avoid giving a terminated worker's case the leverage it needs—proof that the company has made a practice of firing older workers and replacing them with younger ones.

When you are contemplating a large layoff, or seek to reduce your payroll through early retirement incentives, proceed with caution.

With respect to sex discrimination, be aware that the law requires equal pay for equal work and similar employment policies, standards and practices for males and females. Always treat pregnant women who are unable to work the same way as other workers who have other forms of disability.

Avoid firing anyone who complains about sexual harassment or reports a sexual harassment incident. As discussed in more detail in Chapter 3, sexual harassment cases are dangerous to employers because many courts are ruling that some companies are responsible for the acts of their supervisory employees, regardless of whether the company knew or even should have known of the occurrence. In some states, this makes the employer strictly liable for the acts of any supervisor. In cases where the employee is subjected to slur, insult, or innuendo, the courts are allowing claimants to prevail if they can prove that sexual harassment incidents took place which were neither isolated nor trivial. Some courts have even ruled that companies are liable for incidents which they should have known about (but didn't) if no effective action is taken to end the harassment, even when the companies' official policies prohibit sexual harassment.

Counsel Comments: *Management should remind key executives of these and other potential legal hazards. For example, companies should disseminate a periodic reminder to employees in policy manuals, journals and letters that the company does not tolerate sex discrimination or harassment of any kind on the job, that anyone who experiences or observes such treatment should report it to management (or their immediate supervisor) immediately, and that all communications will be held in the strictest confidence with no direct or indirect reprisals against the informant and/or complainant. In addition, supervisors should be educated as to what constitutes sexual harassment and other forms of sex discrimination, what the adverse effects to the company could be, and ways to handle problems if they arise.*

All supervisors should be instructed to:

* *Address themselves promptly to all complaints;*
* *Remain objective and responsive to problems;*
* *Consult with the complainant immediately to resolve problems before they get out of hand.*

Retirement plans and pension programs that favor one sex over the other are illegal. Speak with experienced labor counsel immediately if you have any doubts about the application of fringe benefit plans such as vacations, insurance coverage, pensions, profit-sharing plans, bonuses, holidays, or disability leave policies you may be considering.

> **Counsel Comments:** *In the absence of state or federal law, your company may be free to determine what benefits will be given and the nature of those benefits. If benefits are offered, publish them in a company handbook or policy manual so that employees will have advance notification of what is available. For your company's protection, your manuals and handbooks should always state that the benefits offered may be rescinded, discontinued or modified at any time without advance notice. Thus you may avoid being committed to granting such benefits by contract and giving your employees the legal right to rely upon them.*

Potential problems regarding race, handicap, and religious discrimination arise every time your company fires someone in a protected class. For example, employers have an obligation to make reasonable accommodations of the religious needs of employees. An employer must give time off for the sabbath or holy day observance, except in an emergency. The employer may give leave without pay, may require equivalent time to be made up, or may allow the employee to charge the time against any other leave with pay except sick pay. Exempted from this protection, however, are employees in certain health and safety occupations, or any employee whose presence is essential on any given day. It also does not apply to private employers who can prove that an employee's absence would cause severe business hardship.

In summary, management's ability to recognize what constitutes discrimination can go a long way toward protecting the company from such charges. In the event a private lawsuit is instituted, or formal charges are filed with the EEOC, the State Division of Human Rights, or other agency, take prompt steps to enforce the company's rights. A carefully drafted response should be forwarded within several weeks after formal charges are received. Decide whether it makes economic sense to offer some form of restitution or money settlement early on, out of court. However, perhaps the best way to avoid legal exposure and involvement in this area is to consider carefully (before the firing) whether there is a strong possibility that a discrimination charge will be brought. If so, you may wish to reconsider your decision before taking action.

Advantages Of An Independent Review

Never underestimate the advantages of discussing the decision to fire with a trusted advisor before taking action. A procedure for independent review of all termination decisions can be an important step in reducing the risks associated with employee terminations.

An effective independent reviewer must be well-versed both in the legal principles that govern employee terminations and in the company's personnel policies and practices. Equally important, the reviewer must have actual authority to reject proposed terminations if they do not meet legal requirements or company standards.

> **Counsel Comments:** *The independent reviewer should consider all of the strategies previously mentioned in this chapter and should inquire into the following:*
>
> * *Would the payment of a small amount of severance (e.g., two weeks in lieu of notice, or one week per year of employment) reduce animosity and the chances of a lawsuit?*
> * *Are there any mitigating factors that may excuse or explain the employee's poor performance or misconduct?*
> * *How long has the employee worked for the company?*
> * *What kind of overall record does the employee have?*
> * *Is termination appropriate considering all of the circumstances? Does the punishment fit the crime?*
> * *Has the company followed a consistent policy of terminating workers with similar infractions?*

* *Is the threat of legal repercussions in a given instance greater than with other terminations in the past?*

* *Is the company retaliating against the employee because of a refusal to commit illegal or unethical acts (e.g., falsifying records, for serving on extended jury duty or in the military, or for obeying a subpoena), rather than for a bona fide business reason, disciplinary problem, or poor performance?*

Choosing a qualified person within the company to evaluate independently the decision to fire may protect your company from committing illegal discrimination toward employees.

PLANT CLOSINGS

Be aware of the ramifications of the federal Worker Adjustment and Retraining Notification act (WARN) when contemplating closing a plant or discharging workers en masse. This law requires employers with more than 100 workers to give employees and their communities at least 60 days notice, or comparable financial benefits, of plant closings and large layoffs that affect 50 or more workers at a job site. The law is unique in its provisions that deal with retraining of displaced workers. It is also extremely technical and must be thoroughly understood before you take action. The following thumbnail sketch highlights important aspects of the act together with analysis of the law's possible effects on companies throughout the United States.

Section 3(a) of WARN prohibits employers from ordering a plant closing or mass layoff until 60 days after the employer has given written notice of this to:

- Affected employees or their representatives;
- The state dislocated worker unit; and
- The chief elected official of the unit of local government where the closing or layoff is to occur.

Employers are defined as business enterprises that employ more than 100 full-time workers (part-timers are characterized as those working fewer than 20 hours per week or less than six months in the preceding year), or who employ more than 100 employees who in the aggregate work at least 4,000 hours per week, excluding overtime.

The act calls for covered employers to give notice of a plant closing or mass layoff. A plant closing is defined as the "permanent or temporary shutdown of a single site of employment, or one or more facilities or operating units within a single site of employment if the shutdown results in an employment loss at the single site of employment during any 30-day period for 50 or more employees excluding part-time employees." Employment loss is defined under the law as "a termination other than for cause, voluntary departure or retirement, or a layoff for more than six months or a reduction in hours of work of more than 50 percent during each month of any six month period."

The term "mass layoff" means a reduction in force different from a plant closing resulting in employment loss during any 30-day period for 50 full-time employees who constitute at least 33 percent of the full-time employees at a single site of employment, or 500 employees.

The law does not affect government, nonprofit and service organizations. Also, many layoffs of small and very large companies may not be affected by the act's requirements due to the numbers of persons. In addition, if the plant closing or massive layoff was caused by a natural disaster (e.g., flood, earthquake or severe drought), or the closing of a temporary facility or completion of a project whose employees were hired with the understanding that their work was of limited duration, the law will not adversely affect the employer. The same is true for problems caused by strikes, lockouts or permanent replacement of economic strikers. Other exceptions include: the 60-day rule does not have to be strictly followed if the employer, reasonably and in good faith, is forced to shut down the plant more quickly to obtain needed capital or business, or if the closing or mass layoff is caused by business circumstances not reasonably foreseeable at the time the required notice was to be given.

Finally, the law apparently does not protect workers who lose their jobs less than 60 days after the effective date of a sale because the act was intended to protect workers only from closings or layoffs prior to a sale. The law appears merely to obligate the seller to give notice until the sale is completed; it is still unclear to what extent, if any, the buyer would be liable thereafter.

Any employer who orders a plant closing or mass layoff without furnishing appropriate notice may be liable in a civil action to each affected employee for:

- One day's back pay for each day of violation up to 60 days. This amount is calculated at the higher of the employee's average regular rate or final regular rate of pay less any wages paid during the layoff period and any voluntary or unconditional payments (e.g., severance) paid to the affected worker which were not legally required;
- The value of medical expenses and other benefits paid directly to the affected employee; and
- The value of actual payments made to third parties on behalf of the affected employee.

Employers are also subject to fines not to exceed $500 per day to the appropriate unit of local government where the closing or layoff occurs unless the employer continues to pay benefits to affected employees as described above within three weeks of the shutdown or layoff. However, this fine may be reduced by a showing that a "complaint of wrongful act or omission" was in good faith and that the employer had reasonable grounds for believing that the act or omission was not a violation of law.

Critics contend that the law is weak, since federal courts do not have the authority to enjoin plant closings and layoffs—in other words, cannot force an employer to reopen or rehire. The act awards only the above cited economic sanctions plus reasonable attorney fees and costs to the prevailing party. Some legislators interested in protecting the rights of employees are arguing that the act has no teeth and, at best, merely gives workers notice of the firing, and possibly some severance pay if a job is eliminated prior to the 60-day notice period.

Counsel Comments*: Companies covered by the law must now carefully orchestrate all moves before closing marginally profitable plants. Obviously, affected workers and the community must be notified properly and additional benefits will have to be given to comply with the act's provisions. All of these considerations, and others, should be reviewed by a knowledgeable company officer before action is taken.*

EMPLOYER LEGAL OPTIONS AND STRATEGIES

There are ways to fire employees without encountering legal battles. A little time and education on the part of your company's executives can result in legal hiring and firing procedures that protect the company. Keep in mind the following points.

For-Cause Firing

Understand problems of proof associated with "for-cause firings." Many employers employ union workers who are covered under collective bargaining agreements stating that they can only be fired "for cause." Other companies use written employment contracts or company manuals with non-union employees. Some of these contracts subscribe to either a "firing for cause" or "hiring for a definite term" practice. This distinction—hiring an employee with the promise of secure employment unless there are grounds for termination, as opposed to being hired at will which means the worker can be fired at any time, with or without notice and reason—is a critical one, yet many companies apparently do not appreciate the difference.

When a terminated worker consults a labor lawyer, one of the first questions asked is whether he or she was hired at will. If so, the chances of obtaining damages from a company based on legal theories that include wrongful discharge and breach of contract are dramatically reduced. However, if an employee was hired under an agreement that he or she could only be fired "for cause," the company must then be able to justify the firing with sufficient legal reasons (e.g., fighting on the job, etc). Many companies have difficulty proving this.

Although such cases may appear to be fairly straightforward, it is often difficult to prove that the infractions occurred with sufficient intensity to justify a firing. Arbitrators and judges look first to see whether a legitimate company rule was violated and whether that rule was justified. Sometimes, an act or behavior cited as the reason for termination may not even fit in a "for cause" category—for example, some labor contracts do not specifically define drug or alcohol abuse as unacceptable workplace conduct.

Counsel Comments: *One standard manual that arbitrators use to assist them in rendering employment decisions lists standards for "just cause" firings. Every company official entrusted with* *hiring and firing employees should be familiar with these guidelines:*

* *Did the company have a clear rule against the kind of employee behavior for which the discipline was administered?*
* *Is the rule reasonably related to the orderly, efficient and safe operation of the company's business?*
* *Has the company granted employees reasonable opportunity to learn the company's rules?*
* *Has the company provided employees with reasonable opportunity to learn the possible consequences of disregarding the rules?*
* *Has the company administered and enforced the rules even-handedly and without discrimination among the employees?*
* *Did the company investigate fairly the circumstances involved in an alleged offense?*
* *Did the company, through its investigation, obtain substantial evidence of guilt?*
* *Was the penalty imposed for a fairly investigated, fact-supported offense reasonably related to the seriousness of the proven offense and/or the nature of the guilty employee's past record?*

The burden of proving these points typically rests with the company. Because that burden is usually one of "clear and convincing" proof rather than the "preponderance of the evidence" standard which is typically required in other kinds of lawsuits, companies must be careful to maintain accurate records before firing workers whose jobs are secure. Always follow necessary procedures spelled out in any handbooks or manuals that were previously distributed to employees. Finally, avoid hiring employees under any other circumstance than at will. This is the best preventive advice of all.

Legal Opinions In Sensitive Situations

Consider obtaining a formal legal opinion in sensitive and difficult situations including employee terminations that appear headed toward confrontation and possible litigation, or those which pose complicated legal questions. Large-scale terminations or layoffs due to business reorganizations should always be planned with counsel before implementation. The same is true for mandatory retirement programs the company wishes to institute. Early consultation with counsel may reduce the legal risks associated with employee terminations, as well as develop defenses to subsequent litigation stemming from employee firings.

Peer Review

As previously discussed in the section entitled "Advantages Of An Independent Review" in this chapter, consider utilizing a peer review system before the actual firing takes place. In evaluating a proposed termination, the reviewer should consider a list of major issues. Among the points to be included are the following:

- What is the employee's seniority? What kind of overall record does the employee have?
- Is the termination consistent with the employee's performance appraisals?
- Has the employee received progressive discipline before the discharge?
- Is the proposed termination consistent with the company's actions in similar circumstances in the past?
- Is the company disciplining the worst offenders first?
- Are there any mitigating factors that may explain or excuse the employee's prior performance or misconduct?
- Are there mitigating circumstances which suggest that less drastic action be taken?
- Was the employee aware of the performance standards, work rules, or other standards for which he or she is to be terminated?
- Are there any statutory problems such as race, sex, age, pregnancy discrimination, or

violations of whistleblowing laws or exceptions to the employment-at-will doctrine?

- Do any of the circumstances suggest actual or apparent problems under the National Labor Relations Act, or other employment statutes?
- Have any representations been made to the employee concerning job security? If so, is the proposed termination consistent with those representations?
- What does the employment contract say about firings? Were all provisions (e.g., sending a formal notice by certified mail) followed?
- Are there any public policy concerns? For example, has the employee recently exercised a legal right (i.e., attended jury duty) that your company complained about?
- Has the employee been involved in any controversial events that may include misconduct on the company's behalf (e.g., wrongful surveillance, eavesdropping, excessive interrogations or other violations of employee rights of privacy)?
- Has the supervisor complied with relevant portions of the personnel policies and procedures?
- Is the employee close to earning substantial financial benefits such as a vested pension, large commission or bonus? If so, will the firing deprive the employee of that expected financial benefit?
- Under all of the circumstances, does this case present a fair and honest reason, regulated by good faith, for termination?
- Are there legitimate adverse business conditions or other bona fide economic reasons necessitating the elimination of the employee's position?

Counsel Comments: *Although this list does not cover all considerations, it is fairly inclusive. Certainly companies must recognize that all terminations should be handled in a consistent manner in accordance with a well-defined policy.*

Determine HowThe Firing Will Occur

Once the decision to terminate has been made and approved by management, companies must determine how the firing will occur. Most termination decisions should be announced to the employee personally. Avoid communicating the message by letter or memorandum if you can help it. Issues such as who should tell the employee, when the conversation should take place, and where the conversation should take place should be decided on a case-by-case basis.

Break The News Properly

In general, employers should decide how to terminate the employee with an eye to minimizing the employee's discomfort, including embarrassment, and maximizing the chances that the employee will have an opportunity to regain his or her composure and begin taking steps to find employment elsewhere. Once the decision to terminate has been made and approved by management, companies must be careful about how the news is broken to the terminated worker. There is no single, best way to tell a worker that his/her services are no longer needed. However, certain rules can help you break the news properly. How an employer elects to inform the employee of the termination can dramatically affect the risk of wrongful termination litigation, because it can determine the degree of anger, frustration and hostility with which the news is received. In addition, the way the employee was told may reflect on the company's degree of humanity, a consideration that can influence a jury if litigation arises.

An employee should be told the specific reasons for the firing. Some states, including Florida, Indiana, Kansas, Maine, Missouri and Montana, have passed laws called service letter statutes that give fired workers additional legal protection. Generally, under the laws in these states, employers are required to give a terminated worker a true written statement regarding the cause of his or her dismissal. Once such an explanation is received, the employer cannot furnish prospective employers or others with reasons which deviate from those given in the service letter. In those states, an employer can be sued for damages for refusing to tell a worker why he or she was fired, for providing the worker with false reasons, or for changing its story and offering additional reasons to outsiders or during legal proceedings (i.e., at a trial or arbitration).

Counsel Comments: *Since workers may have the right to demand and receive a true reason for the firing, avoid potential exposure by furnishing the truthful reason to the discharged worker from the onset. In the event of litigation, a jury* *may well believe that decency and compassion require, at the minimum, that the employer tell the employee why he or she is being terminated; be consistent in holding to the first reason offered.*

Some supervisors are embarrassed to say negative things which reveal true personal facts regarding the employee's character (such as honesty traits, etc.). Instruct them to be as direct and honest as possible since the company will have to be able to prove the true business reason for the termination at a trial. Avoid being apologetic when telling the news, since this could be interpreted as a sign of weakness. On the other hand, avoid being overly specific or detailed in explaining the reason for the termination because the more information you give, the greater the chances that some of it may be incorrect and could hurt the company at a trial. In the uncomfortable setting of a termination interview, the supervisor may well get the facts wrong.

An article on wrongful terminations by attorney Ralph H. Baxter, Jr., given at the Practising Law Institute's 17th Annual Institute of Employment Law and quoted in the Nov. 1, 1988 issue of *Your Business and the Law,* recommends that all companies be compassionate, yet firm. Avoid confrontations. If the terminated worker begins to shout, do not respond angrily. Wait for the outburst to end. If the employee persists, call security if necessary. Never accuse or make derogatory comments about the ex-employee in front of non-essential third parties because you may be creating a ready-made defamation claim.

Make sure the employee knows the decision is final and non-negotiable. Give workers a specific date and time on which they are no longer employees. If they are eligible for any benefits, and if other matters need to be clarified (such as how references will be handled, outplacement counseling, the time frame for leaving, etc.), spell these out at the final termination session. If the person handling the firing is not knowledgeable about all the benefits due the individual, refer the ex-employee to the appropriate administrator in the personnel department.

Treat the individual with dignity. Avoid telling the fired person to clear out his/her desk immediately except in cases of blatant insubordination or theft. However, be sure to recover all company property before he/she departs. This may include such items as automobile keys, samples, company brochures and literature, customer lists and other information. Some companies expedite this process by holding back *voluntary* payments (such as severance) until company property has been returned.

Counsel Comments: *However, avoid holding back final accrued wages, salary, vacation and other payments previously earned and due to avoid an investigation and other penalties imposed by your state's Department of Labor. In many states, earned payments such as wages and other monies must be paid immediately upon a firing and presented to the terminated employee in the form of a check at the time of the exit interview. Since substantial fines, penalties and other problems can ensue, including* personal *liability for officers and directors of companies in some situations, avoid holding back such payments unless counsel has recommended or approved that such action be taken.*

Statements To Current Employees

One of the most overlooked items on management's agenda is what to say to the employees left behind. Offer your employees a frank presentation of the situation where warranted but never badmouth the terminated worker ("he was fired because he was a crook") because word of such statements may get back to the ex-employee and create defamation problems. And, if the reason was because of a layoff and you advise present workers of this fact, other employees may be fearful of losing their job (creating potential morale and productivity problems). Thus, consider carefully all the ramifications of what will be said to current employees.

Advantages Of Non-Monetary Benefits

Consider offering non-monetary benefits to "sweeten" the termination if necessary. For example, if grounds exist to deny unemployment compensation (because the individual was terminated due to misconduct), the company may elect to avoid filing charges sufficient to deny unemployment compensation to the individual or appear at an unemployment hearing as a way of minimizing conflict caused by the termination. Or, the company can advise the individual that although it has no legal obligation to provide prospective employers with references, favorable or otherwise, it will do so provided the employee accepts the termination graciously.

Other options include continued use of a company office, telephone, secretary, resume preparation, outplacement guidance, waiving the enforcement of a previous non-compete agreement, and so forth. You can be surprised by their effectiveness in reducing the chances of post-termination litigation.

Planning Ahead

The best planned terminations are typically orchestrated by a team, including a manager and a human resources person. Experts recommend that it be formal and clear; the manager should present the facts for the termination and the human resources person should discuss the severance package and field any questions. Some companies hand the employee a formal termination letter and a written description of the severance terms. Where warranted, the employee might be asked to sign a waiver.

If the employee wants to stall or requests that the decision be reconsidered until another day, insist that the offer is non-negotiable and is the same as is offered to others. This may persuade the terminated individual that any negotiation for more severance and other benefits will be futile. In many situations, companies favor firing workers in the early afternoon so that the employee has plenty of time to leave the premises by the end of the day.

Using Releases

Consider the signing of releases when appropriate. A properly executed general release, provided it was not signed under circumstances suggestive of fraud, duress or mistake, can protect your company against lawsuits by prohibiting a terminated individual from instituting a lawsuit to collect damages stemming from the firing. If you are seeking to be released from potential *discrimination claims,* the release must also contain language giving the employee a significant amount of time (typically seven days after signing) to rescind it before it becomes effective. Examples of such releases are included in the Appendix.

Counsel Comments*: Since many individuals are reluctant to sign releases without first obtaining proper legal counsel, and the entrance of a lawyer into the picture may create further problems (such as a request for more benefits before the release is signed), the decision to request a signed release sometimes makes sense only in cases where significant, additional benefits (such as generous severance pay) are being offered up-front. In such situations, it may be difficult for the employee to refuse to sign a release when the package is too good to pass up.*

Dealing With Potential Employers

Take a conservative approach with potential employers. People with a new job are less likely to sue former employers. Avoid standing in the way of a terminated person's future employment if possible. Adopt a policy of simply confirming the facts of employment, dates, duties, and positions held. The more derogatory information you supply a prospective employer (such as "The ex-employee is not eligible for re-hire because..."), the greater the chance you will face a defamation lawsuit. Remember, bad references lead to expensive lawsuits! More information on this subject is included in the section "Defamation Concerns" in this chapter.

Many states have enacted anti-blacklisting statutes that punish employers for maliciously or willfully attempting to prevent former employees from finding work. Also, as mentioned previously, some states, including Florida, Indiana, Kansas, Maine, Missouri and Montana, require employers to give an employee a written statement of the cause of their dismissal. Under this legislation, the employer cannot furnish prospective employers with reasons for the dismissal that deviate from those in the service letter. In those states, if the employer refuses to give written reasons for the firing, or the reasons stated are untrue, the individual may bring a lawsuit for damages.

The Exit Interview

Use the exit interview to your company's advantage. At the exit interview, supervisors should be prepared to answer reasonable questions and to spend time in discussion with the employee following announcement of the termination. It is also a good idea to conduct exit interviews with employees who resign from their jobs.

Properly conducted exit interviews serve several purposes. By questioning the employee, the employer can learn about the individual's dissatisfaction with company policies and procedures. If the individual is planning to sue, you may gain valuable information that can assist the company in building a proper defense or in taking corrective action before a suit is filed. You may also gain information about other employees that can be used to the company's benefit.

Enforcement Of Restrictive Covenants

If the employee is an important executive who has acquired confidential trade information or company secrets, defined as "any formula, pattern, device, or compilation of information used in business that gives a competitor an advantage over competitors that do not know or use it," try to learn the identity of the company the individual plans to work for. If he/she signed a contract containing a covenant not to work for a competitor or to use confidential information against your company, such information could help you monitor the situation more closely and could be extremely useful.

Counsel Comments: *The enforcement of post-termination restrictive covenants varies on a state-by-state basis and generally depends on the unique facts of each case. Many states, such as New York, have left the issue to the courts for resolution. Other states, including Oregon, Louisiana and Texas, have responded legislatively by enacting statutes regulating the enforceability of such clauses.*

Assuming the company can prove that trade secrets or confidential information is involved (which is often difficult because companies often confuse such information with mere general data acquired by the individual from his/her business experience), the company took precautions to guard the secrecy of such data or information, and the time limit and geographic scope limitations of the covenant are reasonable, many courts will enforce confidentiality agreements previously signed by key employees to prevent them from using or disclosing this information. Depending on state law, confidentiality agreements should be drafted when dealing with outside companies such as independent research and development firms, subcontractors and others with access to confidential information including licensees and suppliers.

However, it is generally more difficult to enforce covenants not to compete (such as restricting a key executive from working for a competitor, starting a competing business, or soliciting current or former employees away from your organization) unless the restriction is reasonable in terms of geographic scope and time limitation and a court is persuaded that the request is proper and necessary to protect the interests of your company. Certainly keeping the time restriction short (i.e., six months or less) and paying the executive additional consideration before the written covenant was signed can enhance your company's chances of success in this area. However, since the law varies so, always speak to experienced counsel before considering the drafting of such clauses in an pre-employment or post-employment agreement.

Efficient exit procedures include taking preventive steps to reduce the dangers of disloyal ex-employees using confidential information against your company. All material (including copies of relevant documents) containing company secrets should be returned before the employee departs. The individual, whether he/she resigns or is fired, should be advised of his/her continuing obligation not to disclose trade secrets and should be requested to sign a document confirming this. When the situation warrants, some companies withhold *gratuitous* (not previously earned) severance benefits until they have proof that trade secrets have not been taken and/or conveyed.

If applicable, send both the individual and his or her new employer (your competitor) a letter reminding them of the ex-employee's continuing obligation to secrecy and the fact that a restrictive covenant is in effect. If you learn that this letter is ignored, a cease and desist letter must be sent by counsel advising them of the seriousness of the situation. Strategies such as these can persuade them that it might be risky to violate the covenant and may demonstrate your resolve to fight it out in court if necessary.

Severance Policy

Consider offering a modest severance policy in your manual or handbook to reduce the chance of having to make a larger severance payment after the individual is fired. Some companies reduce the chances of paying larger settlements after a firing by establishing a limited policy that is followed consistently. For example, your company could state that upon termination for any reason other than for cause, a flat two weeks is paid in lieu of severance for workers with less than five years of service and flat four weeks for workers with more than five years service. Then, when all terminated workers receive these sums, regardless of length of service or seniority, a fired worker will have difficulty claiming that he/she has been treated unfairly and is entitled to more. Offering a sufficient amount of severance to all employees and sticking to that policy may be effective.

TAX RAMIFICATIONS OF STRUCTURING SETTLEMENTS

No matter how carefully employers run their businesses, many companies face the prospect of paying settlements or court-ordered judgments as a result of legal actions brought by former employees. These payments arise from various causes of action such as claims for race, age or sex discrimination, wrongful discharge, defamation, and breach of contract, among others. Besides payment for traditional compensatory damages, portions of these settlements or court-awarded judgments often go to cover the employee's attorney fees, costs and disbursements, interest, mental and emotional distress, and punitive damages.

The tax consequences of employee-related court awards and settlement payments present many opportunities for companies since properly structured settlements can save companies money while putting more after-tax dollars into an employee's pocket. Employers can avoid common pitfalls in this area and, by following certain strategies, decrease the chances that the proposed settlement or judgment (which has been structured to your company's benefit) will be disturbed by the IRS.

According to the IRS, money received by a judgment or settlement, in a lump sum or periodic payments as damages for personal injuries, emotional pain, suffering, inconvenience, mental anguish, loss of enjoyment of life, and other non-pecuniary losses or sickness (such as in a sex harassment case) is not taxable. On the other hand, any money paid to an employee in settlement or judgment as compensation for lost wages, back pay and front pay, severance payments or fringe benefits is subject to withholding taxes. If such money is paid in lost wages, then the employer is required to withhold income taxes and FICA taxes from the payment. The employer would also be required to pay additional sums for FUTA and the employer's portion of FICA.

The potential liability to companies here arises when the IRS finds that the parties improperly treated an amount paid as excludable income (i.e., for pain and suffering) or non-wage income. In such cases, employers are liable for the employee's failure to pay FICA and income taxes together with interest and penalties unless the IRS can receive the amounts owed from the employee. Such penalties may also be assessed against certain corporate officers if the employee fails to pay said amounts. But note that the employer's portion of FICA taxes as well as FUTA tax cannot be paid by the employee and thus the employer is *always* liable for these taxes.

Furthermore, the United States Supreme Court ruled in its Spring 1992 term that employers are required to treat *some* portion of settlement proceeds in discrimination cases as taxable lost wages and make deductions from the proceeds regardless of whether the discrimination claimant is a current employee.

A company is allowed to deduct the portions of attorney fees and interest spent defending the interests of its business. This applies particularly to contesting demands made by the terminated worker for wages for breach of contract. Conversely, attorney fees incurred by an ex-employee to prosecute his/her alleged defamation of character claims are not deductible, since money received for such claims is for personal injuries and is therefore excludable from being taxed. This includes punitive damages and damages arising from wrongful discharge claims.

After understanding what is and is not tax deductible, you may then design the settlement to produce tax advantages for both the company and the employee. As the following example shows, the advantage comes from allocating legal fees, interest and related expenses in a way that increases the tax exemption for both parties. Once you know what you want to do, be sure to put all settlements in writing with specific allocations for specific payments. Identifying the underlying basis for any payments can help avoid problems with the IRS.

Counsel Comments: *The IRS is not bound by any allocation but it may be honored if it is reasonable. To determine what is reasonable, Attorneys Alan M. Koral and*

Neil Capobianco write in the September 1992 issue of the New York State Bar Association's Labor and Employment Law Section Newsletter that the IRS will refer to any lawsuit's complaint to determine the true scope of the remedies sought by the plaintiff. Understandably, the IRS will look with suspicion upon attempts by the parties to diminish their tax liabiity, such as amending the complaint just prior to settlement to eliminate or decrease a demand for back pay.

For example, when settling a firing with potential sex discrimination ramifications, instead of paying $50,000 in back pay or severance, try to structure the settlement in terms of attorney fees, interest, liquidated damages and back pay. Assume this is allocated as follows: attorney fees, $10,000; interest, $2,000; back pay, $30,000; and liquidated damages, $8,000. By structuring the arrangement in this fashion, the parties would eliminate the need to pay FICA and FUTA taxes on 40 percent of the settlement.

Counsel Comments*: Take advantage of the after-tax consequences to offer less money in settlement to the employee. Whenever you are in the process of negotiating a payment or settlement,* always *attempt to put together a package that saves the company real dollars while creating a greater after-tax benefit for the employee receiving the settlement. Be as specific as possible when drafting settlement agreements and releases and write these with care. In addition to reducing the particular settlement allocation to writing, be sure to use specific language that complies with IRS Code language.*

Be sure that all settlements are based on economic realities and good business practices, and that the parties will abide by them. In a recent case, the parties agreed on a certain allocation in the settlement agreement, yet the taxpayer claimed a different amount on his tax return. This triggered an IRS audit and both parties suffered substantial penalties and unnecessary expenses. To avoid this, you may wish to request in the settlement agreement a copy of the terminated employee's next tax return to be sure that the settlement allocation is followed per the agreement. Some lawyers also draft indemnification and hold harmless clauses protecting the company from individuals who fail to follow their promises in settlement agreements or releases.

Finally, in view of the recent Supreme Court ruling requiring some reasonable allocation of a portion of any discrimination settlement as wages, be sure to make such an allocation in discrimination-oriented case settlements and withhold federal, FICA and FUTA income taxes to avoid IRS assessed penalties.

DEFAMATION CONCERNS

Avoid discussing the decision to terminate or criticize the fired individual in front of non-essential third parties. Companies across the country are facing a new kind of potential liability: defamation actions. Fired employees are increasingly suing former employers for libel and slander. In fact, libel suits filed by discharged employees against their former bosses now account for approximately one-third of all defamation actions and the average winning verdict in such cases exceeds $112,000, according to Jury Verdict Research Inc., a company that monitors this kind of litigation.

The Minnesota Supreme Court recently awarded four employees $570,000 because they had to reveal in job applications that their former employers had fired them. The plaintiffs had been fired for gross insubordination for failing to comply with their manager's request to falsify certain expenditure reports. Following termination, the employees sought other positions of employment. In response to inquiries about their previous positions, the four employees stated that they had been fired for gross insubordination.

The Minnesota Court ruled that a defamation had occurred since the terminated employees, when asked, would truthfully reply that they were fired for insubordination. Any explanations the plaintiffs tried to provide to prospective employers could not compensate for the highly negative impression caused by the word "insubordination." To make matters worse, the company's policy of withholding information after a job referral request only added to the innuendos. This case is significant because it indicates that, in some states, employees fired on false charges of bad conduct can sue their former employers for defamation, even if it is the workers themselves who reveal the charges.

To reduce the risk of defamation claims by ex-employees, consider the following strategies:

1. **Never stand in the way of a terminated employee's future employment.** Juries take a dim view of companies that deliberately prevent an employee from obtaining work elsewhere. You may wish to offer outplacement counseling to terminated employees to reduce the odds of wrongful termination and defamation lawsuits. Remember that disgruntled ex-employees who find new jobs are far less likely to sue.

2. **Maintain tight control over personnel files and avoid distributing personal information without an employee's consent.** Managers and supervisors should be instructed to avoid distributing copies of damaging records, such as memos in personnel files or poor performance evaluations. Untrue written comments that are distributed to third parties may give rise to potential defamation and libel claims as well as invasion of privacy lawsuits. Many states, including Connecticut, Illinois and Michigan, have passed strict laws prohibiting employers from divulging disciplinary information, including information concerning a disciplinary discharge, unless a copy of the statement is mailed to the affected employee.

In some cases, the conveyance of damaging oral or written information has caused juries to award large verdicts to injured ex-employees. In one case, a terminated employee sued his former boss on the basis of defamation because letters describing the employee's poor performance had been distributed and read by several executives. The individual was awarded $90,000 after proving that company officials distributed the letters, knowing they were false.

3. **Advise management and personnel entrusted with the authority to fire to keep their lips sealed whenever possible.** Your company can also minimize problems by limiting access to personnel files to only those people who require access; consider even limiting the kinds of documents (i.e., harmful memos, letters and other documents) which are contained in such files.

4. **Avoid giving negative references to prospective employers.** Anxious to avoid the high cost and aggravation of defamation suits, many companies are now confirming only an individual's former employment, the dates of employment, and the last salary grade and position held. Most important, many labor lawyers advise employers never to offer their opinions about a former employee's work performance ("The individual is not permitted to reapply here") unless it's conclusively positive. Although some states have ruled that employers have a qualified privilege when discussing an ex-employee's job performance with a prospective employer, a qualified privilege can be lost if abused. For example, the company can be liable if an executive knowingly makes false defamatory comments about a former employee due either to reckless disregard for the truth, ill will, or spite.

> **Counsel Comments:** *The less information an employer reveals, and the less subjective that information is, the safer your company will be.*

In many states, including Connecticut, *any* dissemination of employment data to prospective employers (other than the dates of employment, last position held and latest salary figures) is illegal without the ex-employee's consent. Many states prohibit the dissemination of confidential medical information as well.

5. **Avoid criticizing an individual in front of others, particularly at the exit or firing interview.** Defamation occurs not only by the dissemination of information to prospective employers, but also on-site within your company. For example, if you are about to fire someone suspected of stealing company property, and you accuse him/her in front of non-essential third parties (making comments such as "You are a crook") an action for defamation (slander) may be taken if the remarks are proven false. For further protection, consider your exit and firing interviews to take place between the individual and *one* company official when the circumstances surrounding the termination are likely to be "nasty."

6. **Remember that protection for defamation may also extend to physical acts.** For example, an employee working for a large automobile manufacturer was suspected of theft. Hundreds of workers observed him being forcibly searched and interrogated when leaving the premises. After proving the charges were unfounded, the man sued the company, arguing that the rough treatment observed by other workers defamed his reputation and held him up to ridicule and scorn (since the treatment

implied that he was guilty of theft). He was awarded $25,000 in damages.

7. **Understand that the rights of terminated workers are expanding rapidly throughout the U.S., and a defamation action against your company may be brought if a person's business reputation is impugned in and of itself by the firing.** In one case, a man was discharged after he incorrectly failed a polygraph test. The employee proved his company defamed him by firing him under circumstances that strongly implied he was guilty of theft; he was awarded $150,000 for his troubles.

8. **Recognize that some states, including Arkansas, Maine, Nebraska, New Mexico and Utah, treat untruthful job references as *crimes*.** Missouri permits civil actions against employers for compensatory damages for untruthful statements. The following states provide criminal penalties and civil damage lawsuits against former employers: California, Florida, Iowa, Kansas, Montana, North Carolina and Texas. In California and Texas, triple damages are awarded in certain situations; Montana and North Carolina statutes provide for additional punitive damages.

9. **Give truthful reasons for the termination.** In any defamation lawsuit, truth is an absolute defense. This means that if you disseminate something harmful about a person to a prospective employer which is true, or fire someone for a documented, legitimate reason (i.e., stealing, repeated inexcusable absences), the odds are high your company will prevail in a defamation lawsuit. Of course, your company will still be out-of-pocket for substantial legal fees and costs. But it is essential to conduct regular and comprehensive performance appraisals so that your reasons for the firing are documented and truthful. This is your first line of defense in any libel action.

10. **Remember that if your company refrains from releasing negative information, it may still be vulnerable in a suit if the terminated worker is forced to tell a prospective employer a reason why he or she was let go, and the reason given later proves to be false.**

11. **Consider an ex-employee's demand to review the contents of his or her personnel file where applicable.** A recent trend allows terminated workers access to and inspection of their personnel files. In California, Connecticut, Delaware, Illinois, Maine, Michigan, Nevada, New Hampshire, Ohio, Oregon, Pennsylvania, Washington and Wisconsin, for example, people now have the right to inspect their files. Some states even allow them to place rebuttals in their files which can refute company action or comments and may be read by prospective employers. In some states, people are even authorized to expunge false information contained in such files.

12. **Consider executing a general release if you think you may have a problem.** In some cases, employers can be reasonably certain at the time of termination that defamation litigation will later ensue. In those cases, the employer should consider buying out the claim with severance pay beyond the norm in exchange for a release from all claims. In order to be valid, the employer must confer some valuable consideration on the employee to which he or she would not otherwise be entitled, and the release or "separation agreement" should be signed voluntarily, free from fraud or duress.

Counsel Comments*: General releases signed for this purpose need not meet the stringent requirements of agreements releasing a company from age discrimination lawsuits and related discrimination exposure. In other words, it may not be necessary that the release:*

* *Clearly state all of the rights and claims available to the employee which are being waived, such as the specific names of all federal and state discrimination laws.*
* *Contain language that the individual has the right to reflect and confer with an attorney.*
* *State that the individual may revoke the release within seven days after signing it.*

But offering an employee additional severance in consideration for signing a general release can backfire against your company because the offer may be construed as a sign of weakness, causing the employee to seek the advice of counsel who may force an increase in your offer by the time the release is signed. Therefore, this strategy should never be attempted without the advice and approval of labor counsel. As this text demonstrates, any firing may have defamatory repercussions in the hands of an experienced labor attorney, so be careful.

HIDDEN LABOR ISSUES WHEN BUYING OR SELLING A BUSINESS

During the purchase of a business, both the buyer and seller are understandably concerned with financial considerations affecting the terms of sale and financing. However, after the deal is structured satisfactorily from the financial end, many labor issues come into play which should be carefully considered but are sometimes overlooked.

The buyer of an ongoing business must decide which employees will stay on board. For those who will not be rehired under the new regime, issues of severance, vacation pay, and other post-termination benefits come into play. Pension and profit-sharing plan obligations must also be examined and followed to comply with federal law and to adhere to collective bargaining obligations. Discrimination laws must be considered to insure that older workers are not being displaced by younger workers with lower salaries and earned benefits. The following are some important issues to consider in this area.

Severance Pay And Related Benefits

When workers are laid off, issues of severance and other post-termination benefits must be addressed. As a business grows, informal pay policies are frequently relied upon by terminated workers as a contract right. Often, the buyer of a business will view such payments as discretionary and gratuitous. This thinking may clash with the view of terminated workers, who consider such benefits guaranteed.

Many state courts have ruled that employees have rights that cannot be modified by buyers or sellers of businesses. With the enactment of the Employee Retirement Income Security Act of 1974 (ERISA), most severance plans fall under its protection. As a result, terminated workers have recently won major cases imposing severance obligations. For example, in cases where the buyer retains the services of a worker for a short time, then fires that worker, the worker may be able to sue and collect severance benefits as if he or she were still working for the former employer.

Counsel Comments: *Thinking ahead before a sale, companies that adopt formal severance rules forbidding the payment of excessive severance and limiting the amount of severance to be paid if a company is sold are better served in this area. In addition, your company may reserve the right to modify or terminate a severance policy and should consider doing so where appropriate.*

Collective Bargaining Agreements

In many cases, collective bargaining agreements already in effect protect union employees from modified working arrangements following the sale. When the seller does not comply with these agreements, workers typically request a court to impose "successor involuntary liability" on the buyer, even if the buyer only purchased assets, without any of the seller's obligations. Thus, a buyer must consider whether it will be forced to negotiate and deal with the labor union recognized by the seller or be bound by the existing collective bargaining agreement.

Counsel Comments: *The U.S. Supreme Court has ruled that when the buyer wants to lay off the entire workforce or substantially change the company's method of operations, it does not have to bargain with the union representing the seller's employees. The key issue is whether the buyer can be held liable as a successor, either because it failed to change operations substantially or because it used the services of the seller's workers in some significant way.*

Discrimination Concerns

When anticipating layoffs due to mergers or acquisitions of a company, special attention must be paid to age discrimination laws. Violations often occur when employers attempt to soften the impact and encourage voluntary resignations of elderly workers by offering early retirement incentives and enhanced severance packages. One area of age discrimination involves forced retirement, which occurs when companies exert pressure on older workers to opt for early retirement or face firing, demotion, cuts in pay or poor recommendations. Many older employees are successfully challenging company retirement plans stemming from large layoffs.

Thirty years ago, companies were generally free to cut payroll costs by laying off large numbers of employees. But because layoffs generally affect those with the least seniority, many employees who left were at the low end of the wage scale (which didn't solve a company's problem). Using early retirement packages, companies found that they could get rid of fewer workers at a higher cost savings, because those leaving were generally at the top of the wage scale because of their seniority. Although by nature such plans are discriminatory, since they target older employees, the ADEA generally allows early retirement programs (since they are perceived as an employee benefit). However, employees cannot be forced or coerced into taking advantage of them (except for bona-fide executives in certain limited situations).

Counsel Comments: *To increase the chances that an early retirement or "golden parachute" offer will be legally valid after acceptance, companies should require terminated workers to execute releases and waivers to resolve all potential employment claims. Care must also be taken in selecting personnel for layoff to avoid charges of actual or perceived discrimination based on age, sex, race, religion, or national origin. Terminating those most recently hired may reduce problems.*

Engage a qualified individual to analyze all relevant data, such as the respective ages of all employees considered for termination, to be sure that the ages are not unfairly skewed toward older workers. This is important when considering the discharge of a large number of employees due to a layoff or reorganization.

Warning Requirements

As discussed in a previous section in this chapter entitled "Plant Closings," the federal Worker Adjustment and Retraining Notification Act (WARN) requires employers with more than 100 workers to give employees and their communities at least 60 days notice of plant closings and large layoffs that affect 50 or more workers at a job site. Strict compliance with this federal law is essential to avoid potential problems.

UNEMPLOYMENT HEARINGS

After firing a worker for a valid reason (i.e., for cause), many companies out of kindness regularly fail to oppose the ex-employee's application for unemployment benefits. Such a move sometimes comes back to haunt them when the terminated worker files a lawsuit asserting a variety of legal causes of action stemming from the firing, and it is determined that the failure to oppose the unemployment claim constitutes a waiver of a legitimate reason for the firing or represents an employer's tacit admission of wrongdoing. When companies do not know how to defend themselves at unemployment hearings and lose the case, they risk additional legal exposure. For example, if a company argued that a minority worker was terminated due to misconduct and loses the unemployment hearing, this makes it easier for a disgruntled ex-employee to file a lawsuit claiming that he or she was fired due to discrimination. Furthermore, the company faces a direct economic result of losing its case by being charged a higher rate and paying more for unemployment insurance coverage.

Companies often underestimate the importance that unemployment hearings can play in reducing other forms of post-termination litigation. This section will instruct employers how to prepare properly and assert strategies to maximize the chances of success at the initial hearing.

State Requirements

Each state has different standards for collecting unemployment benefits and the standards of proof required from the employer in denying such benefits. Your company must know all of the essential details to properly contest any claim, such as how quickly to respond to the ex-employee's application for benefits, whether a detailed written statement must be submitted and made a part of the employer's file, whether the company has the opportunity to review the employee's position and other documentation submitted in favor of his/her request for benefits before the hearing, whether a stenographic record or tape recording will be made at the hearing, whether the company has the right to be represented by counsel, whether the decision can be appealed, and what formal rules of evidence, if any, will be followed at the hearing. A proper defense begins by planning ahead and being aware of all essential details before the hearing date; contact the nearest unemployment office for pertinent information when in doubt.

Standards For Benefits

In most states, a terminated worker may receive unemployment benefits as a result of a business reorganization, massive layoff, job elimination and other "no-fault" reasons. In some situations, this also includes being unsuited or unskilled for the job and even for overall poor work performance. However, a worker generally may not collect benefits caused by a voluntary resignation or a termination due to misconduct. The following are common examples of acts that often justify the denial of unemployment benefits based on misconduct:

- Insubordination or fighting on the job;
- Habitual lateness or excessive absence;
- Intoxication or drug abuse on the job;
- Disobedience of company work rules or policies;
- Gross negligence or neglect of duty;
- Dishonesty or unfaithfulness.

Although these examples appear to be relatively straightforward, employers often have difficulty proving that such acts reached the level of misconduct. This is because hearing examiners typically seek to determine whether a legitimate company rule was violated and whether that rule was justified.

Counsel Comments: *To maximize the company's defense, it is best to have a clear rule in place against the kind of behavior that resulted in the firing. The rule should be reasonably related to the orderly operation of the employers' business, and the employer should be able to produce credible witnesses who can prove the charges and demonstrate that the employer administered and enforced the rules fairly and consistently.*

The Hearing

Most unemployment hearings are no different from a trial. Witnesses typically testify under oath. Documents, including personnel information, warnings, performance appraisals, etc. are submitted as exhibits. The atmosphere is rarely friendly. Thus, it is essential to prepare in advance what you will say and how your company will handle tough questions from the worker and judge.

When preparing for the hearing, be certain that all your friendly witnesses (if any) will attend and testify on the company's behalf. If necessary, ask a representative from the unemployment office to issue a subpoena compelling the attendance of key disinterested witnesses who refuse to attend and testify voluntarily. Appoint one person responsible for organizing the company's defense before the hearing day to maximize your chances of success. Collect all evidence so it can be produced easily at the hearing. Discuss the testimony of co-workers and other witnesses to help organize and prepare the important facts. It is also wise to prepare an outline of key points to be discussed and questions to ask the ex-employee.

Arrive early on the day of the hearing and advise a scheduling clerk of your company's appearance. When the case is called, wait until the judge asks a question or requests information. Speak directly and with authority. Make your answer direct and to the point. Avoid arguing with the ex-employee and avoid interrupting his or her presentation. Once the ex-employee finishes testifying, a company representative or attorney may cross-examine such testimony and refute what was said.

Counsel Comments: *Labor lawyers are mindful of the standards that hearing examiners, judges and arbitrators use in making decisions at unemployment hearings and arbitrations. Since many of these guidelines are relevant to understanding and successfully defending an ex-employee's claim for unemployment benefits as well as prevailing at arbitration hearings and trials, they are repeated here:*

* *Did the employer have a clear rule against the kind of behavior which resulted in the firing?*
* *Is the rule reasonably related to the orderly, efficient and safe operation of the employer's business?*
* *Did the employer provide all employees with a reasonable opportunity to learn the company's rules?*
* *Did the employer provide all employees with reasonable notice regarding the consequences of violating such rules?*
* *Has the employer administered and enforced the rules consistently and without discrimination among all employees?*

* *Did the employer take steps to fairly investigate the circumstances involved in the alleged offense?*

* *Did the employer obtain substantial evidence of the alleged act through this investigation?*

* *Was it proper to discharge the employee for the incident or should a warning or suspension have been given?*

* *Does the worker have a history of committing similar acts?*

* *Did the employer do anything to contribute to the employee's offensive act (i.e., a supervisor provoking an employee to fight by directing racial slurs at the worker)?*

* *Did such acts meet the standard of law required to prove misconduct?*

* *Are there mitigating factors which reasonably explain the employee's conduct?*

* *Was the firing fair under all of the circumstances?*

* *In cases alleging theft, did the company prove its case clearly and convincingly by the evidence?*

* *Were the employer's witnesses credible in proving the action taken?*

At unemployment hearings and arbitrations, the employer typically has the burden of proving the facts and demonstrating that the acts are serious enough to rise to the level of misconduct. Often, where it appears that the facts seem to be equally balanced in favor of and against the ex-employee, the employee will probably win since the employer was unable to sustain its burden of proof.

These and other considerations demonstrate the degree of sophistication that is often required to prevail at unemployment hearings (and arbitrations and trials). Due to the *res judicata effect* unemployment verdicts cast on subsequent litigation, it is often advantageous for employers to be represented by competent counsel at all stages of the unemployment hearing.

Obtaining A Decision

Decisions are not usually obtained immediately after the hearing. Your company will probably be notified by mail a few weeks later. If you lose the decision, read the notice carefully. Most judges and hearing examiners give specific, lengthy reasons for their rulings. If the ruling was incorrect or you disagree with the judge's opinion, consider filing an appeal and have the case reheard, particularly if new material facts come to light or new relevant witnesses are willing to come forward and testify at the appeal hearing.

Seek Legal Advice

Speak to an experienced labor attorney for an opinion because appeals are not granted automatically. In many states, if a group of judges on the Appeals Board believe that the hearing judge's decision was correct factually and/or as a matter of law, the decision will go undisturbed. Often, the amount of time needed to review the transcript or tape of the proceeding(s), prepare an appeal brief, and reargue the case makes it too expensive and time-consuming.

> **Counsel Comments:** *Depending on the particular facts of the case and the consequences of not appealing (such as the possibility that the unfavorable decision will impact on another significant case brought by the ex-employee or create a harmful precedent), appealing the matter may not be justified. That is why it is important to sufficiently prepare for the first hearing to maximize the chances of obtaining a successful decision the first time around.*

APPENDIX A

SAMPLE EMPLOYMENT APPLICATION

APPLICATION FOR EMPLOYMENT

NAME ______________________ SOC. SEC. NO. __________________

ADDRESS ____

TELEPHONE (   ) ________________ Are you 18 years or older? YES   NO

If hired, can you provide the documents required to prove that you are authorized to work in the U.S.? YES   NO

EDUCATION

Type	Name/ Location	Course	No. Years Completed	Degree/ Diploma
Elementary & Jr. High				
High School				
College				
Technical Training				
Other				

EMPLOYMENT RECORD

	Company/ Name/ Address	Kind of Work	Date Started/ Left	Pay	Reason for Leaving
1					
2					
3					
4					
5					

Type of Work desired ____________________________ Desired Pay ______

How were you referred to our organization? ___________________________

Is there any information we would need about your name or use of another name for us to be able to check your work record? YES   NO

Please specify ____

U.S MILITARY SERVICE

Branch of Service ____

Rank & Type of Service ____________________________________

Traning/Experience Received ________________________________

REFERENCES

Name	Occupation	Yrs. Known	Address
1			
2			
3			

Please list any additional information such as licenses, professional degrees, that you consider important for the job to which you have applied:

____

____

I understand that the employer follows an employment-at-will policy, in that I or the employer may terminate my employment any time, or for any reason consistent with applicable state or federal law. I understand that this application is not a contract of employment. I understand that to be employed I must be lawfully authorized to work in the United States, and I must show the employer documents that will prove this if I am offered the job.

I understand that the company will thoroughly investigate my work and personal history and verify all data given on the application, on related papers, and in interviews. I authorize all individuals, schools and firms named within to provide any information requested about me, and I release them from all liability for damage in providing this information.

I certify that all the statements herein are true and understand that any falsification or willful omission shall be sufficient cause for dismissal or refusal of employment.

(Your Signature) ________________________ Date ____________________

APPLICANTS PLEASE DO NOT WRITE BELOW THIS LINE

Interviewed by (1) ____________ (2) ______________ (3) ________________

Starting Date __________ Rate ____________ Classification ______________

Relocation Information ____

Agency Fee Arrangements _______________________________________

Other Commitments ____

Approved by: (1) ____________ (2) ______________ (3) ________________

APPENDIX B

REFERENCE CHECK FORM

(COMPANY LETTERHEAD)

To Whom It May Concern:

____ ❑ has been employed by us
❑ has applied for employment

and given the following information covering employment in your organization. We have been authorized to communicate with you for verification and such reference information as you care to give us.

(Please check if correct or change if incorrect)

Employment dates: _______________________ _______________________

Position: _______________________________ _______________________

Last earning rate: $____________ per _______ _______________________

Reason for leaving: _______________________ _______________________

____ _______________________

Is applicant eligible for rehire? ____

____
Your signature

____
Title

On the back of this letter we would appreciate any helpful comments you care to make, and will respect your confidence in this matter. The enclosed duplicate is for your own files.

Sincerely yours,

____
Personnel Department

APPENDIX C

SAMPLE CONFIDENTIALITY AND NON-COMPETITION AGREEMENT

In consideration of my employment or continued employment by [Name of Company] (the ''Company''), together with its affiliates and subsidiaries, and any subsidiaries or affiliates which hereafter may be formed or acquired and in recognition of the fact that as an employee of the Company I will have access to the Company's customers and to confidential and valuable business information of the Company and of its parent company, [specify], together with its affiliates and subsidiaries, and any subsidiaries or affiliates which hereafter may be formed or acquired, I hereby agree as follows:

1. The Company's Business. The Company is [specify] a consulting firm. The Company is committed to quality and service in every aspect of its business. I understand that the Company looks to and expects from its employees a high level of competence, cooperation, loyalty, integrity, initiative, and resourcefulness. I understand that as an employee of the Company, I will have substantial contact with the Company's customers and potential customers.

I further understand that all business and fees including insurance, bond, risk management, self insurance, insurance consulting and other services produced or transacted through my efforts shall be the sole property of the Company, and that I shall have no right to share in any commission or fee resulting from the conduct of such business other than as compensation referred to in paragraph 3 hereof. All checks or bank drafts received by me from any customer or account shall be made payable to the Company, and all premiums, commissions or fees that I may collect shall be in the name of and on behalf of the Company.

2. Duties Of Employee. I shall comply with all Company rules, procedures and standards governing the conduct of employees and their access to and use of the Company's property, equipment and facilities. I understand that the Company will make reasonable efforts to inform me of the rules, standards and procedures which are in effect from time to time and which apply to me.

3. Compensation And Benefits. I shall receive the compensation as is mutually agreed upon, which may be adjusted from time to time, as full compensation for services performed under this Agreement. In addition, I may participate in such employee benefit plans and receive such other fringe benefits, subject to the same eligibility requirements, as are afforded other Company employees in my job classification. I understand that these employee benefit plans and fringe benefits may be amended, enlarged, or diminished by the Company from time to time, at its discretion.

4. Management Of The Company. The Company may manage and direct its business affairs as it sees fit, including, without limitation, the assignment of sales territories, notwithstanding any employee's individual interest in or expectation regarding a particular business location or customer account.

5. Termination Of Employment. My employment may be terminated by the Company or me in accordance with the Company Personnel Policy on termination. Upon termination of my employment, I shall be entitled to receive incentive payments in accordance with the provisions of the Company's Incentive Plan, as it may be modified by the Company from time to time, less any adjustments for amounts owed by me to the Company. I understand that I may also receive additional compensation at the discretion of the Company and in accordance with the published Company Personnel Policy on Termination Pay.

6. Agreement Not To Compete With The Company.

A. As long as I am employed by the Company, I shall not participate directly or indirectly, in any capacity, in any business or activity that is in competition with the Company.

B. In consideration of my employment rights under this Agreement and in recognition of the fact that I will have access to the confidential information of the Company and that the Company's relationships with their customers and potential customers constitute a substantial part of their good will, I agree that for One (1) year from and after termination of my employment, for any reason, unless acting with the Company's express prior written consent, I shall not, directly or indirectly, in any capacity, solicit or accept insurance business from, provide insurance consulting services of any kind to, or perform any of the services offered by the Company for, any of the Company's customers or prospects with whom I had business dealings in the year next preceding the termination of my employment.

7. Unauthorized Disclosure Of Confidential Information. While employed by the Company and thereafter, I shall not, directly or indirectly, disclose to anyone outside of the Company any Confidential Information or use any confidential Information (as hereinafter defined) other than pursuant to my employment by and for the benefit of the Company.

The term ''Confidential Information'' as used throughout this Agreement means any and all trade secrets and any and all data or information not generally known outside of the Company whether prepared or developed by or for the Company or received by the Company from any outside source. Without limiting the scope of this definition, Confidential Information includes any customer files, customer lists, policy expiration dates, policy terms, conditions and rates; familiarity with customers' risk characteristics; sources with which insurance is placed; information concerning the insurance markets for large or unusual commercial risks; manuals; computer programs, disks or data; any business, marketing, financial or sales record, data, plan, or survey; and any other record or information relating to the present or future business, product or service of the Company. All Confidential Information and copies thereof are the sole property of the Company.

Notwithstanding the foregoing, the term Confidential Information shall not apply to information that the Company has voluntarily disclosed to the public without restriction, or which has otherwise lawfully entered the public domain.

8. Prior Obligations. I have informed the Company in writing of any and all continuing obligations that require me not to disclose to the Company any information or that limit my opportunity or capacity to compete with any previous employer.

9. Employee's Obligation To Cooperate. At any time upon request of the Company (and at the Company's expense), I shall execute all documents and perform all lawful acts the Company considers necessary or advisable to secure its rights hereunder and to carry out the intent of this Agreement.

10. Return Of Property. At any time upon request of the Company, and upon termination of my employment, I shall return promptly to the Company, including all copies of all Confidential Information or Developments, and all records, files, blanks, forms, materials, supplies, and any other materials furnished, used or generated by me during the course of my employment, and any copies of the foregoing, all of which I recognize to be the sole property of the Company.

11. Special Remedies. I recognize that money damages alone would not adequately compensate the Company in the event of breach by me of this Agreement, and I therefore agree that, in addition to all other remedies available to the Company at law or in equity, the Company shall be entitled to injunctive relief for the enforcement hereof. Failure by the Company to insist upon strict compliance with any of the terms, covenants, or conditions hereof shall not be deemed a waiver of such terms, covenants or conditions.

12. Miscellaneous Provisions. This Agreement contains the entire and only agreement between me and the Company respecting the subject matter hereof and supersedes all prior agreements and understandings between us as to the subject matter hereof; and no modification shall be binding upon me or the Company unless made in writing and signed by me and an authorized officer of the Company.

My obligations under this Agreement shall survive the termination of my employment with the Company regardless of the manner of or reasons for such termination, and regardless of whether such termination constitutes a breach of this

Agreement or of any other agreement I may have with the Company. If any provisions of this Agreement are held or deemed unenforceable or too broad to permit enforcement of such provision to its full extent, then such provision shall be enforced to the maximum extent permitted by law. If any of the provisions of this Agreement shall be construed to be illegal or invalid, the validity of any other provision hereof shall not be affected thereby.

This Agreement shall be governed and construed according to the laws of [specify State], and shall be deemed to be effective as of the first day of my employment by the Company.

BY SIGNING THIS AGREEMENT, I ACKNOWLEDGE THAT I HAVE READ AND UNDERSTOOD ALL OF ITS PROVISIONS AND THAT I AGREE TO BE FULLY BOUND BY THE SAME.

Employee:__________________________________ Date:

Accepted By:______________________________ Date:

[Name and Title of Officer]

APPENDIX D

SAMPLE EMPLOYMENT AGREEMENT—LONG VERSION
(Typically given to executives with a definite term of employment)

Employment Agreement dated as of [specify], by and between [specify Name of Company], a [specify state] corporation with its principal place of business at [specify address] (the ''Company''), and [specify Name of Employee] (the ''Employee'').

WHEREAS, effective January 1, 1990 the Company and the Employee entered into an employment agreement, which agreement terminated December 31, 1992; and

WHEREAS, the Company desires to continue to employ the Employee, and the Employee desires to continue his employment with the Company; and

WHEREAS, the Company and the Employee wish to set forth the terms and conditions of the Employee's employment with the Company.

NOW, THEREFORE, in consideration of the mutual promises, warranties and covenants set forth below, the parties hereto, intending to be legally bound, hereby agree as follows:

1. Employment. Effective as of the commencement date described in Section 2 below, the Company employs the Employee and the Employee accepts employment by the Company upon the terms and conditions hereafter set forth.

2. Term of Employment. The employment of the Employee under this Agreement shall commence as of January 1, 1993 and terminate on December 31, 1994. Thereafter, this Agreement shall be extended automatically for successive terms of One (1) year unless (i) the Company or the Employee shall give written notice of termination to the other party hereto at least Sixty (60) days prior to the termination of the initial term of employment hereunder or any renewal term thereof, or (ii) unless earlier terminated as herein provided. The initial term of this Agreement and any renewal term thereof are hereinafter collectively referred to as the ''Employment Period.''

3. Scope of Duties. During the Employment Period, the Employee shall be employed as [specify] as well as such other duties and responsibilities which may be assigned to him by a Company manager or official. The Employee shall perform such service in good faith and comply with all rules, regulations and policies established or issued by the Company.

4. Extent of Service. The Employee shall devote his entire time, attention and energies to the business of the Company, and shall not during the Employment period engage in any other business activity which in the judgment of the Company conflicts with the duties of the Employee hereunder.

5. Compensation. In consideration of the services rendered by the Employee hereunder, the Company shall pay the Employee an aggregate base salary of [specify] per annum (the ''Base Salary''), payable weekly. In addition to the Base Salary, the Employee shall also be paid (specify). The Employee shall also be entitled to (i) the use of an automobile provided by the Company, and (ii) medical, life insurance, disability and other such benefits which the Company may from time to time make available generally to its employees in accordance with the terms of such benefit and welfare plans.

6. Business Expenses. During the Employment period, the Company shall reimburse the Employee for all reasonable and necessary travel expenses and other disbursements incurred by him for or on behalf of the Company in the performance of his duties hereunder (hereinafter referred to as ''Business Expenses'') upon presentation by the Employee to the Company of appropriate expense reports.

7. Death. If the Employee dies during the Employment Period, his employment hereunder shall be deemed to terminate as of the last day of the month during which his death occurs. Upon the death of the Employee, neither the Employee nor his beneficiaries or estate shall have any further rights or claims against the Company, except the right to receive:

A. The unpaid portion of the Base Salary, computed on a *pro rata* basis to the date of termination;

B. Any earned, but unpaid commissions or other sales incentives;

C. Unused personal and vacation days to which the Employee is entitled in accordance with Company policy;

D. Reimbursement for any unpaid business expenses; and

E. Life insurance and other post-termination benefits in accordance with the Company welfare and benefit plans.

8. Termination for Cause. Upon furnishing of notice to the Employee, the Company may terminate the employment of the Employee for cause at any time during the Employment period by reason of the Employee's (i) neglect of his duties hereunder, (ii) breach of or negligence with respect to his obligations under this Agreement, (iii) engaging in misconduct injurious to the company, or (iv) the Employee's commission of an act constituting common law fraud or a felony. If the Employee's employment is terminated by the Company for cause as herein defined, his Base Salary and his eligibility for all other benefits provided by the Company shall cease as of his termination date, after which time the Company shall have no other further liability or obligation of any kind to the Employee under this Agreement, except the Employee shall have the right to receive:

A. The unpaid portion of the Base Salary, computed on a *pro rata* basis to the date of termination;

B. Reimbursement for any unpaid business expenses;

C. Any earned but unpaid commission or other sales incentives;

D. Unused personal and vacation days to which the Employee is entitled in accordance with Company policy; and

E. Any post-termination benefits in accordance with the Company welfare and benefit plans.

9. Employee Acknowledgments. Employee recognizes and acknowledges that in the course of Employee's employment it will be necessary for Employee to acquire information which could include, in whole or in part, information concerning the Company's sales, sales volume, sales methods, sales proposals, customers and prospective customers, suppliers and prospective suppliers, identity, practices and procedures of key purchasing and other personnel in the employ of customers and prospective customers and suppliers and prospective suppliers, amount or kind of customer's purchases from the Company, research reports, the Company's computer program, system documentation, special hardware, related software development, the Company's manuals, methods, ideas, improvements or other confidential or proprietary information belonging to the Company or relating to the Company's affairs (collectively referred to herein as ''Confidential Information'') is the property of the Company). Employee further agrees that the use, misappropriation or disclosure of the Confidential Information would constitute a breach of trust and could cause irreparable injury to the Company, and it is essential to the protection of the Company's good will and to the maintenance of the Company's competitive position that the Confidential Information be kept secret and the Employee agrees not to disclose the Confidential Information to others or use the Confidential Information to Employee's own advantage or the advantage of others.

Employee further recognizes and acknowledges that it is essential for the proper protection of the business of the Company that Employee be restrained from soliciting or inducing any employee of the Company to leave the employ of the Company, or hiring or attempting to hire any employee of the Company.

10. Non-Disclosure of Confidential Information. Employee shall hold and safeguard the Confidential Information in trust for the Company, its successors and assigns and shall not, without the prior written consent of the Company, misappropriate or disclose or make available to anyone for use outside the Company organization at any time, either during his employment with the Company or subsequent to the termination of his employment with the Company for any reason, including, without limitation, termination by the Company for cause or without cause, any of the Confidential Information, whether or not developed by Employee, except as required in the performance of Employee's duties to the Company.

11. Return of Materials. Upon the termination of Employee's employment with the Company for any reason, including without limitation termination by the Company for cause or without cause, Employee shall promptly deliver to the Company all correspondence, manuals, orders, letters, notes, notebooks, reports, programs, proposals and any documents and copies concerning the Company's customers or concerning products or processes used by the Company and, without limiting the foregoing, will promptly deliver to the Company any and all other documents or material containing or constituting Confidential Information.

12. Non-Solicitation of Customers and Suppliers. Employee shall not during his time of employment with the Company, directly or indirectly, solicit the trade of, or do business with, any customer or prospective customer, or supplier or prospective supplier of the Company for any business purpose other than for the benefit of the Company. Employee further acknowledges that, in consideration of the promises contained in the Agreement and to induce the Company to enter into this Agreement, he shall not for One (1) year following the termination of his employment with the Company, including, without limitation, termination by the Company for cause or without cause, directly or indirectly, solicit the trade of, or do business with, any person or entity whatsoever who or which is or was a customer or supplier of the Company in any of the territory or territories assigned to the Employee during the Employment Period, with respect to products of the same or similar kind as those presently or in the future distributed by the Company.

13. Non-Solicitation of Employees. The Employee shall not during his employment with the Company and for One (1) year following termination of Employee's employment with the Company, including, without limitation, termination by the Company for cause or without cause, directly or indirectly, solicit or induce, or attempt to solicit or induce, any employee, current or future, of the Company to leave the Company for any reason whatsoever, or hire any current or future employee of the Company.

14. Advice of Counsel/Restrictive Covenants. The Employee has had the opportunity to consult with independent counsel and understands the nature of and the burdens imposed by the restrictive covenants contained in this Agreement. The Employee represents and acknowledges that such covenants are reasonable, enforceable, and proper in duration, scope and effect.

Moreover, Employee represents and warrants that his experience and capabilities are such that the restrictive covenants set forth herein will not prevent him from earning his livelihood and that Employee will be fully able to earn an adequate livelihood for himself and his dependents if any of such provisions should be specifically enforced against Employee.

15. Authorization to Modify Restrictions. The Employee acknowledges that the remedies at law for any breach by Employee of the provisions of the restrictive covenants will be inadequate and that the Company shall be entitled to injunctive relief against the Employee in the event of any such breach, in addition to any other remedy and damage available. The Employee acknowledges that the restrictions contained herein are reasonable, but agrees that if any court of competent jurisdiction shall hold such restrictions unreasonable as to time, geographic area, activities, or otherwise, such restrictions shall be deemed to be reduced to the extent necessary in the opinion of such court to make them reasonable.

16. No Prior Agreements. Employee represents and warrants that he is not a party to or otherwise subject to or bound by the terms of any contract, agreement or understanding which in any manner would limit or otherwise affect his ability to perform his obligations hereunder, including, without limitation, any contract, agreement or understanding containing terms and provisions similar in any manner to those contained in Section 12 hereof. Employee further represents and warrants that his employment with the Company will not require the disclosure or use of any Confidential Information.

17. Covenants of the Essence. The covenants of the Employee set forth herein are of the essence of this Agreement; they shall be construed as independent of any other provision in this Agreement and the existence of any claim or cause of action of the Employee against the Company, whether predicated on this Agreement or not, shall not constitute a defense to the enforcement by the Company of these covenants.

18. Tolling Period. If it should become desirable or necessary for the Company to seek compliance with the restrictive covenants by judicial proceedings, the period during which the Employee will not engage in the activities prohibited by Sections 12 and 13 hereof shall be extended to the first anniversary of the date of the judicial order requiring such compliance.

19. Arbitration. The parties expressly agree that all disputes or controversies arising out of this Agreement, its performance, or the alleged breach thereof, if not disposed of by agreement, shall be resolved by arbitration in accordance with this section. Either party must demand such arbitration only within Nine (9) months after the controversy arises by sending a notice of demand to arbitrate to the American Arbitration Association (the ''Association''), with a copy thereof to the other party. The dispute shall then be arbitrated by a three-arbitrator panel pursuant to the Commercial Rules of the Association at the Association office in [specify state/place]. In the disposition of the dispute, the arbitrators shall be governed by the express terms of this Agreement and otherwise by the laws of the State of [specify] which shall govern the interpretation of the Agreement. The decision of the arbitrators shall be final and conclusive on the parties and shall be a bar to any suit, action or proceeding instituted in any federal, state or local court or before any administrative tribunal. Notwithstanding the foregoing, judgment on any award by the arbitrators may be entered in any court of competent jurisdiction. This arbitration provision shall survive any expiration or termination of the Agreement.

20. Notices. Any notice required or permitted to be given under this Agreement shall be sufficient if in writing, personally delivered, mailed or telecopied, if to the Employee, to the Employee's residence as contained in Company records, and if to the Company, to its principal place of business set forth in the first paragraph of this Agreement.

21. Assignment. This Agreement is personal in its nature and the Employee shall not without the prior written consent of the Company, assign or transfer this Agreement or any rights, duties or obligations hereunder.

22. Entire Agreement. This Agreement constitutes the full and complete understanding and agreement of the parties hereto with respect to any employment of the Employee by the Company and supersedes all prior agreements and understanding with respect to the subject matter hereof, whether written or oral. This Agreement may not be changed orally, but only by an agreement in writing signed by the party against whom enforcement of any waiver, change, modification or discharge is sought.

23. Governing Law. This Agreement shall be governed by, and construed in accordance with, the laws of the State of [specify].

24. Remedies. All remedies hereunder are cumulative, are in addition to any other remedies provided by law and may be exercised concurrently or separately, and the exercise of any one remedy shall not be deemed to be an election of such remedy or to preclude the exercise of any other remedy. No failure or delay in exercising any right or remedy shall operate as a waiver thereof or modify the terms of this Agreement.

IN WITNESS WHEREOF, the parties have executed this Agreement as of the date first above written.

(NAME OF COMPANY)	(NAME OF EMPLOYEE)
(''The Company'')	(''The Employee'')
By: ______________________	By: ______________________
(NAME TITLE)	[NAME OF EMPLOYEE

APPENDIX E

SAMPLE EMPLOYMENT AGREEMENT—LONG VERSION (For Executives)

The parties to this Agreement dated [specify] are [Name of Company] a [specify State and type of company] (the ''Company''), and [Name of Employee] (the ''Executive'').

The Company wishes to employ the Executive, and the Executive wishes to accept employment with the Company, on the terms and subject to the conditions set forth in this Agreement. It is therefore agreed as follows:

1. Employment. The Company shall employ the Executive, and the Executive shall serve the Company, as a [specify] of the Company, with such duties and responsibilities as may be assigned to the Executive by the President of the Company and as are normally associated with a position of that nature. The Executive shall devote his best efforts and all of his business time to the performance of his duties under this Agreement and shall perform them faithfully, diligently and competently and in a manner consistent with the policies of the Company as determined from time to time by an officer of or President of the Company. The Executive shall report to the General Manager, [specify] Office of the Company. The Executive shall not engage in activities outside the scope of his employment if such activities would detract from or interfere with the fulfillment of his responsibilities or duties under this Agreement or require substantial time or services on the part of the Executive. The Executive shall not serve as a director (or the equivalent position) of any company or other entity and shall not receive fees or other remuneration for work performed either within or outside the scope of his employment without the prior written consent of the President of the Company. This consent shall not be unreasonably withheld.

2. Term of Employment. The Executive's employment by the Company under this Agreement shall commence on the date of this Agreement and, subject to earlier termination pursuant to section 5 or 7, shall terminate on [specify date]. This Agreement may also be extended as needed by a written amendment as discussed in section 16.

3. Compensation. As full compensation for all services rendered by the Executive to the Company under this Agreement, the Company shall pay to the Executive the compensation set forth in Schedule A attached hereto. This schedule may be amended from time to time in writing by the Company and the Executive.

4. Fringe Benefits; Expenses.

A. The Executive shall be entitled to receive all health and pension benefits, if any, provided by the Company to its employees generally and shall also be entitled to participate in all benefit plans, if any, provided by the Company to its employees generally.

B. The Company shall reimburse the Executive for all reasonable and necessary expenses incurred by him in connection with the performance of his services for the Company in accordance with the Company's policies, upon submission of appropriate expense reports and documentation in accordance with the Company's policies and procedures. The Company will reimburse the Executive for the expenses involved with his acquisition and business related use of a portable cellular telephone.

C. The Executive shall be entitled to Three (3) weeks paid vacation time annually, to be taken at times selected by him, with the prior concurrence of the General Manager to whom the Executive is to report.

5. Disability or Death.

A. If, as the result of any physical or mental disability, the Executive shall have failed or is unable to perform his duties for a period of Sixty (60) consecutive days, the Company may, by notice to the Executive subsequent thereto, terminate his employment under this Agreement as of the date of the notice without any further payment or the furnishing of any benefit by the Company under this Agreement (other than accrued and unpaid base salary and commissions and expenses and benefits which have accrued pursuant to any plan or by law).

B. The term of the Executive's employment under this Agreement shall terminate upon his death without any further payment or the furnishing of any benefit by the Company under this Agreement (other than accrued and unpaid base salary and commissions and expenses and benefits which have accrued pursuant to any plan or by law).

6. Non-Competition; Confidential Information; Inventions.

A. During the term of the Executive's employment under this Agreement, the Executive shall not, directly or indirectly, engage or be interested (as a stockholder, director, officer, employee, salesperson, agent, broker, partner, individual proprietor, lender, consultant or otherwise), either individually or in or through any person (whether a corporation, partnership, association or other entity) which engages, anywhere in the United States, in a business which is conducted by the Company on the date of termination of his employment, except that he may be employed by an affiliate of the Company and hold not more than 2% of the outstanding securities of any class of any publicly held company which is competitive with the business of the Company.

B. The Executive shall not, directly or indirectly, either during the term of the Executive's employment under this Agreement or thereafter, disclose to anyone (except in the regular course of the Company's business or as required by law), or use in any manner, any information acquired by the Executive during his employment by the Company with respect to any clients or customers of the Company or any confidential or secret aspect of the Company's operations or affairs unless such information has become public knowledge other than by reason of actions (direct or indirect) of the Executive. Information subject to the provisions of this paragraph shall include, without limitation:

(i) procedures for computer access and passwords of the Company's clients and customers, program manuals, user manuals or other documentation, run books, screen, file, or database layouts, systems flow charts, and all documentation normally related to the design or implementation of any computer programs developed by the Company relating to computer programs or systems installed either for customers or for internal use;

(ii) lists of present clients and customers and the names of individuals at each client or customer location with whom the Company deals, the type of equipment or computer software they purchase or use, and information relating to those clients and customers which has been given to the Company by them or developed by the Company, relating to computer programs or systems installed;

(iii) lists of or information about personnel seeking employment with or who are employed by the Company;

(iv) prospect lists for actual or potential clients and customers of the Company and contact persons at such actual or potential clients and customers;

(v) any other information relating to the Company's research, development, inventions, purchasing, accounting, engineering, marketing, merchandising and selling.

C. The Executive shall not, directly or indirectly, either during the term of the Executive's employment under this Agreement or for a period of One (1) year thereafter, solicit, directly or indirectly, the services of any person who was a full-time employee of the Company, its subsidiaries, divisions or affiliates, or solicit the business of any person who was a client or customer of the Company, its subsidiaries, divisions or affiliates, in each case at any time during the last year of the term of the Executive's employment under this Agreement. For purposes of this Agreement, the term ''person'' shall include natural persons, corporations, business trusts, associations, sole proprietorships, unincorporated organizations, partnerships, joint ventures and governments or any agencies, instrumentalities or political subdivisions thereof.

D. All memoranda, notes, records, or other documents made or composed by the Executive, or made available to him during the term of this Agreement concerning or in any way relating to the business or affairs of the Company, its subsidiaries, divisions, affiliates or clients shall be the Company's property and shall be delivered to the Company on the termination of this Agreement or at any other time at the request of the Company.

E. (i) The Executive hereby assigns and agrees to assign to the Company all of his rights to and title and interest to all Inventions, and to applications for United States and foreign patents and United States and foreign patents granted upon such Inventions and to all copyrightable material or other works related thereto.

(ii) The Executive agrees for himself and his heirs, personal representatives, successors and assigns, upon request of the Company, to at all times do such acts, such as giving testimony in support of the Executive's inventorship, and to execute and deliver promptly to the Company such papers, instruments and documents, without expense to him, as from time to time may be necessary or useful in the Company's opinion to apply for, secure, maintain, reissue, extend or defend the Company's worldwide rights in the Inventions or in any or all United States patents and in any all patents in any country foreign to the United States, so as to secure to the Company the full benefits of the Inventions or discoveries and otherwise to carry into full force and effect the text and the intent of the assignment set out in section 6E(i) above.

(iii) Notwithstanding any provision of this Agreement to the contrary, the Company shall have the royalty-free right to use in its business, and to make, have made, use and sell products, processes and services to make, have made, use and sell products, processes and services derived from any inventions, discoveries, concepts and ideas, whether or not patentable, including, but not limited to, processes, methods, formula and techniques, as well as improvements thereof and know-how related thereto, that are not inventions as defined herein, but which are made or conceived by the Executive during his employment by the Company or with the use or assistance of the Company's facilities, materials or personnel. If the Company determines that it has no present or future interest in any invention or discovery made by the Executive under this paragraph, the Company shall release such invention or discovery to the Executive within Sixty (60) days after the Executive's notice in writing is received by the Company requesting such release. If the Company determines that it does or may in the future have an interest in any such invention or discovery, such information will be communicated to the Executive within the 60-day period described above.

(iv) For purposes of this Section 6E, ''Inventions'' means inventions, discoveries, concepts and ideas, whether patentable or not, including, but not limited, to processes, methods, formula and techniques, as well as improvements thereof or know-how related thereto, concerning any present or prospective activities of the Company with which the Executive becomes acquainted as a result of his employment by the Company.

F. The Executive acknowledges that the agreements provided in this Section 6 were an inducement to the Company entering into this Agreement and that the remedy at law for breach of his covenants under this section 6 will be inadequate and, accordingly, in the event of any breach or threatened breach by the Executive of any provision of this Section 6, the Company shall be entitled, in addition to all other remedies, to an injunction restraining any such breach.

7. Termination. The Company shall have the right to terminate this Agreement and the Executive's employment with the Company for cause. For purposes of this Agreement, the term ''cause'' shall mean:

A. Any breach of the Executive's obligations under this Agreement;

B. Fraud, theft or gross malfeasance on the part of the Executive, including, without limitation, conduct of a felonious or criminal nature, conduct involving moral turpitude, embezzlement or misappropriation of assets;

C. The habitual use of drugs or intoxicants to an extent that it impairs the Executive's ability to properly perform his duties;

D. Violation by the Executive of his obligations to the Company, including, without limitation, conduct which is inconsistent with the Executive's position and which results or is reasonably likely to result (in the opinion of the President of the General Partner of the Company) in an adverse effect (financial or otherwise) on the business or reputation of the Company or any of its subsidiaries, divisions, or affiliates;

E. The Executive's failure, refusal or neglect to perform his duties contemplated herein within a reasonable period under the circumstances after written notice from the General Manager, or the President of the Company, describing the alleged breach and offering the Executive a reasonable opportunity to cure same;

F. Repeated violation by the Executive of any of the written work rules or written policies of the Company after written notice of violation from the General Manager or the President of the Company;

G. Breach of standards adopted by the Company governing professional independence or conflicts of interest.

If the employment of the Executive is terminated for cause, the Company shall not be obligated to make any further payment to the Executive (other than accrued and unpaid base salary and commissions and expenses to the date of termination), or continue to provide any benefit (other than benefits which have accrued pursuant to any plan or by law) to the Executive under this Agreement.

8. Miscellaneous.

A. This Agreement shall be governed by and construed in accordance with the laws of the State of [specify], applicable to agreements made and to be performed in [specify State], and shall be construed without regard to any presumption or other rule requiring construction against the party causing the Agreement to be drafted.

B. This Agreement contains a complete statement of all the arrangements between the Company and the Executive with respect to its subject matter, supersedes all previous agreements, written or oral, among them relating to its subject matter and cannot be modified, amended or terminated orally. Amendments may be made to this Agreement at any time if mutually agreed upon in writing.

C. Any amendment, notice or other communication under this Agreement shall be in writing and shall be considered given when received and shall be delivered personally or mailed by Certified Mail, Return Receipt Requested, to the parties at their respective addresses set forth below (or at such other address as a party may specify by notice to the other): [specify addresses]

D. The failure of a party to insist upon strict adherence to any term of this Agreement on any occasion shall not be considered a waiver or deprive that party of the right thereafter to insist upon strict adherence to that term or any other term of this Agreement. Any waiver must be in writing.

E. Each of the parties irrevocably submits to the exclusive jurisdiction of any court of the State of [specify] sitting in [specify] County or the Federal District Court of [specify State] over any action, suit or proceeding relating to or arising out of this

Agreement and the transactions contemplated hereby. EACH OF THE PARTIES IRREVOCABLY AND UNCONDITIONALLY WAIVES THE RIGHT TO A TRIAL BY JURY IN ANY SUCH ACTION, SUIT OR PROCEEDING. Each party hereby irrevocably waives any objection, including, without limitation, any objection to the laying of venue or based on the grounds of *forum non conveniens* which such party may now or hereafter have to the bringing of any such action, suit or proceeding in any such court and irrevocably agrees that process in any such action, suit or proceeding may be served upon that party personally or by Certified or Registered Mail, Return Receipt Requested.

F. The invalidity or unenforceability of any term or provision of this Agreement shall not affect the validity or enforceability of the remaining terms or provisions of this Agreement which shall remain in full force and effect and any such invalid or unenforceable term or provision shall be given full effect as far as possible. If any term or provision of this Agreement is invalid or unenforceable in one jurisdiction, it shall not affect the validity of enforceability of that term or provision in any other jurisdiction.

G. This Agreement is not assignable by either party except that it shall inure to the benefit of and be binding upon any successor to the Company by merger or consolidation or the acquisition of all or substantially all of the Company's assets, provided such successor assumes all of the obligations of the Company, and shall inure to the benefit of the heirs and legal representatives of the Executive.

By:

[Name and Title of Employer]
[NAME OF COMPANY]
(''The Company'')

By: ______________________________

[NAME OF EMPLOYEE]

(''Executive'')

APPENDIX F

SAMPLE EMPLOYMENT AGREEMENT—LONG VERSION (Typically given to sales employees working in the telemarketing industry)

This EMPLOYMENT AGREEMENT (''Agreement'') is made and entered into as of [specify] by and between [specify Name of Company] (''Company''), and [specify Name of Employee] (''Employee'').

RECITALS

A. Company is engaged in the business of telemarketing and desires to obtain the services of Employee as a sales associate upon the terms and conditions provided herein.

B. Employee desires to be employed by Company as a sales associate upon the terms and conditions provided herein.

AGREEMENT

NOW, THEREFORE, for good and valuable consideration, the receipt and sufficiency of which are hereby acknowledged, Company and Employee agree as follows:

1. Retention Of Employee.

1.1 Engagement. Company hereby engages the services of Employee as a sales associate of Company, and Employee hereby agrees to provide such services, all upon the terms and conditions set forth in this Agreement.

1.2 No Interference. Employee hereby represents and warrants to Company that Employee is free to enter into this Agreement and has no prior or other obligations or commitments to any third party which would or might interfere with the acceptance or the full, uninhibited and faithful performance of the services to be provided hereunder.

1.3 Exclusivity. During the term of this Agreement, Employee shall not provide services in the telemarketing business or otherwise for compensation except to Company.

1.4 At-Will Employee. THE EMPLOYMENT OF EMPLOYEE BY COMPANY SHALL BE AT-WILL. SPECIFICALLY, EMPLOYEE MAY QUIT HIS OF HER EMPLOYMENT WITH COMPANY AT ANY TIME, FOR ANY REASON OR FOR NO REASON AT ALL, AND COMPANY MAY TERMINATE EMPLOYEE'S EMPLOYMENT AT ANY TIME, FOR ANY REASON OR FOR NO REASON AT ALL. It is the intent of Company and Employee in executing this Agreement that the provisions of this Section 1.4 may be amended or modified only by a writing signed by both Company and Employee which specifically refers to this Section 1.4 and which states that the provisions of this Section 1.4 are being amended or modified. This Section 1.4 may not be modified by an oral agreement, and Employee agrees that any conduct, past or future, of Company or its officers, employees or agents shall not be deemed to give rise to an implied covenant or agreement which is contrary to the provisions of this Section 1.4.

2. Duties. Employee shall diligently, faithfully and legally solicit prospective customers in an endeavor to secure sales for Company. Employee shall utilize Employee's best efforts to obtain business exclusively for Company and to exclusively promote Company's business operations.

3. Term.

3.1 Commencement. The term of this Agreement and Employee's obligation to provide services hereunder shall commence on the date entered by the parties on Exhibit ''A'' hereto.

3.2 Termination. Employee's obligation to provide services hereunder may be terminated at any time by one party giving written or oral notice to the other. All of the other terms and conditions of this Agreement, including the obligation of Company to pay compensation pursuant to Section 4 for services heretofore provided to Company and the obligation of Employee to maintain the confidentiality of Company's Confidential Information pursuant to Section 7, shall survive the termination of Employee's services hereunder.

4. Compensation.

4.1 Computation of Amount. In consideration of Employee's services and Employee's other agreements and covenants hereunder, Company shall periodically pay

Employee compensation computed in accordance with the terms of Exhibit ''B'' hereto. Notwithstanding anything to the contrary contained in that Exhibit ''B,'' Employee's compensation shall at no time be less than the minimum wage required by law.

5. Expenses. In its sole discretion, the Company may reimburse Employee for such reasonable business and travel expenses as Employee may incur in connection with Employee's services hereunder and which Company has approved in writing in advance.

6. Regulatory Compliance.

6.1 Acknowledgment. Employee acknowledges that the business of telemarketing is subject to substantial regulation and that serious and adverse consequences to Company, Company's business and Employee might result if Employee fails to strictly comply with such regulations. Accordingly, Employee agrees to act in compliance with such regulations.

6.2 Sales Presentation Policy Statement. Company has adopted a Sales Presentation Policy Statement, the most recent version of which is attached hereto as Exhibit ''C.'' Employee agrees to strictly comply with the instructions of this Sales Presentation Policy Statement, as the same may be modified or amended from time to time.

6.3 Employee Information Sheet. Company is required to provide to various governmental entities and periodically update information about Company's business and the persons acting on Company's behalf, including Employee. Accordingly, at Company's request, Employee has completed Company's standard Employee Information Sheet, which is attached hereto as Exhibit ''D.'' Employee represents and warrants to Company that the information contained thereon is complete and accurate. Employee agrees that Company may use such information (and any updating information) in documents which Company provides to governmental entities. Employee recognizes that it is extremely important for Company to have current information in order to make accurate filings with governmental entities. Accordingly, Employee agrees that Employee shall notify Company in writing at any time if any of the information provided on Exhibit ''D'' hereto changes and that Employee will, upon the request of Company, at any time, complete a new

Employee Information Sheet.

6.4 Prohibition Against Misrepresentations. Company has advised Employee that the principal purpose of the governmental regulation of telemarketing is to prevent fraud upon persons solicited by telephone. Accordingly, Employee agrees that, while employed by Company, Employee will not make any misrepresentation or misleading statement to any person, including without limitation, any misrepresentation or misleading statement concerning Company's identity and location, or the price, quantity or quality of any product offered for sale, or sold or shipped by Company.

6.5 Immediate Termination for Breach. COMPANY MAY IMMEDIATELY TERMINATE EMPLOYEE'S RELATIONSHIP WITH COMPANY FOR ANY VIOLATION OF THE PROVISIONS OF THIS SECTION 6.

7. Confidential Information.

7.1 Definition. Employee acknowledges that Company's operations, techniques, forms, documents, computer printouts, invoices, methods of doing business, clients, customer lists, the identity of suppliers or goods sold by Company, the prices paid by Company for its goods, and Company's accounts receivable are trade secrets and confidential information (herein ''Confidential Information'').

7.2 Duty to Preserve Confidential Information. Employee may receive certain Confidential Information during the term of this Agreement. Employee agrees to preserve the confidentiality of such information, and to make every effort to ensure that the confidentiality of such information is not compromised by any action or omission of Employee. Employee specifically agrees that he will not at any time, whether during or subsequent to the term of Employee's employment by Company, in any fashion, form, or manner, unless specifically consented to in writing by Company, either directly or indirectly, use or divulge, disclose, or communicate to any person, firm, or corporation, in any manner whatsoever, any Confidential Information of any kind, nature or description.

7.3 Specific Prohibitions. Employee shall not:

7.3.1 Disclose, grant, assign, license, sell, give away, or otherwise transfer to any third party, or develop, produce, promote, or otherwise exploit any idea, proprietary information, trade secret or Confidential Information, the knowledge of which Employee obtains by reason of Employee's relationship with Company hereunder;

7.3.2 Remove from Company's business premises any original or any copy of any Company document or form, including, without limiting the generality of the foregoing, computer printouts, or all or any portion of the Confidential Information, or

7.3.3 Undertake planning for or organization of any business activity competitive with Company's business or combine or join with other employees, representatives, or independent contractors of Company's business for the purpose of organizing any such competitive business activity.

7.4 Return of Confidential and Order Material. Upon the termination of Employee's employment with Company hereunder, Employee will immediately return to Company any Confidential Information in Employee's possession or control.

8. Indemnification.

Employee shall indemnify and hold the Company harmless against any claim, demand, damage, debt, liability, account, reckoning, obligation, cost, expense, lien, action or cause of action (including the payment of attorneys' fees and costs actually incurred whether or not litigation is commenced) arising from the breach of this Agreement.

9. Additional Covenants.

9.1 Other Business Interests. During Employee's employment with Company, Employee agrees that he will not, directly or indirectly, own an interest in, operate, join, control, or participate in, or be connected as an officer, employee, agent, independent contractor, partner, shareholder, or principal of any corporation, partnership, proprietorship, firm, association, person, or other entity producing, designing, providing, soliciting orders for, selling, distributing, or marketing products, goods, equipment, or services that directly or indirectly compete with Company's products or Company's business.

9.2 Subsequent Activities. For Six (6) months following termination as an employee, Employee agrees not to undertake any employment or activity competitive with Company's business in which the loyal and complete fulfillment of the duties of the competitive employment or activity would call on Employee to reveal, to make judgments on, or otherwise to use any trade secrets of Company's business to which Employee had access by reason of Company's business.

9.3 Solicitation Requirements. During the term of this Agreement, Employee agrees that he will not, directly or indirectly, either for himself or for any other person, firm, or corporation, divert or take away or attempt to divert or take away (and following termination as an employee, call on or solicit or attempt to call on or solicit) any of Company's customers or patrons, including but not limited to those on whom he called or solicited or with whom he became acquainted while engaged as an employee in Company's business.

9.4 Non-Waiver. Nothing in this Paragraph 9 shall be deemed a waiver of Employee's obligations under Paragraph 7; in the event of any conflict or inconsistency between provisions of Paragraph 9 and Paragraph 7, the provisions in Paragraph 7 shall control.

10. Miscellaneous.

10.1 Entire Agreement, Waiver and Amendment. This Agreement embodies and constitutes the entire understanding between the parties hereto with respect to the transactions contemplated herein, and all prior and contemporaneous agreements, understandings, representations, and statements, oral and written, are merged herein. No provision of this Agreement shall be waived, modified, amended, discharged or terminated, except by an instrument in writing signed by the party against which the enforcement of such waiver, modification, amendment, discharge or termination is sought and then only to the extent set forth in such written instrument.

10.2 Applicable Law. This Agreement shall be governed by and construed in accordance with the laws of the State of [specify].

10.3 Paragraph Headings. Descriptive paragraph headings are for convenience only and shall not control or affect the meaning or construction of the provisions of the Agreement.

10.4 Gender. Whenever the context herein shall so require, the singular shall include the plural, the male gender shall include the female gender and the neuter, and vice versa.

10.5 Unenforceability. In case any one or more of the provisions contained in this Agreement shall for any reason be held to be invalid, illegal or unenforceable in any respect, such invalidity, illegality or enforceability shall not affect any other provisions hereof, and this Agreement shall be construed as if such invalid, illegal or unenforceable provision had never been contained herein.

10.6 Waiver. No waiver by Company of any breach of this Agreement shall be deemed a waiver of any preceding or succeeding breach of the same or of any other provision hereof. Each and all of the several rights, remedies, and options of Company hereunder shall be construed as cumulative and no one of them is exclusive of the other or of any right, remedy or priority allowed by law or in equity.

10.7 Exhibits. All exhibits attached hereto are incorporated herein by this reference.

IN WITNESS WHEREOF, Company and Employee have executed this Standard Telemarketer Employment Agreement as of the date above written.

[NAME OF COMPANY]
''Company:''

By:__________________________
Title:________________________

[NAME OF EMPLOYEE]
''Employee:''

____

EXHIBIT "A"

ENGAGEMENT AND TERMINATION DATES UNDER EMPLOYMENT AGREEMENT

Date of Agreement:______________________________, 19___

''Company:'' ____

''Employee:''____

Date Engagement Began:__________________________, 19___

Initials of Initials of

Company Officer _______ Employee _______

Date of Termination: ___________________________, 19___

Initials of

Company Officer _______

EXHIBIT "B"
(INSERT COMPENSATION TERMS HERE)

EXHIBIT "C"
SALES PRESENTATION POLICY STATEMENT

Only those sales presentations that are specifically authorized by the Company may be used. Use of an unauthorized sales presentation is grounds for immediate termination. Any false or misleading statements made in connection with the sale, or offering for the sale, of any product is also grounds for immediate termination. Among other things, all salespersons are required to observe the following guidelines when soliciting customers:

1. Stick to the script. Any deviation from it may result in your termination.

2. You must represent yourself as calling from the Company.

3. You must state where Company is located pursuant to the script.

4. You must not suggest or imply that a customer should withhold any information from the verification department.

5. You must accurately advise the customer of the shipping time on the product. If they are expecting it sooner than it arrives, they may fear it is not going to come and cancel their order. Our standard shipping time is [specify days/weeks] from receipt of payment for the product.

6. Avoid rude behavior. Any substantiated reports of customer harassment or verbal abuse will result in your immediate termination.

The kinds of statements, omissions or other conduct that constitute misrepresentations or deceitful conduct and will result in your immediate dismissal include:

A. Failure to properly identify the Company or misrepresenting the name or identity of the Company for whom you are calling.

B. Statements or the omission of statements made for the purpose of misleading the customer as to the nature of the product being sent to the customer.

C. Statements made to the customer that are intended to lead the customer to believe that the customer has had prior dealings with the Company when the customer has not had such dealings.

D. Misleading the customer as to the purpose of the telephone call.

7. You must make the customer realize that the Company is not selling and shipping merchandise subject to the customer's approval.

Obviously, these are only a few of the possible ways a customer can be misled, and this list is not intended to be exclusive. You may not make any statement intended or likely to mislead a customer. If you are in doubt as to whether a particular statement is misleading, ask yourself, ''Is what I am saying untrue?,'' and, ''Even if what I am saying is technically correct, is my purpose in saying it to lead the customer to believe something other than what is in fact true?'' If your answer to either question is ''yes'' do not make the statement. Not only are you violating Company Policy, you are violating the law!

In order to further ensure that these standards will be followed by all salespeople, the Company will have a manager or assistant manager on the floor at all times monitoring your sales efforts. In addition, from time to time, ''test'' leads will be inserted into the group of leads that you happen to be working from. The customer will be fictitious, but you won't know that. Management evaluation of your performance will be based in part on how you interact with these fictitious customers.

AGREED AND ACCEPTED

''Employee''

____

____

DATE

EXHIBIT "D"
EMPLOYEE INFORMATION SHEET

NAME: ____

HOME TELEPHONE #: __________________________________

PERMANENT ADDRESS: _________________________________

____

DRIVER'S LICENSE #: ________________________________

STATE: ________

SOCIAL SECURITY #: _________________________________

APPENDIX G

SAMPLE EMPLOYMENT AGREEMENT—SHORT VERSION

THIS EMPLOYMENT AGREEMENT (the ''Agreement'') made and entered into on [specify date], by and between [Name of Employee] (the ''Employee''), an individual residing at [specify address] and [Name of Company] (the ''Company), a [specify the state] corporation having offices at [specify address].

W I T N E S S E T H:

WHEREAS, the Employee is willing to enter into this Agreement and employment with the Company upon the conditions and terms herein set forth;

NOW THEREFORE, for the valuable consideration set forth in this Agreement and intending to be legally bound, the Employee and the Company mutually promise and agree as follows:

1. Position and Duties. During the time this Agreement is in effect, the Company will employ the Employee and the Employee will accept such employment, in such capacities and with such powers and duties as may from time to time be determined by the President of the Company. The Employee will devote substantially all of his time and attention to, and will use his best energies and abilities in the performance of, his duties and responsibilities as prescribed in this Paragraph 1, and will not engage as a director, officer, employee, partner, shareholder, or any other capacity, in any business which competes, conflicts or interferes with the performance of his duties hereunder in any way, or solicit, canvass or accept any business or transaction for any other such competing business.

2. Compensation and Incentives.

A. For all services to be rendered by the Employee pursuant to Paragraph 1 of this Agreement, and in part of the consideration for the other obligations and promises of the Employee as set forth in this Agreement, the Company will compensate the Employee at the annual rate of [specify] (''Base Compensation'') with it being intended that such Base Compensation shall be reviewed annually hereafter, with the changes in Base Compensation to be determined by the President from time to time based on the performance of the Employee and the results of the Company. The Base Compensation shall be paid to the Employee in equal installments and shall be subject to applicable income tax withholding deductions required by law and other deductions authorized by the Employee. The Employee will be entitled to reasonable vacation and sick leave in accordance with Company policy.

B. In addition to his Base Compensation, the Employee will be entitled to the following performance incentives during the time he is employed by the Company:

i) A sales commission of [specify] percent of the gross amount of all sales to new customers with whom it was the Employee who made the initial contact on behalf of the Company. From time to time, the Company may also designate existing customers as accounts of the Employee, for which the Employee will earn Sales Commissions at the above rate. Sales Commissions earned will be paid upon the completion of each respective project (i.e., when all engineering work has been completed and the customer's invoices relating thereto have been fully paid).

3. Term. This Agreement for employment by and between the parties shall be an agreement for employment at will commencing on the date hereof, subject to immediate termination by either party.

Nothing contained in this Agreement shall be construed to prevent the Company from terminating the employment of the Employee hereunder at any time for cause. As used in this Agreement, ''termination for cause'' shall mean a termination based upon the dishonesty, gross negligence, incompetence or moral turpitude of the Employee or any failure to perform his duties hereunder or otherwise comply with and observe the covenants and agreements made by him herein.

4. Non-Competition. During the time of his employment by the Company, and for a period of One (1) year thereafter, the Employee shall not, directly or indirectly, acting alone or in conjunction with others:

A. Request any customers of any business then being conducted by the Company to curtail or cancel their business with the Company;

B. Solicit, canvass or accept any business or transaction for any other person, firm or corporation or business similar to the business of the Company, from any past or existing customers of the Company;

C. Induce, or attempt to influence, any employee of the Company to terminate employment with the Company or to enter into any employment or other business relationship with any other person (including the Employee), firm or corporation; or

D. Act or conduct himself in any manner which is contrary to the best interests of the Company.

The Employee recognizes that immediate and irreparable damage will result to the Company if the Employee breaches any of the terms and conditions of this Paragraph 4 and, accordingly, the Employee hereby consents to the entry by any court of competent jurisdiction of an injunction against him to restrain any such breach, in addition to any other remedies or claims for money or damages which the Company may seek. The Employee represents and warrants to the Company his experience and capabilities are such that he can obtain employment in business without breaching the terms and conditions of this Paragraph 4, and that his obligations under the provisions of this Paragraph 4 (and the enforcement thereof by injunction or otherwise) will not prevent him from earning a livelihood. The Employee agrees to pay any and all reasonable attorney fees sustained by the Company in connection with any breach of this Agreement.

5. Trade Secrets/Confidential Information. The Employee agrees that he will not at any time or in any manner divulge, disclose or communicate to any person, firm or corporation any trade, technical or technological secrets; any details of the Company's organization or business affairs, its manner of operation, its plans, processes, and/or other data; any names of past or present customers of the Company; or any other information relating to the business of the Company, without regard to whether all of the foregoing matters will be deemed confidential, material, or important. With respect to the foregoing, the Employee hereby stipulates and agrees that the same are confidential, material, and important, and any breach of this Paragraph 5 will adversely affect the business of the Company, its effective and successful management, and its inherent good will.

6. Assignment. The benefits of this Agreement are and shall be personal to the Employee, and none thereof shall inure to the benefit of his heirs, personal representatives, or assigns. The obligations and duties of the Employee hereunder shall be personal and not assignable or delegable by him in any manner, whatsoever. This Agreement shall be binding upon and inure to the benefit of the Company and it shall be assignable by the Company to any entity which may acquire substantially all of the business and assets of the Company, or with or into which the Company may be merged or consolidated.

7. Entire Agreement, Amendment. This Agreement constitutes the entire agreement between the parties with respect to the employment of the Employee by the Company and shall be deemed to supersede and cancel any other written agreements between the parties hereto relating to the transactions herein contemplated. No representation, inducement or condition set forth herein has been made or relied upon by any party. This Agreement may be amended, modified or waived only by an instrument in writing signed by the Employee and an authorized executive officer of the Company.

8. General. The headings of the Articles and Paragraphs of this Agreement are for the convenience of reference and not to be used to interpret or construe any provisions of this Agreement. This Agreement shall be construed and enforced in accordance with and governed by the laws of [specify state].

IN WITNESS WHEREOF, the parties have executed this Agreement on the date first above written.

[NAME OF EMPLOYEE] (''Employee'')

____

Signature

[NAME OF EMPLOYER] (''Employer'')

By: ____________________________

Title: __________________________

APPENDIX H

SAMPLE EMPLOYMENT AGREEMENT—SHORT VERSION

THIS AGREEMENT made and entered into as of [specify], by and between [Name of Company], a [specify state] corporation (herein called the ''Company'') and [Name of Employer] (herein called ''Employee'').

W I T N E S S E T H

1. The Company hereby employs Employee for a term commencing on the date of this Agreement [specify], and Employee hereby accepts such employment.

2. During his employment hereunder Employee shall:

A. devote such business, time and services to the affairs of the Company as may be reasonable required by the President and the Board of Directors of the Company to carry out his duties;

B. not engage in any other business or as a consultant to any other business entity or to other individuals during the term of this Agreement, without the written consent of the Company's President; and

C. perform such duties as Vice President as may be reasonably assigned to him from time to time by the President and Board of Directors of the Company.

3. For his services performed pursuant to this Agreement, the Company shall pay to the Employee:

A. During the period of his employment, annual compensation equal to the sum of: [specify formula]

B. For a period of Two (2) years commencing on (specify), the Employee will receive an additional bonus of ten percent (10%) of commission revenue received by the Company from principals listed on Exhibit A. This payment will be made quarterly commencing with the quarter ending [specify], and continuing each quarter thereafter through the quarter ending [specify].

C. For the purpose of sub-paragraph A. hereof, annual compensation shall include the cost of all fringe benefits provided to the Employee by the Company, including, without limitation, medical, hospitalization, disability and life insurance, employee paid FICA and similar taxes, travel expenses, car allowance and other related expenses.

D. For the purpose of sub-paragraph A:

i) A monthly draw against the annual compensation plan will be established at the rate of Three Thousand Dollars ($3,000.00) per month;

ii) A car allowance against the annual compensation plan will be established at the rate of Five Hundred Dollars ($500.00) per month; and

iii) Travel expenses will be reimbursed on a monthly basis.

e) The Company shall pay the Employee pursuant to subparagraph A. quarterly, based upon commission revenue received, less advances, pursuant to subparagraph D. Within ninety (90) days after the close of each calendar quarter, the Company or the Employee, as the base may be, shall pay or repay any deficiency or excess of compensation advanced.

4. Employee agrees that during the period of his employment by the Company and for a further period of One (1) year after termination of such employment or through [specify date], whichever period is the shorter, he will not directly or indirectly as an owner, stockholder, partner, employee or otherwise engage in the business of acting as a broker of products customarily sold by the Company within the States of [specify]. Employee further agrees that during such period he will not, directly or otherwise, engage in any business on behalf of any principal or customer of the Company.

5. Employee recognizes that the business of the Company involves the use of information of a confidential nature which constitutes an asset of substantial value. Accordingly, Employee hereby covenants and agrees that during the term of this Agreement and thereafter he will not, directly or indirectly, disclose to others any such confidential information or render any service to others which would in any way involve the divulging of such information. Employee further covenants and agrees that he will not remove, without the Company's written consent, any figures, calculations, letters, papers, drawings, blueprints or copies thereof.

6. Employee agrees that the Company, at its own discretion, may apply for and procure in its own name and for its own benefit life insurance and disability insurance in any amount considered advisable; and, that he shall have no right, title or interest therein; and, further agrees to submit to any medical or other examination and to execute and deliver any application or other instrument in writing, reasonably necessary to effectuate such insurance.

7. In the event of the merger or consolidation of the Company into or with another corporation or in the event of the sale or transfer of substantially all of the Company's stock or assets to another entity, the Company shall have the right to assign all of its right, title and interest under this Agreement to the successor to its business.

8. At any time the Company may, upon delivery of written notice to the Employee, discharge him for cause or for no cause. Discharge of the Employee for cause shall mean discharge because of a) dishonesty, b) breach of this Agreement or c) other misconduct which in the judgment of the Board of Directors of the Company is detrimental to the best interests of the Company.

9. A. Employee's employment thereunder shall terminate (i) in the event of his death, as of the date of such death; (ii) in the event of Employee's discharge pursuant to Section 8 hereof, as of the date of such discharge; (iii) in the event of the Employee's inability to perform all or any substantial portion of the duties prescribed in or assigned pursuant to this agreement for a period of Thirty (30) consecutive days, Ten (10) days following written notice of such fact from the Company to the Employee; and, (iv) in the event Employee leaves the employment of the Company for any cause or reason (whether voluntary or involuntary on his or the Company's part).

B. Upon termination of the Employee's employment, all rights and obligations of the Company and Employee hereunder shall terminate except (i) any rights or causes of action arising out of the occurrences which constituted the cause of termination, (ii) the obligation not to disclose pursuant to Section 5 of this

Agreement, (iii) the covenant not to compete set forth in Section 4 of this Agreement, (iv) the right of the Employee or his heirs to receive any salary or bonus which had been earned prior to termination, but not yet paid.

10. This Agreement shall be interpreted and its validity and effect determined under and in accordance with the laws of the State of [specify].

11. This Agreement embodies the entire agreement and understanding between the Company and Employee and supersedes all prior agreements and understandings relating to the matter of employment of Employee by the Company. This Agreement may be modified or amended only in writing signed by Employee and by an officer of the Company on behalf of the Company.

12. Until advised otherwise in writing, all notices, demands and other communications hereunder shall be in writing and shall be deemed to have been duly given if sent by registered mail to the following addresses:

If to the Company: [specify address]

If to the Employee: [specify address]

13. This Agreement may be executed in as many counterparts as desired by the parties; any one of which shall have the force and effect of an original.

IN WITNESS WHEREOF, the Company has caused this Agreement to be signed and its corporate seal to be hereunto affixed by its duly authorized officers, and Employee has hereto set his hand and seal on the date first above written.

Attest: [NAME OF EMPLOYER]
(''the Company'')

By______________________________
its [specify title]

[NAME OF EMPLOYEE]
(''the Employee'')

____

APPENDIX I

SAMPLE EMPLOYMENT AGREEMENT—SHORT VERSION

Date

Name of Sales Manager
Address
City, State, Zip

Dear [Name of Sales Manager]:

This letter confirms that [Name of Company] (''The Company'') has hired you as its sales manager. In consideration thereto, you agree to be employed under the following terms and conditions:

1. You agree to work full-time and use your best efforts while rendering services for the Company. As our sales manager, you will be responsible for: [specify in detail]

2. You will make no representations, warranties, or commitments binding the Company without our prior consent nor do you have any authority to sign any documents or incur any indebtedness on the Company's behalf.

3. You shall assume responsibility for all samples, sales literature and other materials delivered to you and you shall return same immediately upon the direction of the Company.

4. THE COMPANY EMPLOYS YOU AT WILL AND MAY TERMINATE YOUR EMPLOYMENT AT ANY TIME, WITHOUT PRIOR NOTICE, WITH OR WITHOUT CAUSE. LIKEWISE, YOU ARE FREE TO RESIGN AS OUR SALES MANAGER AT ANY TIME, WITH OR WITHOUT NOTICE.

5. The Company shall pay you a salary of [Specify $X] per [specify] as consideration for all services to be rendered pursuant to this Agreement. In addition, the Company shall provide you with health insurance coverage for you and your family, and you will be eligible to participate in the Company pension plan. You will also receive Two (2) weeks paid vacation each year, provided you give the Company appropriate notice and the Company reserves the right to schedule your vacation(s) so as not to conflict with its normal business operations.

6. You shall also be paid for absences due to illness up to a maximum of Two (2) weeks per year, provided you submit a doctor's authorization indicating the reason for extended illness and the treatment received.

7. The Company shall also provide you time off with pay for the following holidays: [specify].

8. You agree and represent that you owe the Company the highest duty of loyalty. This means that you will never make secret profits at the Company's expense, will not accept kickbacks or special favors from Customers or Manufacturers, and will protect Company property.

9. While acting as a sales manager for the Company, you will not directly or indirectly, own an interest in, operate, control, or be connected as an employee, agent, independent contractor, partner, shareholder or principal in any company which markets products, goods or services which directly or indirectly compete with the business of the Company.

10. All lists and other records relating to the Customers of the Company, whether prepared by you or given to you by the Company during the term of this Agreement, are the property of the Company and shall be returned immediately upon termination or resignation of your employment.

11. You further agree that for a period of Six (6) months following the termination or resignation of your employment, you shall not work for, own an interest in, or be connected with as an employee, stockholder or partner, any company which directly or indirectly competes with the business of the Company.

12. There shall be no change, amendment or modification of this Agreement unless it is reduced to writing and signed by both parties. This Agreement cancels and supersedes all prior agreements and understandings.

13. If any provision of this Agreement is held by a court of competent jurisdiction to be invalid or unenforceable, the remainder of the Agreement shall remain in full force and shall in no way be impaired.

Your signature in the lower right corner of this Agreement will indicate the acceptance of the terms and conditions herein stated.

Sincerely yours,

By: ______________________________

[specify Name and Title]
[NAME OF COMPANY]
(''The Company'')

I, [Name of Sales Manager], the Employee stated herein, have read the above Agreement, understand and agree with its terms, and have received a copy.

____

[NAME OF SALES MANAGER]

APPENDIX J

SAMPLE SALES EMPLOYEE AGREEMENT—LETTER VERSION

Date

Name of Employee
Address
City/State/Zip

Dear [Name of Employee]:

This will confirm your engagement as our employee, pursuant to the terms and conditions set forth herein.

1. **Employment.** The Company hereby employs [Name of employee] (''The Employee'') to loyally render exclusive and full-time services as a sales employee for the Company.

2. **Duties.** The Employee shall work an eight-hour day, five days per week, excluding holidays, out of the Company's premises located at [specify], and throughout the Employee's territory as more fully described herein. the Employee shall devote his/her best efforts to the affairs of the Company and shall perform such duties as shall be directed by the supervisors and officers of the Company.

3. **Acceptance.** In consideration of the Company's employing or continuing to employ The Employee, The Employee hereby accepts such employment and agrees to render such services. As an exclusive and full-time employee, the Employee will not, during the term hereof, render any services for other corporations, businesses or entities directly or indirectly in competition with the Company.

4. **Terms of Employment.** THE COMPANY EMPLOYS THE EMPLOYEE AT WILL AND MAY TERMINATE THE EMPLOYEE AT ANY TIME WITHOUT PRIOR NOTICE WITH OR WITHOUT CAUSE.

5. Compensation. The Company agrees to pay the Employee a salary at the rate of [specify $X] per [specify] as consideration for services rendered pursuant to this Agreement. Salary increases will be at The Company's discretion and may be based, among other things, on productivity. The salary set forth hereinabove shall be payable in accordance with the regular payroll practices of the Company.

In addition, the Company shall pay The Employee a commission as listed on Exhibit A of this Agreement. Said commission shall be paid on all shipped orders paid by Customers in the Employee's designated territory. Bad debts, defined as non-payments by the Customer after a period of One Hundred and Twenty (120) days, shall be deducted from the Employee's commission for each order which remains unpaid to the extent of commission credited to the Employee for that particular order.

6. Expenses. The Company shall pay or reimburse the Employee for all necessary and reasonable expenses incurred or paid by the Employee in connection with the performance of services under this Agreement, upon presentation of expense statements or vouchers or such other supporting information as it may from time to time request, evidencing the nature of such expense, and, if appropriate, the payment thereof by the Employee, and otherwise in accordance with Company procedures from time to time in effect.

7. Additional Benefits. The Employee shall be entitled to participate in any group insurance, qualified pension, hospitalization, medical health and accident, disability or similar plan or program of the Company now existing, or hereafter established, to the extent that he is eligible under its general provisions hereof. NOTWITHSTANDING ANYTHING HEREIN TO THE CONTRARY, HOWEVER, THE COMPANY SHALL HAVE THE RIGHT TO AMEND OR TERMINATE ANY SUCH PLANS OR PROGRAMS WITHOUT PRIOR NOTICE. In addition, the Company reserves the right to schedule vacations so as to not conflict with normal business operations.

8. Maintenance of Business Automobile. The Employee shall purchase and operate an automobile to be used in connection with his selling duties. The Company shall be notified of the make and model of said vehicle in a timely fashion.

The Employee covenants that he shall maintain a valid driver's license at all times and carry automobile liability insurance for no less than One Million Dollars ($1,000,000). The Employee shall submit a certificate of insurance from his insurance carrier documenting said coverage upon the Company's request and the failure to comply with said request shall be grounds for immediate dismissal.

9. Representations And Warranties. The Employee will make no representations, warranties, or commitments binding the Company without the Company's prior consent.

10. Price And Product Changes. The Company will provide product specifications, prices, delivery schedules and discounts, and will give the Employee timely notice of any and all changes.

11. Acceptance Of Orders. All orders are subject to acceptance or rejection by the Company at its home office. The Company shall also provide the Employee with the names of all persons and companies within his/her territory requesting information.

12. Duty Of Loyalty. The Employee covenants and represents that he owes the Company the highest duty of loyalty with respect to his/her duties. This means that he/she will, among other things, maintain a constant vigil over the Company's property, never make secret profits at the Company's expense, never service customers of the Company but bill them himself, never accept kickbacks or special favors from Customers, dress in a proper fashion, not use drugs or alcohol while on the job, and maintain his/her personal automobile in good condition together with a valid driver's license.

13. Protection Of Confidential Information. In view of the fact that the Employee's work will bring him into close contact with many confidential matters such as information about costs, profits, vendors, inventory, service techniques, technical manuals, customer needs and lists, markets, sales, discounts and other information not readily available to the public, and in consideration of the Company's employing or continuing to employ the Employee, the Employee hereby covenants and agrees, as an essential condition of his/her employment or continued employment by the Company, as follows:

A. To keep secret all confidential matters of the Company and its affiliates and not to disclose them to anyone outside of the Company, either during or after the Employee's employment with the Company, except with the Company's consent;

B. To avoid discussing any matters of a confidential nature with competitors or their employees. The includes discussions regarding the Company's customers, pricing, and policies. The Employee is reminded that any such discussions may cause the Company, and the Employee personally, to have violated anti-trust laws including the Sherman and Clayton Acts. Sanctions of up to Three (3) years imprisonment and fines up to $100,000 have been imposed on individual employees who violate such laws.

C. To deliver promptly to the Company upon termination of the Employee's employment, or at any time the Company may so request, all memoranda, notes, records, reports, technical manuals and other documents (and all copies thereof) relating to the Company's and its affiliate's businesses which the Employee may then possess or have under the Employee's control.

14. Obligations After Termination. The Employee agrees that for a period of Six (6) months after the termination of his/her employment with the Company, he/she shall not work for, own and interest in, operate, join, control, participate in or be connected, either directly or indirectly, as an officer, employee, agent, independent contractor, shareholder or principal of any of the Principals of the Company, whom you sold for during the past Two (2) years while acting as our sales employee. The Employee further agrees to notify any prospective employer of the existence of this Agreement, in writing, with a copy of such notice to an officer of the Company.

If the Employee is unable to obtain employment consistent with his abilities and education solely because of the provisions of this paragraph, the Employee shall promptly notify the Company and the Company shall have the option of waiving the requirements of this paragraph or making payments to the Employee equal to [specify] of the weekly base pay at termination, provided the Employee has made and continues to make, conscientious and aggressive efforts to find other employment. Documentation of these efforts will be required on a regular and consistent basis.

15. Right To Seek Injunctive Relief. The Employee agrees that any breach of any of the covenants contained in Paragraphs 12, 13 and 14 of this Agreement constitutes substantial and irreparable harm to the Company, and that such harm could not be adequately compensated by the Company's recovery of monetary damages. Therefore, the Employee agrees that the Company may seek injunctive relief, or any other relief which it deems necessary and appropriate, in order to protect its rights under this Agreement and other common law rights, and that such injunctive proceeding shall not limit or in any way restrain the Company from seeking any other relief or damages.

16. Right To Seek Other Relief Or Damages. Notwithstanding the right to seek injunctive relief, the Company may, upon finding by it that the Employee has violated his covenant of Duty Of Loyalty as more fully defined in Paragraph 12 of the Agreement:

A. Terminate the Employee without notice and without severance pay or other benefits not previously earned; and

B. Recover all monies paid in salary, commission and other benefits to the Employee for the period of time said Duty Of Loyalty was violated.

17. Resignation Of Employee. The Employee shall give the Company written notice of his decision to resign from said employment no less than Two (2) weeks prior to the effective termination date.

Said notice shall be in writing, and sent Certified Mail or hand-delivered to the (headquarter) office of the Company.

18. Final Accounting. At the termination of the Agreement, The Company shall pay the Employee his/her final commission due, as calculated more fully on Exhibit A attached hereto. Said commission shall be earned on all accepted orders in house at the date of termination which are shipped within one (1) month after the termination date.

19. Non-Affiliate. Nothing in this Agreement shall be construed to constitute the Employee as a partner or affiliate of the Company.

20. Prior Agreement. This Agreement forms the entire understanding between the parties. It cancels and supersedes all prior agreements and understandings.

21. Modifications. There will be no change, amendment, or modification of any of the terms in this Agreement unless it is reduced to writing and signed by both parties. The Employee shall not be excused from compliance with the provisions of this Agreement by the failure of the Company to protest any changes instituted by either the Company or the Employee.

22. Enforceability. If any provision of this Agreement is held by a court of competent jurisdiction to be unenforceable, the remainder of the Agreement shall remain in full force and effect and shall in no way be impaired.

Dated this _____ day of ___________________

Sincerely yours,

By ____________________________
[specify Name and Title]

NAME OF COMPANY
(''The Company'')

I, [Name of Employee], the Employee, have read the above letter, understand and agree with its terms, and have received a copy.

____
[NAME OF EMPLOYEE]

APPENDIX K

SAMPLE CONSULTING AGREEMENT

This Consulting Agreement (the ''Agreement'') is entered into this [specify date] by and between [Name of Consultant], an individual, (''Consultant'') and [Name of Company] (the ''Company'').

RECITALS

WHEREAS, the Company is in need of assistance in the computer systems support area; and WHEREAS, Consultant has agreed to perform consulting work for the Company in providing computer systems support and consulting services and other related activities as directed by the Company;

NOW, THEREFORE, the parties hereby agree as follows:

1. Consultant's Services. Consultant shall be available and shall provide to the Company professional consulting services in the area of computer systems support (''Consulting services'') as requested.

2. Consideration.

A. RATE. In consideration for the Consulting Services to be performed by Consultant under this Agreement, the Company will pay Consultant at the rate of One Hundred Dollars ($100.00) per hour for time spent on Consulting Services. Consultant shall submit written, signed reports of the time spent performing Consulting Services, itemizing in reasonable detail the dates on which services were performed, the number of hours spent on such dates and a brief description of the services rendered. The Company shall pay Consultant the amounts due pursuant to submitted reports within 14 days after such reports are received by the Company.

B. EXPENSES. Additionally, the Company will pay Consultant for the following expenses incurred while the Agreement between Consultant and the Company exists:

- All travel expenses to and from all work sites
- Meal expenses;

- Administrative expenses;

- Lodging Expenses if work demands overnight stays; and

- Miscellaneous travel-related expenses including parking and tolls.

Consultant shall submit written documentation and receipts where available itemizing the dates on which expenses were incurred. The Company shall pay Consultant the amounts due pursuant to submitted reports within 14 days after a report is received by the Company.

3. Independent Contractor. Nothing herein shall be construed to create an employer-employee relationship between the Company and Consultant. Consultant is an independent contractor and not an employee of the Company or any of its subsidiaries or affiliates. The consideration set forth in Section 2 shall be the sole consideration due Consultant for the services rendered hereunder. It is understood that the Company will not withhold any amounts for payment of taxes from the compensation of Consultant hereunder. Consultant will not represent to be or hold herself out as an employee of the Company.

4. Confidentiality. In the course of performing Consulting Services, the parties recognize that Consultant may come in contact with or become familiar with information which the Company or its subsidiaries or affiliates may consider confidential. This information may include, but is not limited to, information pertaining to the Company computer systems, which information may be of value to a competitor. Consultant agrees to keep all such information confidential and not to discuss or divulge it to anyone other than appropriate Company personnel or their designees.

5. Term. This Agreement shall commence on [specify date] and shall terminate on [specify date], unless earlier terminated by either party hereto. Either party may terminate this Agreement upon Thirty (30) days prior written notice. The Company may, at its option, renew this Agreement for an additional One (1) year term on the same terms and conditions as set forth herein by giving notice to Consultant of such intent to renew on or before [specify date].

6. Notice. Any notice or communication permitted or required by this Agreement shall be deemed effective when personally delivered or deposited, postage prepaid, in the first class mail of the United States properly addressed to the appropriate party at the address set forth below:

1. Notices as to Consultant: [specify address]

2. Notices to the Company: [specify address]

7. Miscellaneous.

7.1 Entire Agreement and Amendments. This Agreement constitutes the entire agreement of the parties with regard to the subject matter hereof, and replaces and supersedes all other agreements or understandings, whether written or oral. No amendment or extension of the Agreement shall be binding unless in writing and signed by both parties.

7.2 Binding Effect, Assignment. This Agreement shall be binding upon and shall inure to the benefit of Consultant and the Company and to the Company's successors and assigns. Nothing in this Agreement shall be construed to permit the assignment by Consultant of any of its rights or obligations hereunder, and such assignment is expressly prohibited without the prior written consent of the Company.

7.3 Governing Law, Severability. This Agreement shall be governed by the laws of the State of [specify]. The invalidity or unenforceability of any provision of the Agreement shall not affect the validity or enforceability of any other provision.

WHEREFORE, the parties have executed this Agreement as of the date first written above.

[COMPANY:]

By:_______________________________

[CONSULTANT:]

____

[DATE]

APPENDIX L

SAMPLE INDEPENDENT SALES REPRESENTATIVE AGREEMENT (LONG VERSION)

This Agreement is made in [specify State] as of [specify], between [Name of Company], a [specify State] corporation, having its principal place of business at [specify address] (hereinafter called ''the Company'') and [Sales Representative's Full Legal Name and D/B/A (if different from Legal Name)] having its principal place of business at [specify address] (hereinafter called ''Representative'').

A. The Company markets various [specify] products in the United States.

B. The Company desires to obtain the services of Representative, and Representative desires to provide services to the Company in accordance with the terms, conditions and covenants set forth in this Agreement. Accordingly, in consideration of the mutual covenants and undertakings set forth herein, the parties hereby agree as follows:

1. Appointment and Acceptance.

A. The Company hereby appoints Representative as one of the Company's independent sales representatives to solicit orders for those [specify] products marketed from time to time by the Company. Representative's appointment shall not be applicable to any other products marketed by the Company.

B. Representative shall solicit orders for Company Products in the geographic territory designated on Exhibit ''A'' (hereinafter called ''the Territory''). Representative shall not solicit orders for Company Products in any other geographic territory. The Company shall have the right, from time to time, at its sole discretion, to change the scope of the Territory. In any such instance, the Company shall issue a new Exhibit ''A'' to Representative reflecting such change, which shall, as of the effective date stated thereon, supersede the prior Exhibit ''A''. Representative acknowledges and agrees that it neither has, nor will acquire, any vested or proprietary right or interest with respect to the Territory, any Company customers in the Territory, or any Company customer lists. Representative further acknowledges and agrees that any goodwill accruing in the Territory during the term of this Agreement with respect to the Company or Company Products shall be considered the property of the Company rather than Representative.

C. Notwithstanding anything contained herein, unless specifically authorized by the Company in writing, Representative shall not solicit orders for the Products from any O.E.M. or private label accounts, it being understood and acknowledged by Representative that the Company may solicit orders from such accounts directly (in which case they shall be considered ''Reserved Factory Accounts'') or may authorize other specially appointed Company sales representatives to solicit orders from such accounts. Further, the Company shall have the right, from time to time, at its sole discretion, to designate other account categories and/or specific accounts within the Territory as accounts which shall be serviced by the Company directly as Reserved Factory Accounts, or by other Company sales representatives, regardless of whether Representative previously has serviced such account categories or accounts on the Company's behalf.

D. Representative hereby accepts its appointment hereunder.

2. Responsibilities of Representative. Representative shall satisfy the following responsibilities at all times during the term of this Agreement:

A. Representative and its staff shall conduct themselves in a manner consistent with the high image, reputation and credibility of the Company and Company Products, and shall engage in no activities which reflect adversely on the Company or the Products.

B. Representative shall use its best efforts to solicit orders for the Products, shall promote the sale of the Products in a diligent and aggressive manner, and shall forward all orders to the Company promptly.

C. Representative shall maintain an office in the Territory which shall be open and staffed adequately during normal business hours. Representative shall employ and maintain adequately trained and competent personnel in numbers sufficient to carry out and perform properly and fully all of Representative's responsibilities under this Agreement.

D. In the event that Representative becomes aware of any actual or potential claim against the Company by any person or entity, Representative shall notify the Company immediately.

E. Representative shall use its best efforts to achieve sales quotas assigned periodically by the Company to Representative. The Company shall have the right to adjust or revise any assigned sales quotas, from time to time, at its sole discretion, by written notice to Representative. Representative understands that sales volume is only one factor which will be considered by the Company in evaluating Representative's performance, and that the achievement of any sales quota(s) shall not preclude the Company from exercising its non-extension or termination rights pursuant to paragraph 14 of this Agreement.

F. Representative shall furnish the Company, on a timely basis, with sales call reports, sales forecasts, and such other information pertinent to Representative's performance hereunder, as the Company may request.

G. Representative shall attend any and all meetings and trade shows required by the Company.

H. Representative shall comply with all applicable federal, state and local laws and regulations in performing its responsibilities hereunder.

I. Representative shall assist the Company in obtaining relevant financial information concerning Company accounts and potential accounts within the Territory.

J. Representative shall keep the Company informed as to competitive and economic conditions within the Territory which may affect the marketing or sales of the Company Products therein.

K. To the extent not otherwise required herein, Representative shall provide complete cooperation to the Company in order to assist the Company in maximizing the Company's success within the Territory.

3. Relationship of the Parties. Representative acknowledges that it has its own independently established business which is separate and apart from the Company's business. Representative at all times shall be considered an independent contractor with respect to its relationship with the Company. Nothing contained in this Agreement shall be deemed to create the relationships of employer and employee, master and servant, franchisor and franchisee, partnership or joint venture between the parties.

4. Scope and Limitations of Representative's Authority.

A. Representative has authority to solicit orders only and has no authority to accept orders. All orders solicited by Representative shall be subject to acceptance or rejection by the Company, in whole or in part, at the Company's sole discretion.

B. The Company shall have the sole right to determine the accounts to whom the Products shall be sold, and Representative shall have no right or authority to obligate the Company to sell the Products to any account.

C. Prices, credit terms, sales programs and other terms and conditions of sale governing transactions between the Company and its customers shall be those adopted by the Company from time to time, at its sole discretion. Representative shall have no authority to modify any such prices, credit terms, sales programs or other terms or conditions of sale, to authorize any customer to return the Products to the Company for credit, or to obligate or bind the Company in any other manner.

D. Representative at no time shall engage in any unfair trade practices with respect to the Company or the Products, and shall make no false or misleading representations with respect to the Company or the Products. Representative shall refrain from communicating any information with respect to guarantees or warranties regarding the Products, except such as are expressly authorized by the Company or are set forth in the Company's literature or other promotional materials.

E. Except as authorized by the Company, Representative shall have no authority to make collections from customers, but shall assist the Company in collections upon the Company's request, and shall remit any collected funds to the Company immediately.

F. Representative shall not use the Company's tradenames or trademarks or any names closely resembling same as part of Representative's corporate or business name, or in any manner which the Company in its sole discretion, may consider misleading or otherwise objectionable.

G. Representative shall not attempt to fix the prices at which any account or prospective account of the Company may resell the Company Products, it being acknowledged and understood that the Company accounts are free to determine resale prices at their sole discretion.

5. Commissions.

A. The sole and exclusive compensation to be paid by the Company to Representative in consideration for all services rendered by Representative as an independent sales representative for the Company shall be commissions on sales of the Products in accordance with the commission schedule set forth on Exhibit ''B'' (''the Commission Schedule''), which is attached hereto and shall be considered an integral part of this Agreement. The Company shall have the right, from time to time, at its sole discretion, to modify the Commission Schedule, in whole or in part. In any such instance, the Company shall issue a new Exhibit ''B'' to Representative reflecting such change(s), which shall, as of the effective date stated thereon, supersede the prior Exhibit ''B''. Anything contained herein or on Exhibit ''B'' notwithstanding, the Commission Schedule shall not govern close-out sales, sales made at less than regular prices or sales involving terms different from the Company's standard terms of sale. The Company shall have the right to determine the commissions on such sales at its sole discretion, on a case by case basis, without the requirement of advance notice to Representative.

B. Commissions shall be computed on the net invoice price of the Products. The ''net invoice price'' shall be computed by deducting from the gross sales price, all taxes, freight, insurance charges, credits (arising from returns or other adjustments), discounts, rebates or allowances of any kind, except prompt payment discounts.

C. Subject to the final settlement procedures set forth in paragraph 6 and to the debit provisions of subparagraph E hereof, commissions shall become earned and due to Representative in accordance with the following provisions:

i) Except as otherwise provided in this Agreement, commissions on commissionable orders shall be considered earned and due to Representative on the [specify time] following the [specify time] in which the order is shipped and invoiced to the Company's customer. For example, commissions on commissionable orders shipped in [specify] shall be considered earned and due to Representative on [specify].

ii) Commissions on any shipment(s) made subsequent to any expiration or termination of this Agreement shall be considered earned and due to Representative only if the shipment relates to an order received and accepted by the Company prior to the expiration or termination date, is made within Thirty (30) days of such expiration or termination date, and otherwise becomes earned and due pursuant to the provisions of Paragraph 6 hereof.

iii) No commissions shall be considered earned and due to Representative under any circumstances with respect to:

a) Sales to any Reserved Factory Accounts or to any other accounts from which Representative is not authorized by the Company to solicit orders; or

b) Sales of parts or promotional items, sales of any products not covered by this Agreement, accommodation sales, sales made to Representative or to any of its employees, or sales to any other entity in which Representative or any principal(s) of Representative has any ownership or other financial interest; or

c) Any unfilled orders; or

d) Any shipments made more than Thirty (30) days after any expiration or termination of this Agreement, regardless of whether the order(s) in question has been submitted to the Company prior to the expiration or termination date; or

e) Any orders submitted to the Company after any expiration or termination of this Agreement; or

f) Any orders or portions thereof as to which the Company is obligated to pay the commissions to any other Company sales representative.

D. In those cases in which the Company ships an order to an account's outlets in more than one territory, or to an account's central redistribution to more than one territory, the Company, at its sole discretion, may apportion such commissions to more than one representative, in proportions deemed by the Company, in its sole judgment, to be equitable. All such determinations in any particular instance shall not be binding on the Company in subsequent instances.

E. The monthly commissions otherwise payable to Representative shall be offset by any debits issued against Representative's commission account. Debits shall be issued in accordance with the following provisions of Paragraph 6 hereof:

i) If any credits, discounts, rebates or allowances (except prompt payment discounts) are granted to an account after merchandise has been shipped and invoiced, a debit will be issued for the commissions allocable thereto.

ii) A debit will be issued for the commissions allocable to any amounts which are more than Ninety (90)days past due, and/or are written off by the Company as bad debts. Any subsequent collection of all or any portion of such amounts shall not serve to reduce, offset, or reverse the debit. In situations in which the Company engages an attorney or collection agency, the provisions of subparagraph iii) will be controlling.

iii) If the Company incurs any legal expense or pays any collection agency for the collection or attempted collection of any unpaid amounts from accounts serviced by Representative, a debit will be issued for the commissions allocable to the entire amount sought to be collected, and the collection of all or any portion of the indebtedness shall not serve to reduce, offset, or reverse the debit.

iv) If Representative (or any other business entity in which Representative or any of its principals has any ownership or other financial interest) becomes indebted to the Company, regardless of the basis or nature of the indebtedness, the Company shall have the right to issue a debit against Representative's commission account for the full amount of such indebtedness or any portion thereof.

v) Debits shall be issued during the term of this Agreement and thereafter, until the completion of the final reconciliation, as provided in Paragraph 6 hereof. All debits issued in any particular calendar month shall serve to reduce the commissions payable to Representative in succeeding calendar months until said debits have been offset in their entirety against commissions. If the debits issued against Representative's commission account at any time exceed the commissions then due Representative, the Company may require, in lieu of offsetting said debits against future commissions, that Representative pay said excess amount to the Company. In such event, payment shall be made by Representative to the Company within Thirty (30) days after receipt of the Company's written demand therefor.

D. The Company shall furnish Representative periodically with statements reflecting the status of Representative's commission account. If Representative has objections with respect to any such statement, whether regarding its accuracy, completeness or any other matter, Representative shall make such objection(s) known to the Company in writing within thirty (30) days after the date of the statement. ANY AND ALL OBJECTIONS AS TO WHICH WRITTEN NOTICE IS NOT RECEIVED BY THE COMPANY WITHIN THE THIRTY (30) DAY PERIOD SHALL BE DEEMED WAIVED AND ABANDONED.

6. Final Settlement Procedures. Notwithstanding anything contained in Paragraph 5, any commissions otherwise becoming earned and due to Representative as of the expiration or termination date of this Agreement, or thereafter, may be withheld by the Company and shall become due, if at all, only after a final reconciliation is performed by the Company One Hundred Fifty (150) days subsequent to the expiration or termination date (''the Reconciliation Date''). In lieu of withholding the entire amount of such commissions, the Company may, at its option, withhold only that portion as the Company deems necessary for its financial protection. The Company shall debit Representative's commission account on the Reconciliation Date for the commissions allocable to any outstanding invoices applicable to customers serviced by Representative, which the Company believes are uncollectable or in jeopardy of non-payment. If the debits allocable to such invoices, together with any other debits not previously offset against commissions do not exceed the amount of any remaining commissions otherwise payable to Representative, the difference between the remaining commissions and the outstanding debits then shall be considered earned and due, and thereupon shall be paid by the Company to Representative. If all outstanding debits exceed the remaining commissions, no additional commissions shall be considered earned and due, and Representative shall be required to pay the Company the difference between such outstanding debits and the remaining commissions, upon receipt of the Company's statement therefor. After the Reconciliation Date, no additional commissions shall become earned and due to Representative, and the Company shall not be entitled to issue any additional debits against Representative's commission account.

7. Competitive Products.

A. Unless authorized by the Company in writing, neither Representative nor any other entity in which Representative or any of its principals has any ownership or other financial interest, shall act, at any time during the term of this Agreement, as a sales representative for any products or product lines which are in any way similar in design, function or intended use to Company Products, or which otherwise are competitive, in the Company's sole judgment, with the Company Products.

B. In order to ensure Representative's compliance with subparagraph A. hereof, Representative shall identify, from time to time, when requested by the Company, all products or product lines other than the Company Products, for which Representative (or any other business entity in which Representative or any of its principals has any ownership or other financial interest) is acting as a sales representative. Representative, in any event, shall notify the Company in writing, whenever Representative or any such other business entity is contemplating the commencement of representation for any additional products or product line(s).

8. Product Changes. The Company shall have the right, at its sole discretion, to modify or discontinue selling any or all of the Products at any time, without incurring any liability to Representative.

9. Purchases for Resale. In the event that the Company and Representative agree that Representative shall purchase quantities of the Company's Products for resale, any such purchases shall be at such prices and upon such other terms and conditions of sale as are determined by the Company from time to time, at its sole discretion. The Company shall have the right to cease selling the Company Products to Representative at any time.

10. Submission of Ideas to the Company. In consideration for the Company's execution of this agreement, Representative agrees that any and all business ideas, materials, procedures, policies and plans (hereinafter called collectively ''the ideas'') as may be submitted by Representative to the Company during the term of this Agreement and which pertain directly or indirectly to the business of the Company, shall belong to and be deemed to be the property of the Company. Unless otherwise agreed expressly in writing by an officer of the Company, the Company shall not be required to compensate Representative in any manner for the ideas, regardless of whether the Company utilizes or does not utilize the ideas, in whole or in part. Representative agrees to execute any additional documents as may be necessary to effectuate these provisions.

11. Proprietary Information. All financial, engineering, sales, marketing or other information disclosed by the Company to Representative as a consequence of Representative's relationship with the Company shall be treated by Representative as the Company's trade secrets and shall not be disclosed by Representative to any other person, firm or entity, during the term of this Agreement or thereafter, without the prior written consent of the Company, except to the extent that such information is in the public domain at the time of its disclosure to Representative or thereafter becomes in the public domain through no fault of Representative.

12. Representative's Business Expenses. Representative shall bear the entire responsibility for any and all expenses incurred in connection with its business (including, but not limited to leaseholding expenses, salaries, telephone and traveling expenses), and the Company shall not be obligated to pay any such expenses or to reimburse Representative therefore.

The Company shall have no responsibility for the payment of withholding, Social Security or unemployment taxes, or any similar taxes or other payments, with respect to commissions earned by Representative hereunder. If, notwithstanding the provisions of this paragraph, any such taxes or payments ever are assessed against the Company, Representative shall reimburse the Company promptly for all sums paid by the Company, including any interest or penalties.

14. Duration of Agreement/Termination.

A. This Agreement shall remain in effect until midnight of the last day of [specify] immediately following the date shown at the beginning of this Agreement, unless terminated sooner as provided in subparagraph B., or unless extended for an additional period. Any such extension shall be operative only if effectuated by a written instrument executed by both parties. NEITHER PARTY SHALL BE OBLIGATED TO EXTEND THE DURATION OF THIS AGREEMENT UPON THE EXPIRATION OF THE INITIAL TERM OR ANY SUCCEEDING TERM. Although either party may elect to provide the other with advance notice of any intention not to extend this Agreement upon its expiration, such notice shall not be required, it being understood that the notice provisions of subparagraph B apply solely to termination prior to expiration.

B. Either Representative or the Company may terminate this Agreement, at will, at any time during the initial term or any succeeding term, and such termination may be either with or without cause. If the termination is without cause, Thirty (30) days advance written notice must be provided by the terminating party to the other party. EACH PARTY ACKNOWLEDGES THAT SUCH THIRTY (30) DAY PERIOD IS ADEQUATE TO ALLOW IT TO TAKE ALL ACTIONS REQUIRED TO ADJUST ITS BUSINESS OPERATIONS IN ANTICIPATION OF TERMINATION. If the termination is for cause, no advance notice shall be required, but may be provided at the option of the terminating party. ''Cause'' for purposes of this paragraph shall include, but not necessarily be limited to, the following:

i) In the case of termination by Representative, cause shall exist if the Company materially breaches any provision of this Agreement.

ii) In the case of termination by the Company, cause shall exist:

a) If Representative fails to achieve any sales quota(s) assigned by the Company, fails to satisfy any of its other responsibilities provided in Paragraph 2 hereof, breaches Paragraph 7 of this Agreement, or breaches any other provision of this Agreement; or

b) If Representative is unable, by reason of illness or disability of any of its employees, to perform any of its responsibilities hereunder; or

c) If Representative sells its business or merges its business with another company, or if there is any other change in the management or control of Representative's business.

iii) Cause shall exist for termination by either party if the other party assigns or attempts to assign this Agreement, except as permitted hereunder, liquidates or terminates its business, is adjudicated a bankrupt, makes an assignment for the benefit of creditors, invokes the provisions of any law for the relief of debtors, or files or has filed against it any similar proceeding.

C. Upon any expiration or termination of this Agreement, Representative shall cease holding itself out in any fashion as a sales representative for the Company, and shall return to the Company, all sales literature, price lists, customer lists and any other documents, materials or tangible items pertaining to the Company's business, with the exception of any Company Product, which may have been purchased by Representative.

D. THIS AGREEMENT IS EXECUTED BY BOTH THE COMPANY AND REPRESENTATIVE WITH THE KNOWLEDGE THAT IT MAY BE TERMINATED OR NOT EXTENDED. NEITHER REPRESENTATIVE NOR THE COMPANY SHALL BE LIABLE TO THE OTHER FOR COMPENSATION, REIMBURSEMENT FOR INVESTMENTS OR EXPENSES, LOST PROFITS, INCIDENTAL OR CONSEQUENTIAL DAMAGES, OR DAMAGES OF ANY OTHER KIND OR CHARACTER, BECAUSE OF ANY EXERCISE OF ITS RIGHT TO TERMINATE THIS AGREEMENT, AS PROVIDED HEREUNDER, OR BECAUSE OF ANY ELECTION TO REFRAIN FROM EXTENDING THE DURATION OF THIS AGREEMENT UPON THE EXPIRATION OF THE INITIAL TERM OR ANY SUCCEEDING TERM.

15. Applicable Law, Forum Selection and Consent to Jurisdiction. This Agreement shall be governed and construed in all respects in accordance with the laws of the state of [specify]. Any litigation instituted by Representative against the Company pertaining to any breach or termination of this Agreement, or pertaining in any other manner to this Agreement, must be filed by Representative before a court of competent jurisdiction in [specify state] and Representative hereby consents irrevocably to the jurisdiction of the [specify state] courts over its person. Service of process may be made upon Representative as provided by [specify state] law, or shall be considered effective if sent by Certified or Registered Mail, Return Receipt Requested, Postage Prepaid.

16. Miscellaneous.

A. Representative may not assign, transfer or sell all or any of its rights under this Agreement (or delegate all or any of its obligations hereunder), without the prior written consent of the Company. If a sale or other transfer of Representative's business is contemplated (whether by transfer of stock, assets or otherwise), Representative shall notify the Company in writing no less than Thirty (30) days prior to effecting such transfer, but such notice shall not obligate the Company in any manner. The Company may assign this Agreement only to a parent, subsidiary or affiliated firm or to another entity in connection with the sale or other transfer of all or substantially all of its business assets. Subject to these restrictions, the provisions of this Agreement shall be binding upon and shall inure to the benefit of the parties, their successors and permitted assigns.

B. The waiver by either party of any of its rights or any breaches of the other party under this Agreement in a particular instance shall not be construed as a waiver of the same or different rights or breaches in subsequent instances. All remedies, rights, undertakings and obligations hereunder shall be cumulative, and none shall operate as a limitation of any other remedy, right, undertaking or obligation hereunder.

C. Representative shall maintain automobile

insurance, general liability insurance, and any other insurance required by applicable laws or regulations.

D. All notices and demands of any kind which either the Company or Representative may be required or desire to serve upon the other under the terms of this Agreement shall be in writing and shall be served by personal delivery or by mail, at the addresses set forth in this Agreement or at such other addresses as may be designated hereafter by the parties in writing. If by personal delivery, service shall be deemed complete upon such delivery. If by mail, service shall be deemed complete upon mailing.

E. The paragraph headings contained herein are for reference only and shall not be considered substantive provisions of this Agreement. The use of a singular or plural form shall include the other form, and the use of a masculine, feminine or neuter gender shall include the other genders.

F. In the event that any of the provisions of this Agreement or the application of any such provisions to the parties hereto with respect to their obligations hereunder shall be held by a court of competent jurisdiction to be unlawful or unenforceable, the remaining portions of this Agreement shall remain in full force and effect and shall not be invalidated or impaired in any manner.

G. This Agreement supersedes any and all other agreements between the parties pertaining in any manner to the subject matter hereof, and contains all of the covenants and agreements between the parties with respect to said subject matter. Each party to this Agreement acknowledges that no written or oral representations, inducements, promises or agreements have been made which are not embodied herein. IT IS THE INTENTION AND DESIRE OF THE PARTIES THAT THIS AGREEMENT NOT BE SUBJECT TO IMPLIED COVENANTS OF ANY KIND. Except as otherwise provided in this Agreement, this Agreement may not be amended, modified or supplemented, except by a written instrument signed by both parties hereto.

H. This Agreement has been executed in multiple counterparts, each of which shall be deemed enforceable without production of the others.

IN WITNESS WHEREOF, the parties hereto have executed this Agreement as of the date and year first hereinabove written.

ACCEPTED AND CONSENTED TO:

[Sales Representative's Full Legal Name] and [D.B.A (if different from Legal Name)]	[Name of Corporation]
''The Representative''	''The Company''
By: ______________________ Signature	By: ______________________ Signature
Title: ______________________	Title: ______________________ [Corporate officer (indicate office), Partner, Owner]

EXHIBIT "A"
FOR INDEPENDENT
SALES REPRESENTATIVE AGREEMENT

BETWEEN [NAME OF COMPANY] AND [SALES REPRESENTATIVE'S FULL LEGAL NAME AND D.B.A (IF DIFFERENT FROM LEGAL NAME)]

TERRITORY. Representative's appointment is applicable in the following geographic territory: In the state of [specify], includes the counties of [specify].

This Exhibit is effective as of [specify], and supersedes any prior Exhibits concerning the subject matter hereof.

[Sales Representative's Full Legal Name] and [D.B.A (if different from Legal Name)]	[Name of Corporation]
''The Representative''	''The Company''
By: ______________________ Signature	By: ______________________ Signature
Title: ____________________	Title: __________________ [Corporate officer (indicate office), Partner, Owner]

EXHIBIT "B"
FOR INDEPENDENT
SALES REPRESENTATIVE AGREEMENT

BETWEEN [NAME OF COMPANY] AND [SALES REPRESENTATIVE'S FULL LEGAL NAME AND D.B.A (IF DIFFERENT FROM LEGAL NAME)]

COMMISSION SCHEDULE: The commission rate shall be [specify] percent of the net invoice price.

This Commission Schedule is subject to modification by the Company pursuant to the provisions of Paragraph 5A of the Independent Sales Representative Agreement.

This Exhibit is effective as of [specify date], and supersedes any prior Exhibits concerning the subject matter hereof.

[Sales Representative's Full Legal Name] and [D.B.A (if different from Legal Name)]	[Name of Corporation]
''The Representative''	''The Company''
By: ____________________ Signature	By: ____________________ Signature
Title: ____________________	Title: ____________________ [Corporate officer (indicate office), Partner, Owner]

APPENDIX M

SAMPLE INDEPENDENT SALES REPRESENTATIVE AGREEMENT LETTER VERSION

Name

Title

Street Address

City, State, Zip

Dear [Name of Officer],

This will confirm your engagement as an independent sales representative for [Name of Company] (hereinafter referred to as ''the Company'') under the following terms and conditions:

1. You will devote your best efforts for the solicitation of orders resulting in sales of our [specify product] to the [specify type of industry] located in the States of [specify], in which you shall have exclusive territorial rights.

2. You are hereby retained as an independent contractor and not as an employee of the Company. As an independent contractor, you shall be solely responsible to pay all applicable taxes arising from payments made to you by the Company, including, but not limited to, social security, self-employment taxes and disability insurance. Neither you nor your employees shall be entitled to participate in any Company plans, arrangements or distributions pertaining to any pension, stock, bonus, profit sharing or similar benefits.

3. You agree to indemnify and hold the Company harmless from any and all liability, claims, demands or requirements imposed by federal or state law upon self-employed individuals arising from payments made to you under this Agreement.

4. You agree to bear all expenses incurred in your sales endeavors except those which the Company agrees to pay for in writing.

5. You agree to make no representations, warranties or commitments binding the Company without the Company's prior consent. You will execute no agreement on behalf of the Company nor shall you hold yourself out as having such authority. In addition, you warrant and represent to the Company that you are free to enter into this Agreement and that this does not violate any agreement heretofore made by you.

6. You agree that if you or your employees shall operate a motor vehicle during the term of this Agreement, the Company is not responsible for any damage or loss sustained by the use of said automobile during the term hereof. If you or your employees shall operate a motor vehicle in the performance of your duties hereunder, you will maintain public liability insurance in limits not less than $300,000/$500,000, and shall promptly furnish the Company with documentation evidencing same upon our request.

7. The Company has the sole right to establish, alter or amend product specifications, prices, delivery schedules and discounts, and the Company will give you timely notice of any and all changes.

8. In full payment for all services to be rendered by you, the Company shall pay you a commission of [specify percentage] of all orders shipped into your exclusive territory, with the following exception:

The Company shall pay a split commission for any accepted orders taken from a customer in your territory but shipped to an affiliate, subsidiary or designee of said customer in another sales representative's territory. In addition, you shall receive a split commission for any accepted orders taken from a customer in another sales representative's territory but shipped into your territory. The Company reserves the right to allocate or split the [specify percentage] commission in a manner it deems most reasonable to best reward the sales representative who had greatest influence on the sale.

9. All orders are subject to acceptance by the Company at our home office and the Company may reject an order at any time for any reason.

10. The Company shall furnish you with copies of all invoices for shipments of our product into your territory and shall keep an accurate set of books and records regarding commissions due. Exceptions to this policy are split commissions whereby only the representative servicing the ''Bill to'' address will receive invoice copies. Commission statements and payments shall be sent to your offices at [specify City and State] no later than the Twentieth (20th) day of the month following the month the goods are shipped. Commission statements presented to you shall be deemed correct unless objections in writing are received by the Company within Thirty (30) days from the issuance of same.

11. You agree to assist the Company in all collection efforts from non-paying customers in your territory upon our request. Notwithstanding the foregoing, the Company shall deduct commission on credits, returns, and bad debts from your commission statement as they become due. For the purposes of this Agreement, bad debts are defined as uncollectable invoices exceeding 120 days.

12. You covenant and agree that during the term of this Agreement, you shall not sell, promote or offer for sale, directly or indirectly, any product which might in any way be deemed competitive to our [specify] line and that you presently carry no line which is competitive with said product. Notwithstanding the foregoing, you agree to notify the Company in writing of all future products with the name of the manufacturer you intend to carry, competing, or otherwise, before your representation of same. This covenant shall become a material part of this Agreement.

13. The Company hereby employs you at will and this Agreement may be terminated by either party at any time for any reason. Said termination will be effective after either party sends to the other, by Certified Mail, Return Receipt Requested, a written notice of intent to terminate at the expiration of Thirty (30) days from the date upon which such notice is mailed to the other. Such termination will then occur at the end of the Thirty (30) day notice period. Notwithstanding the foregoing, the Company shall be able to terminate this Agreement immediately, without the sending of the aforesaid written Thirty (30) day notice, upon your death, bankruptcy, or in the event you breach any of the material terms of this Agreement.

14. In the event you send the Company written notice of your intent to terminate this Agreement pursuant to Paragraph 13, you shall continue to solicit orders for the Company during the aforesaid Thirty (30) day period. Notwithstanding the foregoing, if the Company sends you written notice of its intent to terminate this Agreement pursuant to Paragraph 13, you shall cease soliciting orders for the Company immediately on the day said notice of termination is received by you.

15. At the termination of this Agreement, a final accounting will be made between the Parties. In the event you send the Company notice of your intent to terminate this Agreement pursuant to Paragraph 13, you will receive full commission on all accepted orders shipped within your territory during the Thirty (30) day notice period prior to the effective termination date of this Agreement.

16. Notwithstanding the provisions contained in Paragraph 15, if the Company sends you written notice of its intent to terminate this Agreement pursuant to Paragraph 13, and you are not terminated for cause, the Company will pay you severance compensation as additional consideration for entering into this Agreement. The amount of severance to be paid shall be computed by calculating the average monthly commission earned by you during the preceding full year, multiplied by the following formula:

Years Representing Company	**Amount of Severance Compensation**
0 through 5 years	1 month
6 through 10 years	2 months
11 through 15 years	3 months
16 through 20 years	4 months
21 through 25 years	5 months
more than 25 years	6 months

The following example will illustrate the aforesaid: A representative is notified of termination by the Company on October 1, 1993, and the termination is without cause. The representative was employed by the Company for Four (4) years and earned $48,000 in commissions during 1992, or an average of $4,000 per month. Therefore, upon termination, the representative would receive full commission on all orders shipped into his territory during October 1993, and severance compensation of $4,000 upon termination of this Agreement.

17. The aforesaid severance compensation shall be paid in equal monthly installments with the first payment due commencing the effective termination date of this Agreement, provided you have complied with all terms and conditions of this Agreement. Said severance compensation shall represent full and final payment of all services rendered by you and benefits received by the Company from your efforts, and you shall have no claims for re-orders, territorial rights, or otherwise.

18. At the termination of this Agreement, you shall cease using any sales materials and product samples in your possession or under your control and shall return same, including all catalogs, brochures, advertising, literature and other property of the Company, immediately upon our request. Final severance compensation due, if any, shall not be paid until such property is received by us and has been returned in reasonably good condition, together with a duly executed general release.

19. Both parties acknowledge that the Company is entering into this Agreement due to the special, unique and extraordinary skills of [Name of Employee]. Accordingly, this Agreement may not be transferred, sold or assigned to any other individual, corporation, partnership or joint venture without the Company's prior approval. Notwithstanding the foregoing, the Company shall be notified in writing of your intention to cease selling the Company's product, an intention to liquidate your business, sell its assets, or sell or transfer more than 50% of the capital stock of the business, no less than Five (5) business days prior to the occurrence of same. In no event will the Company be bound to continue this Agreement under the same terms and conditions to your transferee, successor or majority stockholder, or in the event that [specify] is no longer personally and actively involved in selling the Company's products.

20. You shall notify the Company of all employees you intend to hire who shall assist you in representing the Company's products no less than Five (5) working days prior to their representation of same.

21. You hereby covenant, warrant and represent that both you and your employees will keep confidential, both during the term of this Agreement and forever after its termination, all information obtained from the Company with respect to all trade secrets, proprietary matters, business procedures, customer lists, needs of customers, manufacturing processes and all matters which are competitive and confidential in nature, and will not disclose this information to any person, firm, corporation or other entity for any purpose or reason whatsoever. The Company shall be entitled to an injunction restraining you from disclosing this information in the event of a breach or threatened breach of the provisions of this paragraph.

22. You agree that while this Agreement is in effect and for a period equal to the length of time you continue to receive severance compensation as more fully defined in Paragraph 17, that you and your employees shall not, directly or indirectly, for yourself or any other individual, partnership, corporation, or entity, solicit, represent, act on behalf of, sell or provide solicitation to any individual, partnership, corporation or entity competing against the Company. The Company agrees to pay, and you agree to receive the aforementioned severance compensation, as fair and reasonable consideration and an adequate bargained-for exchange so that a court of competent jurisdiction will enforce the provisions of this restrictive covenant as aforesaid.

23. Any claim or controversy arising among or between the parties hereto and any claim or controversy arising out of or respecting any matter contained in this Agreement or any difference as to the interpretation of any of the provisions of this

Agreement shall be settled by arbitration in [specify City and State] by Three (3) arbitrators under the then prevailing rules of the American Arbitration Association.

24. In any arbitration involving this Agreement, the arbitrators shall not make any award which will alter, change, cancel or rescind any provision of the Agreement and their award shall be consistent with the provisions of this Agreement. Any such arbitration must be commenced no later than One (1) year from the date such claim or controversy arose. The award of the arbitrators shall be final and binding and judgement may be entered in any court of competent jurisdiction. In addition to the foregoing, the Company may apply to any court of appropriate jurisdiction for any of the provisional remedies it may be entitled to, including but not limited to injunction, attachment or replevin, pending the determination of any claim or controversy pursuant to the arbitration provisions of this Agreement.

25. Service of process and notice of arbitration of any and all documents and papers may be made either by Certified or Registered mail, addressed to either party at the addresses listed in the Agreement.

26. The Agreement is being made by each of the parties after each party has had an opportunity to fully review, analyze, and obtain legal counsel with respect to this Agreement and all of its terms.

27. Nothing in this Agreement shall be construed to constitute you as a partner, affiliate or employee of the Company.

28. This Agreement forms the entire understanding between the parties. It cancels and supersedes all prior agreements and understandings.

29. There shall be no change, amendment or modification of any of the terms of this Agreement unless it is reduced to writing and signed by both parties.

30. If any provision of this Agreement is held by a court of competent jurisdiction or arbitration to be unenforceable, the remainder of the Agreement shall remain in full force and effect and shall in no way be impaired.

31. This Agreement shall be governed by the laws of the State of [specify].

Your signature in the lower left-hand corner of the copy hereof will indicate the acceptance of the terms and conditions herein stated, and thereafter this letter shall constitute our whole and complete agreement concerning your engagement which may not be orally modified or extended.

Very truly yours,

[NAME OF COMPANY]

(''The Company'')

____

By: [Name OF OFFICER]

[TITLE]

Consented and Agreed to:

By: [NAME OF REP OR REP FIRM]

Signature:______________________

[DATE]

APPENDIX N

SAMPLE PERFORMANCE APPRAISAL

NAME_______________________ DEPARTMENT ______________

POSITION __________________ TIME IN POSITION ___________

REVIEW PERIOD COVERED ________________________________

STEP 1—RATING OF JOB DUTIES AND RESPONSIBILITIES

List significant duties, responsibilities, and requirements of the job. Rate employee's ability to perform these duties.

A—Technical Knowledge

B—Analytical Ability and Judgment

C—Attitude and Personal Characteristics

D—Other

E—Overall Rating and Reasons Why

Poor

Satisfactory

Good

Outstanding

STEP 2—PERFORMANCE EVALUATION

A—Identify employee's strengths and weaknesses: ______________________

____

____

____

____

B—Set goals to further utilize the employee's strengths and develop plans for improving deficiencies	Timetable

Other comments by evaluator: ______________________

____

____

____

____

Comments of staff member being evaluated: ______________________

____

____

____

____

Signatures:

Evaluated Staff Member: ______________________ Date: ____________

Evaluator: ______________________ Date: ____________

APPENDIX O

SAMPLE STATEMENT OF COMPANY POLICY

NEED FOR POLICY

[Name of Company] maintains certain policies to guide its employees with respect to standards of conduct expected in areas where improper activities could damage the Company's reputation and otherwise result in serious adverse consequences to the Company and to employees involved. The purpose of this Policy is to affirm, in a comprehensive statement, required standards of conduct and practices with respect to certain types of payments and political contributions.

An employee's actions under this Policy are significant indications of the individual's judgement and competence. Accordingly, those actions constitute an important element in the evaluation of the employee for position assignments and promotion. Correspondingly, insensitivity to or disregard of the principles of this Policy will be grounds for appropriate management disciplinary action.

STATEMENT OF POLICY

Prohibition of Improper Payments

The Company expects all employees to use only legitimate practices in commercial operations and in promoting the Company position on issues before governmental authorities. As stated below, "kickbacks" or "bribes" intended to induce or reward favorable buying decisions and governmental actions are unacceptable and prohibited.

No employee of the Company or any Controlled Affiliate acting on the Company's behalf shall, in violation of any applicable law, offer or make directly or indirectly through any other person or firm, any payment of anything of value (in the form of compensation, gift, contribution or otherwise) to:

- any person or firm employed by or acting for or on behalf of any customer, whether private or governmental, for the purpose of inducing or rewarding any favorable action by the customer in any commercial transaction; or any governmental entity, for the purpose of inducing or rewarding action (or withholding of action) by a governmental entity in any governmental matter;
- any governmental official, political party or official of such party, or any candidate for political office, for the purpose of inducing or rewarding favorable action (or withholding of action) or the exercise of influence by such official, party or candidate in any commercial transaction or in any governmental matter.

In utilizing consultants, agents, sales representatives or others, the Company will employ only reputable, qualified individuals or firms under compensation arrangements which are reasonable in relation to the services performed. The International Franchising Operation will issue from time to time criteria and procedures to be utilized in international transactions with respect to the selection and compensation of sales representatives. Consultants, agents or representatives retained in relation to the provision of goods or services to the federal government must agree to comply with all laws, regulations and Company policies governing employee conduct.

The provisions of this section are not intended to apply to ordinary and reasonable business entertainment or gifts not of substantial value, customary in local business relationships and not violative of law as applied in that environment. In some countries (but not in all countries--and particularly not in the United States), it may be acceptable to make such insubstantial gifts to minor government officials where customary in order to expedite or secure routine administrative action required in the orderly conduct of operations. Managers are expected to exercise sound discretion and control in authorizing such business entertainment and gifts.

When customer organizations, governmental agencies, or others have published policies intended to provide guidance with respect to acceptance of entertainment, gifts, or other business courtesies by their employees, such policies shall be respected.

Political Contributions

The Company will not make any contribution to any political party or to any candidate for political office in support of such candidacy except as provided in this Policy and as permitted by law.

In the United States, federal law strictly controls corporate involvement in the federal political process. Generally, federal law provides that no corporation may contribute anything of value to any political party or candidate in connection with any federal election.

While similar laws apply in some states and their political subdivisions, in many jurisdictions in the United States corporate contributions to candidates and political parties in connection with state and local election campaigns are lawful.

The laws governing participation by corporations in the political process of countries other than the United States vary widely. In certain countries, contributions to the political process (including contributions to political parties) are lawful and expected as a matter of good corporate citizenship.

In foreign jurisdictions and in state and local jurisdictions of the United States where corporate political contributions are lawful, contributions by the Company or by a Controlled Affiliate may be appropriate if prudent in amount and otherwise consistent with good judgment. Company contributions shall be governed by written guidelines. Contributions by a Controlled Affiliate shall also be governed by written guidelines or other form of written authority as established by the affiliate's Board of Directors. Any contribution by the Company or by a Controlled Affiliate shall comply in all respects with the provisions of local applicable law and shall be reported as part of the annual review process provided by this Policy.

This Policy is not intended to prevent the communication of Company views to legislators, governmental agencies, or to the general public with respect to existing or proposed legislation or governmental policies or practices affecting business operations. Moreover, under this Policy, reasonable costs incurred by the Company to establish or administer political action committees or activities organized to solicit voluntary political contributions from individual employees are not regarded as contributions to political parties or candidates, where such costs may lawfully be incurred by the Company.

Reports and Periodic Reviews

Any employee who is requested to make, authorize, or agree to any offer or payment which is, or may be, contrary to this Policy will promptly report such information to the employee's manager, to assigned Company legal counsel, or to the manager in the component having responsibility for financial activity.

Any employee who acquires information (for example, newspaper reports, reports from customers, or statements of individuals involved) that gives the employee reason to believe that any employee is engaged in conduct forbidden by this Policy, or that any sales representative, distributor, or other person or firm representing the Company in any transaction is engaged in the type of conduct (whether or not in connection with a transaction involving the Company or its products) which, if engaged in by an employee of the Company, would violate this Policy, will promptly report such information to the employee's manager, to assigned company legal counsel, or to the manager in the component having responsibility for financial activity.

Any manager receiving a report as cited above will promptly consult with assigned Company legal counsel and thereafter will, after appropriate investigation, take timely remedial or other action as warranted under the provisions of this Policy. Such manager will also promptly report the matter to higher management.

COMPLIANCE WITH THE ANTITRUST LAWS

NEED FOR POLICY

For many years [Name of company] has recognized a need to single out compliance with the antitrust laws of the United States and other countries as a subject requiring a specific Company policy. The antitrust laws are relevant to many business decisions, and the consequences of violations anywhere can be seriously injurious to the Company and to the individuals involved.

Several provisions of the antitrust laws of the United States contain penal provisions under which employees who authorize or engage in acts in violation of such laws are personally subject to substantial fines and imprisonment. There are also in existence a number of antitrust decrees affecting the Company and its employees. Violation of any one of the provisions of these decrees is an offense which may subject the Company and the individuals involved to severe penalties.

Each manager must accept the challenge to have the Company excel competitively at the point of market confrontation; for, apart from legal penalties, Company growth and profitability objectives would be frustrated by arrangements with other business firms which restrict its competitive initiative.

Officers, managers and other key employees are expected to develop in employees a sense of commitment to comply with this policy. The antitrust compliance environment within such a key employee's assigned area of responsibility will be a significant factor in evaluating the quality of that individual's performance.

STATEMENT OF POLICY

General

It is the objective of the Company:

- to comply with the antitrust laws of the United States and other countries applicable to its business operations, and
- to hold employees in management positions personally and strictly accountable for taking the measures necessary to achieve this objective within their areas of responsibility.

Compliance With Section 1 Of the Sherman Act

In furtherance of this Policy and specifically in furtherance of compliance with Section 1 of the Sherman Act:

A. No employee shall enter into any understanding or agreement--whether expressed or implied, formal or informal, written or oral--with a competitor limiting or restricting any of the following aspects of the competitive strategy of either party or of the business offering of either party to any third party or parties:

prices
costs
profits
product or service offerings
terms or conditions of sale
production or sales volume
production facilities or capacity
market share
decisions to quote or not to quote
customer or supplier classification or selection
sales territories
distribution methods

B. No employee shall enter into any understanding or agreement with a purchaser or lessee of a product sold or leased by the Company which restricts the right of the purchaser or lessee to determine the price at which to resell or lease such product; nor shall any employee enter into such an agreement when the Company is the purchaser or lessee of a product.

C. The following understandings may be violative of the antitrust laws under certain circumstances and may be entered into by an employee of the Company only if the agreement has been reviewed by Company legal counsel in advance of execution and in the opinion of counsel is not in violation of law:

(1) Understandings with any customer or supplier which condition the sales or purchases of The Company on reciprocal purchases or sales by the customer/supplier;

(2) Understandings with any purchaser or lessee of a product of the Company which in any way restrict the discretion of the customer to use or resell the product as the customer sees fit;

(3) Understandings with anyone which restrict the discretion of either party to manufacture any product or provide any service, or to sell to, or buy from, any third party.

Discussions And Exchange Of Information With Competitors

Communication with a competitor on subjects as to which an understanding with the competitor would be illegal is, in antitrust litigation, likely to serve as important evidence of the existence of an understanding, particularly if the communication is accompanied or followed by similarity of action. The prohibitions set forth below are thus intended to avoid antitrust prosecutions which, though based on merely circumstantial evidence, may nevertheless be difficult to defend successfully.

Accordingly, no employee shall discuss with a competitor or any third party acting for a competitor, or otherwise furnish to or accept from a competitor or any third party acting for a competitor, information on any subject as to which an understanding with the competitor is prohibited by paragraph A. above on compliance with Section 1 of the Sherman Act unless, in the opinion of Company legal counsel, such discussions or transmittal of information would neither violate the antitrust laws nor furnish a reasonable basis for inferring such a violation.* This paragraph does not preclude obtaining competitive information from independent third-party sources who are not acting for a competitor in transmitting the information. However, certain other legal and policy restrictions applicable to transactions with the federal government limit the competitive information that may be obtained from a third-party source.

Participation in Trade Associations and Other Meetings with Competitors

A. No employee shall attend or remain present:

(1) at any surreptitious meeting of competitors;

(2) at any meeting where there is a discussion by competitors of any subject which the Company's employee is precluded from discussing by the paragraph above on Discussions and Exchange of Information with Competitors; or

(3) at any informal meeting of competitor members of a trade association held for the purpose of discussing business matters without observing the formal procedural requirements established by such trade association for its business meetings.

B. Employees should also be aware that participation in standard development and product certification activities which impact competitors or suppliers may raise antitrust concerns. Before participating in committees or organizations which develop standards or certify products, employees should consult with Company legal counsel.

Violations of the Policy

A. Violations of the Policy are grounds for discharge or other disciplinary action, adapted to the circumstances of the particular violation and having as a primary objective furtherance of the Company's interest in preventing violations and making clear that violations are neither tolerated nor condoned.

B. Disciplinary action will be taken, not only against individuals who authorize or participate directly in a violation of the Policy, but also against:

(1) any employee who may have deliberately failed to report a violation of the Policy;

(2) any employee who may have deliberately withheld relevant and material information concerning a violation of this Policy; and

(3) the violator's managerial superiors, to the extent that the circumstances of the violation reflect inadequate leadership and lack of diligence.

C. Where an employee is accused of violating the antitrust laws, and the employee has relied in good faith on the advice of Company legal counsel after full disclosure of the material facts, no disciplinary action may be taken against the employee under this Policy; and the Company may, within the limits permitted by law, assist in the employee's defense.

RESPONSIBILITY AND AUTHORITY

Reports and Periodic Reviews

A. Any employee who is requested to engage in any activity which is or may be contrary to this Policy will promptly report such information to the manager whom the individual reports, or, if the employee was so directed by the manager, then to assigned Company legal counsel.

B. Any employee who acquires information that gives the employee reason to believe that any other employee is engaged in conduct forbidden by the Policy will promptly report such information to the manager to whom the employee reports or, if the manager is engaged in such conduct, then to the assigned Company legal counsel.

APPENDIX P

SAMPLE NOTICE OF TERMINATION

TO: [Name of Terminated Employee]

SUBJECT: Separation Arrangements

In connection with your separation, your attention is called to the following matters:

1. Your coverage under ____________ will be continued for [specify] days from date of termination. Under federal law (COBRA), you may be covered under this policy for up to 18 months by paying the Company the premium amount specified below within 30 days of termination and by subsequently continuing to pay the premium in a timely fashion. Failure to pay the premium within any 30-day period will result in discontinuance of the insurance.

Your GROUP PREMIUM RATE is:____________________

Your HEALTH PLAN NUMBER is:____________________

Use this number in all correspondence concerning your benefits.

2. Your GROUP LIFE INSURANCE policy terminates on the last day of your employment, but it can be converted without a physical examination and at a higher individual rate within 30 days of termination. If you wish to convert, contact the [specify insurance company] within the next 30 days.

3. Your WEEKLY SICKNESS and ACCIDENT DISABILITY INSURANCE terminates on the last day of employment and is not convertible to an individual policy.

4. (IF APPLICABLE.) When the next PROFIT SHARING DIVIDEND is determined, a check for you proportionate share of the dividend will be mailed to you within 60 days thereafter.

OR

5. (IF APPLICABLE.) Since you have not satisfied the vesting requirements under our PENSION PLAN, you do not have any vested rights in the plan.

If you have any questions about these matters, please call.

____

Personnel Director

APPENDIX Q

PERSONNEL ACTION FORM

PERSONNEL ACTION FORM

EMPLOYEE ____
first name last name

INSTRUCTIONS

Check the appropriate box and fill in the information in the blanks below. Employee signs only if he/she initiates action or payroll deduction is required. Supervisor signs in all cases.

- ❑ Payroll Increase
- ❑ Payroll Decrease
- ❑ Transfer
- ❑ Payroll Deduction
- ❑ Promotion
- ❑ Leave of Absence
- ❑ Separation
- ❑ Change of address
- ❑ Change in dependents
- ❑ Classification change

CHANGE IN PAY OR CLASSIFICATION

From **To**

Pay ____________________per_______ ____________________per___

Classification ______________________ __________________________

TO BE EFFECTIVE _________

SEPARATION

- ❑ Laid off for lack of work
- ❑ Left work voluntarily
- ❑ Discharged for repeated willful misconduct
- ❑ Discharged for felonious conduct
- ❑ Other reason

Remarks (Final pay check, date, amount, etc.)

____

Eligible for rehire? ❑ Yes ❑ No

Other (changes, deductions, etc.)

____

____

____

______________________________ ______________________________
Employee Signature Supervisor Signature

______________________________ ______________________________
Date Date

APPENDIX R

SAMPLE JOB ELIMINATION NOTIFICATION

DATE: [specify]

TO: [Name of Terminated Employee]

As you know, our business is a dynamic one and change is inevitable. Reorganizations, productivity initiatives, market demands, profitability issues—any one of these situations may require organization redesign and reallocation of resources. As a business, we've had to make a very difficult but necessary decision to realign our business for improved workflow efficiencies and focus on our customers.

This decision requires us to eliminate your position located at [specify Company address]. As a consequence, unfortunately, you will be involuntarily terminated on [specify date] if you are unable to secure a position within the Company by that date. You will receive your last paycheck on [specify date] for all hours worked up to that date. Special severance related benefits will commence after [specify date].

Information regarding your eligibility for post-employment payments and benefits are in your Package enclosed. In addition to the post-employment payments and health benefits under the Plan, you are entitled to continuation of health coverage under the Consolidated Omnibus Budget Reconciliation Act of 1986 (COBRA).

Attached to this letter you will find important documents. **Please read them carefully.**

I realize that this will be a difficult time for you; however, I urge you to direct your attention and energies to your future. We want to help you understand your special payment package, assist in positioning you to source new opportunities, and ensure as smooth a transition as possible.

In this regard, feel free to contact me at [specify] if you have any questions. I thank you for your contributions to our business in the past and wish you well in your future endeavors.

Sincerely,

Attachments

[NAME OF OFFICER]

SEPARATION AGREEMENT AND RELEASE

In consideration of the fact that I, [specify Name of Employee] (the ''Employee''), have voluntarily and of my own free will, elected to accept a bonus payment (''Release Bonus'') in the amount of [specify $], separation pay in the amount of [specify $], and that [specify Name of Company], or its subsidiaries and affiliates (hereinafter ''the Company'') has agreed to pay me the above amounts, I acknowledge and agree to the following:

1. I understand that as of [specify date] my employment with the Company will cease.

2. I have been advised by the Company that I am being separated from the payroll pursuant to the terms of the Company's Reduction-in-Force Management Plan and that I am entitled to a severance payment in accordance with the following schedule:

Net Credited Service In Years	**Length of Severance Pay Period in Months**
Less than 2	1
2 but less than 4	1.5
4 but less than 6	2
6 but less than 8	2.5
8 but less than 10	3
10 but less than 12	4
12 but less than 14	5
14 but less than 16	6
16 but less than 18	7
18 but less than 20	8
20 and over	9

The Release Bonus is 33 1/3% of the Severance Pay.

3. I understand that the Release Bonus is being paid as consideration for my signing this Separation Agreement and Release and that these are benefits to which I would not have been entitled had I not signed this Separation Agreement and Release.

4. I also understand that, pursuant to the Older Workers Benefit Protection Act of 1990, I have the right to consult with an attorney before signing this Separation Agreement and Release, I have 45 days to consider the Release before signing it, and I may revoke the Release within 7 calendar days after signing it.

5. I realize that there are various State and Federal laws that govern my employment relationship with the Company and/or prohibit employment discrimination on the basis of age, color, race, gender, sexual preference/orientation, marital status, national origin, mental or physical disability, religious affiliation or veteran status and that these laws are enforced through the courts and agencies such as the Equal Employment Opportunity Commission, Department of Labor and State Human Rights Agencies. Such laws include, but are not limited to, Title VII of the Civil Rights Act of 1964, the Age Discrimination in Employment Act of 1967, as amended, the Employee Retirement Income Security Act, 29 U.S.C. 1001, et seq., 42 U.S.C. Section 1981, etc. In consideration of the Release Bonus provided for in this Agreement, I intend to give up any rights I may have under these or any other laws with respect to my employment and termination of employment at the Company and acknowledge that the Company has not discriminated against me, breached any express or implied contract with me, or otherwise acted unlawfully toward me.

6. Subject to paragraph 7 herein, on behalf of myself, my heirs, executors, administrators, successors and assigns, I release and discharge the Company, its successors, assigns, subsidiaries, affiliates, directors, officers, representatives, agents and employees (''Releasees'') from any and all claims, including claims for attorney's fees and costs, charges, actions and causes of action with respect to, or arising out of, my employment or termination of employment with the Company. This includes, but is not limited to, claims arising under federal, state, or local laws prohibiting age, color, race, gender, sexual preference/orientation, marital status, national origin, mental or physical disability, religious affiliation or veteran status or any other forms of discrimination or claims growing out of the Company's termination of its employees. With respect to any charges that have been or may be filed concerning events or actions relating to my

employment or the termination of my employment and which occurred on or before the date of this Agreement, I additionally waive and release any right I may have to recover in any lawsuit or proceeding brought by me, an administrative agency, or any other person on my behalf or which includes me in any class. If I breach this paragraph, I understand that I will be liable for all expenses, including costs and reasonable attorney's fees, incurred by any Releasee in defending the lawsuit or charge of discrimination, regardless of the outcome. I agree to pay such expenses within Thirty (30) calendar days of written demand. This paragraph is not intended to limit me from instituting legal action for the sole purpose of enforcing this Agreement.

7. I understand that this Separation Agreement and Release in no way affects any rights I may have for benefits under the Company's Pension Plan or any other applicable benefit plan.

8. In accordance with my existing and continuing obligations to the Company, I have returned or will immediately return to the Company, on or before my termination date, all Company property, including, but not limited to, files, records, computer access codes, computer programs, instruction manuals, business plans, and other property which I prepared or helped to prepare in connection with my employment with the Company.

9. I affirm my obligation to keep all proprietary Company information confidential and not to disclose it to any third party in the future. I understand that the term ''proprietary Company information'' includes, but is not necessarily limited to, technical, marketing, business, financial or other information which constitutes trade secret information or information not available to competitors of the Company, the use or disclosure of which might reasonably be construed to be contrary to the interest of the Company or its subsidiaries or affiliates.

10. The construction, interpretation and performance of this Agreement shall be governed by the laws of the state in which I am working on the date of my separation from the Company's payroll.

11. In the event that any one or more of the provisions contained in this Agreement shall for any reason be held to be unenforceable in any respect under the law of any state or of the United States of America, such unenforceability shall not affect any other provisions of this Release, but, with respect only to that jurisdiction holding the provision to be unenforceable, this Release shall then be construed as if such unenforceable provision or provisions had never been contained herein.

12. This Separation Agreement and General Release contains the entire agreement between the Company and me and fully supersedes any and all prior agreements or understandings pertaining to the subject matter hereof. I represent and acknowledge that in executing this Separation Agreement and Release I have not relied upon any representation or statement not set forth herein made by any of the Releasees or by any of the Releasee's agents, representatives or attorneys with regard to the subject matter of this Agreement.

BY SIGNING THIS SEPARATION AGREEMENT AND RELEASE, I STATE THAT: I HAVE READ IT; I UNDERSTAND IT AND KNOW THAT I AM GIVING UP IMPORTANT RIGHTS; I AGREE WITH EVERYTHING IN IT; I AM AWARE OF MY RIGHT TO CONSULT AN ATTORNEY BEFORE SIGNING IT; AND I HAVE SIGNED IT KNOWINGLY AND VOLUNTARILY.

DATE:

____
EMPLOYEE SIGNATURE

____
[EMPLOYEE NAME PRINTED]

PRELIMINARY PAYMENT CALCULATION SHEET

[DATE]

NAME:
SOCIAL SECURITY #:
SALARY BAND:

HIRE DATE:
YEARS OF SERVICE:

NOTIFICATION DATE:
OFF-PAYROLL-DATE:

BENEFITS COVERAGE THROUGH:

YOU MAY ELECT TO CONTINUE HEALTH INSURANCE COVERAGE FOR AN EXTENDED PERIOD UNDER C.O.B.R.A. FEDERAL BENEFITS CONTINUATION REGULATIONS. ENROLLMENT INFORMATION AND MATERIALS WILL BE MAILED TO YOUR HOME.

BASE SALARY:
INCENTIVE AMOUNT:

TOTAL:

WEEKLY RATE:

SEVERANCE:
POST-EMPLOYMENT PAYMENT:
POST-EMPLOYMENT SUPPLEMENT
(IF APPLICABLE):
TOTAL:

RELEASE BONUS (IF APPLICABLE)
(20% OF TOTAL SEVERANCE):

TOTAL OF SEVERANCE AND RELEASE:

*PAY FOR UNUSED VACATION DAYS,
PERSONAL DAYS, AND FLOATING
HOLIDAYS:
UNUSED DAYS:

GRAND TOTAL:

If you feel that any of the data on this sheet is inaccurate, please contact [specify Name] at [specify address and/or phone number].

APPENDIX S

SAMPLE LEAVE OF ABSENCE LETTER

[DATE]

Name of Employee

Address

Apt.

City, State, Zip

Dear [Name of Employee]:

[Name of Company] is pleased to offer you a Leave of Absence. This Leave is based on your years of service and overall contribution to the Company. Your Leave will commence on September 1, 1993 and end with your retirement on September 1, 1995.

During your Leave, you status with [Name of Company] (the ''Company'') will be that of an inactive employee on a Leave of Absence. The Company will pay your salary, on a semi-monthly basis based on your annual salary of [specify] per year. All salary paid to you by the Company during your Leave will be subject to applicable federal, state, city, and/or other local income taxes, social security deductions, and all other applicable withholdings and deductions. These taxes and deductions will be made whether your residence is in or out of New York State. During your Leave, the Company must comply with any changes in laws affecting the amount of involuntary deductions from your salary.

The Company will also provide you with the employment benefits you have selected under the Company's Benefits program with limitations as described in this letter. You will continue to be responsible for all premiums which will be deducted from salary payments made to you during your leave, and are subject to the same changes in premiums or in the benefits provided that affect active employees. In addition, while you are on Leave, you will not be eligible for any new benefits the Company will introduce.

The list of benefits available under the [specify] Benefit Program while on Leave are as follows:

* Medical and dental benefits

* Employee Life Insurance

* Dependent Life Insurance

[Specify Name of spending account]. If you are currently enrolled in [Name of spending account], you may file claims for expenses in incurred up to the end of the year in which your Leave ends. If claims are not submitted by January 31 of the year following the year in which claim was incurred, you will forfeit your [spending account] balance pursuant to the terms of the [spending account] plan.

During your Leave you may continue to make salary redirection deposits to your [spending account] on the same basis as you could as an active employee.

* On the effective date of your Leave, your benefit program will be changed as follows: You will no longer receive credits currently used to select and fund your benefits. You will receive a rate sheet describing the cost of each benefit. These rates are subsidized by the Bank to offset the credits you no longer will receive.

Your Savings Plan will continue with the following restrictions:

* You will retain your Savings Plan account during your Leave. However, no further allocations to your fund will be made during the Leave. While on Leave, you are eligible to transfer your funds from one investment fund to another and/or apply for a hardship withdrawal. These are the only two Savings Plan transactions you can make while on Leave. Final settlement of your Savings Plan account will be according to your election at the completion of your Leave.

* Any payment due from you with respect to loans from your Savings Plan account will continue to be due until the loan is repaid or the end of your Leave, whichever comes first. At the final distribution of your Savings Plan account, any unpaid balance must be settled before final payout is made.

Some of your current benefits will discontinue when you are transferred to the Leave, and are as follows:

* Long Term Disability
* Business Travel Accident Insurance
* Accidental Death and Dismemberment Insurance
* You will not accrue vacation during your Leave period. At the beginning of your Leave, you will be paid for any unused entitled vacation time for the year in which you start your Leave.

If you die while on Leave, all salary and benefits payable to you under this Leave agreement will cease, although if you are married or legally separated at the time of your death, your spouse will receive spouse's benefits to the same extent that your spouse would have received them if you had been an active employee, contingent upon your enrollment in and entitlement under the Company's various benefits plans.

Before your Leave begins, you may choose to continue any or all of your voluntary deductions, such as Employee Stock Purchase Plan, Holiday Club, IRA's, voluntary insurance programs, Payroll Savings, and Savings Bonds.

All of your personal bank accounts, such as [spending account] privilege checking, savings accounts, mortgage, Visa/Mastercard, installment loans, and safe deposit boxes will remain available to you during your Leave on the same terms on which they are presently available to you.

If you are an Officer, you will be required to resign your Corporate title at the start of your Leave. You may not, as an inactive employee, conduct Company business during your Leave, except that you agree to cooperate with requests for reasonable assistance to cover matters or events relating to your employment with the Company. If you choose to secure employment elsewhere during your Leave, you will not forfeit any of the benefits, including the salary payments.

Approximately three to six months prior to the end of your Special Leave, the Retirement Center will contact you to discuss the various options offered.

If you have any questions, please call me at [specify].

Sincerely,

[NAME AND TITLE]

RELEASE AND MEMORANDUM OF UNDERSTANDING CONCERNING LEAVE OF ABSENCE

In consideration of the benefits set forth in the attached letter from [specify] dated [specify] (hereinafter ''the attached letter''), I hereby acknowledge and agree to the following Release and Memorandum of Understanding (hereinafter ''Agreement'').

I have reviewed and voluntarily agree to accept the benefits, obligations, terms and conditions that have been offered to me by the Company as set forth in the attached letter.

I fully understand that, after the date of my execution of this Agreement, I may not change my decision or request from the Company re-instatement and/or re-employment or any other remuneration in any form.

In return for my entitlements under the Agreement, to which I acknowledge that, but for this Agreement, I would not be entitled to under any Company personnel policies or practices, I hereby RELEASE AND DISCHARGE the Company, its affiliated companies, and its and their officers, directors, and employees from any and all claims, obligations, or causes of action, whether or not now known to me, that I or anyone else acting on my behalf may have, based upon any conduct up to and including the date of this Agreement, except for the Company's obligations under this Agreement. I RELEASE AND DISCHARGE all such claims, obligations or causes of action including but not limited to:

* Those claims arising under any federal, state, or local human or civil rights law (including, but not limited to, Title VII of the Civil Rights Act of 1964, the Vocational Rehabilitation Act of 1973, the Age Discrimination in Employment Act of 1967, the Civil Rights Acts of 1866 and 1871 including Section 1981 of the Civil Rights Act), the New York Human Rights (Executive) Law, and the Administrative Code of the City of New York; and

* Those claims arising under any federal, state, or local wage-hour or wage-payment, pension or labor laws [including, but not limited to, the National Labor Relations Act, the Fair Labor Standards Act, and the Employment Retirement Income Security Act of 1974 (ERISA) (except that I do not release claims concerning payment of any and all vested, accrued benefits or

amounts, if any due me under the terms of the Company Retirement and/or Savings Plans)]; and

* Those claims arising under any rule, regulation, constitution or ordinance and/or public policy, contract or tort law, or any claim or retaliation under any of the above referenced laws, or any claim of breach of any contract (whether express, oral, written or implied from any source), or any claim of intentional or negligent infliction of emotional distress, tortous interference with contractual relations, wrongful or abusive discharge, defamation, prima facie tort, fraud, negligence, loss of consortium, or any action similar thereto; and

* Any claim from attorney's fees pursuant to any of the above-referenced claims.

I further agree that I shall not seek or in any way obtain or accept any award, recovery, settlement or relief from any source or proceeding pursuant to such claims.

The parties agree that this Agreement does not constitute an admission of wrongdoing by either party.

Notwithstanding this release, the Company acknowledges that on the date applicable that my status as an active employee of the Company ceases, I will be fully vested in retirement benefits. This release will not, in any manner whatsoever, affect my entitlement to those benefits, except as may be provided in the attached letter.

I agree that I will not seek re-employment with the Company and waive any claim with respect to the Company's failure for refusal to hire or re-employ me at any time in the future.

I further agree that, except as may be required and not merely permitted by law, I will not hereafter publish, publicize or disseminate or cause to permit to be published, publicized or disseminated in any way the existence or terms of this Agreement.

This Agreement and the terms and conditions described in the attached letter, may not be amended except by written agreement signed by both parties, and must be construed in accordance with the laws of the State of [specify], and the parties will submit to the jurisdiction of the state and/or federal courts located within the State of [specify] for the resolution of any dispute which may arise hereunder.

The parties further agree that if any of the provisions, terms, clauses, or waivers or releases of claims contained in this Agreement are declared illegal, unenforceable, or ineffective in a legal forum of competent jurisdiction, such provisions, terms, clauses, waivers or releases of claims or rights shall be deemed severable, such that all other provisions, terms, clauses, and waivers and releases of claims and rights contained herein shall remain valid and binding upon both parties.

I have been given a full and fair opportunity to seek advice of an attorney in connection with my decision whether to accept the benefits that have been offered to me pursuant to the Leave of Absence Program and I have either consulted with an attorney or else consciously and freely decided not to consult an attorney before assenting to the Agreement, without duress, coercion or undue influence and with full and free understanding of its terms.

To signify their agreement to the terms of this Agreement, the parties hereto executed and notarized this document on the date set forth under their signatures which appear below.

The Company

By: ______________________

Sworn to this [specify] of [specify month, year]

____
Notary Public

By: ______________________
Employee's Signature

Sworn to this [specify] of [specify month, year]

____
Notary Public

APPENDIX T

CONFIDENTIAL SETTLEMENT AGREEMENT MUTUAL RELEASE AND COVENANT NOT TO SUE

This Confidential Settlement Agreement, Mutual Release and Covenant Not to Sue (''Agreement'') is entered into this [specify date] by and among [specify company] (''the Company''), on the one hand, and [specify company] (''Sales Rep'') on the other hand.

I. RECITALS

A. WHEREAS, on or about May 1, 1992, Sales Rep entered into a sales representative contract with [specify] (the ''Sales Representative Contract'');

B. WHEREAS, after the Sales Representative Contract was executed, the Company acquired certain of the assets of [specify];

C. WHEREAS, by letter dated June 14, 1993, the Company confirmed that the Sales Representative Contract had already been terminated and outlined a superseding commission and finder's fee schedule (the ''June 14, 1993 letter'');

D. WHEREAS, Sales Rep claims an entitlement to a commission or other monetary consideration in connection with an order placed by [specify], and the Company denies Sales Rep's entitlement to same;

E. WHEREAS, the parties desire to settle, pursuant to the terms and conditions set forth herein below, all claims between them in any way related to the Sales Representative Contract, the June 14, 1993 letter, the relationship between the parties, any claim to commissions, finder's fees or other monetary consideration and wish to terminate any relationship which may have existed.

II. AGREEMENT

NOW, THEREFORE, the parties mutually agree as follows:

1. Consideration. The Company shall:

A. Execute and deliver to counsel for Sales Rep a

check in the amount of Fifty Thousand ($50,000.00), made payable to the Law Offices of Steven Mitchell Sack, which sum is being paid collectively to Sales Rep and its counsel and which sum they are to divide between themselves as they see fit;

B. Execute and deliver to counsel for Sales Rep a signed original of this Agreement.

2. Consideration. Sales Rep shall:

A. Execute and deliver to counsel for the Company a signed original of this Agreement, thereby fully and forever releasing the Company on the terms described in this Agreement;

B. Accept the single sum of $7,500.00 as the sole monetary consideration for the execution of this Agreement and the release herein.

3. Mutual Release of Claims.

A. Conditioned upon receipt of the consideration set forth in Section 1 hereof, Sales Rep, on behalf of itself and on behalf of its affiliates, subsidiaries, officers, directors, employees, sales personnel, agents, attorneys, accountants, insurers, representatives, successors and assigns, hereby releases and forever discharges the Company and past and present affiliates, subsidiaries, officers, directors, partners, principals, employees, attorneys, insurers, agents, servants, successors, heirs and assigns (''the Released Parties''), from any and all claims, demands, obligations, losses, causes of action, costs, expenses, attorneys' fees and liabilities of any nature whatsoever, whether based on contract, tort, statutory or other legal or equitable theory of recovery, whether known or unknown, which Sales Rep has, had or claims to have against any or all of the Released Parties, including but not limited to any and all claims which relate to, arise from, or are in any manner connected to i) the Sales Representative Contract, ii) the June 14, 1993 Letter and/or iii) any claimed commissions, ''finder's fees'' or other monetary consideration, whether accrued or not.

B. Conditioned upon payment of the consideration set forth in Section 1 hereof, the Company, on behalf of itself and its past and present partners, principals, employees, agents, servants, attorneys, insurers, representatives, affiliates, successors, heirs and assigns, hereby releases and forever discharges Sales

Rep and its respective agents, attorneys, accountants, insurers, successors and assigns, from any and all claims, demands, obligations, losses, causes of action, costs, expenses, attorneys' fees and liabilities of any nature whatsoever, whether based on contract, tort, statutory or other legal or equitable theory of recovery, whether known or unknown, which the Company has, had, claims or could claim to have against Sales Rep, including but not limited to any and all claims which relate to, arise from, or are in any manner connected to A. the Sales Representative Contract, B. the June 14, 1991 Letter and/or C. any claimed commissions, ''finder's fees'' or other monetary consideration, whether accrued or not.

4. Termination of Agreements. The parties hereto agree and confirm that, except for this Settlement Agreement, any and all agreements, written or oral, including but not limited to the Sales Representative Agreement and/or the June 14, 1993 letter, have already been and are terminated and are of no further force and effect. All parties hereto agree that none of the terms, conditions or obligations, if any, have survived termination, and that this Agreement supersedes any of the terms of such agreements. All parties expressly release each other from any continuing rights, duties and/or obligations under any agreements, and Sales Rep shall make no further claim for any compensation even if such allegedly entitling sale was disclosed pursuant to the June 14, 1993 letter or otherwise falls within the terms of the agreements.

5. Waiver of California Civil Code §1542 and New York counterpart, if any. Each party knowingly and intentionally waives any protection afforded to them by California Civil Code §1542, which provides:

A general release does not extend to claims which the creditor does not know or suspect to exist in his favor at the time of executing the release, which if known by him must have materially affected his settlement with the debtor

Each party further waives any protection under any new York counterpart to California Civil Code §1542. Each party agrees that this Agreement is intended to cover all claims or possible claims arising out of or related to those matters referenced or impliedly covered in the general release referenced above, whether the same are known, unknown or hereafter discovered or ascertained, and the provisions of §1542 of the California Civil Code and the New York counterpart (if any) are hereby expressly waived. The parties hereto expressly acknowledge that they have been advised by their counsel of the contents and effect of such provisions, and with such knowledge they hereby expressly waive whatever benefits they may have pursuant to such provisions.

6. Covenants.

A. Sales Rep covenants and agrees that it will not, at any time hereafter, either directly or indirectly, initiate, assign, maintain or prosecute, or in any way knowingly aid or assist in the initiation, maintenance or prosecution of any claim, demand or cause of action at law or otherwise, against the Released Parties, or any of them, for damages, loss or injury of any kind arising from, related to, or in any way connected to any activity with respect to which a release has been given pursuant to Section 3 of this Agreement.

B. The terms of this Agreement, and the very existence of this Agreement itself, shall remain strictly confidential. Each signatory to this Agreement individually covenants not to disclose any of the terms of this Agreement, whether generally or specifically, to any third party, except as may be required by a party's accountants or insurers, or by order of a court of competent jurisdiction. Each signatory further covenants that he or it will be personally liable for any and all damages that may be caused to any other party by his unauthorized disclosure of any of the terms of this Agreement.

7. Agreement Not an Admission of Liability. The parties hereto agree and acknowledge that this Agreement is a compromise settlement of each party's disputed claims, and that the sums and covenants given in consideration of this Agreement, as well as the execution of this Agreement, shall not be construed to be an admission of liability on the part of any party with respect to the disputed matters set forth above.

8. Parties to Bear Own Costs and Attorneys' Fees. Each party to this Agreement will bear its own costs, expenses, claims to interest and attorneys' fees, whether taxable or otherwise, incurred in or arising out of, or in any way connected with the matters which are referenced or covered in the mutual releases referenced above or which were otherwise related to the subject of this Agreement.

9. Entire Agreement. This Agreement represents and contains the entire agreement and understanding among the parties hereto with respect to the subject matter of this Agreement, and supersedes any and all prior oral and written agreements and understandings. No representation, warranty, condition, understanding or agreement of any kind with respect to the subject matter shall be relied upon by the parties except those contained herein. This Agreement may not be amended or modified except by an agreement signed by the party against whom enforcement of any modification or amendment is sought.

10. Advice of Counsel. In entering into this Agreement, the parties each acknowledge and represent that they have sought and obtained the legal advice of their attorneys, who are the attorneys of their own choice. They further represent that the terms of this Agreement have been completely read by them, and that those terms are fully understood and voluntarily accepted by them.

11. Counterparts. This Agreement may be executed in any number of counterparts, each of which shall be deemed an original, and all of which together shall be deemed one and the same instrument.

12. Attorneys' Fees. In the event litigation is necessary to enforce a provision or provisions of this Agreement, all costs, expenses and attorneys' fees, whether taxable or not, shall be paid by the non-prevailing party or parties to the prevailing party or parties.

13. No Assignment. The parties each represent and warrant to one another that they have not sold, assigned, transferred, conveyed or otherwise disposed of any claim or demand covered by this Agreement.

14. Heirs, Successors and Assigns. This Agreement

shall be binding upon and inure to the benefit of the parties' respective legal heirs, successors and assigns.

15. Severability. Should any portion (word, clause, phrase, sentence, paragraph or section) of this Agreement be declared void or unenforceable, such portion shall be considered independent and severable from the remainder, the validity of which shall remain unaffected.

Dated:
[NAME OF SALES REP]
(''Sales Rep'')

____

By: [NAME AND TITLE]
Its: [specify]

Dated:
[NAME OF COMPANY]
(''The Company'')

____

By: [Name and Title]

APPROVED AS TO FORM AND CONTENT:

LAW OFFICES OF STEVEN MITCHELL SACK
Counsel to [specify]

____

By: Steven Mitchell Sack

[NAME OF LAW FIRM]

____

By: [COUNSELOR]

APPENDIX U

SAMPLE SEPARATION AGREEMENT AND RELEASE

[DATE]

Name of Employee

Street Address

City, State, Zip

Dear [Name of Employee]:

This letter confirms your termination as [specify title] of [Name of Company] (the ''Company'') effective [specify date].

Our understanding and agreement with respect to your separation is as follows:

1. Your total and final compensation from the Company shall be provided to you as follows:

A. You will receive a lump sum payment of [specify amount] (less statutory deductions) in the form of a Company check to be sent to you Seven (7) days following the execution of this letter.

B. You will continue to be covered under the Company's group medical, dental, vision and life insurance programs until [specify date], which expense shall be covered by the Company and you at the same proportionate rates as are being paid on the date of separation. Thereafter, you may continue to be covered under the Company's group health insurance program, at your expense, for a period of 18 months (or such longer period as may be required by law) or until you become covered by any other group health plan, whichever occurs first. This continued coverage will be subject to and in accordance with the terms of the documents governing the program.

C. A check in the amount of [specify amount], representing all accrued but unused vacation (less statutory deductions), will be mailed to you on [specify day and date].

D. The Company agrees to provide you with a letter of reference attached hereto.

E. Other than as set forth herein, you will not receive any compensation or benefits of any kind from the Company and you expressly acknowledge and agree that you are not entitled to any such payment or benefit, with the exception of any vested benefit to which you have or will become entitled under the [specify company] Pension Plan.

2. You understand and agree that the compensation and benefits provided for herein are being provided to you in consideration for the covenants undertaken and the releases contained in this Agreement.

3. A. You agree to accept the compensation and benefits provided for herein in full resolution and satisfaction of, and hereby IRREVOCABLY AND UNCONDITIONALLY RELEASE, REMISE AND FOREVER DISCHARGE the Company from any and all liabilities, actions, causes of action, contracts, agreements, promises, claims and demands of any kind whatsoever, in law or equity, whether known or unknown, suspected or unsuspected, fixed or contingent, apparent or concealed, which you, your heirs, executors, administrators, successors or assigns ever had, now have or hereafter can, shall or may have for, upon, or by reason of any matter, cause or thing whatsoever, from the beginning of the world to the day of the date of this Agreement and Release, including, without limitation, any and all claims arising out of or relating to your employment, compensation and benefits with the Company and/or the termination thereof including, without limitation, contract claims, benefit claims, tort claims, harassment, defamation and other personal injury claims, fraud claims, whistleblower claims, unjust, wrongful or constructive dismissal claims and any claims under any municipal, state or federal wage payment, discrimination or fair employment practices law, statute or regulation, and claims for costs, expenses and attorneys' fees with respect thereto.

B. By signing this Agreement and Release and by acceptance of the compensation and benefits provided for herein, you hereby WAIVE, RELEASE AND COVENANT NOT TO SUE the Company with respect to any matter relating to or arising out of your employment, compensation and benefits with the Company and/or the termination thereof, and you agree that neither you nor any person organization or entity acting on your behalf will (i) file or participate or join in, encourage, assist, facilitate or permit the bringing or maintenance of any claim or cause of action against the Company, whether in the form of a federal, state or municipal court lawsuit or administrative agency action or otherwise, on the basis of any claim arising out of or relating to your employment, compensation, and benefits with the Company and/or the termination thereof or (ii) seek reinstatement, reemployment or any other relief from the Company, however that relief might be called, whether back pay, compensatory damages, punitive damages, claims for pain and suffering, claims for attorneys' fees, reimbursement of expenses or otherwise, on the basis of any such claim, except for claims for a breach of this Agreement and Release.

4. Nothing contained herein shall be deemed to constitute an admission or evidence of any wrongdoing or liability on the part of the Company.

5. Any breach of any provision of this Agreement and Release by you shall constitute a forfeiture of all compensation and benefits set forth herein and, if any such compensation and benefits have already been conveyed as of the time of your breach, you agree to return and/or repay the same to the Company.

6. You agree that you will not provide consulting advice or counsel to or otherwise cooperate with or assist employees, agents or independent contractors, or former employees, agents or independent contractors of the Company to pursue legal actions against the Company or its owners, stockholders, agents, directors, officers, employees, representatives, attorneys, divisions, parents, subsidiaries, trustees, predecessors, successors or assigns (together, ''the Releasees'') on or in connection with any matters relating to their employment or the termination thereof. You further agree that you will not participate, directly or indirectly, as a party, witness or otherwise, in any action at law, proceeding in equity, or in any administrative proceeding in which Releasees or Releasees' personnel are parties or attempt to offer into evidence against Releasees or Releasees' personnel any fact of or concerning any act or motion of Releasees or Releasees' personnel prior to the date of this

Agreement, unless compelled to do so by force of law.

7. Should you commence or prosecute any action or proceeding contrary to the provisions of this Agreement, you agree to indemnify Releasees and/or Releasees' affected personnel for all court costs and attorney's fees incurred by Releasees' personnel in the defense of such action or in establishing or maintaining the application or validity of this Agreement or provisions thereof.

8. You will not issue any communication, written or otherwise, that disparages, criticizes or otherwise reflects adversely or encourages any adverse action against the individuals or entities that are the Releasees except if testifying truthfully under oath pursuant to subpoena or otherwise.

9. You acknowledge that by reason of your position with the Company you have been given access to lists of subscribers, prices, plans, and similar confidential or proprietary materials or information respecting the Company's business affairs. You represent that you have held all such information confidential and will continue to do so, and that, unless you first secure the Company's written consent, you shall not directly or indirectly publish, market or otherwise disclose, advise, counsel or otherwise procure any other person or entity, directly or indirectly, to publish, disclose, market or use, any such secret, confidential or proprietary information or relationships of the Company (''Trade Secrets''), of which you became aware or informed during your employment with the Company, unless the Company shall have first given its express written consent to such publication, disclosure, marketing or use, except to the extent that such Trade Secrets a) were known to you at the time of their receipt, b) were in or have become part of the public domain (otherwise than through you), c) were known to the recipient prior to the disclosure, or d) are required to be disclosed by a court or governmental agency. Such Trade Secrets are and shall continue to be the exclusive proprietary property of the Company whether or not they were disclosed to or developed in whole or in part by you.

Such ''Trade Secrets'' include, without limitation, subscriber lists, marketing plans and programs, studies, and strategies of or about the Company or its business, customers or suppliers, which derives independent economic value, actual or potential, from not being generally known to, and not being readily ascertainable by proper means by, other persons who can obtain economic value from its disclosure.

10. You represent you have returned to the Company any and all files, calendars, distribution lists and any other information and records in your possession or under your control containing confidential or proprietary information concerning the Company or its operations. You also represent that you have no such information and records in your possession or under your control at this time. You further represent that you have returned all keys or other Company property in your possession.

11. It is expressly understood and agreed that this Agreement and Release shall act as a complete bar to any claim, demand or action of any kind whatsoever brought by you against the Company including, without limitation, any claim, demand or action under, or relating to your employment, compensation and benefits with the Company and/or the termination thereof, except for claims for breach of this Agreement and Release.

12. This Agreement and Release may not be changed orally, and no modification, amendment or waiver of any of the provisions contained in this Agreement and Release nor any future representation, promise or condition in connection with the subject matter of this Agreement and Release, shall be binding upon any party hereto unless made in writing and signed by such party.

13. This Agreement and Release shall be subject to, governed by and interpreted in accordance with the laws of the State of [specify].

14. This Agreement and Release and the terms hereof shall be kept confidential.

15. This Agreement and Release contains the entire agreement between the parties with respect to the subject matter hereof and supersedes and terminates any and all previous agreements of any kind whatsoever between the parties, whether written or oral, relating to your employment, compensation and benefits with the Company and/or the termination thereof. This is an integrated document.

16. The parties agree that this Agreement and Release may be specifically enforced in court and may be used as evidence in a subsequent proceeding in which any of the parties allege a breach of this Agreement and Release. In the event of litigation in connection with or concerning the subject matter of this Agreement and Release, the prevailing party shall recover all the party's costs, expenses and attorneys' fees incurred in each and every such action, suit or other proceeding, including any and all appeals or petitions therefrom.

17. In the event that any provision of this Agreement and Release should be held to be void, voidable, unlawful or, for any reason, unenforceable, the remaining portions hereof shall remain in full force and effect.

18. If this Agreement and Release is acceptable to you, please indicate your agreement by signing and dating the enclosed copy of this Agreement and Release in the space provided below and returning it to me on or before [specify date]. YOU WILL THEN BE PERMITTED TO REVOKE THIS AGREEMENT AND RELEASE AT ANY TIME DURING THE PERIOD OF SEVEN DAYS FOLLOWING THE EXECUTION HEREOF, AND THIS AGREEMENT AND RELEASE WILL NOT BE EFFECTIVE OR ENFORCEABLE AND NO PAYMENTS WILL BE MADE HEREUNDER UNTIL THE SEVEN-DAY REVOCATION PERIOD HAS EXPIRED. In the event you elect to revoke this Agreement and Release, this Agreement and Release will be of no further force or effect, and neither you nor the Company will have any further rights or obligations hereunder.

19. You shall have Seven (7) calendar days following the execution of this Agreement in which to revoke said Agreement. This Agreement may be revoked only in writing and only during the seven (7) day period stated in this paragraph. To be effective, written revocation must, within the Seven (7) day period, be hand-delivered or telecopied to [specify]. This Agreement shall not become effective or enforceable until the expiration of the revocation period.

20. THIS IS A LEGAL DOCUMENT. YOU SHOULD CONSULT WITH AN ATTORNEY PRIOR TO SIGNING THIS AGREEMENT AND RELEASE AND THE ATTACHMENTS HERETO. BY SIGNING THIS AGREEMENT AND RELEASE YOU ACKNOWLEDGE AND AFFIRM THAT YOU ARE COMPETENT, THAT YOU HAVE BEEN AFFORDED A TIME PERIOD OF 21 DAYS TO REVIEW AND CONSIDER THIS AGREEMENT AND RELEASE WITH AN ATTORNEY OF YOUR CHOICE, THAT SUCH TIME PERIOD IS A REASONABLE AND SUFFICIENT TIME FOR SUCH REVIEW, THAT YOU HAVE READ AND UNDERSTAND AND ACCEPT THIS DOCUMENT AS FULLY AND FINALLY WAIVING ANY AND ALL CLAIMS, DEMANDS AND DISPUTES AND DIFFERENCES OF ANY KIND WHATSOEVER WHICH YOU MAY HAVE AGAINST THE COMPANY (AS DEFINED IN PARAGRAPH 3 ABOVE), *INCLUDING ANY AND ALL CLAIMS UNDER THE AGE DISCRIMINATION AND EMPLOYMENT ACT,* THAT NO PROMISES OR INDUCEMENTS HAVE BEEN MADE TO YOU EXCEPT AS SET FORTH IN THIS AGREEMENT AND RELEASE, AND THAT YOU HAVE SIGNED THIS DOCUMENT FREELY AND VOLUNTARILY, INTENDING TO BE LEGALLY BOUND BY ITS TERMS.

[NAME OF EMPLOYER]

By: [NAME OF EMPLOYER]
[Title]

Accepted and Agreed:
[NAME OF EMPLOYEE]

On [specify date], before me personally came [Name of Employee], to me known and known to me to be the individual described in and who executed the foregoing Agreement and Release, and he duly acknowledged to me that he executed the same.

____
Notary Public

APPENDIX V

SAMPLE SEVERANCE LETTER AND RELEASE

[DATE]

Name Of Terminated Employee

Street Address

City/State/Zip

Dear [NAME OF TERMINATED EMPLOYEE]:

As you are aware, [specify company] (the ''Company'') has undergone a reduction in the working force that has resulted in the termination of your employment. In order to assist you in your transition, the Company is willing to provide you with a severance payment, which the Company is offering to make in its sole discretion. The severance payment will be provided subject to the terms contained in this letter. If you wish to receive the severance payment, please sign the last page of this letter and return the signed letter to the Company.

1. As a severance payment, the Company agrees to provide you with an amount equal to your regular base salary for a period of Three (3) months, less all applicable withholding taxes. Such amount shall be paid to you on a regular payroll basis at such times as payroll checks are normally issued, and will be forwarded to you by mail at your mailing address set forth above. You and your eligible dependents will also be extended an opportunity to purchase continued medical benefits in accordance with federal law. As part of the severance package offered to you in this Agreement, if you or your eligible dependents elect such continued coverage, the Company will pay the premiums for the first Three (3) months of coverage elected.

2. In consideration of the payment and premium benefits described in paragraph 1 above, you voluntarily, knowingly and willingly release and forever discharge the Company, its parents, subsidiaries and affiliates together with their respective officers, directors, partners, shareholders, employees and agents, from any and all charges, complaints, claims, promises, agreements, controversies, causes of action and demands of any nature whatsoever against them which you or your executors, administrators, successors or assigns ever had, now have or hereafter can, shall or may have by reason of any matter, cause or thing whatsoever arising to the time you sign this Agreement. You further agree that you will not seek or be entitled to any award of equitable or monetary relief in any proceeding of any nature whatsoever brought on your behalf arising out of any of the matters released by this paragraph 2. This release includes, but is not limited to, any rights or claims relating in any way to your employment relationship with the Company or the termination thereof, or under any statute, including the federal Age Discrimination in Employment Act, Title VII of the federal Civil Rights Act of 1964, or any other federal, state or local law.

3. You represent that you have returned or will immediately return to the Company all ''Company Information,'' including without limitation, mailing lists, reports, files, memoranda, records and software, credit cards, door and file keys, computer access codes or disks and instructional manuals, and other physical or personal property which you received or prepared or helped prepare in connection with your employment with the Company, and that you will not retain any copies, duplicates, reproductions or excerpts thereof. The term ''Company Information'' as used in this Agreement means A. confidential information of the Company, including without limitation, information received from third parties under confidential conditions; and B. other technical, business or financial information or trade secrets, the use of disclosure of which might reasonably be construed to be contrary to the interests of the Company or its affiliates.

4. We agreed that in the course of your employment with the Company you have acquired Company Information as defined in paragraph 3. You understand and agree that such Company Information has been disclosed to you in confidence and for the use of only the Company. You acknowledge that you have no ownership right or interest in any Company Information used or developed during the course of your employment. You understand and agree that (i) you will keep such Company Information confidential at all times after your employment with the Company, and (ii) you will not make use of Company Information on your own behalf, or on behalf of any third party. You agree that in the event of any actual or threatened breach by you of the provisions of paragraphs 3 and 4 hereof, the Company shall be entitled to an immediate injunction against such breach or threatened breach without the necessity of posting any bond or security. You further agree that the Company shall be entitled to terminate any further payments hereunder in the event of such breach or threatened breach, and that such termination shall not impair the validity of the remainder of this Agreement.

5. The Company's offer to you of this Agreement and the severance pay set forth herein is not intended to, and shall not be construed as, any admission of liability by the Company to you or of any improper conduct on the Company's part with respect to your employment, all of which the Company specifically denies.

6. The Company advises you to consult with an attorney of your choosing prior to signing this Agreement. You understand and agree that you have the right and have been given the opportunity to review this Agreement and, specifically, the release in paragraph 2, with an attorney of your choice should you so desire. You also understand and agree that the Company is under no obligation to offer you the severance payment and premium benefits set forth in paragraph 1 and that you are under no obligation to consent to the release set forth in paragraph 2 and that you have entered into this Agreement freely and voluntarily.

7. You have Forty Five (45) days to consider the terms of this Agreement, although you may sign and return it sooner if you wish. Furthermore, once you have signed this Agreement, you have Seven (7) additional days from the date you sign it to revoke your consent. This Agreement will not become effective until Seven (7) days after the date you have signed it. Once this Agreement becomes effective, we will commence making the payments set forth in paragraph 1. Annex A to this

Agreement contains information concerning the individuals eligible and not eligible for severance pay. You acknowledge that you have received and had an opportunity to review the information contained in Annex A prior to entering into this Agreement.

8. The terms described in this letter constitute the entire agreement between us and may not be altered or modified other than in a writing signed by you and the Company. This Agreement will be governed by the law of New York, without reference to its choice of law rules.

If the above sets forth our agreement as you understand it and consent to it, please so signify by signing this letter in the space provided below, and return it to the undersigned. The enclosed copy is for your records.

Very truly yours,

[NAME AND TITLE OF COMPANY REP]

Agreed to and Accepted

[NAME OF TERMINATED EMPLOYEE]

Dated: ____________, 1992

APPENDIX W

GENERAL RELEASE

FOR GOOD AND VALUABLE CONSIDERATION, the adequacy of which is hereby acknowledged, in the form of payment to [Name of Employee] of a severance benefit in the amount of [specify] salary less withholding for federal and state taxes, FICA and any other amounts required to be withheld, Employee agrees that he/she, or any person acting by, through or under Employee, RELEASES AND FOREVER DISCHARGES [Name of Employer], and its parent company and its subsidiaries, affiliates, predecessors, successors, and assigns, as well as the officers, employees, representatives, agents and fiduciaries, *de facto* or *de jure* (hereinafter collectively referred to as ''Released Parties''), and covenants and agrees not to institute any action or actions, causes or causes of action (in law unknown) in state or federal court, based upon or arising by reason of any damage, loss, or in any way related to Employee's employment with any of the Released Parties or the termination of said employment. The foregoing includes, but not by way of limitation, all claims which could have been raised under common law, including retaliatory discharge and breach of contract, or statute, including, without limitation, the Age Discrimination in Employment Act of 1967, 42 U.S.C. Sections 621-634, as amended by the Older Workers Benefit Protection Act of 1990, Title VII of the Civil Rights Act of 1964, 42 U.S.C. Sections 2000e *et. seq.* and the Employee Retirement Income Security Act of 1974, 29 U.S.C. Sections 1001 *et. seq.* or any other Federal or State Law; except that this General Release is not intended to cover any claim arising from computational or clerical errors in the calculation of the severance benefit provided to Employee, or retirement benefit to which Employee may be entitled from any plan or other benefits to which Employee may be entitled under any plan maintained by any of the Released Parties.

Employee covenants and agrees to forever refrain from instituting, pursuing, or in any way whatsoever aiding any claim, demand, action or cause of action or other matter released and discharged herein by Employee arising out of or in any way related to Employee's employment with any of the Released Parties and the rights to recovery for any damages or compensation awarded as a result of any lawsuit brought by any third party or governmental agency on Employee's behalf.

Employee further agrees to indemnify all Released Parties from any and all loss, liability, damages, claims, suits, judgments, attorneys' fees and other costs and expenses of whatsoever kind or individually, they may sustain or incur as a result of or in connection with the matters hereinabove released and discharged by Employee. Employee warrants that he/she has not filed any lawsuits, charges, complaints, petitions, or accusatory pleadings against any of the Released Parties with any governmental agency or in any court, based upon, arising out of or related in any way to any event or events occurring prior to the signing of this General Release, including, without limitation, his/her employment with any of the Released Parties or the termination thereof.

Employee acknowledges, understands and affirms that:

A. This General Release is a binding legal document;

B. (i) Released Parties advised him/her to consult with an attorney before signing this General Release, (ii) he/she had the right to consult with an attorney about and before signing this General Release, (iii) he/she was given a period of at least 21 calendar days in which to consider this General Release prior to signing, and (iv) he/she voluntarily signs and enters into this General Release without reservation after having given the matter full and careful consideration; and

C. (i) Employee has a period of seven days after signing this General Release in which he/she may revoke this General Release, (ii) this General Release does not become effective or enforceable and no payment shall be made hereunder until this seven-day-revocation period has elapsed, and (iii) any revocation must be in writing by Employee and delivered to the Vice-President, Human Resources within the seven-day-revocation period.

IN WITNESS WHEREOF, the Employee signs this General Release this [specify date].

[EMPLOYEE'S NAME]
(please print)

WITNESS:
[Name of Witness] Signature:______________________

[DATE]

TO: Severed Employee

FROM:

RE: Older Workers Benefit Protection Act

This communication apprises you of your rights under the Older Workers Benefit Protection Act (''OWBPA'') which amends the Age Discrimination in Employment Act (''ADEA''), that Congress recently passed. The OWBPA establishes certain standards as regards waivers that the employer obtains from its employees.

The OWBPA amends the ADEA by adding a new section which establishes standards for a ''knowing and voluntary'' waiver. The OWBPA sets forth seven basic requirements for a knowing and voluntary waiver:

(1) The 'waiver has to be part of an agreement between the employee and the employer and it has to be written in understandable English;

(2) The waiver must refer specifically to rights or claims arising under the ADEA;

(3) The waiver cannot cover rights or claims that may arise after the date on which it is signed;

(4) The waiver must be exchanged for consideration, and the consideration must be in addition to anything of value to which the employee is already entitled;

(5) The employee must be advised in writing to consult with an attorney before signing the agreement;

(6) The employee has to be given a period of at least (21) days to decide whether to sign the waiver; and

(7) The employee is entitled to revoke the waiver within seven days after signing it, and the waiver does not become effective or enforceable until the revocation period has expired.

APPENDIX X

GENERAL RELEASE

KNOW ALL MEN BY THESE PRESENTS THAT I, [Name of Employee], for and in consideration of the payment to me of [specify amount], do for myself, my heirs, executors, administrators, successors and assigns, in addition to all the promises made herein, hereby release and forever discharge [Name of Employer] and its parents, divisions, successors, predecessors, subsidiaries, affiliates, assigns, and the directors, officers, servants, agents and employees of each of them, and each of their heirs, executors and administrators, and all of them (hereinafter collectively ''Releasees'') from any and all actions and causes of action, claims and demands, suits, damages, costs, attorneys' fees, expenses, debts due, contracts, agreements, and claims for any compensation or benefits whatsoever, in law or in equity, which I or anyone claiming by, through or under me in any way might have or could have against Employer and Releases, including, but not *limited to,* any claims whatsoever which arose out of, or which could be claimed to have arisen out of, my employment with, or the separation of my employment from, Employer that I ever had or now have against Employer or Releasees from the beginning of the world to the date of this Release.

This Release includes, but is not limited to, claims under the Age Discrimination In Employment Act of 1967, as amended (''ADEA'').

I expressly acknowledge that I have read this Release and have had at least Twenty-one (21) days to discuss it with legal counsel of my choice before signing and that I realize and understand that it applies to and covers all claims, demands, and causes of action, including those under ADEA, against Employer or Releasees or any of them, whether or not I know or suspect them to exist at the present time. I further understand that this Release will not be accepted by Employer if I sign it prior to the expiration of 21 days from the date I received it.

I further acknowledge that this Release is not part of a program being offered to a group or class of employees and that my execution of this Release is made voluntarily without coercion in any way.

I understand that I shall have a period of Seven (7) days from the date I sign this Release to revoke it. If I decide to revoke this Release, the revocation must be in writing signed by me and received by Employer before the expiration of the Seventh (7th) calendar day following the date I sign this Release. Consequently, this Release shall have no force and effect until the expiration of Seven (7) calendar days following the day on which I sign it, and Employer shall likewise have no obligation hereunder until after that time.

I understand that nothing herein waives any rights or claims I may have arising under ADEA after the date on which I sign this Release.

I will not apply for or otherwise seek re-employment with Employer at any time.

I will keep the terms, amount and fact of this Release and the payment hereunder confidential and will not hereafter state the facts or terms of this Release to anyone (except my attorney and wife), including, but not limited to, any past, present or prospective employee or applicant for employment with Employer.

Nothing herein nor the payment hereunder shall be construed as an admission of any liability on the part of anyone for any matter, all liability being denied.

I have not relied on any representation, expressed or implied, made by Employer or any of its representatives.

This Release constitutes the entire understanding between myself and Employer and cannot be modified except in writing signed by both myself and [Employer].

I intend that this Release shall not be subject to any claim of fraud, duress, deception, or mistake of fact, and that it expresses a full and complete settlement of any claims whatsoever I ever had or may have against Employer or any Releasee.

I will not file any complaint, suit, claim or charge against Employee or any Releasee with any local, state or federal agency or court. If any agency or court assumes jurisdiction of any complaint, suit, claim or charge against Employer or any Releasee on my behalf, I will request such agency or court to dismiss the matter.

I understand this Release is contractual and based on my representation that I will comply with the terms set forth herein. Should I breach any of the terms of this Release, I shall repay to Employer all sums paid to me hereunder, plus reasonable attorneys' fees incurred in connection with the enforcement of the terms of this Release, in addition to any other damages caused by my breach of any of the terms of this Release. Nothing herein shall be construed to limit any other remedies Employer or Releasees may have under law or in equity.

I, intending to be legally bound, hereby apply my signature voluntarily with full understanding of the contents of this Release.

[WITNESS]

[DATE]

I, [Name of Attorney], am an attorney licensed to practice law in the State of [specify]. I represent [Name of Client], I have explained to him the consequences of signing this Release and he has indicated to me an understanding thereof and that he is signing this Release of his own free will.

APPENDIX Y

DISCHARGE CHECKLIST

Date____________

Name______________________

Dept.______________________

For Department Supervisor

Check return of relevant items below:

- ❑ SAFETY EQUIPMENT
- ❑ CREDIT CARDS
- ❑ MANUALS
- ❑ UNIFORM
- ❑ BADGE
- ❑ TOOLS
- ❑ KEYS
- ❑ OTHER______________________

____

Supervisor Date

For Accounting Department

Last work day ________________ Sick leave pay ____________

Vacation pay? ________________ Other ________________

Bonds, loans, savings, expense account balances ______________________

____

TOTAL FINAL CHECK: $ ______________________

(For Accounting Dept.) Date

For Personnel Department

PINK SLIP to read:

- ❑ Laid off for lack of work
- ❑ Discharged for repeated willful misconduct
- ❑ Left work voluntarily
- ❑ Discharged for felonious assault
- ❑ Other reason ______________________

TERMINATION LETTER to employee has been ❑ mailed ❑ delivered

EMPLOYEE ELIGIBLE FOR REHIRE? ❑ Yes ❑ No

____

Supervisor Date

APPENDIX Z

SALES REP PROTECTION STATUTES

STATE	TIME LIMIT	NON-COMPLIANCE PENALTY	WRITTEN CONTRACT	LEGAL REFERENCE
Alabama	Within 7 working days after termination if no written agreement	Triple damages plus reasonable attorney fees and costs	Required	Code of Alabama 1975, Vol. 6, §§8-24-1 through 8-24-5
Arizona	Within 30 days after termination of contract	Damages sustained by the sales representative plus cost of suit including reasonable attorney fees	Required	§1. Title 44, Chap. 11, Arizona Rev. Statutes, Art. 15, §§ 44-1798 through 44-1798.03
Arkansas	Within 30 working days after termination of contract	Liable in civil action for three times damages sustained by sales rep plus attorney fees and costs	Required	Arkansas Code, §§ 4-70-301 through 4-70-306
California	Within 72 hours after termination if no written agreement	Liable in civil action for triple damages	No	California Statutes 1937, c.90 p.197,§202;1963, c. 1088, p.2549, §§ 1,2
Florida	Within 14 days of termination	Commission amount plus exemplary damages up to twice commissions owed, plus reasonable attorney fees	Required	Official Florida Statues, §686.201
Georgia	Within 14 days after termination if no contract	Commission amount plus exemplary damages up to twice commissions owed, plus reasonable attorney fees	Required	Official Code of Georgia Annotated, Article 24, §§10-1-700 through 10-1-704
Iowa	Within 30 days after commission earned; upon termination, within 30 days	Commission plus liquidated damages (5% of commission due times number of days past due), including court costs and attorney fees	No	Code of Iowa, Vol. 1, 1989, Chap. 91A, §§91A.1 through 91A.13
Kansas	Within 30 days after commission earned	The commission amount	No	Kansas Statutes Annotated, 1987 Cumulative Supplement, Chap. 44, Art. 3, §§44-341 through 44-347
Kentucky	Within 30 Working days after effective date of termination	Commission plus exemplary damages not to exceed two times commission due plus attorney fees and court costs; if a sales rep action found frivolous, Principal will be awarded attorney fees and court costs	No	Kentucky Rev. Statutes, chap. 371, §§371.370-371.375 and 371.380-371.385

STATE	TIME LIMIT	NON-COMPLIANCE PENALTY	WRITTEN CONTRACT	LEGAL REFERENCE
Louisiana	Within 30 working days after termination if no contract; otherwise as in written agreement	Triple damages plus attorney fees and costs	No	Louisiana Rev. Statutes (West 1988), Title 51, R.S. 51:441 through 445
Illinois	Within 13 days of termination or when commission earned	Up to three times commission amount plus reasonable attorney fees and court costs	No	Illinois Rev. Statutes, Chap. 48, para. 2251, 2252, 2253
Indiana	Within 14 days after payment would have been due under contract	Exemplary damages up to three times commission, plus reasonable attorney fees and costs	No	Indiana Code, 1988 Ed., §§24-4-7-1 through 24-4-7-6
Maryland	Within 45 days after payment would have been due if contract not terminated	Exemplary damages not to exceed three times commission plus court costs, provided Principal furnished written notice 10 days prior of intent to file civil action for exemplary damages	No	Annotated Code Maryland, Art. 100, §§127 through 131
Massachusetts	Within 7 days after termination	The commission amount	Required	Massachusetts Gen. Laws Annotated (West, 1988), Chap. 104, §§7 through 9
Minnesota	Within 3 working days of salesperson's last day of work	Commission plus 1/15th of commission for every day of nonpayment	No	Minnesota Statutes 1988, Chap. 181.13m 181.14, 181.145
Mississippi	Within 21 days after effective date of termination	Up to triple commission due plus reasonable attorney fees and costs	No	1988 Mississippi Gen. Laws, Chap. 588, §§75-87-1, 75-87-3, 75-87-5, and Notes
New Hampshire	Within 45 days after date of termination of contract	In civil action, damages, exemplary damages, plus reasonable attorney fees and costs	Required	Amendments to RSA 339-E:1 through 339-E:4 to SB 16, New Hampshire
New Jersey	Within 30 days after payment would have been due under contract if contract had not been terminated	Commissions plus exemplary damages not to exceed two times the amount of the commissions due plus reasonable attorney fees and court costs	Required	New Jersey Act concerning sales representatives supplementing Title 56 of the Rev. Statutes
New York	Within 5 business days after termination, or when commission earned	Two times commission, plus reasonable attorney fees, court costs, and disbursements	Required	Labor Law Book No. 30, chap. 451, §§191-a, 191-b, 191-c

STATE	TIME LIMIT	NON-COMPLIANCE PENALTY	WRITTEN CONTRACT	LEGAL REFERENCE
North Carolina	Within 45 days after effective date of contract termination	In civil action, amounts due plus exemplary damages not to exceed amount of commissions, plus reasonable attorney fees and court costs	Required	§1. chapter 66, Art. 27, §§66-190 through 66-193
Ohio	All commissions must be paid within 13 days of when due, or as specified by contract	Liable in civil action for triple damages plus reasonable attorney fees and costs	No, but strongly recommended	Ohio Rev. Code 1988, § 1355.1
Oklahoma	If contract, within 14 calendar days; without contract, according to past practice or industry custom and usage	Commissions plus reasonable attorney fees and court costs	No	Oklahoma Statutes, Title 15 §§675 through 680
Pennsylvania	Within 14 days after payment due if contract not terminated	In civil action, commissions plus exemplary damages not to exceed two times commission plus reasonable attorney fees and court cost	Required	Pennsylvania Laws of 1988, Act 184
South Carolina	As required by contract or upon termination if there is no contract	In civil action, all amounts due plus punitive damages not to exceed three times commissions plus attorney fees and court costs	No	Cumulative Suppl. of Code of Laws of South Carolina, Vol 13A, Chap. 65, pp. 59, 60, §§39-65-1-, through 39-65-80
Tennessee	Within 14 days of salesperson's termination	Up to three times commission, plus reasonable attorney fees and court costs	No	Tennessee Code Annotated, §47-50-114
Texas	Within 30 working days after termination date, or as specified in contract	In civil action, triple damages plus reasonable attorney fees and costs	Required	Texas Business & Commerce Code Annotated (Vernon, 1987), §§35.81 through 35.86

Glossary of Terms

Abuse of process A cause of action which arises when one party intentionally misuses the legal process to injure another.

Accord and satisfaction An agreement by the employee and his or her company to compromise disputes concerning outstanding debts, compensation or terms of employment. Satisfaction occurs when the terms of the compromise are fully performed.

Action in accounting A cause of action in which one party seeks a determination of the amount of money owed by another.

Admissible Capable of being introduced in court as evidence.

Advance Sometimes referred to as "draw," it is a sum of money which is applied against money to be earned.

Affidavit A written statement signed under oath.

Allegations Written statements of a party to a lawsuit which charge the other party with wrongdoing. In order to be successful, these must be proven.

Answer The defendant's reply to the plaintiff's allegations in a complaint.

Anticipatory breach A breach of contract that occurs when one party, i.e., the employee, states in advance of performance that he or she will definitely not perform under the terms of his or her contract.

Appeal A proceeding whereby the losing party to a lawsuit applies to a higher court to determine the correctness of the decision.

Arbitration A proceeding whereby both sides to a lawsuit agree to submit their dispute to arbitrators, rather than judges. The arbitration proceeding is expeditious and is legally binding on all parties.

Assignment The transfer of a right or interest by one party to another.

Attorney in fact A person appointed by another to transact business on his or her behalf; the person does not have to be a lawyer.

At-will-employment See Employment-at-will.

Award A decision made by a judicial body to compensate the winning party in a lawsuit.

Bill of particulars A document used in a lawsuit which specifically details the loss alleged by the plaintiff.

Breach of contract A legal cause of action for the unjustified failure to perform a duty or obligation specified in an agreement.

Brief A concise statement of the main contentions of a lawsuit.

Burden of proof The responsibility of a party to a lawsuit to provide sufficient evidence to prove or disprove a claim

Business deduction A legitimate expense that can be used to decrease the amount of income subject to tax.

Business slander A legal wrong committed when a party orally makes false statements which impugn the business reputation of another (e.g., imply that the person is dishonest, incompetent or financially unreliable).

Calendar A list of cases to be heard each day in court.

Cause of action The legal theory upon which the plaintiff seeks to recover damages.

Caveat emptor A Latin expression frequently applied to consumer transactions; translated as "Let the buyer beware."

Cease-and-desist letter A letter, usually sent by a lawyer, notifying an individual to stop engaging in a particular type of activity, behavior or conduct which infringes upon the rights of another.

Certificate of incorporation A document which creates a corporation.

Check A negotiable instrument; the depositor's written order requesting his or her bank to pay a definite sum of money to a named individual, entity or to the bearer.

Civil court Generally, any court which presides over noncriminal matters.

Claims court A particular court which hears tax disputes.

Clerk of the court A person who determines whether court papers are properly filed and court procedures followed.

Closely held business A business typically owned by fewer than ten co-owners.

Collateral estoppel See Estoppel. Collateral estoppel is where a prior but different legal action is conclusive in a way to bring about estoppel in a current legal action.

Common law Law which evolves from reported case decisions which are relied upon for their precedential value.

Compensatory damages A sum of money awarded to a party which represents the actual harm suffered or loss incurred.

Complaint A legal document which commences the lawsuit; it alleges facts and causes of action which the plaintiff relies upon to collect damages.

Conflict of interest The ethical inability of a lawyer to represent a client because of competing loyalties, e.g. representing both employer and employee in a labor dispute.

Consideration An essential element of an enforceable contract; something of value given or promised by one party in exchange for an act or promise of another.

Constitutional Recognized as legal or valid.

Contempt A legal sanction imposed when a rule or order of a judicial body is disobeyed.

Contingency fee A type of fee arrangement whereby a lawyer is paid a percentage of the money recovered. If unsuccessful, the client is only responsible for costs already paid by the lawyer.

Continuance The postponement of a legal proceeding to another date.

Contract An enforceable agreement, either written, oral, or implied by the actions or intentions of the parties.

Contract modification The alteration of contract terms.

Counterclaim A claim asserted by the defendant in a lawsuit.

Covenant A promise.

Credibility The believability of a witness as perceived by a judge or jury.

Creditor The party to whom money is owed.

Cross-examination The questioning of a witness by the opposing lawyer.

Damages An award, usually money, given to the winning party in a lawsuit as compensation for the wrongful acts of another.

Debtor The party who owes money.

Decision The determination of a case or matter by a judicial body.

Deductible The unrecoverable portion of insurance proceeds.

Defamation An oral or written statement communicated to a third party which impugns a person's reputation in the community.

Default judgment An award rendered after one party fails to appear in a lawsuit.

Defendant The person or entity who is sued in a lawsuit.

Defense The defendant's justification for relieving himself or herself of fault.

Definite term of employment Employment for a fixed period of time.

Deposition A pretrial proceeding in which one party is questioned, usually under oath, by the opposing party's lawyer.

Disclaimer A clause in a sales, service, or other contract which attempts to limit or exonerate one party from liability in the event of a lawsuit.

Discovery A general term used to describe several pretrial devices (e.g., depositions and interrogatories) that enable lawyers to elicit information from the opposing side.

District court A particular court that hears tax disputes.

Dual Capacity A legal theory, used to circumvent Worker's Compensation laws, that allows an injured employee to sue his or her employer directly in court.

Due process Constitutional protections which guarantee that a person's life, liberty or property cannot be taken away without the opportunity to be heard in a judicial proceeding.

Duress Unlawful threats, pressure, or force that induces a person to act contrary to his or her intentions, if proved, it allows a party to disavow a contract.

Employee A person who works and is subject to an employer's scope, direction and control.

Employment-at-will Employment which does not provide an employee with job security, since the person can be fired on a moment's notice with or without cause.

Employment discrimination Conduct directed at employees and job applicants that is prohibited by law.

Equity Fairness; usually applied when a judicial body awards a suitable remedy other than money to a party (e.g., an injunction).

Escrow account A separate fund where lawyers are obligated to deposit money received from or on behalf of a client.

Estoppel Estoppel is a legal bar to prevent a party from asserting a fact or claim inconsistent with that party's prior position which has been relied on or acted on by another party.

Evidence Information in the form of oral testimony, exhibits, affidavits, etc., used to prove a party's claim.

Examination before trial A pretrial legal device; also called a "deposition."

Exhibit Tangible evidence used to prove a party's claim.

Exit agreements Agreements sometimes signed between employers and employees upon resignation or termination of an employee's services.

Express contract An agreement whose terms are manifested by clear and definite language, as distinguished from those agreements inferred from conduct.

False imprisonment The unlawful detention of a person who is held against his or her will without authority or justification.

Filing fee Money paid to start a lawsuit

Final decree A court order or directive of a permanent nature.

Financial statement A document, usually prepared by an accountant, which reflects a business' (or individual's) assets, liabilities and financial condition.

Flat fee A sum of money paid to a lawyer as compensation for services.

Flat fee plus time A form of payment in which a lawyer receives one sum for services and then receives additional money calculated on an hourly basis.

Fraud A false statement that is relied upon and causes damages to the defrauded party.

General denial A reply contained in the defendant's answer.

Ground The basis for an action or an argument.

Guaranty A contract where one party agrees to answer for or satisfy the debt of another.

Hearsay evidence Unsubstantiated evidence that is often excluded by a court.

Hourly fee Money paid to a lawyer for services, computed on an hourly basis.

Implied contract An agreement that is tacit rather than expressed in clear and definite language; an agreement inferred from the conduct of the parties.

Indemnification Protection or reimbursement against damage or loss. The indemnified party is protected against liabilities or penalties from that party's actions; the indemnifying party provides the protection or reimbursement.

Infliction of emotional distress A legal cause of action in which one party seeks to recover damages for mental pain and suffering caused by another.

Injunction A court order restraining one party from doing or refusing to do an act.

Integration The act of making a contract whole by integrating its elements into a coherent single entity. An agreement is considered integrated when the parties involved accept the final version as a complete expression of their agreement.

Interrogatories A pretrial device used to elicit information; written questions are sent to an opponent to be answered under oath.

Invasion of privacy The violation of a person's constitutionally protected right to privacy.

Judgment A verdict rendered by a judicial body; if money is awarded, the winning party is the "judgment creditor" and the losing party is the "judgment debtor."

Jurisdiction The authority of a court to hear a particular matter.

Legal duty The responsibility of a party to perform a certain act.

Letter of agreement An enforceable contract in the form of a letter.

Letter of protest A letter sent to document a party's dissatisfaction.

Liable Legally in the wrong or legally responsible for.

Lien A claim made against the property of another in order to satisfy a judgment.

Lifetime contract An employment agreement of infinite duration which is often unenforceable.

Liquidated damages An amount of money agreed upon in advance by parties to a contract to be paid in the event of a breach or dispute.

Malicious interference with contractual rights A legal cause of action in which one party seeks to recover damages against an individual who has induced or caused another party to terminate a valid contract.

Malicious prosecution A legal cause of action in which one party seeks to recover damages after another party instigates or institutes a frivolous judicial proceeding (usually criminal) which is dismissed.

Mediation A voluntary dispute-resolution process in which both sides attempt to settle their differences without resorting to formal litigation.

Misappropriation The unlawful taking of another party's personal property.

Misrepresentation A legal cause of action which arises when one party makes untrue statements of fact that induce another party to act and be damaged as a result.

Mitigation of damages A legal principle which requires a party seeking damages to make reasonable efforts to reduce damages as much as possible; for example, to seek new employment after being unfairly discharged.

Motion A written request made to a court by one party during a lawsuit.

Negligence A party's failure to exercise a sufficient degree of care owed to another by law.

Nominal damages A small sum of money awarded by a court.

Noncompetition clause A restrictive provision in a contract which limits an employee's right to work in that particular industry after he or she ceases to be associated with his or her present employer.

Notary Public A person authorized under state law to administer an oath or verify a signature.

Notice to show cause A written document in a lawsuit asking a court to expeditiously rule on a matter.

Objection A formal protest made by a lawyer in a lawsuit.

Offer The presentment of terms, which, if accepted, may lead to the formation of a contract.

Opinion letter A written analysis of a client's case, prepared by a lawyer.

Option An agreement giving one party the right to choose a certain course of action.

Oral contract An enforceable verbal agreement.

Parol evidence Oral evidence introduced at a trial to alter or explain the terms of a written agreement.

Partnership A voluntary association between two or more competent persons engaged in a business as co-owners for profit.

Party A plaintiff or defendant in a lawsuit.

Perjury Committing false testimony while under oath.

Petition A request filed in court by one party.

Plaintiff The party who commences a lawsuit.

Pleading A written document that states the facts or arguments put forth by a party in a lawsuit.

Power of attorney A document executed by one party allowing another to act on his or her behalf in specified situations.

Pretrial discovery A legal procedure used to gather information from an opponent before the trial.

Process server An individual who delivers the summons and/or complaint to the defendant.

Promissory note A written acknowledgement of a debt whereby one party agrees to pay a specified sum on a specified date.

Proof Evidence presented at a trial and used by a judge or jury to fashion an award.

Punitive damages Money awarded as punishment for a party's wrongful acts.

Quantum meruit An equitable principle whereby a court awards reasonable compensation to a party who performs work, labor or services at another party's request; also referred to as "unjust enrichment."

Rebuttal The opportunity for a lawyer at a trial to ask a client or witness additional questions to clarify points elicited by the opposing lawyer during cross-examination.

Release A written document which, when signed, relinquishes a party's rights to enforce a claim against another.

Remedy The means by which a right is enforced or protected.

Reply A written document in a lawsuit conveying the contentions of a party in response to a motion.

Restrictive covenant A provision in a contract which forbids one party from doing a certain act, e.g., working for another, soliciting customers, etc.

Retainer A sum of money paid to a lawyer for services to be rendered.

Service letter statutes Laws in some states that require an employer to furnish an employee with truthful written reasons for his discharge.

Sex harassment Prohibited conduct of a sexual nature which occurs in the workplace.

Shop rights The rights of an employer to use within the employer's facility a device or method developed by an employee.

Slander Oral defamation of a party's reputation.

Small claims court A particular court that presides over small disputes (e.g., those involving sums of less than $2,500).

Sole proprietorship An unincorporated business.

Statement of fact Remarks or comments of a specific nature that have a legal effect.

Statute A law created by a legislative body.

Statute of frauds A legal principle requiring that certain contracts be in writing in order to be enforceable.

Statute of limitations A legal principle requiring a party to commence a lawsuit within a certain period of time.

Stipulation An agreement between parties.

Submission agreement A signed agreement whereby both parties agree to submit a present dispute to binding arbitration.

Subpoena A written order requiring a party or witness to appear at a legal proceeding; a subpoena duces tecum is a written order requiring a party to bring books and records to the legal proceeding.

Summation The last part of the trial wherein both lawyers recap the respective positions of their clients.

Summons A written document served upon the defendant giving notification of a lawsuit.

Temporary decree A court order or directive of a temporary nature, capable of being modified or changed.

Testimony Oral evidence presented by a witness under oath.

"Time is of the essence" A legal expression often included in agreements to specify the requirement of timeliness.

Tort A civil wrong.

Unfair and deceptive practice Illegal business and trade acts prohibited by various federal and state laws.

Unfair discharge An employee's termination without legal justification.

Verdict The decision of a judge or jury.

Verification A written statement signed under oath.

Void Legally without merit.

Waiver A written document that, when signed, relinquishes a party's rights.

Whistleblowing Protected conduct where one party complains about the illegal acts of another.

Witness A person who testifies at a judicial proceeding.

Worker's compensation A process in which an employee receives compensation for injuries sustained in the course of employment.

Index